Lecture Notes in Computer Science

Lecture Notes in Computer Science

Edited by G. Goos and J. Hartmanis

332

D. Sannella A. Tarlecki (Eds.)

Recent Trends in Data Type Specification

5th Workshop on Specification of Abstract Data Types
Gullane, Scotland, September 1–4, 1987
Selected Papers

Springer-Verlag
Berlin Heidelberg New York London Paris Tokyo

Editors

Donald Sannella
Department of Computer Science, University of Edinburgh
Edinburgh EH9 3JZ, Scotland

Andrzej Tarlecki
Institute of Computer Science, Polish Academy of Sciences
PKiN, P.O. Box 22, 00-901 Warsaw, Poland

CR Subject Classification (1987): D.2.1–2, D.2.4, D.2.m, D.3.1–3, F.3.1–2

ISBN 3-540-50325-0 Springer-Verlag Berlin Heidelberg New York
ISBN 0-387-50325-0 Springer-Verlag New York Berlin Heidelberg

Printed in Germany

Printing and binding: Druckhaus Beltz, Hemsbach/Bergstr.
2145/3140-543210

Preface

The algebraic specification of abstract data types has been a flourishing research topic in computer science since 1974. The main goal of work in this area is to evolve a methodology to support the design and formal development of reliable software. The particular approach taken builds upon concepts from universal algebra and elementary category theory. The core of this work has now stabilized to a great extent and is mature enough to find application in real-life software engineering and to related topics such as concurrency, databases, and even hardware design. Such applications are becoming more feasible because of the emergence of integrated specification/development environments which include tools such as theorem provers based on fast term rewriting engines. Researchers are also exploring ways of widening the scope of the theory to make it applicable to (for example) higher-order functions and non-deterministic programs. Another trend is toward taking a more general view which allows superficially different approaches having the same general aims and methods to be unified.

The Fifth Workshop on Specification of Abstract Data Types took place 1-4 September 1987 in the small town of Gullane, about 20 miles from Edinburgh, organized by Don Sannella. This series of workshops, including meetings at Sorpesee (1981), Passau (1983), Bremen (1984) and Warberg (1986), has become the chief international series of meetings devoted to this topic. Participants came from Denmark, East Germany, France, Hong Kong, Italy, the Netherlands, Norway, Poland, Portugal, Spain, Switzerland, the U.K., the U.S. and West Germany. Successors in Berlin (1988) and Dresden (1990) are already planned.

The general feeling was that the workshop was extremely successful and that a number of very promising new results and ideas were presented which reflected the general trends indicated above. Following the example of Hans-Jörg Kreowski who edited a volume of papers based on talks given at the Bremen workshop,[1] we selected a number of talks which in our view represented the most interesting ideas and reflected the main trends in current research and asked their presenters to contribute papers. The result is this volume. All the papers underwent a careful refereeing process.

We are grateful to the following people who agreed to referee the papers despite our tough deadlines:

J. Bergstra, M. Bidoit, C. Choppy, H.-D. Ehrich, W. Fey, A. Geser, H. Hansen, R. Harper, M. Hermann, H. Hußmann, H.-J. Kreowski, T. Lehmann, J. Loeckx, M. Löwe, T. Maibaum, B. Möller, E. Moggi, L. Moss, T. Nipkow, F. Orejas, P. Padawitz, A. Poigné, H. Reichel, D. Rydeheard, O. Schoett, S. Sokołowski, J. Tucker, J. Winkowski, M. Wirsing

Our special thanks to Hartmut Ehrig who arranged for the submission contributed by one of us to be anonymously refereed. Thanks also to Monika Lekuse for helping with the workshop organization and Joan Ratcliff for secretarial support. The workshop was sponsored by Edinburgh University and received financial support from the British Council.

Don Sannella
Andrzej Tarlecki

[1] *Recent Trends in Data Type Specification*, Springer Informatik-Fachberichte Vol. 116 (1985)

Table of contents

The stratified loose approach: A generalization of initial and loose semantics.

Michel Bidoit *

Laboratoire de Recherche en Informatique
C.N.R.S. U.A. 410 "Al Khowarizmi"
Université Paris-Sud · Bât. 490
F 91405 ORSAY Cedex
France

Abstract

Besides the respective advantages and drawbacks of the initial and loose approaches to algebraic semantics, the choice of either initial semantics or loose semantics for a given specification language often relies on methodological considerations. In this paper, we briefly recall the main features of the **Pluss** specification language, the semantics of which was originally designed following the loose approach. Then we study how far some basic concerns, such as modularity and reusability, interact with the design of the semantics of the **Pluss** specification-building primitives. We show that neither the initial approach nor the loose one is powerful enough to reflect our intuition and needs about software reusability and modularity, and we introduce a more sophisticated framework, the ***stratified loose semantics***, which can be considered as a generalization of both loose and initial semantics.

1 Introduction.

Among all approaches to algebraic semantics, two candidates are especially promising: the initial approach [28,38,21,24,25] and the loose approach [29,39,36,2]. Most algebraic specification languages developed up to now rely on one of these two approaches.

The main statements argued in favor of the initial algebraic semantics are the following:

- First of all, the mathematical foundations of initial algebraic semantics are well-established [28,24].
- The initial approach has turned out to be the most appropriate framework to define specification correctness criteria such as sufficient completeness and hierarchical consistency [4].

However, the counterparts of this approach are still worth considering:

*This work is partially supported by ESPRIT Project 432 METEOR and C.N.R.S. GRECO de Programmation.

- The formalization of parameterization cannot be done in a strict initial way, since the semantics of a formal parameter cannot be restricted to an initial model. Thus, the models of a parameterized specification are not strictly speaking initial ones, but must combine in some sense initial and loose parts. This can be achieved by using *data constraints* [33]. Another solution is to consider that parameterized specifications are not at the same "level" as ordinary specifications; in that case the semantics of a parameterized specification is merely defined by means of synthesis functors and pushouts.

- Another serious drawback of the initial approach is that it requires the existence of initial models ! As a first consequence, axioms must be restricted to be (positive) conditional equations. Moreover, to extend the standard theory to cope with more sophisticated features such as e.g. exception handling requires non trivial mathematical developments (consider for instance the initial semantics of exception algebras [5] or of order-sorted algebras [27]).

The main statements argued in favor of the loose semantics are the following:

- Axioms should not be restricted to be positive conditional equations, but may be any kind of logical formulae, including existential quantifiers. This greatly improves the power of expression of the specification language. Moreover, exception handling features can be introduced in a more easy and intuitive way [7].

- Specification-building primitives to structure and modularize large specifications can be easily designed. The best example being **ASL** [39,36,2], where some kind of lambda-calculus over specifications is defined. Parameterized specifications can be dealt with as ordinary specifications, and recursive parameterized specifications may even be considered.

The most serious drawback of the loose approach is the following: as soon as one is interested in using specifications for prototyping purposes, it is necessary to refer to some standard model in order that symbolic evaluation (e.g. term rewriting) makes sense.[1]

Since both initial and loose approaches to algebraic semantics have (nice) positive aspects and (serious) drawbacks, the ultimate argument to choose one or another is often a methodological one. This is the case of the **Pluss** specification language, which relies on the loose approach (see Section 2). In this paper, we consider two major roles algebraic specifications are often argued to be usable for, **modular software development** and **software reusability**. It is often claimed that formal specifications are a key concept for software reusability, since a formal specification is the most appropriate way (if not the only one) to know whether or not some piece of software is reusable to achieve a given goal. However, claiming that formal (algebraic) specifications may play a crucial role with respect to software reusability is a short argument in the lack of a formal theory of software reusability.

The aim of this paper is not to define a formal framework for software reusability, but to explain why and how far software reusability paradigms as well as modularity considerations may interact with the semantics of the specification-building primitives. More precisely, we detail why neither the loose nor the initial approach can reflect in a powerful enough way our needs with respect to software modularity and reusability. Then we introduce a new kind of semantics, the "stratified loose semantics", who generalizes the main concepts of both initial and loose semantics. The basic definitions of a formal theory of software reusability, built on top of our stratified loose semantics,

[1] For instance, when we want to use a set of conditional equations as a conditional term rewriting system, the "operational" semantics associated to exp1 = exp2 ⇒ t1 = t2 is: if exp1 and exp2 (instantiated) both reduce to the same normal form, then t1 (instantiated) rewrites into t2 (instantiated). This is correct only with respect to initial semantics [31].

are described in [26].

The paper is organized as follows. In Section 2 we briefly recall the main features of the **Pluss** specification language and we outline why specification reusability and software reusability should be carefully distinguished. In Section 3 we detail various software reusability and modularity paradigms and we study how far they are or can be reflected by the algebraic semantics of the specification language. In Section 4 we describe an example who demonstrates that the loose approach is not powerful enough, and in Section 5 we define the stratified loose semantics.

It should be noted that, in this paper, we have deliberately chosen to put emphasis on the intuitive aspects involved by software reusability and modularity. Our claim (based on our previous attempts in drawing up the formal semantics of **Pluss**) is that it is far more difficult to capture these intuitive aspects (and to fully understand their implications and consequences) than to develop the appropriate mathematical machinery.

2 A short introduction to the Pluss algebraic specification language.

In this section we briefly recall the main features of the **Pluss**[2] algebraic specification language.

Pluss means "a Proposition of a Language Usable for Structured Specifications". This language provides a way of structuring algebraic specifications, i.e. any kind of specifications for which a formal semantics can be given by means of a signature and a class of algebras. **Pluss** is the result of a broad range of experiments in writing large specifications: a Pascal Compiler [20], part of a Telephone Switching System [13,15,9], Protocols [14], an interpreter of conditional rewrite rules [19], a subset of the Unix[3] file system [12], the specification data base of the **Asspegique** specification environment [17,11].

An important aspect of **Pluss** is that it is, to some extent, a *meta specification language*, since the structuring features are not (or little) dependent on the kind of algebras under consideration. That means that several variants of the **Pluss** specification language are (or can be) defined [17], depending on whether partial algebras [16], standard algebras, E,R-algebras [7,10], exception-algebras [5], etc. are considered. These "institution independent" aspects of **Pluss** are mainly due to the fact that this language was originally built on top of **ASL** [39,36,35].

A specification is supposed to describe a future or existing system in such a way that the properties of the system (**what** the system does) are expressed, and the implementation details (**how** it is done) are omitted. Thus a specification language aims at describing classes of possible implementations. In contrast a programming language aims at describing specific implementations. The loose semantics seems to be especially appropriate with that respect: an algebraic specification defines a class of algebras (also called models), i.e. a set of operations on various sets of values. Thus, an algebra is just a possible *implementation* of the sorts and operation names which occur in the specification. This point, which can be considered as a very naïve and oversimplified understanding of implementations, takes also into account the fact that a specific implementation may have more properties than those strictly required by the specification. However, this does not preclude more refined views about implementations [34,37], such as the abstract implementation of

[2]The first design of the **Pluss** specification language was done by M.-C. Gaudel at the Laboratoires de Marcoussis (C.G.E.).

[3]Unix is a trademark of Bell Laboratories.

one specification by another (more concrete) one [22,6], or the stepwise refinement and transformation of a specification into a piece of software [3]. Thus, in **Pluss** the semantics of a specification is not restricted to initial algebras, but will be defined as some class of (non-isomorphic) algebras, i.e. the **Pluss** algebraic specification language mainly follows the loose approach. By convention, in this paper we shall consider that the class of algebras associated to a **Pluss** specification is exactly the set of all allowed implementations for this specification. Our claim is that keeping in mind the analogy between the various models of a specification and its various possible implementations helps to better understand how the formal semantics of the algebraic specification language under consideration should be designed. As a matter of fact, we shall thoroughly use this analogy in this paper to better illustrate our motivations and needs for "a new semantics".

The main originality of the **Pluss** specification language is to state a careful distinction between completed specification components and specification components under design. By completed specification components we mean the following strong property: the class of possible implementations is fixed. Practically that means that such a specification component is either already implemented or may be implemented without taking care of its context (for instance the other components of a specification where this completed specification component is used). By specification component under design we mean a preliminary specification component where the signature and the axioms are not fully fixed and may be further refined: at this early stage, implementing the specification component is premature since the implementation choices may have to be reconsidered later, depending on the further refinements of the specification. Note that the distinction between completed specification components and specification components under design is basically a methodological one, and is left to the specifier. What is important is that it is possible to precise the state of achievement of a specification component with the **Pluss** specification language. Moreover, the semantics of the **Pluss** specification language should be designed in such a way that this distinction is correctly reflected with respect to both the specification and the software development processes.

Specification components are either obtained by an enrichment of already defined specifications by new sorts and/or new operations and/or new axioms, or as an instance of a parameterized specification. Thus the primary specification-building primitives are enrichment and instantiation. Other specification-building primitives are defined in **Pluss**, such as renaming, visibility control primitives (to avoid name clashes when putting together several specification components) and primitives to convert a specification component under design into a completed specification component.

According to this distinction between completed specification components and specification components under design, the reusability concept should be split into two distinct ones: software component reusability (through their formal, completed specifications), and specification component reusability. Specification reusability mainly concerns specification components under design and can be achieved by means of various specification-building primitives (such as enrichment and parameterization) and inheritance mechanisms. In this paper we shall focus on the enrichment specification-building primitive for completed specification components and we shall discuss how its semantics should be designed with respect to software reusability and modularity.

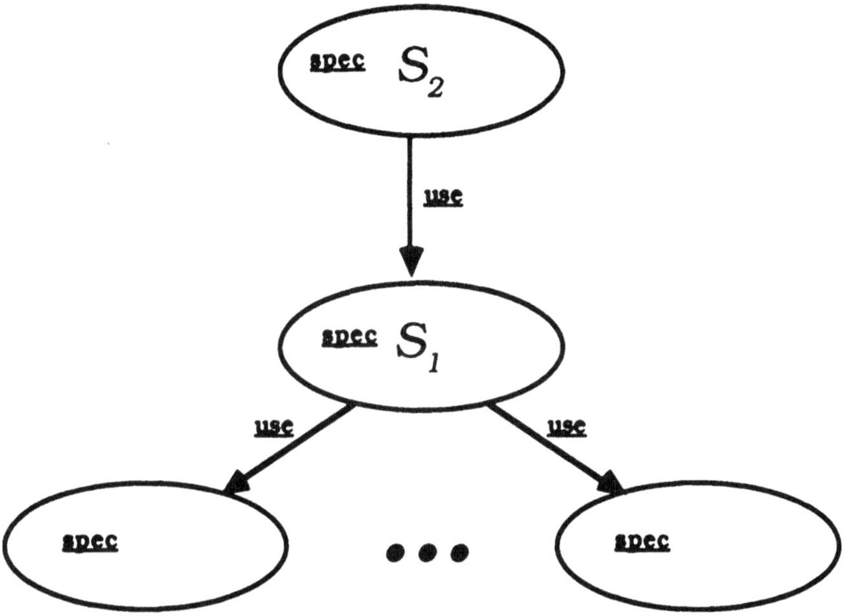

Figure 1: Basic enrichment situation.

3 Understanding some software reusability and modularity paradigms inside the scope of the loose approach.

In this section we explain how far some basic requirements about software reusability and modularity can be successfully reflected by various constraints on the semantics of the specification-building primitives. Indeed, as explained in the previous section, we shall focus on the enrichment specification-building primitive, which is called **use** (for completed specifications) in **Pluss**. Moreover, in order to better reflect our intuition and needs about software reusability and modularity (more precisely, about the way software reusability and modularity interacts with the **use** semantics), we shall deliberately stay at an (as far as possible) intuitive level, using oversimplified examples.

The results contained in this section are by no means new, but they can be thought of as being positive arguments in favor of the loose approach with respect to reusability and modularity. This is the reason why we consider they must be recalled in this paper, or at least reinterpreted by means of software reusability and modularity paradigms. However we give in the next section a counter-example which points out where the loose approach fails.

3.1 Hypotheses, notations and basic constraints.

For sake of simplicity, we shall assume throughout this section (unless otherwise specified) that we are in the basic case pictured by Figure 1, i.e. we consider a specification module S_2 who enriches only one specification module S_1 (which in turn may enrich other specification modules). All specification modules considered here are supposed to be "completed" ones, i.e. they are supposed to be either already implemented or ready to be implemented. In **Pluss** such completed specification modules are introduced by the keyword **spec**.

The specification module S_1 determines the specification $\widetilde{S_1}$, the semantics of which is some class of models (or algebras). The signature associated to $\widetilde{S_1}$ is denoted by Σ_1, while the distinguished subset[4] of Σ_1 corresponding to the generators of the defined sorts is denoted by Ω_1. The class of models associated to $\widetilde{S_1}$ is denoted by $\mathcal{M}_1$. Similar notations hold for the S_2 specification module. Note that we have $\Sigma_1 \subseteq \Sigma_2$, and $\Omega_1 \subseteq \Omega_2$. $\mathcal{U}$ denotes the usual forgetful functor from Σ_2-algebras to Σ_1-algebras; the image $\mathcal{U}(\mathcal{M}_2)$ of the class $\mathcal{M}_2$ by the forgetful functor $\mathcal{U}$ will also be denoted by $\mathcal{M}_2|_{\Sigma_1}$, as well as the image by $\mathcal{U}$ of some model M_2 of $\mathcal{M}_2$ is denoted by $M_2|_{\Sigma_1}$.

The first two constraints that the models associated to a specification $\tilde{S}$ must verify are independent of the modular structure of the specification.

Constraint C 1

$\forall M \in \mathcal{M} : M$ *is a Σ-algebra finitely generated w.r.t.* Ω.

Constraint C 2

$\forall M \in \mathcal{M} : M \models \mathcal{A}x(\tilde{S})$.

where $\mathcal{A}x(\tilde{S})$ denotes the set of axioms of $\tilde{S}$.

The second constraint does not require any further comment. The first constraint expresses that the carrier sets associated to the sorts introduced by $\tilde{S}$ only contain values denotable by a ground term built with function symbols from Ω. This means that in **Pluss**, the **spec** construct implicitly embodies the **ASL reachable** primitive [39,2]. From a theoretical point of view, the most important consequence of this constraint is that *structural induction* using the operations in Ω is a correct proof principle. But this constraint has many practical consequences too, since reasoning by means of constructors helps writing the axioms in a structured way [8]. In the next sub-section we shall see also that this constraint, when combined with other ones, can be used to write "incomplete" specifications.

As a matter of fact, this constraint also reflects the fundamental distinction between completed specifications and specifications under development: to fix the class of possible implementations of some specification we must at least fix the various sets of values (while most of the time, these sets of values are not yet known at the beginning of a specification process).

3.2 Reusing "complex" software for "simpler" purposes.

The very first attempt to capture our intuition about software reusability and modularity embodies the following naïve and simple idea:

Informal Requirement 1 (Reusability by restriction)
If some piece of software fulfills (i.e. is a correct implementation of) a "complex" specification, then it must be reusable for simpler purposes (i.e. it must also be a correct implementation of a sub-specification of the "complex" one).

[4] In **Pluss**, this distinguished subset is specified apart from the other operations and is introduced by the keyword **generated by**.

Keeping in mind our simplified view about implementations (i.e. implementations are just models, see Section 2), the informal requirement above can be translated into our algebraic framework as follows:

Algebraic Translation 1
When forgetting the (new) part specified by the specification module S_2, *any model* M_2 *of the specification* $\widetilde{S_2}$ *should be a model of the sub-specification* $\widetilde{S_1}$.

This indeed is exactly what the standard loose semantics of enrichment (e.g. the **ASL enrich** primitive [39,36,2]) guarantees. More precisely:

Constraint C 3 (ASL enrich semantics)
The class $\mathcal{M}_2$ *of the* $\widetilde{S_2}$ *models must verify:*

$$\forall M_2 \in \mathcal{M}_2 : M_2|_{\Sigma_1} \in \mathcal{M}_1 \text{ i.e. } \mathcal{M}_2|_{\Sigma_1} \subseteq \mathcal{M}_1.$$

It is important to note that this constraint, when combined with the constraint C **1** above, automatically implies that the "old" sort carrier sets (i.e. the carrier sets of the sorts defined in $\widetilde{S_1}$) will contain no "new" value (hence the so-called **no junk** property holds). Roughly speaking, that means that the constraints C **1** and C **3** together behave as if some kind of *sufficient completeness* of the module S_2 with respect to the specification $\widetilde{S_1}$ was requested. However, here the "no junk" property is achieved by semantical means, without any syntactical restriction on the axioms of S_2.

Remark 1 (Incomplete specifications)
This provides us with a nice way to write incomplete specifications or to define underspecified operations. For instance, if we need to specify a (deterministic) choose operation on sets of natural numbers, the following axiom would be sufficient:

$$S \neq empty \implies member(choose(S), S) = true$$

The constraints C **1** *and* C **3** *will ensure that for any non empty set S, choose(S) is actually a natural number (which must be an element of S from the axiom above), and not a "junk" natural number.*

3.3 Reusing "simple" software for "more complex" purposes.

The second point about software reusability and modularity is less straightforward, and is not necessarily achieved through the previous constraints. Let us first state it in an informal and intuitive way:

Informal Requirement 2 (Reusability by extension)
If some piece of software fulfills (i.e. is a correct implementation of) a "simple" specification, then it must be possible to reuse it for "more complex" purposes, i.e. it must be possible to extend it in a suitable way to obtain a correct implementation of a "more complex" specification.

This informal requirement is translated in our algebraic framework as follows:

Algebraic Translation 2
It should be possible to extend any model M_1 *of a specification* $\widetilde{S_1}$ *to obtain a model of a larger specification* $\widetilde{S_2}$.

What is important here is the ability of reusing **any** implementation of a sub-specification to extend it. The constraint C **3** of the previous sub-section only ensures that the models of the subset $\mathcal{M}_2|_{\Sigma_1}$ of $\mathcal{M}_1$ can be extended, and in general this subset is a strict subset. To fulfill the informal requirement above, we must further constrain the class $\mathcal{M}_2$:

Constraint C 4
The class $\mathcal{M}_2$ of $\widetilde{S_2}$ models must verify:

$$\textit{Either } \mathcal{M}_2 = \emptyset \textit{ or } \forall M_1 \in \mathcal{M}_1, \exists M_2 \in \mathcal{M}_2 \textit{ such that } M_2|_{\Sigma_1} = M_1 \textit{ i.e. } \mathcal{M}_1 \subseteq \mathcal{M}_2|_{\Sigma_1}.$$

It must be noted that this constraint automatically implies some kind of *hierarchical consistency* of the module S_2 with respect to the specification $\widetilde{S_1}$. More precisely, "old" objects who may be distinct before (in at least one model of $\mathcal{M}_1$) should not be forced to be equal by the new axioms (the so-called **no confusion** property).

Moreover, this constraint implies also some methodological side-effects on the way large specifications should be structured into modules. Typically, adding new observers on "old" sorts in S_2 will lead to inconsistent specifications (i.e. specifications with the empty class of models as semantics). This is due to the fact that with these new observers, it may be possible to distinguish "old" values (i.e. to prevent them from being equal), while these "old" values could have been equal in some model M_1 of $\widetilde{S_1}$. Such a model M_1 cannot be extended to obtain a model of $\widetilde{S_2}$. Thus, these new observers should rather have been defined at the appropriate level (e.g. in the module S_1 or in another lower module). Note that this remark on the way specifications should be structured into modules turns out in practice to be more a fruitful guide in writing large specifications than a restriction.

Another major motivation for the constraint **C 4** is related with our understanding of the role of completed specification modules with respect to the software development process. As soon as one agrees with our distinction between completed specifications and specifications under development, it becomes clear that this distinction only makes sense as far as a completed specification can be implemented independently of any "specification context". That means that it should be possible to implement a completed specification $\widetilde{S_1}$ without considering the "potential" specification modules who may **use** S_1. This can only be achieved by a careful distinction between completed specifications and specifications under development, and by embedding the constraint **C 4** in the semantics of the (completed) specification-building primitives.

Remark 2 (Pluss use semantics – old version)
In the **Pluss** *specification language, the formal semantics of the* **use** *enrichment specification-building primitive for completed specifications was up to now based on the combination of the four constraints* **C 1** *to* **C 4** *above.*

It should be noted that this choice contrasts with all other major algebraic specification languages, such as e.g. **ACT ONE** [21], **ASL** [39,36,2], **LARCH** [29] or **OBJ2** [25]. As a matter of fact, even if these languages offer a full range of various enrichment primitives who reflect more or less (various combinations of) the constraints defined above (e.g. the enrichment primitives "using", "extending" and "protecting" in **OBJ2**, or the enrichment primitives "assumes", "imports" and "includes" in **LARCH**), it is still not possible in these languages **to decide whether or not a specification module can be implemented without considering its specification context**, since these various enrichment primitives (those who "protect" the sub-modules and those who do not) can be applied to **any** specification module. Hence it is clear that the distinction between completed specifications and specifications under development should be reflected not only at the level of the enrichment specification-building primitives, but also by some (syntactical) distinction between the specification modules themselves. This is achieved in **Pluss** by using distinct keywords (**spec**, **draft**, **sketch**) to introduce the various kinds of modules, and by adding appropriate syntactical rules who prevent to enrich completed specifications with too permissive

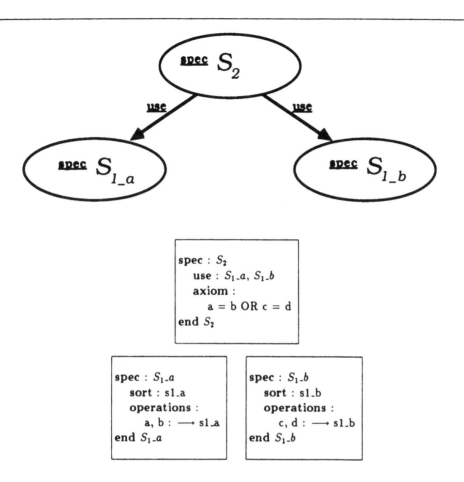

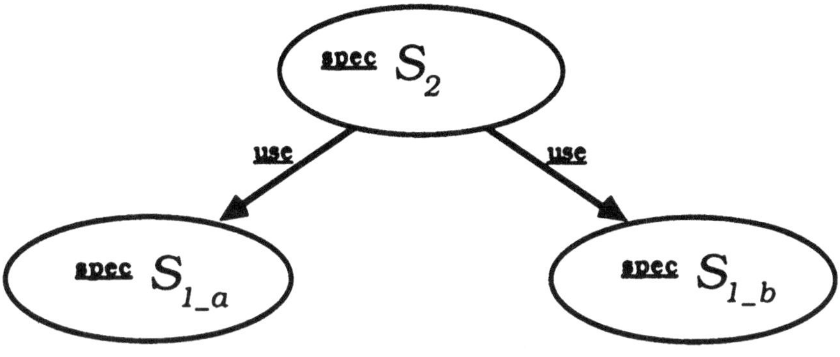

spec : S_2
  use : S_1_a, S_1_b
  axiom :
    a = b OR c = d
end S_2

spec : S_1_a
  sort : s1_a
  operations :
    a, b : $\longrightarrow$ s1_a
end S_1_a

spec : S_1_b
  sort : s1_b
  operations :
    c, d : $\longrightarrow$ s1_b
end S_1_b

Figure 2: Multiple enrichment example.

enrichment specification-building primitives (e.g. only the **use** enrichment specification-building primitive can be applied to **specs**[5]).

3.4 Extension to multiple enrichments.

If we now consider a more complex situation than the one described in this section up to now, i.e. if we assume that the module S_2 uses more than one module but k ones, say $S_1\_a, \ldots, S_1\_k$, we have to carefully generalize the constraint **C 4**. In such cases we do not only require that any models of a sub-specification $\widetilde{S_1\_i}$ is reusable as a basis to obtain a model of the larger specification $\widetilde{S_2}$, but also that **any combination** of them is reusable. A typical (oversimplified) example of such a situation is given in Figure 2.

In the example described in Figure 2, any of the two models of $\widetilde{S_1\_a}$ (resp. $\widetilde{S_1\_b}$) can be extended into a model of $\widetilde{S_2}$, but the combination of the two "initial" models of $\widetilde{S_1\_a}$ and $\widetilde{S_1\_b}$ cannot.

[5]In order to avoid trivial models, i.e. models where all values are collapsed together, *basic completed specification components* (i.e. those who do not **use** any other **specs**) are introduced with a specific construct **basic spec**, the semantics of which is restricted to the initial model.

However, here the solution is quite easy:[6]

Constraint C 5 (Generalization of the constraint C 4 to multiple enrichments)
Let S_2 be a (completed) specification module who enriches multiple modules $S_1\_a, \ldots, S_1\_k$. The class $\mathcal{M}_2$ of $\widetilde{S_2}$ models must verify:

> *Either $\mathcal{M}_2 = \emptyset$ or $\forall M_1\_a \in \mathcal{M}_1\_a, \ldots, \forall M_1\_k \in \mathcal{M}_1\_k$, $\exists M_2 \in \mathcal{M}_2$ such that: $M_2|_{\Sigma_1\_a} = M_1\_a$ and … and $M_2|_{\Sigma_1\_k} = M_1\_k$.*

4 Reusability by software module exchanges: Where the loose approach fails.

In this section we explain why the loose approach is not powerful enough to capture our needs and intuition about software reusability and modularity in a satisfactory way, even with the constraints introduced in the previous section.

Remember that in the previous section, we have emphasized the fact that some given achieved, completed specification should be implementable independently of any "specification context". This requirement was achieved both by embedding the constraint C 4 in the semantics of the **use** enrichment primitive and by using distinct keywords to introduce the various kinds of specification modules. However, to really fulfill our goal, we must also take into account the complementary point of view:

Informal Requirement 3 (Modularity, reusability and interchangeability)
Assume that we are in the basic case pictured by Figure 1. It should be possible to implement the achieved, completed specification module S_2 without knowing which peculiar implementation of the sub-specification $\widetilde{S_1}$ has been (or will be) chosen.

Some comments are necessary to better understand the previous requirement:

- First of all, "the implementation of a specification module" has no precise meaning (i.e. algebraic interpretation) so far, since we only have suggested to interpret "the various implementations of some specification" by "its various models". This is due to the fact that in an algebra, all sorts and operations are at the same level, hence there is no way to distinguish in the algebra M_2 the "new" part, i.e. the part of M_2 who corresponds to the specification module S_2. We can just forget it using the forgetful functor $\mathcal{U}$! More precisely, the "new" part is "$M_2 - \mathcal{U}(M_2)$", but this expression does not denote an algebra.

  However, a closer look to the program side provides us with a natural, intuitive interpretation of what "the implementation of a specification module" means. Assume for instance that we implement our specifications in a modular programming language such as *Ada* [1], *CLU* [32] or *Standard ML* [30], and that the program structure reflects the specification structure. Then to the specification modules $S_2, S_1, \ldots$ are associated program modules $P_2, P_1, \ldots$ (see Figure 3). Roughly speaking, it is the collection of program modules $P_2, P_1, \ldots$ *linked together* who produces an implementation of the (whole) specification $\widetilde{S_2}$, but we may think as well of each program module P_i as being an implementation of the corresponding specification module S_i. Thus, the requirement above means nothing but that a programmer should be able to design the program module P_2 only with the help of the specification modules $S_2, S_1, \ldots$ (and the hierarchical structure of the specification $\widetilde{S_2}$), without looking at the actual code of the program module P_1 who implements the specification module S_1.

[6] The generalization of the constraint C 4 given here is oversimplified and must itself be refined to take care of shared sub-specification modules of the specification modules $S_1\_a, \ldots, S_1\_k$ …

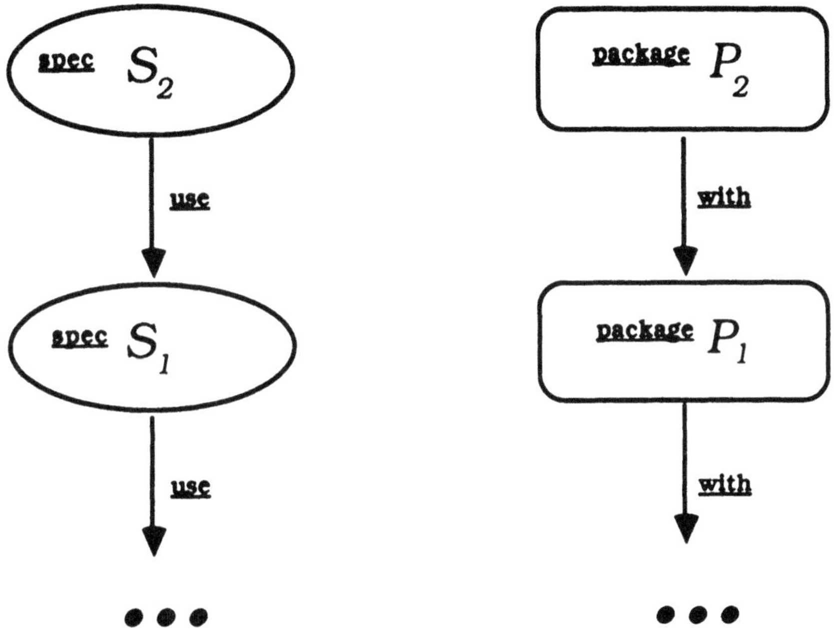

Figure 3: Correspondence between a modular specification and its modular implementation.

- Putting emphasis on modularity, the requirement above can be understood as a very strong requirement about the role of achieved, completed specifications with respect to modular software development: As soon as the specification is structured into completed specification modules, these modules should be implementable independently of each other, may be simultaneously by separate programmer teams. The "correctness" of the global implementation (obtained by *linking together* the implementation modules) with respect to the global specification should only rely on the correctness of each implementation module with respect to the appropriate specification module. Note again that if we can (for sake of simplicity) understand "global correctness" as "being a model of", we have no way up to now to formalize what "modular correctness" should be.

- If we now put emphasis on reusability, the requirement above can be understood as follows. If we have at our disposal some (correct) implementation of the specification module S_2, this implementation should be reusable in conjunction with any (correct) implementation of the sub-specification $\widetilde{S_1}$ (i.e. with any piece of software who fulfills $\widetilde{S_1}$). Moreover, if the collection of program modules $P_2, P_1, \ldots$ produces a correct implementation of the specification $\widetilde{S_2}$, then exchanging the module P_1 for another (correct) implementation module of S_1, say P_1', should still produce a correct implementation of $\widetilde{S_2}$.

As pointed out by the above comments, the first difficulty to solve is to better reflect modularity in our algebraic semantics. It is clear that the standard loose approach is not the appropriate framework in any respect, since this loose approach only allows us to reason by means of (classes of) models, and models can be related to specifications, not to specification modules. Before going into the details of the solution we propose, we would like to give a concrete example of the problem

```
spec : S2                "containers"
      use : S1
   sort : Container
   generated by :
      empty : ⟶ Container
      add : Nat Container ⟶ Container
   operations :
      belongs : Nat Container ⟶ Bool
      remove : Nat Container ⟶ Container
   axioms :
      belongs-1 : belongs(n,empty) = false
      belongs-2 : n = m ⟹ belongs(n,add(m,C)) = true
      belongs-3 : n ≠ m ⟹ belongs(n,add(m,C)) = belongs(n,C)
      remove-1 : remove(n,empty) = empty
      remove-2 : n = m ⟹ remove(n,add(m,C)) = remove(n,C)
      remove-3 : n ≠ m ⟹ remove(n,add(m,C)) = add(m,remove(n,C))
      where :  n, m : Nat,  C : Container
end S2
```

```
spec : S1                "natural numbers"
      use : BOOLEAN
   sort : Nat
   generated by :
      zero : ⟶ Nat
      s : Nat ⟶ Nat
   operations :
      _ + _ : Nat Nat ⟶ Nat
      _ less _ : Nat Nat ⟶ Bool
   axioms :
      less-1 : x less x = false
      less-2 : x less y = true ⟹ y less x = false
      less-3 : x less y = true & y less z = true ⟹ x less z = true
      less-4 : zero less s(zero) = true
      +-1 : x + zero = x
      +-2 : x + s(y) = s(x + y)
      where :  x, y, z : Nat
end S1
```

Figure 4: The "containers of natural numbers" specification.

```
signature NAT-SIG =
  sig
    type Nat
    • • •
  end

abstraction NAT : NAT-SIG =
  struct
    datatype Nat = nat of int
    val zero = nat 0
    • • •
  end
```

```
signature CONTAINER-SIG =
  sig
    structure N : NAT-SIG
    type Container
    val empty : Container
    val add : N.Nat * Container → Container
    val belongs : N.Nat * Container → bool
    val remove : N.Nat * Container → Container
  end

abstraction CONTAINER : CONTAINER-SIG =
  struct
    structure N = NAT
    datatype Container = cont of N.Nat list
    val empty = cont nil
    fun add(n, cont L) = • • •
    fun belongs(n, cont nil) = false
      | belongs(n, cont(m::L)) =
          if n=m then true else belongs(n, cont L)
    fun remove(n, cont L) =
      let fun delete(n, nil) = nil
            | delete(n, m::L) =
                if n=m then delete(n,L)
                else m::delete(n,L)
      in cont(delete(n, L)) end
  end
```

Figure 5: The "containers of natural numbers" implementation scheme.

we want to solve.

Assume that the specification $\widetilde{S_1}$ describes natural numbers, and that the class $\mathcal{M}_1$ of the models of $\widetilde{S_1}$ exactly contains the model of standard natural numbers ($\mathcal{N}$) together with the models of natural numbers modulo n (Z/nZ). Assume that the specification module S_2, built as an enrichment of S_1, describes "containers" of natural numbers in a rather flexible way (i.e. we can imagine various non-isomorphic models of $\widetilde{S_2}$). The specification modules S_1 and S_2 are given in Figure 4.

It is quite easy to figure out various implementations of these containers. To make our discussion more concrete, we shall describe some of them, using as implementation language *Standard ML*, following the scheme pictured in Figure 5, where we have voluntarily left some parts incomplete.[7]

Let us first make a few comments about the implementation scheme described in Figure 5:

- The first point is that we use the **abstraction** construct of *ML* in order to hide the implementation details.[8] This is not only safe from the point of view of encapsulation, but reflects also the fact that we are not interested in all integer values (neither in all lists of integers),

[7] It is a pleasure to acknowledge *Jordi Farrés* who helps me in writing these small *ML* examples during his visit in Orsay. However, errors (if any) should be considered as mine.

[8] The **abstraction** construct of *Standard ML* is described in [30].

but only in those obtained by arbitrary compositions of `s` and `zero` (resp. of `add` and `empty`). As a complementary remark, it is important to note that, despite the fact that we describe here actual implementations (written in *Standard ML*), what we should really consider in the scope of this paper are algebras. Thus the examples given here should only be considered as a convenient way to describe various algebras of $\mathcal{M}_2$. More precisely, in any case the carrier of the sort *Container* is the set of the lists built from arbitrary composition of `empty` and `add`, and we shall obtain various implementations of our containers of natural numbers by changing the definitions of the `s` and `add` functions.

- The second point is that we have deliberately chosen not to use the **functor** construction of *ML* to implement containers. This is due to the fact that we are only interested here in various implementations of containers of natural numbers, and not in various implementations of containers of "anything".

Let us now describe more precisely some implementations of our containers (and of our natural numbers):

1. If we want to implement the specification $\widetilde{S_1}$ by standard natural numbers, then we may define the `s` function in the *NAT* structure by: `s(nat x) = nat(x+1)` while we may define it by: `s(nat x) = nat((x+1) mod 2)` if we want for instance to implement the specification $\widetilde{S_1}$ by natural numbers modulo 2.

2. A straightforward implementation of containers is obtained by directly using lists to represent containers, i.e. we fill in the *CONTAINER* structure with:

```
fun add(n, cont L) = cont(n::L)
```

3. It is also possible to implement containers by ordered lists, with:

```
fun add(n, cont L) =
  let fun plus(n, nil) = [n]
        | plus(n, m::L) = if N.less(n,m) then n::m::L else m::plus(n,L)
    in cont(plus(n, L)) end
```

   Note that in that case the implementation may further depend on the actual implementation of the *less* operation.

4. We may also want to implement containers by lists without duplicates, i.e. we define:

```
fun add(n, cont L) = if belongs(n, cont L) then cont L else cont(n::L)
```

5. One can also imagine to implement containers by lists with at most k duplicates of the same natural number (where k is an arbitrary fixed constant), i.e. we have:

```
fun add(n, cont L) =
  let fun count(n, nil) = 0
        | count(n, m::L) = if n=m then count(n,L)+1 else count(n,L)
    in if count(n,L) < k then cont(n::L) else cont L end
```

   Note that in that case the arity of the `count` auxiliary function is:
   `count : N.Nat * (N.Nat) list -> int .`
   Thus, if we take $k = 3$ for instance, the value of *add(s(s(s(zero))), add(s(zero), add(s(s(s(zero))), add(s(zero), add(s(s(s(zero))), add(s(s(s(zero))), empty))))))* is `cont([nat 1, nat 3, nat 1, nat 3, nat 3])` if we have implemented *Nat* by standard natural numbers and `cont([nat 1, nat 1, nat 1])` if we have implemented *Nat* by natural numbers modulo 2.

6. We may also want to implement containers by lists with at most n duplicates of the natural number n:

```
fun add(n, cont L) =
  let fun count(n, nil) = N.zero
        | count(n, m::L) = if n=m then N.s(count(n,L)) else count(n,L)
    in if N.less(count(n,L), n) then cont(n::L) else cont L end
```

   Note that in this last example, the maximum number of duplicates actually depends on the implementation chosen for natural numbers, since the arity of the count auxiliary function is: `count : N.Nat * (N.Nat) list -> N.Nat` .
   More precisely, if we implement natural numbers by $\mathcal{N}$ then the maximum number of duplicates of $s(s(s(zero)))$ in any container is 3, while if natural numbers are implemented by $Z/2Z$, the maximum number of duplicates of $s(s(s(zero)))$ is 1 (since $s(s(s(zero)))$ = `nat 1`). Thus, the value of the expression above is `cont([nat 3, nat 1, nat 3, nat 3])` when *Nat* is implemented by $\mathcal{N}$ and `cont([nat 1])` when *Nat* is implemented by $Z/2Z$.

The examples given above are just a few ones among all the algebras of $\mathcal{M}_2$. The point is that, in all these examples, the carrier of the sort *Container* is in some sense "parameterized" by the carrier of the sort *Nat*. However, it is also quite correct (with respect to the old version of the **Pluss use** semantics) to implement the specification $\widetilde{S_2}$ by implementing the sort *Nat* by $Z/2Z$, and containers by lists of booleans as follows:

```
abstraction CONTAINER : CONTAINER-SIG =
  struct
    structure N = NAT
    datatype Container = cont of bool list
    val empty = cont nil
    fun add(n, cont L) = if n=N.zero then cont(false::L) else cont(true::L)
    fun belongs(n, cont nil) = false
      | belongs(n, cont(b::L)) =
          let val b1 = if n=N.zero then false else true
            in if b1=b then true else belongs(n, cont L) end
    fun remove(n, cont L) =
      let fun delete(b, nil) = nil
            | delete(b, b1::L) = if b=b1 then delete(b,L)
                                 else b1::delete(b,L)
        in let val b = if n=N.zero then false else true
             in cont(delete(b, L)) end end
  end
```

As far as the sort *Nat* is actually implemented by $Z/2Z$, the implementation above leads to a correct model of $\widetilde{S_2}$. This is obviously not the case if another implementation (e.g. $\mathcal{N}$) is chosen for the sort *Nat*.

It is clear that all the previous models reflect the specification $\widetilde{S_2}$ itself plus additional properties that we would like to call implementation choices in our context. What distinguish two implementations (models) of $\widetilde{S_2}$ are exactly these implementation choices. According to the structuration of the specification $\widetilde{S_2}$ into the specification modules S_2 and S_1, we may attempt to further classify these implementation choices (hence the various models of $\widetilde{S_2}$) according to the following criteria:

- The implementation choices intrinsic to the sub-specification $\widetilde{S_1}$:
  Does the carrier set of the sort Nat contain standard natural numbers or natural numbers modulo n?

- The implementation choices intrinsic to the specification module S_2:
Are containers implemented by lists, ordered lists, lists without duplicates, lists with at most k duplicates?

- The implementation choices related to the specification module S_2, but who take into account (in a general way) the implementation choices made for the sub-specification $\widetilde{S_1}$:
Implementations of containers by lists with at most n duplicates of the natural number n.

- The implementation choices related to the specification module S_2, but who take into account the implementation choices made for some specific model of the sub-specification $\widetilde{S_1}$:
Implementation of containers by lists of booleans and of natural numbers by natural numbers modulo 2.

These various kinds of implementation choices can be directly related to the various ways we can imagine to implement the specification modules S_1 and S_2 by program modules P_1 and P_2: the implementation choices intrinsic to the sub-specification $\widetilde{S_1}$ are the implementation choices for the program module P_1 (or the modules below); the implementation choices intrinsic to the specification module S_2 are the implementation choices who can be made for the program module P_2 in a relatively arbitrary way. We may consider the third kind of implementation choices as implementation choices for the program module P_2, "parameterized" (in a general way) by the program module P_1. The last example, however, corresponds to a specific implementation of S_2 by a program module P_2 who **must** be combined with a specific implementation of $\widetilde{S_1}$ to lead to a correct implementation of the whole specification $\widetilde{S_2}$. In this last case, it is not possible to exchange the implementation of $\widetilde{S_1}$ with another one. In other words, extensive use of the knowledge about the implementation of $\widetilde{S_1}$ has been made while implementing the specification module S_2.

The previous discussion and examples can be summarized as follows:

- The algebraic semantics of achieved, completed specifications must better reflect the modular structure of these specifications: we need a framework which permits to reason about the "models" (i.e. implementations) of a specification **module** as well as about the models of a specification. The standard loose approach does not seem to be suitable for that purpose.

- As shown by the examples, the "models" of the specification module S_2 must be *parameterized* by the models of the enriched sub-specification $\widetilde{S_1}$. This is necessary as soon as we want that the implementations of the specification module only relies on the specification, not on some specific implementation of $\widetilde{S_1}$. This will also be useful to better reflect software reusability.

- The class $\mathcal{M}_2$ of the models of $\widetilde{S_2}$ must be further constrained in order to reject some too specific models (such as the implementation of containers by lists of booleans). More precisely, it is the class of the "models" of the specification module S_2 that must be constrained to reject such models.

In the next section we show how a suitable framework can be obtained by combining the loose approach with the initial one.

5 The stratified loose approach.

In this section we propose a solution to the problems raised in the previous section. This solution will be obtained by embedding the ideas of the initial approach into the loose one, leading to what we will call the "stratified loose approach".

In the very earliest works about the initial approach (e.g. [28]), the semantics of an abstract data type was defined as the initial model (defined up to isomorphism) of the class (category) of all the models of the abstract data type presentation. The existence of such an initial model is ensured as soon as the axioms are restricted to (positive) conditional equations. However, the necessity to structure large abstract data type presentations into smaller units, as well as the necessity of some parameterization mechanisms, have led very soon to generalize this oversimplified view to hierarchical and parameterized abstract data types. The initial semantics was then defined by means of the so-called "synthesis functor" (i.e. the free functor $\mathcal{F}_s$ from $\mathcal{M}_1$ to $\mathcal{M}_2$, left adjoint to the forgetful functor $\mathcal{U}$) and "pushouts" (to cope with shared sub-modules) (see e.g. [38,23,8,24]). The best representative of algebraic specification languages built on top of this initial approach is **ACT ONE** [21].

What is important to note is that this synthesis (free) functor provides a semantics to the piece of specification related to what is usually called "the type of interest" (i.e. the specification module S_2 in our context). Moreover, even if one is just interested in the initial objects, i.e. in the image of the initial object I_1 of $\mathcal{M}_1$ by $\mathcal{F}_s$ (which is exactly the initial object I_2 of $\mathcal{M}_2$), it is still the case that since $\mathcal{F}_s$ is a functor, it is defined over the whole category $\mathcal{M}_1$. Remember also that under suitable assumptions over the axioms, the classes $\mathcal{M}_1$ and $\mathcal{M}_2$ are complete lattices; indeed it can be shown that $\mathcal{M}_2$ is structured into sub-classes, each one being a complete sub-lattice and containing the models who are forgotten by $\mathcal{U}$ into a given model of $\mathcal{M}_1$ [40]. This property is used for instance in the terminal approach, where the terminal semantics of $\widetilde{S_2}$ is defined as the terminal object of $\mathcal{M}_2$ over the initial object of $\mathcal{M}_1$ (to avoid the trivial terminal object of $\mathcal{M}_2$).

In our context, initial objects do not necessarily exist, neither free functors. However, we may still benefit from the underlying ideas to obtain a suitable semantics for specification modules:

Definition 1 (Stratified loose semantics)
Let S_2 be a (completed) specification module built as an enrichment of another (completed) specification module S_1 (i.e. we have **spec** S_2 **use** S_1 ... **end** S_2*). Let $\mathcal{M}_1$ be the class of the models of the specification $\widetilde{S_1}$ (according to the current definition), and $\widehat{\mathcal{M}_2}$ be the class of the Σ_2-algebras satisfying the constraints* **C 1**, **C 2** *and* **C 3** *(i.e. $\widehat{\mathcal{M}_2}$ contains the Σ_2-algebras finitely generated w.r.t. Ω_2 for which the axioms $\mathcal{A}x(\widetilde{S_2})$ hold, and who produce $\widetilde{S_1}$ models when the new part specified by the specification module S_2 is forgotten by the forgetful functor $\mathcal{U}$: $\mathcal{U}(\widehat{\mathcal{M}_2}) \subseteq \mathcal{M}_1$).*

- *If $\widehat{\mathcal{M}_2}$ is empty, the enrichment is said to be (hierarchically) inconsistent and the semantics of the specification module S_2 is empty, as well as the semantics $\mathcal{M}_2$ of the whole specification $\widetilde{S_2}$.*
- *Otherwise, the semantics of the specification module S_2 is defined as being the class $\mathcal{F}_1^2$ of all the mappings $\mathcal{F}_i$ such that:*
  1. *$\mathcal{F}_i$ is a (***total***) functor from $\mathcal{M}_1$ to $\widehat{\mathcal{M}_2}$.*
  2. *$\mathcal{F}_i$ is a right inverse of the forgetful functor $\mathcal{U}$, i.e.:*
     $\forall M_1 \in \mathcal{M}_1 : \mathcal{U}(\mathcal{F}_i(M_1)) = M_1$.

  If the class $\mathcal{F}_1^2$ is empty, then the enrichment is also said to be (hierarchically) inconsistent.
- *The semantics of the whole specification $\widetilde{S_2}$ is defined as being the class of all the models image by the functors $\mathcal{F}_i$ of the models of $\mathcal{M}_1$:*
  $$\mathcal{M}_2 = \bigcup_{\mathcal{F}_i \in \mathcal{F}_1^2} \mathcal{F}_i(\mathcal{M}_1)$$

The class $\mathcal{M}_2$ of the models of the specification $\widetilde{S_2}$ is said to be **stratified** *by the functors $\mathcal{F}_i$.*

Some comments are necessary to better understand the previous definition:

- With our stratified loose semantics, all the constraints C **1**, C **2**, C **3** and C **4** are verified:
  - The first three constraints hold by construction, since the class $\mathcal{M}_2$ is obviously included in $\widehat{\mathcal{M}_2}$.
  - Since the functors $\mathcal{F}_i$ are total mappings and right inverses of the forgetful functor $\mathcal{U}$, the constraint C **4** also holds: either the class $\mathcal{F}_1^2$ is empty (and so is $\mathcal{M}_2$), or we have just to pick one functor $\mathcal{F}_i$ in $\mathcal{F}_1^2$ to get the desired result.

- Our stratified loose semantics is modular, and the semantics of a specification module S_2 is formally defined as being the class of functors $\mathcal{F}_1^2$. This semantics is defined only by means of the collection of the specification modules $S_2, S_1, \ldots$ (and the hierarchical structure of $\widetilde{S_2}$).

- Our semantics is loose, since it associates a class of (non-isomorphic) functors (resp. models) to a given specification module (resp. to a given specification). However, our semantics can also be considered as a strict generalization of the initial approach: under suitable assumptions, both $\mathcal{M}_1$ and $\mathcal{M}_2$ are complete lattices with initial models, and the synthesis (free) functor $\mathcal{F}_s$ is just one specific functor in the class $\mathcal{F}_1^2$.

- The choice of some peculiar functor $\mathcal{F}_i$ in the class $\mathcal{F}_1^2$ both reflects the implementation choices intrinsic to the specification module S_2 and the implementation choices who are related to the specification module S_2 and parameterized by the implementation choices of the sub-specification $\widetilde{S_1}$.

- As desired, too specific implementations of the specification module S_2 are excluded by our definition. Keeping on with our implementation of specification modules in *Standard ML*, an implementation of the specification module S_2 is correct as far as it "defines" a suitable functor $\mathcal{F}_i$. For instance, the case where containers are implemented by lists of booleans does not lead to a correct implementation of the specification module S_2, since this implementation can only be combined with the implementation of $\widetilde{S_1}$ by natural numbers modulo 2.

- Since the $\mathcal{F}_i$ are functors, they do not only map objects to objects, but also arrows to arrows. Thus, if two implementations M_1 and M_1' are related by some Σ_1-morphism h_1, then the two corresponding implementations $\mathcal{F}_i(M_1)$ and $\mathcal{F}_i(M_1')$ are related by the Σ_2-morphism $h_2 = \mathcal{F}_i(h_1)$. Therefore, if we know a way to describe the changes between the implementation choices for M_1 and those for M_1' (i.e. if h_1 exists), we can deduce how far these changes are reflected at the level of the implementations of $\widetilde{S_2}$. In other words, relations between implementation choices intrinsic to the sub-specification $\widetilde{S_1}$ can be retrieved at the level of $\widetilde{S_2}$.

- We have emphasized the fact that the models of the specification module S_2 must be "parameterized" by the models of the enriched sub-specification $\widetilde{S_1}$. However, even if our stratified loose semantics embodies some kind of parameterization, it is important to point out that the parameterization mechanism involved is strictly more powerful than standard parameterized specifications:
  - The first point is that to achieve a similar parameterization mechanism with parameterized specifications would require to be able to specify the class $\mathcal{M}_1$ by some appropriate formal parameter specification. This is clearly impossible in general, at least without existential quantifiers and second-order formulas, since the class $\mathcal{M}_1$ is restricted to finitely generated models and is itself the result of iterative applications of our stratified loose semantics, and it is well-known that, in general, model semantics is strictly more powerful than presentation semantics [39].

- On the other hand, with the parameterization mechanism involved by our stratified loose semantics, it is possible to model more sophisticated implementation schemes than it would be with standard parameterization. In fact, since the $\mathcal{F}_i$ only have to be functors, and not necessarily the free synthesis functor, some of them, even if they are defined on the whole class $\mathcal{M}_1$, may still benefit from the peculiarities of some models. For instance, the following implementation of containers:

```
fun add(n, cont L) =
      if N.s(N.s(N.s(N.zero))) <> N.zero then cont(n::L)
      else if belongs(n, cont L) then cont L else cont(n::L)
```

  where containers are implemented by lists if $s(s(s(zero))) \neq zero$ in the actual implementation of natural numbers and by lists without duplicates otherwise, is a correct functor with respect to our definition, thus defines a correct implementation scheme for containers. This is consistent with our intuition, since the implementation of containers sketched above can be combined with any (correct) implementation of natural numbers.

6 Conclusion.

In this paper we have explained why we have originally chosen the loose approach as a basic framework to define the formal semantics of the **Pluss** specification language. We have stressed why it is important to state a careful distinction between achieved, completed specification components and specification components under design. Then we have shown that, despite some promising attempts, the loose approach is not powerful enough to embed our intuition and needs about software reusability and modularity in the semantics of the enrichment specification-building primitive for completed specification components: the crucial point was the ability to implement independently of each other the various specification components of a specification. Therefore, we have introduced a more sophisticated framework, the *stratified loose semantics*, and we have detailed why this framework seems to be better suited to our goals. It turned out that the stratified loose semantics we have introduced can be considered as a generalization of both initial and loose semantics.

It is clear that further extensions of our definition of the stratified loose semantics are needed, at least to cope with multiple enrichments, but also to take into account other specification-building primitives such as parameterization. This is not a difficult task since our framework requires no specific assumptions, hence can be easily mixed with e.g. **ASL** semantics for parameterized specifications. What is important to note here is that our stratified loose semantics has the required compositional properties, thus the formal semantics of the **Pluss** specification language can be described using the same denotational style as in **ASL** [2].

As explained in the introduction, the goal of this paper was not to describe a formal framework for software reusability, but only to study how reusability and modularity interact with the design of the semantics of the specification language. However, it should be noted that the ideas contained in this paper have already been successfully applied to the rigorous definition of "efficient software reusability" [26]. Moreover, the stratified loose semantics described in this paper is not only related to modularity and reusability, but also to other works where the impact of algebraic specifications on various stages of software development is studied. One of the best example is [18], where it is shown how algebraic specifications can be used for integration testing, by mixing standard symbolic evaluation (for those parts of software who are not yet implemented) and direct program execution (for the already implemented software parts). Such an approach only makes sense in the stratified loose framework.

References

[1] *The programming language Ada. Reference Manual.* United States Department of Defense, January 1983.

[2] E. Astesiano and M. Wirsing. An introduction to ASL. In *Proc. of the IFIP WG2.1 Working Conference on Program Specifications and Transformations*, 1986.

[3] F.L. Bauer et al. *The Munich Project CIP. Volume I: The wide spectrum language CIP-L.* Springer-Verlag L.N.C.S. 183, 1985.

[4] G. Bernot. Good functors... are those preserving philosophy ! In *Proc. of the Summer Conference on Category Theory and Computer Science*, pages 182–195, Springer-Verlag L.N.C.S. 283, September 1987.

[5] G. Bernot, M. Bidoit, and C. Choppy. Abstract data types with exception handling: an initial approach based on a distinction between exceptions and errors. *Theoretical Computer Science*, 46(1):13–45, 1986.

[6] G. Bernot, M. Bidoit, and C. Choppy. Abstract implementations and correctness proofs. In *Proc. of the 3rd STACS*, pages 236–251, Springer-Verlag L.N.C.S. 210, January 1986.

[7] M. Bidoit. Algebraic specification of exception handling and error recovery by means of declarations and equations. In *Proc. of the 11th ICALP*, pages 95–108, Springer-Verlag L.N.C.S. 172, July 1984.

[8] M. Bidoit. *Une méthode de présentation des types abstraits: Applications.* Thèse de 3° Cycle, Université Paris-Sud, June 1981.

[9] M. Bidoit, B. Biebow, M.-C. Gaudel, C. Gresse, and G. Guiho. Exception handling: formal specification and systematic program construction. *I.E.E.E. Transactions on Software Engineering*, SE-11(3):242–252, 1985.

[10] M. Bidoit and C. Choppy. *The ALEX-PLUSS Specification Language.* Technical Report, ESPRIT Project FOR-ME-TOO, January 1986.

[11] M. Bidoit, C. Choppy, and F. Voisin. The ASSPEGIQUE specification environment: motivations and design. In *Proc. of the 3rd Workshop on Theory and Applications of Abstract Data Types*, pages 54–72, Springer-Verlag I.F.B. 116, November 1984.

[12] M. Bidoit, M.-C. Gaudel, and A. Mauboussin. *How to make algebraic specifications more understandable ? An experiment with the Pluss specification language.* Technical Report 343, L.R.I., April 1987.

[13] B. Biebow. *Application d'un langage de spécification algébrique à des exemples téléphoniques.* Thèse de 3° Cycle, Université Paris VI, February 1984.

[14] B. Biebow, N. Choquet, and A. Mauboussin. *Spécification par types abstraits algébriques de fonctions caractéristiques d'une unité de raccordement d'abonnés téléphoniques.* Technical Report, DAII Contract 84.35.087, September 1985.

[15] B. Biebow and J. Hagelstein. Algebraic specification of synchronisation and errors: a telephonic example. In *Proc. of the TAPSOFT Conference*, pages 294–308, Springer-Verlag L.N.C.S. 186, March 1985.

[16] M. Broy and M. Wirsing. Partial abstract data types. *Acta Informatica*, 18(1):47-64, 1982.

[17] F. Capy. *ASSPEGIQUE: un environnement d'exceptions...* Thèse de 3° Cycle, Université Paris-Sud, December 1987.

[18] C. Choppy. Formal specifications, prototyping and integration tests. In *Proc. of the 1st European Software Engineering Conference*, pages 185–192, September 1987.

[19] M.-A. Choquer. *Specification of the evaluation tool: leftmost outermost reduction strategy in the equational case.* Technical Report, ESPRIT Project METEOR, November 1986.

[20] J. Despeyroux-Savonitto. An algebraic specification of a Pascal compiler. *SIGPLAN*, 18(12):34–48, 1983.

[21] H. Ehrig, W. Fey, and H. Hansen. *ACT ONE: An algebraic specification language with two levels of semantics.* Technical Report 83-03, Department of Computer Science, TU Berlin, 1983.

[22] H. Ehrig, H. Kreowski, B. Mahr, and P. Padawitz. Algebraic implementation of abstract data types. *Theoretical Computer Science*, October 1980.

[23] H. Ehrig, H. Kreowski, J.W. Thatcher, E.G. Wagner, and J.B. Wright. Parameterized data types in algebraic specification languages. In *Proc. of the 7th ICALP*, 1980.

[24] H. Ehrig and B. Mahr. *Fundamentals of Algebraic Specification 1.* Springer-Verlag, 1985.

[25] K. Futatsugi, J.A. Goguen, J.-P. Jouannaud, and J. Meseguer. Principles of OBJ2. In *Proc. of the 12th ACM Symposium on Principles of Programming Languages*, pages 52-66, January 1985.

[26] M.-C. Gaudel and Th. Moineau. A theory of software reusability. In *Proc. of ESOP'88*, to appear in Springer-Verlag L.N.C.S., March 1988.

[27] J.A. Goguen and J. Meseguer. *Order-Sorted Algebra I: Partial and Overloaded Operators, Errors and Inheritance.* Technical Report, S.R.I., October 1986. Unpublished Draft.

[28] J.A. Goguen, J.W. Thatcher, and E.G. Wagner. *An initial approach to the specification, correctness, and implementation of abstract data types.* Volume 4 of *Current Trends in Programming Methodology*, Prentice Hall, 1978.

[29] J.V. Guttag, J.J. Horning, and J.M. Wing. *Larch in five easy pieces.* Technical Report 5, Digital Systems Research Center, 1985.

[30] R. Harper. *Introduction to Standard ML.* Technical Report ECS-LFCS-86-14, LFCS, Edinburgh, November 1986.

[31] S. Kaplan. Fair conditional term rewrite systems. *Journal of Symbolic Computation*, 1987.

[32] B. Liskov et al. *CLU Reference Manual.* Technical Report MIT-LCS-TR-225, M.I.T., October 1979.

[33] D. MacQueen and D.T. Sannella. Completeness of proof systems for equational specifications. *I.E.E.E. Transactions on Software Engineering*, SE-11(5), 1985.

[34] D.T. Sannella. Implementations revisited. In *Abstracts of the 5th Workshop on Specification of Abstract Data Types*, September 1987.

[35] D.T. Sannella and A. Tarlecki. Building specifications in an arbitrary institution. In *Proc. of the Intl. Symp. on Semantics of Data Types*, Springer-Verlag L.N.C.S. 173, 1984.

[36] D.T. Sannella and M. Wirsing. A kernel language for algebraic specification and implementation. In *Proc. of FCT'83*, Springer-Verlag L.N.C.S. 158, 1983.

[37] Oliver Schoett. *Data abstraction and the correctness of modular programming*. PhD thesis, University of Edinburg, 1987.

[38] J.W. Thatcher, E.G. Wagner, and J.B. Wright. Data type specification: parameterization and the power of specification techniques. In *Proc. of the 10th Annual Symposium on Theory of Computing*, 1979.

[39] M. Wirsing. *Structured Algebraic Specifications: A Kernel Language*. PhD thesis, Techn. Univ. Munchen, 1983.

[40] M. Wirsing and M. Broy. Abstract data types as lattices of finitely generated models. In *Proc. of the 9th Intl. Symp. on Mathematical Foundations of Computer Science*, Springer-Verlag L.N.C.S., September 1980.

ALGEBRAIC DATA TYPE AND PROCESS SPECIFICATIONS BASED ON PROJECTION SPACES *

Hartmut Ehrig Francesco Parisi-Presicce ** Paul Boehm
Catharina Rieckhoff Cristian Dimitrovici Martin Große-Rhode

TU Berlin

ABSTRACT

The algebraic approach to the semantics of (nonterminating) processes based on the metric completion of process algebras is extended in two directions. Instead of adopting the predefined metric, it is proposed to define the metric internally, using a suitable family of projections as part of the specification and deal with projection spaces rather than metric spaces. It is also proposed to define the data type along with the processes, to allow nonconstant actions and internally defined communication functions. Combined data type and process specifications find a suitable basis for their algebraic semantics in projection algebras.

Notation and keywords :

Cat(SPEC)	Category of SPEC-algebras with algebra homomorphisms
Cat(CSPEC)	Category of (constrained) projection-SPEC-algebras with projection-SPEC-algebra homomorphisms
CatCompl(CSPEC)	Category of complete projection-SPEC-algebras with projection-SPEC-algebra homomorphisms
A^{∞}	completion by standard construction of A (for projection spaces and projection algebras)
T_{SPEC}	Initial SPEC-algebra
CT_{SPEC}	Complete initial projection-SPEC-algebra
Hom(A)	process space

* This report was partly supported by the DFG-project "Algebraische Spezifikation verteilter Systeme und asynchron operationale Semantik (DAO)", the project "Kategorielle Methoden in Topologie und Informatik (KAMITI)" and done in cooperation with the University of Southern California. A previous version appeared as TUB-Report Nr. 87-7 (1987).

** University of Southern California/University of L'Aquila

INTRODUCTION

One of the major tasks in defining algebraic semantics for recursively defined processes is to construct a complete algebra which contains also infinite processes. There are two main approaches to solve this problem. The first approach, using partial orders, considers infinite processes as partial functions and obtains the complete algebra by ideal completion. The Knaster-Tarski fixed-point theorem provides a unique least fixed point that may serve as semantics for the recursive processes. Scott et al., the ADJ group (/ADJ77/, /ADJ78/), Möller (/MD86/, /Mö182/, /Mö185/) and Tarlecki/Wirsing (/TW86/) developed a theory of continuous algebras based on partial orders with main applications to program semantics. Bergstra/Klop, however, observed difficulties in the partial order approach for process specifications, as the bottom element ⊥ seems to lead to inconsistencies with the equations (see /BK86/).

The other approach considers infinite processes as infinite trees or graphs. Having defined a metric on this space (see e.g. /AN80/) the complete algebra can be constructed as a projective limit and the Banach´s fixed-point theorem provides a unique fixed point (not only a unique least fixpoint), which solves the recursive equation system defining the processes. DeBakker/Zucker and Bergstra/Klop have been working with this method. The latter have constructed models for some axiom systems for communicating processes introducing a metric externally by projections (where e.g. the n´th projection of a tree consists of all branches of this tree cut to length n).

Since this metric is uniquely determined by the projections we find it more suitable to specify the projections instead of the distance. The metric, which turns out to be an ultrametric, then is internally defined and the algebra together with its metric is given in one specification. This allows to define initial algebra semantics in each step of the development of a recursive process specification and compositionality of the corresponding semantics. The theory of projection spaces including completion of a projection space, fixed-point theorem and categorical properties is treated in the first section of this paper, and in a more detailed version and extended mathematical background in /DEGR87/.

A further difference with the approach of Bergstra/Klop is that process specifications are allowed to have a parameter part for the data type so that actions and communication functions are no longer constant and externally defined respectively but vary over the class of data algebras. Hence process specifications based on projection spaces also yield a suitable semantic basis for Lotos-like languages (see /LOTOS87/, /LOTOS86/, /LOTOS83/). On the other hand, the high level of abstraction makes it much more difficult to give criteria for the existence of a solution of a general recursive process specification. In this paper we introduce recursive process specifications where recursive processes are defined by recursive equations.

A recursive process specification is built up in three steps:

(1) We start with a process specification **process(data)** , which is an actualization of a parameterized process specification **process(action)** with a data type specification **data** . This resulting specification **process(data)** has initial algebra semantics.

(2) For each sort in **process(data)** we specify a projection, which is discrete for the sorts incorporating data and nondiscrete for the sorts that incorporate processes, obtaining an extension of **process(data)** called **proproc(data)** . If the specification is correct, i.e. each sort together with its projection forms a projection space and the operations are continuous (relative to the projections), then the initial algebra in Cat(**proproc(data)**) is a projection algebra. The semantics of **proproc(data)** is then the universal completion of the initial algebra of Cat(**proproc(data)**) and again initial in the category of complete **proproc(data)** algebras.

(3) In the last step, the projection specification **proproc(data)** is enriched by the signature and the equations for the recursive processes proc1,...,procn, obtaining the recursive process specification **recproc(data)** . The semantics of **recproc(data)** is the extension of the semantics of **proproc(data)** by the

fixed point of an operator T corresponding to the equation system, provided that the operator T is contracting. This means that the semantics of **recproc(data)** is a complete initial projection algebra in the category Cat(**recproc(data)**) .

We outline a first example here, given in an ACT ONE like syntax (see e.g. /EM85/).

As basic actions we take the occurrences of natural numbers at certain gates, seen as the data type specification **natact** :

DATA TYPE SPEC - **data**

natact = **nat** +
<u>sorts</u> gate,act
<u>opns</u> g1,...gn:→gate
(_!_):gate nat→act

The processes are built up by a choice operator + and a sequence operator · , together with a coercion _ that declares actions as processes, specified in the parameterized specification (**action**,**bpa(action)**)
(**bpa**=basic process algebra) :

PROCESS SPEC - **process(action)**

action =
<u>sorts</u> action

bpa(action) = **action** +
<u>sorts</u> proc
<u>opns</u> _:action→proc
+,·:proc proc→proc
<u>eqns</u> <u>for all</u> x,y ,z <u>in</u> proc :

$x+x=x$	(idempotent)
$x+y=y+x$	(commutative)
$(x+y)+z=x+(y+z)$	(associative)
$(x \cdot y) \cdot z=x \cdot (y \cdot z)$	(associative)
$(x+y) \cdot z=x \cdot z+y \cdot z$	(left distributive)

The combined data type and process specification is obtained by actualization of the process specification **bpa(action)** with the data type specification **natact**, i.e. the union of **bpa(action)** and **natact**, where the formal sort action in **bpa(action)** is replaced by the sort act from the actual parameter **natact**.

COMBINED SPEC - **process(data)**

bpa(natact) = **bpa(action)** <u>actualized by</u> **natact**
= **natact** +
<u>sorts</u> proc
<u>opns</u> _:act→proc
+,·:proc proc→proc

<u>eqns</u> <u>for all</u> x,y ,z <u>in</u> proc :

x+x=x

x+y=y+x

(x+y)+z=x+(y+z)

(x·y)·z=x·(y·z)

(x+y)·z=x·z+y·z

The combined specification **bpa(natact)** is now extended by the specification of $\mathbf{N}_1$ and the projections for all sorts (the nat1-specification is given at the beginning of section 2). Since a completion is only needed in the sort "proc" of processes, all other projections are discrete, i.e. ps(n,x)=x for all $n \in \mathbf{N}_1, x \in s, s \in S, s \neq proc$.

PROJECTION SPEC - **proproc(data)**

probpa(nat) =

bpa(natact) + **nat1** +

<u>opns</u> ps:nat1 s→s

(for all s∈ sorts(**bpa(natact)**))

<u>eqns</u> <u>for all</u> n <u>in</u> nat1; <u>for all</u> x <u>in</u> s :

ps(n,x)=x

(for all s≠proc)

<u>for all</u> n <u>in</u> nat1; <u>for all</u> a <u>in</u> act; <u>for all</u> x, y <u>in</u> proc :

pproc(n,a)=a

pproc(1,a·x)=a

pproc(n+1,a·x)=a·pproc(n,x)

pproc(n,x+y)=pproc(n,x)+pproc(n,y)

At last, the projection specification **probpa(nat)** is enriched by the operation P that specifies the given recursive process :

RECURSIVE PROCESS SPEC - **recproc(data)**

recbpa(nat) = **probpa(nat)** +

<u>opns</u> P:nat gate gate→proc

<u>eqns</u> <u>for all</u> n <u>in</u> nat; <u>for all</u> g1, g2 <u>in</u> gate :

P(n,g1,g2) =

<u>(g1!n)</u>·P(n+1,g1,g2)+

<u>(g2!n+1)</u>·P(n,g1,g2)

Informally speaking the semantics of the parameterized process P is given by the following infinite PROCESSGRAPH, obtained from the equation of **recbpa(nat)** , where the actions (g1!n), (g2!n+1),... appear as labels of edges between the corresponding states P(n,g1,g2), P(n+1,g1,g2),... and the operation symbol + in the equation for P(n,g1,g2) corresponds to nondeterministic choice and hence to branching of the process graph.

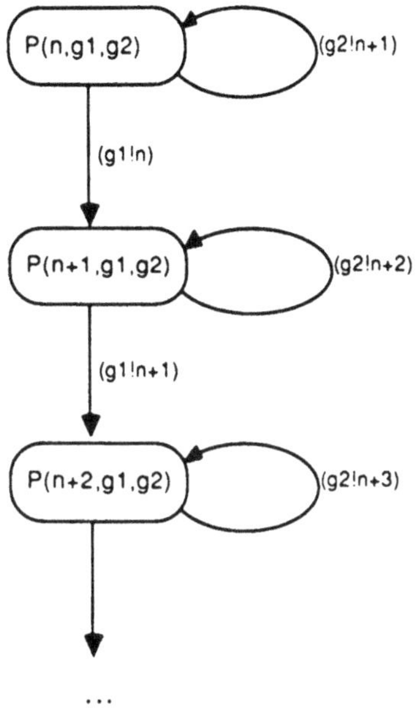

Unwinding the processgraph, we obtain the following infinite ACTIONTREE which is a representative of the equivalence class of P(n,g1,g2) in the complete initial projection algebra of the specification **recbpa(nat).**

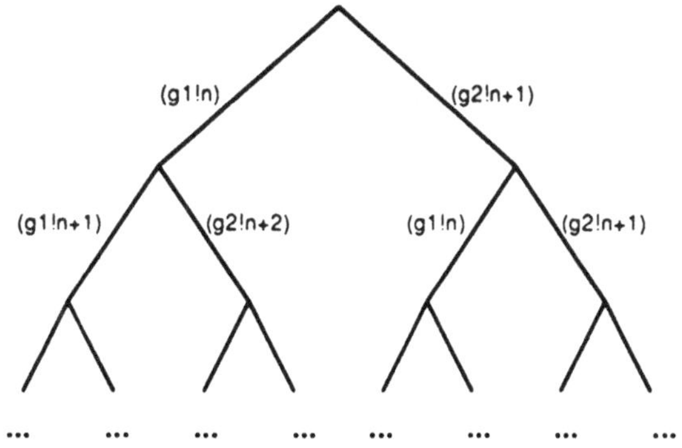

This simple example will be used to illustrate the different points in this paper. More extended examples will be studied in subsequent papers. Finally let us give an overview of the contents of this paper :
Section 1 of this paper treats the preliminary theory of projection spaces, including basic categorical properties, completion of a projection space and a fixed-point theorem for projection spaces. In section 2 projection specifications and projection algebras as a generalization of projection spaces are defined and the results from section 1 are carried over from projection spaces to projection algebras. In section 3 recursive process specifications based on projection specifications are introduced and the algebraic semantics of recursive process specifications is defined. Section 2 and 3 correspond to step (2) and (3) above in building up recursive process specifications.
Concerning the theory of algebraic specifications we refer to /EM85/, the remaining part of the paper is self contained.

1. PROJECTION SPACES

In this section we introduce the basic notions of projection spaces and their morphisms. Projection spaces can be considered as a special case of ultrametric spaces. The algebraic structure of projection spaces however is much more convenient for the purpose of algebraic specifications.

We will give a standard construction for the completion of a projection space that yields one of the presuppositions of a fixed-point theorem for projection spaces related to Banach's fixed-point theorem. Contractions in projection spaces are introduced in order to guarantee a unique fixed point of an operator in a projection space.

1.1 Definition (Projection Space) :

A pair (A,p) consisting of a set A and a function $p:\mathbf{N}_1 \times A \to A$ (where $\mathbf{N}_1$ denotes the natural numbers starting with one) with

(1) $\forall a \in A\ \forall n1,n2 \in \mathbf{N}_1\ p(n1,p(n2,a)) = p(\min(n1,n2),a)$

(2) $\forall a,b \in A\ ((\forall n \in \mathbf{N}_1\ p(n,a)=p(n,b)) \to a=b)$

is called a projection space.

Part (2) of the definition states that each $a \in A$ is completely determined by all its projections p(n,a), also called the approximation induction principle **AIP**. On the other hand if a set A with a function p only fullfills part (1) of the definition, then the factorset A/p together with p is a projection space.

1.2 Example:

(1) Let A^* be the free monoid over a given set A. Define $p:\mathbf{N}_1 \times A^* \to A^*$ by
$p(n,\varepsilon)=\varepsilon$, $p(n,a)=a$, $p(1,aw)=a$ and $p(n+1,aw)=ap(n,w)$ for all $n \in \mathbf{N}_1$, $a \in A$ and $w \in A^*$,
(for short $p(n,w)=w[1...n]$)
Then (A^*,p) is a projection space.
If $L \subseteq A^*$ is a language then (L,p) is a projection space if and only if $p(n,w) \in L$ for all $n \in \mathbf{N}_1$ and all $w \in L$.

(2) Given the set T of finite or infinite trees with nodes from a set A define $p:\mathbf{N}_1 \times T \to T$ by
$p(1,t)=root(t)$
$p(n+1,t)=[nodes(p(n,t)) \cup succ(p(n,t))]$
where succ(t´) is the set of all successors of leaves of t´and the brackets [,] mean the tree spanned by the set of nodes.(I.e. p(n,t) is the tree t cut to length n.)
Then (T,p) is a projection space.

(3) Given a set A define $p:\mathbf{N}_1 \times A \to A$ by $p(n,a)=a$ for all $n \in \mathbf{N}_1$ and $a \in A$. Then (A,p) is a projection space; p is called a discrete projection .

Next we introduce the metric that is induced by the projection of a projection space (A,p).

Recall that a metric on a set X is a function $d:X \times X \to \mathbf{R}$ (**R** denoting the real numbers) with

(i) $d(x,y) \geq 0$ and $d(x,y)=0$ iff $x=y$

(ii) $d(x,y)=d(y,x)$

(iii) $d(x,y) \leq d(x,z)+d(z,y)$ for all $z \in X$ (triangle inequality)

for all $x,y \in X$.

If the triangle inequality can be replaced by the sharper inequality $d(x,y) \leq \max\{d(x,z),d(z,y)\}$ for all $z \in X$, then d is called an ultrametric.

1.3 Definition and Fact (Standard Metric) :

Given a projection space (A,p) the projection p induces an ultrametric d on A, called the standard metric, given by

$d(a,b) = 2^{-i(a,b)}$ if $a \neq b$ and $d(a,b) = 0$ if $a=b$ $\quad (a,b \in A)$

where $i(a,b) = \min\{n : p(n,a) \neq p(n,b)\}$;

(A,d) is called the metric space corresponding to (A,p).

The standard notions of Cauchy sequences and convergence can be viewed in terms of projections.

1.4 Definition :

Given a projection space (A,p), then a sequence $(a_n)_{n \in \mathbf{N}}$, $a_n \in A$, is called

(1) Cauchy in (A,p) if
$\forall m \in \mathbf{N}_1 \exists n \in \mathbf{N} \forall k \in \mathbf{N}\ \ p(m,a_n)=p(m,a_{n+k})$,

(2) convergent with limit $a \in A$, written $\lim_n a_n=a$ if
$\forall m \in \mathbf{N}_1 \exists n \in \mathbf{N} \forall k \in \mathbf{N}\ \ p(m,a)=p(m,a_{n+k})$.

(3) (A,p) is called complete projection space if each Cauchy sequence in (A,p) converges in (A,p).

Cauchy sequences in (A,p) and convergent sequences in (A,p) are equivalent to Cauchy sequences and convergent sequences in the corresponding ultrametric (topological) space:

1.5 Fact :

Given a projection space (A,p) with standard metric d and a sequence $(a_n)_{n \in \mathbf{N}}$, $a_n \in A$, then

(1) $(a_n)_{n \in \mathbf{N}}$ is Cauchy in (A,p) if and only if it is Cauchy in (A,d);

(2) $(a_n)_{n \in \mathbf{N}}$ is convergent with limit a in (A,p) if and only if it is convergent with limit a in (A,d);

(3) (A,p) is a complete projection space if and only if (A,d) is complete (metric space).

Now we can formulate the relation between projection spaces and ultrametric spaces :

1.6 Remark : For every projection space (A,p) the space (A,d), where d is the standard metric, is ultrametric. Conversely for every ultrametric space (U,d) there is a function $p: \mathbf{N}_1 \times U \to U$ so that (U,p) is a projection space and the given ultrametric d is equivalent to the standard metric induced by p as in 1.3. To define this projection choose for each $n \in \mathbf{N}_1$ a system of representatives R_n of the equivalence classes $B(n,a) := \{b \in A : d(a,b) < 2^{-n}\}$, with $R_n \subseteq R_{n+1}$. Then $p(n,a) := a_n \in R_n$, if $a \in B(n,a_n)$. (See /DEGR87/)

The next step is the construction of the completion of a projection space (A,p). As elements of the completion we take sequences $(a_k)_{k \geq 1}$ over A with $p(n,a_{n+1})=a_n$, called projective sequences, and the n'th projection of a projective sequence is the sequence $(a_0,a_1,\ldots,a_{n-1},a_n,a_n,\ldots)$.

1.7 Definition (Completion of a Projection Space by Standard Construction) :

Given a projection space (A,p), then the standard completion (A^∞,p^∞) is defined by

$$A^\infty = \{(a_n)_{n \geq 1} : a_n \in A \text{ and } p(n,a_{n+1})=a_n \text{ for all } n \in \mathbf{N}_1\}$$

$$p^\infty : \mathbf{N}_1 \times A^\infty \to A^\infty,\ p^\infty(k,(a_n)_{n \geq 1}) = (p(k,a_n))_{n \geq 1}.$$

1.8 Fact (Completion) :

Given a projection space (A,p), then the standard completion (A^∞,p^∞) is a projection space and a completion of (A,p); i.e. (A^∞,p^∞) is a smallest complete projection space containing an isometric copy of (A,p).

Proof idea :

The welldefinedness of p^∞ and the projection space properties of (A^∞,p^∞) are easy to show. Note that $(a_k)_{k\geq 1}=(b_k)_{k\geq 1}$ if and only if $\forall k\geq 1\ a_k=b_k$, hence the second projection space property holds in (A^∞,p^∞), even if it does not hold in (A,p).

To show that (A^∞,p^∞) is a completion of (A,p), we define the embedding $i:A\to A^\infty$ by $i(a)=(p(n,a))_{n\geq 1}$. and show that i is isometric (i.e.preserves distances corresponding to the standard metric), i(A) is dense in A^∞ (i.e. each element of A^∞ is a limit of a sequence in i(A)) and that A^∞ is complete, whence the assertion follows.

(i) $p^\infty(n,i(a))=p^\infty(n,i(b)) \Leftrightarrow p(n,a)=p(n,b)$, hence i is isometric;

(ii) Let $(a_k)_{k\geq 1}\in A^\infty$, then $(a_k)_{k\geq 1}=\lim_k i(a_k)$ in (A^∞,p^∞) and i(A) is dense in A^∞;

(iii) Let $(a^n)_{n\in \mathbf{N}}=((a_j^{\,n})_{j\geq 1})_{n\in \mathbf{N}}$ with $a_j^{\,n}\in A$ be a Cauchy sequence in (A^∞,p^∞), i.e.
$\forall m\exists q(m)\forall k\ p^\infty(m,a^{q(m)})=p^\infty(m,a^{q(m)+k})$. Now define $b_m:=a_m^{\,q(m)}$ for $m\geq 1$, then $(b_m)_{m\geq 1}$ is the limit of $((a_j^{\,n})_{j\geq 1})_{n\in \mathbf{N}}$. ⊘

1.9 Remark : In the case of a discrete projection space (A,p), i.e. p(n,a)=a for all $n\in \mathbf{N}_1$, $a\in A$, we have $A^\infty\cong A$ by the isomorphism $i(a)=(a)_{n\geq 1}$. Since the standard metric d of (A,p) is discrete a sequence is Cauchy in (A,d) if and only if it is eventually constant.

Next we define two kinds morphisms of projection spaces and state some of their properties :

1.10 Definition :

Given projection spaces (A_1,p_1), (A_2,p_2), a function $f:A_1\to A_2$ is called

(1) a projection morphism if

$\forall n\in \mathbf{N}_1 \forall a\in A_1\ \ f(p_1(n,a))=p_2(n,f(a))$

(2) projection compatible if

$\forall n\in \mathbf{N}_1 \forall a,b\in A_1\ \ p_1(n,a)=p_1(n,b)\to p_2(n,f(a))=p_2(n,f(b))$

1.11 Fact : Given projection spaces (A_1,p_1), (A_2,p_2) and a function $f:A_1\to A_2$,then we have :

(1) if f is a projection morphism then f is projection compatible;
(the converse does not hold).

(2) if f is projection compatible then f is nonexpansive relative to the standard metric, i.e. $\forall a,b\in A_1\ d_2(f(a),f(b))\leq d_1(a,b)$;

(3) if f is projection compatible then f is continuous, i.e. for any convergent sequence $(a_n)_{n\in \mathbf{N}}$ in (A_1,p_1) we have $f(\lim_n a_n)=\lim_n f(a_n)$;

(4) f is projection compatible if and only if $\forall n\in \mathbf{N}_1\forall a\in A_1\ p_2(n,f(a))=p_2(n,f(p_1(n,a)))$;

(5) Projections are projection morphisms, i.e. for $A=A_1=A_2$, $p=p_1=p_2$ we have $p(m,p(n,\_))=p(n,p(m,\_))$.

As morphisms for a category of projection spaces we do not take the continuous functions but projection morphisms and projection compatible morphisms (see Definition 1.10 above), each a proper subclass of the class of continuous functions. Projection morphisms correspond to the algebraic structure of projection spaces, i.e. if we consider (A_i,p_i) as algebras $(A_i,\mathbf{N}_1,p_i)$, then a projection morphism $f:(A_1,p_1)\rightarrow(A_2,p_2)$ is an algebra homomorphism. Projection compatible morphisms are continuous functions with an additional compatibility property. (Compare definition 2.1(2)(ii))

It is clear that projection morphisms and projection compatible morphisms are preserved under composition and that the identities are projection morphisms, hence projection spaces together with projection (compatible) morphisms define a category.

<u>1.12 Fact</u> (Categories of Projection Spaces) :
Given the class of projection spaces and morphisms as defined in 1.10 we obtain categories

(1) with projection morphisms, called $\underline{\mathbf{PRO}}_m$,

(2) with projection compatible morphisms, called $\underline{\mathbf{PRO}}_c$;

$\underline{\mathbf{PRO}}_m$ is a subcategory of $\underline{\mathbf{PRO}}_c$.

Now that the categories of projection spaces are defined we can state one of the central results of this section. We omit the proof, which can be derived from that of 2.8 in the next section.

<u>1.13 Theorem</u> (Universal Completion, Projective Limit) :

(1) Given a projection space (A,p), then the standard construction (A^{∞},p^{∞}) is the universal completion of (A,p) in $\underline{\mathbf{PRO}}_m$ and also in $\underline{\mathbf{PRO}}_c$, i.e. there is an injective projection morphism $i:A\rightarrow A^{\infty}$ so that for any complete projection space (B,q) and projection (compatible) morphism $f:A\rightarrow B$ there is a unique projection (compatible) morphism $\phi:A^{\infty}\rightarrow B$ with $\phi\circ i=f$.

(2) Define $\pi:\mathbf{N}_1 \times A^{\infty}\rightarrow A$ by $\pi(n,(a_k)_{k\geq 1})=a_n$, then $(A^{\infty},(\pi(n,\_))_{n\geq 1})$ is a projective limit of the diagram

$$A \xleftarrow{p(1,\_)} A \xleftarrow{p(2,\_)} A \text{---}\ldots\text{---} A \xleftarrow{p(n,\_)} A \leftarrow \ldots$$

in each of the categories PROm and $\underline{\mathbf{PRO}}_c$,i.e. for each projection space (B,q) together with a family of projection (compatible) morphisms $f_n:B\rightarrow A$ ($n\in\mathbf{N}_1$) with $p(n,\_)\circ f_{n+1}=f_n$ there is a unique projection (compatible) morphism $f:B\rightarrow A^{\infty}$ with $\pi(n,\_)\circ f=f_n$ for all $n\in\mathbf{N}_1$.

As the second presupposition needed for the fixed-point theorem, we have to define contractions in projection spaces, compatible with that of a contraction in the corresponding metric space.

Banach's fixed-point theorem states that if X is a complete metric space and $f:X\rightarrow X$ is a contraction, then for any $x\in X$ the sequence $(f^n(x))_{n\in\mathbf{N}}$ converges to a fixed point x^* of f (i.e.$f(x^*)=x^*$) and this fixed point is unique (i.e. independent of the starting point x).

<u>1.14 Definition</u> (Contraction in a Projection Space) :
Given a projection space (A,p) with $A\neq\emptyset$ a function $T:A\rightarrow A$ is called a <u>contraction in (A,p)</u> if $\forall a,b\in A \forall n\in\mathbf{N}_1$

$p(1,T(a))=p(1,T(b))$

$p(n,a)=p(n,b) \rightarrow p(n+1,T(a))=p(n+1,T(b))$

The correspondence between this defintion and the classical one is based on the fact that T is a contraction in (A,p) if and only if $d(T(a),T(b))\leq 1/2d(a,b)$ for all $a,b\in A$, where d is the standard metric of (A,p). In the classical case, any constant less than 1 can replace 1/2. Notice also that if T is a contraction, than T is continuous. The requirement $A\neq\emptyset$ in the defintion is needed to guarantee that every contraction in a complete space has a unique fixed point. The function $\emptyset:\emptyset\rightarrow\emptyset$ has none.

1.15 Theorem (Fixed-point Theorem for Projection Spaces) :
Given a nonempty complete projection space (A,p), any contraction $T:A\rightarrow A$ has a unique fixed point $a^* \in A$; moreover we have $\forall n \in \mathbf{N}_1\ p(n,a^*)=p(n,T^n(a))$ for arbitrary $a \in A$.

Proof idea :
The first part of the theorem is Banach's fixed-point theorem stated in terms of projections. The second part is easy to show by induction, using the fact that $a^*=\lim T^n(a)$ for arbitrary $a \in A$. ⊘

2. PROJECTION SPECIFICATIONS AND PROJECTION ALGEBRAS

The intention of projection specifications is to extend the given combined specifications, consisting of data type and process specifications, by projections, one for each sort, to prepare the construction of a complete algebra. Since the domain of the projections contains $\mathbf{N}_1$, the projection specification must contain the specification **nat1** of $\mathbf{N}_1$:

nat1 =

sorts	nat1
opns	1:→nat1
	succ:nat1→nat1
	min:nat1 nat1→nat1
eqns	for all m,n in nat1 :
	min(n,1)=1
	min(1,n)=1
	min(succ(n),succ(m))=succ(min(n,m))

Projection algebras are algebras of projection specifications such that each base set is a projection space and each operation is projection compatible. To ensure that the constraints that guarantee the projection space properties respect the **nat1** reduct of a projection algebra, the projection specification is not allowed to contain additional operation symbols with range nat1 or additional equations between nat1-terms. Since the projection space properties must hold for each base set, we are only concerned with nonparameterized specifications here. The theory for parameterized specifications with appropriate constraints is outside the scope of this paper. The definitions of completion by standard construction and the facts about universal completion and projective limit are carried over from projection spaces to projection algebras.

2.1 Definition (Projection Specification and Projection Algebra) :

(1) A projection specification SPEC=(S,OP,E) is an algebraic specification with :

(i) SPEC⊇**nat1** ,

(ii) for each sort s∈S there is an operation symbol ps:nat1 s→s∈OP ,
and pnat1 is discrete, i.e. pnat1(n,k)=k for all n,k in nat1 ;

(iii) nat1∉range(OP-({pnat1:nat1 nat1→nat1}∪OP(**nat1**))) , i.e. there are no operation symbols N:s1...sn→nat1 in OP except the projection pnat1 and the operation symbols from **nat1** ;

(iv) if t1=t2∈E-E(**nat1**) then sort(t1)≠nat1; i.e. there are no additional equations between nat1-terms

(2) a <u>projection-SPEC-algebra</u> is an algebra of the specification SPEC with the additional properties

(i) (A_s, ps_A) is a projection space for all $s \in S$,

(ii) the operations N_A are projection compatible, i.e.

$\forall N{:}s1...sn \to s\ \forall k \geq 1\ \forall a1 \in A_{s1} ... \forall an \in A_{sn}$

$ps_A(k, N_A(a1,...,an)) = ps_A(k, N_A(ps1_A(k,a1),...,psn_A(k,an)))$;

(iii) $A_{\mathbf{nat1}} \cong \mathbf{N}_1$;

(3) a <u>homomorphism of projection-SPEC-algebras</u> is a homomorphism $f{:}A \to B$, where A,B are projection-SPEC -algebras and f_{nat1} is an isomorphism;

(4) a <u>constrained projection specification</u> CSPEC=(S,OP,E,C) is a projection specification SPEC=(S,OP,E) together with constraints C corresponding to the properties defined in (2) :

$C = C1 \cup C2 \cup C3 \cup C4$, where

$C1_s : \forall n,m \in \mathbf{N}_1\ \forall x \in s\ ps(n,ps(m,x)) = ps(min(n,m),x)$; $\quad C1 = \cup_{s \in S}\{C1_s\}$

$C2_s : \forall x,y \in s\ (\ \forall n \in \mathbf{N}_1\ ps(n,x) = ps(n,y) \to x = y\ )$; $\quad C2 = \cup_{s \in S}\{C2_s\}$

$C3_N : \forall k \in \mathbf{N}_1\ \forall a1 \in A_{s1} ... \forall an \in A_{sn}\ ps_A(k, N_A(a1,...,an)) = ps_A(k, N_A(ps1_A(k,a1),...,psn_A(k,an)))$;

$C3 = \cup_{N \in OP}\{C3_N\}$

C4={initial specification **nat1**} (algebraic constraint) .

<u>2.2 Facts</u> :

(1) If SPEC is a projection specification then SPEC is a conservative extension of **nat1** , i.e. $(T_{SPEC})_{\mathbf{nat1}} \cong T_{\mathbf{nat1}}$;

(2) A is a projection-SPEC-algebra if and only if A is a CSPEC-algebra.

(3) If $f{:}A \to B$ is a homomorphism of projection-SPEC-algebras, then $f_s{:}A_s \to B_s$ for all $s \in S$ is a projection morphism.

<u>2.3 Remarks</u> :

(1) It is of course intended to construct projection specifications SPEC with equations for the projections in such a way that the usual initial algebra T_{SPEC} is already a projection-SPEC-algebra, i.e. $T_{SPEC} \in Cat(CSPEC)$.

(2) Since the **nat1**-part of a projection-SPEC-algebra only serves as domain for the projections and is not allowed to be used by the other operations we could also define projections to be a family of functions $(ps_n{:}s \to s)_{n \in N_1}$ instead of one function ps:nat1 s→s. We preferred the latter version since it provides finite signatures.

(3) The projections $p_A(k,\_){:}A \to A$ need not be homomorphisms of projection-SPEC- algebras, since in general

$ps_A(k, N_A(a1,...,an)) \neq N_A(ps1_A(k,a1),...psn_A(k,an))$.

In /DEGR87/ it is shown that the categories $\underline{\mathbf{PRO}}_m$ and $\underline{\mathbf{PRO}}_c$ are closed under products, whence an operation of a projection-SPEC-algebra $N_A{:}A_{s1} x...x A_{sn} \to A_s$ can be considered as a function of one projection space into another. We do not demand that N_A shall be a projection morphism, for this would exclude for example the sequence operation $\cdot$:proc proc→proc, since $p(1,\underline{a}\cdot\underline{b}) = \underline{a} \neq \underline{a}\cdot\underline{b} = p(1,\underline{a})\cdot p(1,\underline{b})$ (compare the example in the introduction) .

Projection compatibility however seems to be an adequate condition for process operations and still guarantees continuity of the operations.

2.4 Example : The specification **probpa(nat)** is a projection specification.

probpa(nat) =
bpa(natact) + **nat1** +
opns   ps:nat1 s→s   (for all s∈sorts(**bpa(natact)**))
eqns   for all n in nat1; for all x in s :
ps(n,x)=x   (for all s≠proc)
for all n in nat1; for all a in act; for all x,y in proc :
pproc(n,a)=a
pproc(1,a·x)=a
pproc(n+1,a·x)=a·pproc(n,x)
pproc(n,x+y)=pproc(n,x)+pproc(n,y)

The semantics of a constrained projection specification is again given by an initial algebra, whereas in general it is not certain whether a category defined by a specification with constraints has an initial algebra.

2.5 Theorem (Initial Projection-SPEC-Algebra) :
Given a projection specification SPEC, then the category Cat(CSPEC) of projection- SPEC-algebras has an initial object $T_{CSPEC}=T_{SPEC}/_{\approx C}$, where ≈C is the congruence generated by the constraints C.

Proof idea :
The constraints $C1_s$ and $C3_s$ are equations and for algebras with nat1-reduct isomorphic to $\mathbf{N}_1$ $C2_s$ is an infinitary conditional equation, whence the existence of an initial algebra is guaranteed. ⊘

Since the base sets of a projection-SPEC-algebra are projection spaces the completion of a projection space by standard construction (see 1.7) can be carried over to algebras.

2.6 Definition (Completion of a Projection-SPEC-Algebra by Standard Construction) :

(1) Given a projection-SPEC-algebra $A=((A_s)_{s\in S},(N_A)_{N\in OP})$, then the standard completion $A^\infty=((A_s^\infty)_{s\in S},(N_A^\infty)_{N\in OP})$ is defined by
$A_s^\infty=(A_s)^\infty$ (= completion of the projection space (A_s,p_s) by standard construction)
$N_A^\infty((a1_k)_{k\geq 1},\ldots,(an_k)_{k\geq 1})=(ps_A(k,N_A(a1_k,\ldots,an_k)))_{k\geq 1}$;

(2) for n≥1 define the n'th approximation $A^n=((A_s^n)_{s\in S},(N_A^n)_{N\in OP})$ of (A,p) by
$A_s^n=\{ps_A(n,a) : a\in A\}$
$N_A^n(ps1_A(n,a1),\ldots,psk_A(n,ak))=ps_A(n,N_A(a1,\ldots,ak))$;
and define the mapping $\pi(n,\_):A^\infty\rightarrow A^n$ by $\pi(n,(a_k)_{k\geq 1})=a_n$

2.7 Remark :

(1) Since $pnat_1$ is discrete the base set $nat1_A$ is not changed in the standard construction. Hence we write n instead of $(n)_{k\geq 1}$ and $\mathbf{N}_1$ instead of $nat1_A^\infty$.

(2) The projections ps_A^∞ are operations of A^∞ and therefore also defined by $ps_A^\infty(k,(a_j)_{j\geq 1})=(ps_A(k,a_j))_{j\geq 1}$, but this coincides with the definition of p^∞ given in the first section.

(3) The factorization corresponding to the constraints C2 that guarantees **AIP**, the second projection space property is automatically done by the standard construction since it only uses the projections of elements of (A,p).

As in the general case of projection spaces, the standard construction of 2.6 provides the "minimal" complete projection algebra containing A. The assertions of the following theorem can be shown by tedious but straightforward computations.

2.8 Theorem (Universal Completion and Projective Limit) :
Given a projection-SPEC-algebra A, then for the standard construction A^{∞} we have :

(1) A^{∞} is complete projection-SPEC-algebra ;

(2) A^{∞} is universal completion of A in Cat(CSPEC) ,
i.e. there is a homomorphism of projection-SPEC-algebras $i:A \rightarrow A^{\infty}$ so that for any complete projection-SPEC-algebra B and homomorphism of projection-SPEC-algebras $f:A \rightarrow B$ there is a unique homomorphism of projection-SPEC-algebras $\underline{f}:A^{\infty} \rightarrow B$ with $\underline{f} \circ i = f$;

(3) A^n is projection-SPEC-algebra, $\pi(n,\_)$ is a homomorphism of projection-SPEC-algebras and $(A^{\infty},(\pi(n,\_))_{n \geq 1})$ is projective limit of the diagram

$$A^1 \xleftarrow[p_A(1,\_)]{} A^2 \leftarrow \ldots \leftarrow A^n \xleftarrow[p_A(n,\_)]{} A^{n+1} \leftarrow \ldots$$

i.e. for each projection-SPEC-algebra B together with a family of homomorphisms of projection-SPEC-algebras $f_n:B \rightarrow A^n$ $(n \in \mathbf{N}_1)$ with $p_A(n,\_) \circ f_{n+1} = f_n$ there is a unique homomorphism of projection-SPEC-algebras $f:B \rightarrow A^{\infty}$ with $\pi(n,\_) \circ f = f_n$ for all $n \in \mathbf{N}_1$.

As a direct consequence of part (2), we obtain the existence of the initial complete projection algebra of a projection specification SPEC.

2.9 Corollary (Initial Complete Projection-SPEC-Algebra) :
Given a projection specification SPEC and initial projection-SPEC-algebra T_{CSPEC} , then the completion of T_{CSPEC} by standard construction $(T_{CSPEC})^{\infty}$ is initial in the category of complete projection-SPEC-algebras CatCompl(CSPEC) .

Such an algebra is the intended meaning of a projection specification.

2.10 Definition (Semantics and Correctness of a Projection Specification) :
Given a projection specification SPEC, then

(1) the (<u>complete initial projection algebra</u>) <u>semantics</u> CT_{SPEC} of SPEC is the complete initial projection-SPEC-algebra $(T_{CSPEC})^{\infty}$, i.e. $CT_{SPEC}=(T_{CSPEC})^{\infty}$;

(2)

(i) SPEC is <u>correct,</u> if $T_{SPEC} \cong T_{CSPEC}$, i.e. the initial algebra T_{SPEC} satisfies the constraints defined in 2.1(4)

(ii) If SPEC0 is a specification and SPEC⊇SPEC0, then SPEC is <u>correct w.r.t. SPEC0</u> if SPEC⊇SPEC0 is a conservative extension, i.e. $(T_{SPEC})_{SPEC0} \cong T_{SPEC0}$

2.11 Example (Semantics of **probpa(nat)**) :

$$CT_{\mathbf{probpa(nat)}} \cong A:=(A_{\mathbf{nat}}, A_{gate}, A_{act}, A_{proc}, A_{\mathbf{nat1}}, (\_!\_)_A, +_A, \cdot_A, \_{}_A, (ps_A)_{s \in S})$$

(For notational convenience we drop the index $_A$ and the underscore _ .)

$A_{nat}=(\{0,1,2,...\},0,v,+,...) = \mathbf{N}$

$A_{gate}=\{G1,G2,...,Gn\}$

$A_{act}=\{(Gi!m) \mid 1\leq i\leq n,\ m\in\{0,1,...\}\}$

$A_{proc}°$, the set of finite processes, is defined recursively by

$(Gi!n)\in A_{proc}°$, and

if $X_k\in A_{proc}°$ $k=1,...,m$, then $\Sigma(Gi_j!n_j)+\Sigma(Gi_k,n_k)\cdot X_k\in A_{proc}°$

(where one of the sums may be empty)

hence

$A_{proc}=\{(a_n)_{n\geq 1} \mid pproc_A(n,a_{n+1})=a_n\}$

$A_{nat1}=(\{1,2,3,...\},1,v,min) = \mathbf{N}_1$

We define the projection $pproc_A=:p$ again first for the finite processes $x=\Sigma a_j+\Sigma b_k\cdot X_k$, with $(Gi_j!n_j)=a_j$, $(Gi_k,n_k)=b_k$:

$p°(1,\Sigma a_j+\Sigma b_k\cdot X_k)=\Sigma a_j+\Sigma b_k$

$p°(m+1,\Sigma a_j+\Sigma b_k\cdot X_k)=\Sigma a_j+\Sigma b_k\cdot p°(m,X_k)$

then

$p(m,(a_n)_{n\geq 1})=(p°(m,a_n))_{n\geq 1}$;

The other projections are discrete and the definitions of the remaining operations can be taken directly from the equations of **recbpa(nat)** .

We still have to show that

(i) $p(m_1,p(m_2,\_))=p(min(m_1,m_2),\_)$

(ii) $+$ and $\cdot$ are projection compatible .

Proof :

(i) Let $m_1\geq m_2$.

If $m_1=1$, then $p(1,p(1,\Sigma a_j+\Sigma b_k\cdot X_k))=\Sigma a_j+\Sigma b_k=p(1,\Sigma a_j+\Sigma b_k\cdot X_k)$;

for the inductive step, if the assertion holds for $m_1\geq 1$ then

$p(m_1+1,p(m_2,\Sigma a_j+\Sigma b_k\cdot X_k))=\Sigma a_j+\Sigma b_k\cdot p(m_1,p(m_2-1,X_k))=$

$=\Sigma a_j+\Sigma b_k\cdot p(m_2-1,X_k)=p(m_2,\Sigma a_j+\Sigma b_k\cdot X_k)$;

the case $m_1\leq m_2$ is analogous ;

(ii) if $p(m,q_i)=p(m,r_i)$, $i=1,2$, then

$p(m,q_1+r_1)=p(m,q_1)+p(m,r_1)=p(m,q_2)+p(m,r_2)=p(m,q_2+r_2)$;

To show projection compatibility for $\cdot$ we first show it for finite processes $x=\Sigma a_j+\Sigma b_k\cdot X_k$,y :

$p(1,(\Sigma a_j+\Sigma b_k\cdot X_k)\cdot y)=$

$=p(1,\Sigma a_j\cdot y+(\Sigma b_k\cdot X_k)\cdot y)=$

$=\Sigma a_j+\Sigma b_k=$

$=p(1,(\Sigma a_j)\cdot p(1,y)+(\Sigma b_k)\cdot p(1,y))=$

$=p(1,p(1,\Sigma a_j+\Sigma b_k\cdot X_k)\cdot p(1,y))$

For $m\geq 2$ we show by induction on m that

$p(m,x\cdot y)=p(m,p(m,x)\cdot p(m-1,y))$

whence

$p(m,p(m,x)\cdot p(m,y))=p(m,p(m,p(m,x))\cdot p(m-1,p(m,y)))=p(m,p(m,x)\cdot p(m-1,y))=p(m,x\cdot y)$ (•)

For the base case let m=2, then

$p(2,(\Sigma a_j+\Sigma b_k\cdot X_k)\cdot y)=$
$=\Sigma a_j\cdot p(1,y)+\Sigma b_k\cdot p(1,X_k\cdot y)=$
$=\Sigma a_j\cdot p(1,y)+\Sigma b_k\cdot p(1,p(1,X_k)\cdot p(1,y))=$
$=p(2,p(2,(\Sigma a_j+\Sigma b_k\cdot X_k))\cdot p(2,y))$

If the assertion holds for m≥2 then applying the induction hypotheses as in (•) above, we have

$p(m+1,(\Sigma a_j+\Sigma b_k\cdot X_k)\cdot y)=$
$=\Sigma a_j\cdot p(m,y)+\Sigma b_k\cdot p(m,X_k\cdot y)=$
$=p(m+1,p(m+1,(\Sigma a_j+\Sigma b_k\cdot X_k))\cdot p(m,y))$

By 2.8(1) projection compatibility of the operations carries over from the finite to the infinite case. Since the approximation induction principle **AIP** always holds in standard constructions X^∞ the example is complete.

3. TOWARDS RECURSIVE PROCESS SPECIFICATIONS

The projection specification SPEC defined in the previous section can now be enriched by signature and equations for the definition of recursive processes proc1,...procn. The equation system defines an operator T on the space of all projection compatible functions of complete projection-SPEC-algebras on the signature of proc1,...,procn.

If the recursive process specification is correct, i.e. if T is a contraction, then the semantics is given by $((T_{CSPEC})^\infty$,PROC), where $(T_{CSPEC})^\infty$ is the completion by standard construction of the initial projection-SPEC-algebra T_{CSPEC} and PROC is the unique fixed point of T. The semantics $((T_{CSPEC})^\infty$,PROC) is again initial in the category of complete projection-RECSPEC-algebras.

<u>3.1 Definition</u> (Recursive Process Specification RECSPEC) :
Given a projection specification SPEC, then a <u>recursive process specification</u> RECSPEC based on SPEC is a specification of the form :

RECSPEC = SPEC +
<u>opns</u> proci:si1...simi→si
<u>eqns</u> proci(xi1,...,ximi)=Ti (i=1,...,n)

where Ti∈ $T_{SIG(RECSPEC)}(Xi)$, Xi={xi1,...,ximi} .

<u>3.2 Example</u> : recbpa(nat) is a recursive process specification based on **probpa(nat)** .

recbpa(nat) = probpa(nat) +
<u>opns</u> P:nat gate gate→proc
<u>eqns</u> <u>for all</u> n <u>in</u> nat; <u>for all</u> g1, g2 <u>in</u> gate :
P(n,g1,g2) =
(g1!n)·P(n+1,g1,g2)+
(g2!n+1)·P(n,g1,g2)

Next we define the domain for the operator T. It is the cartesian product of n spaces, where each component consists of all the projection compatible functions that can be chosen, based on the signature alone, as the meaning of the corresponding process.

<u>3.3 Definition</u> :

Given RECSPEC as above and a projection-SPEC-algebra A, then

(1) $\text{Homi}(A):=\{fi:A_{si1}{}^{\infty}x...xA_{simi}{}^{\infty}\rightarrow A_{si}{}^{\infty} : fi \text{ is projection compatible}\}$ together with
$pHi:\mathbf{N}_1 x\text{Homi}(A)\rightarrow \text{Homi}(A)$ defined by
$pHi(k,fi)(ai1,...,aimi):=psi_{A^{\infty}}(k,fi(ai1,...aimi))$
for i=1,...,n is called <u>i'th process space</u> ;

(2) $\text{Hom}(A):=\text{Hom1}(A)x...x\text{Homn}(A)$ together with
$pH:\mathbf{N}_1 x\text{Hom}(A)\rightarrow \text{Hom}(A)$ defined by
$pH(k,(f1,...,fn)):=(pH1(k,f1),...,pHn(k,fn))$
is called a <u>process space</u> .

If it is possible to define operations on the given projection-SPEC-algebra A that satisfy the equations for proc1,...,procn, then they are already contained in Hom(A). Thus Hom(A) serves as domain for the operator T that is defined by the equations (see 3.4 below) and the solution is obtained as the unique fixed point of T. But first we need that Hom(A) be a complete projection space. In fact the i'th process spaces (Homi(A),pHi) for i=1,...,n and the process space (Hom(A),pH) are complete projection spaces. The projection space properties are based on the fact that the limit of a Cauchy sequence of projection compatible functions can be taken pointwise. Also it is obvious that each product of projection spaces (A_i,p_i) ($i\in I$ an arbitrary index set) is a projection space $(\Pi A_i,\Pi p_i)$, and that the finite product of complete projection spaces is complete.

Now we are ready to define the operator T as specified by the equations in 3.1.

<u>3.4 Definition</u> :

(1) Given a recursive process specification RECSPEC based on a projection specification SPEC and a projection-SPEC-algebra A, then the operator $T_A:\text{Hom}(A)\rightarrow\text{Hom}(A)$ is defined by

$f=(f1,...,fn)\rightarrow T(f)=f^*=(f1^*,...,fn^*)$

where $fi^*(ai1,...,aimi)=\underline{vali}(T_i)$, (i=1,...,n) and <u>vali</u> is the unique extension of the assignment function $vali:X_i\rightarrow(A^{\infty},f1,...,fn)$ defined by $vali(xij)=aij$, (j=1,...mi) .

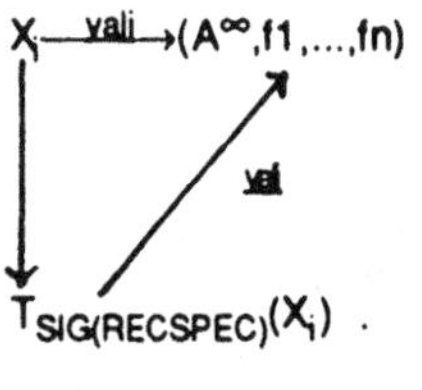

(2) RECSPEC is <u>contracting</u> if $T_{T_{CSPEC}}$ is a contraction (see Definition 1.14).

Before proceeding with the semantics of the equations in 3.1, we need to know that for all projection-SPEC-algebras A the operator T_A is well defined. For the proof, we have to show that if f1,...,fn are projection compatible, then also $f1^*,...,fn^*$ are projection compatible. To this extent it is sufficient to show, by structural induction, the following

Lemma : If A is a projection-SPEC-algebra and $t \in T_{SIG(SPEC),s}(X)$, then for all assignment functions $val: X \to A$ and for all $k \in \mathbf{N}_1$ we have $ps_A(k, \underline{val}(t)) = ps_A(k, \underline{valk}(t))$, with $valk: X \to A$, $valk = ps_A(k,\_) \circ val$.

As an application of the fixed-point theorem to projection spaces we obtain the correctness condition for RECSPEC. Given a recursive process specification RECSPEC and a projection-SPEC-algebra A, if RECSPEC is contracting, then the operator T_A has a unique fixed point PROC∈Hom(A). If RECSPEC is a correct recursive process specification based on a projection specification SPEC, then we can extend each projection-SPEC-algebra A to a complete projection-RECSPEC-algebra using A and the additional equation system for the recursive processes only: First A is completed by standard construction to A^∞, then A^∞ is enriched by the unique fixed point PROC of the operator T_A, which is given as limit of the sequence $(T^n(f))_{n \in N}$ for arbitrary f∈Hom(A). Take as starting point for example any constant function f_0, which is always contained in Hom(A). If we are interested in the n'th projection (i.e. the n'th finite approximation) of PROC, then the fixed-point theorem for projection spaces states that this n'th projection is reached after n applications of T_A to f_0 .

3.5 Theorem :

If RECSPEC is a contracting recursive process specification based on a projection specification SPEC, A a projection-SPEC-algebra and PROC=(PROC1,...,PROCn) the unique fixed point of T_A, then $(A^\infty$,PROC1,...,PROCn) is a complete projection RECSPEC algebra, i.e. $(A^\infty$,PROC1,...,PROCn)∈CatCompl(CRECSPEC).

Proof :

Since each equivalence class of terms in T_{CSPEC} is enlarged by at most one term, RECSPEC is an enrichment of SPEC and the operations PROC1,...,PROCn are projection compatible by definition, hence the assertion follows. ∅

If we take A to be initial in Cat(CSPEC), i.e. $A = T_{CSPEC}$, then the construction given above yields an initial algebra in CatCompl(CRECSPEC), hence we can again define an initial algebra semantics for the recursive process specification RECSPEC.

3.6 Theorem (Initial Algebra in CatCompl(CRECSPEC)) :

Let T_{CSPEC} be initial in the category of projection-SPEC-algebras Cat(CSPEC), RECSPEC, A and PROC as in the previous theorem, then

$CT_{RECSPEC} := ((T_{CSPEC})^\infty$,PROC1,...,PROCn)

is initial algebra in the category of complete projection-RECSPEC-algebras CatCompl(CRECSPEC).

Proof idea :

Since CT_{SPEC} is initial in CatCompl(CSPEC), it remains to be shown that the unique homomorphism of projection-SPEC-algebras $f^*: CT_{SPEC} \to V(B)$ for arbitrary B∈CatCompl(CRECSPEC), V the corresponding forgetful functor, extends uniquely to a homomorphism of projection-RECSPEC-algebras $f: CT_{RECSPEC} \to B$.; i.e. we have to show that the diagram on the following page (with PROCi=:Pi, $proci_B$=:Qi, T_{CSPEC}=:A)

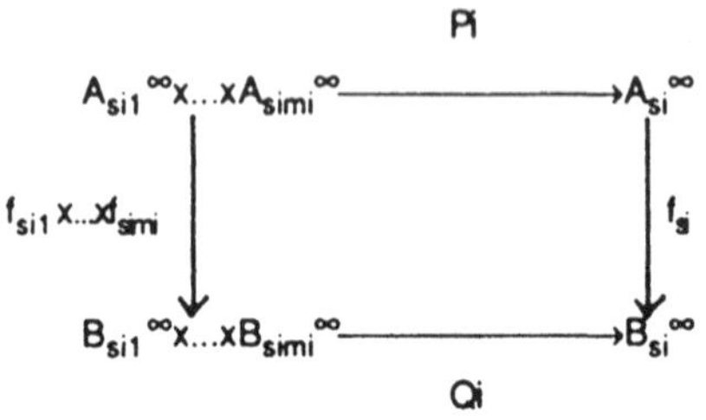

commutes for all i=1,...,n;

Let P0,Q0 be constant functions with values p0,q0 and $f_{si}(p0)=q0$. If Pi is replaced by P0 and Qi by Q0 in (i), then (i) commutes. Furthermore we have :

Lemma: If (i) commutes with P,Q, then (i) commutes with $T_A(P),T_A(Q)$.

Proof of the lemma:

In the diagram

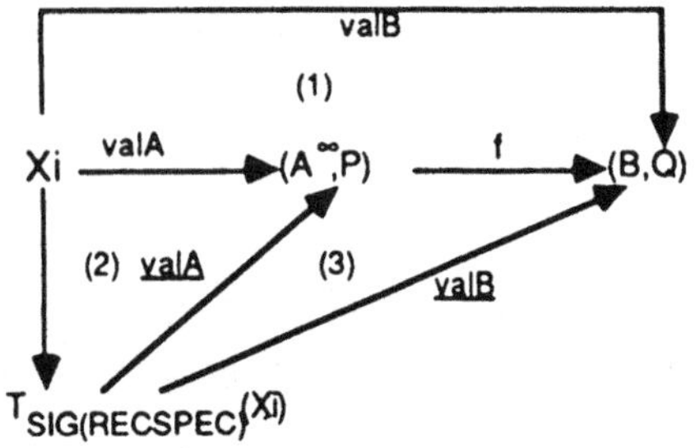

f is a homomorphism by the assumption of the lemma,

(1) commutes by definition of T_A and T_B : $val_A(xij)=aij$, $val_B(xij)=f(aij)$

(2) & (2)∪(3) commute by definition of $\underline{val}_A$ and $\underline{val}_B$,thus

$T_A(P)(ai1,...,aimi)=\underline{val}_A(Ti(xi1,...,ximi))$

$T_B(Q)(f_{si1}(ai1),...,f_{simi}(aimi))=\underline{val}_B(Ti(xi1,...,ximi))=f(\underline{val}_A(Ti(xi1,...,ximi)))$

i.e. (i) commutes with $T_A(P),T_B(Q)$ q.e.d.

Thus (i) commutes with $T^k(P0),T^k(Q0)$ for all $k\in \mathbf{N}$ and

$f_{si}\circ Pi=f_{si}\circ(\lim_k T_A{}^k(P0))=\lim_k (f_{si}\circ T_A{}^k(P0))=\lim_k (T_B{}^k(Q0)\circ(f_{si1}x...xf_{simi}))=Qi\circ(f_{si1}x..xf_{simi})$ ⊘

As result we give the definition of the semantics of RECSPEC :

3.7 Definition (Semantics and Correctness of RECSPEC) :

(1) Given a recursive process specification RECSPEC, then the initial algebra $CT_{RECSPEC}$ defined in theorem 3.6 is called the (complete initial projection algebra) semantics of RECSPEC ;

(2) RECSPEC is correct if it is contracting.

3.8 Example (Semantics of **recbpa(nat)**) :

The semantics of **recbpa(nat)** is the semantics of **probpa(nat)** with an additional operation P .To define P we have to develop the sequence $(T^n(f_0))_{n\in N}$, where $f_0\in Hom(T_{\mathbf{probpa(nat)}})$.

$Hom(T_{\mathbf{probpa(nat)}})=\{f:A_{nat}xA_{gate}xA_{gate}\to A_{proc}$ I f is projection compatible}

First we show that **recbpa(nat)** is correct, i.e. T is a contraction.

Let $f \in Hom(T_{\mathbf{probpa(nat)}})$, then

$T(f)(n,Gi,Gj)=(Gi!n)\cdot f(n+1,Gi,Gj)+(Gj!n+1)\cdot f(n,Gi,Gj)$ and

$pproc_A(1,T(f)(n,Gi,Gj))=(Gi!n)+(Gj!n+1)$ is independent of f .

Now let $f,g \in Hom(T_{\mathbf{probpa(nat)}})$ with $pH(m,f)=pH(m,g)$, then

$pproc_A(m+1,T(f)(n,Gi,Gj))=pproc_A(m+1,(Gi!n)\cdot f(n+1,Gi,Gj)+(Gj!n+1)\cdot f(n,Gi,Gj))=$

$=(Gi!n)\cdot pproc_A(m,f(n+1,Gi,Gj))+(Gj!n+1)\cdot pproc_A(m,f(n,Gi,Gj))=$

$=(Gi!n)\cdot pproc_A(m,g(n+1,Gi,Gj))+(Gj!n+1)\cdot pproc_A(m,g(n,Gi,Gj))=$

$=pproc_A(m+1,T(g)(n,Gi,Gj))$.

Thus T is a contraction and **recbpa(nat)** is correct.

(We remark that in Bergstra's BPA, PA (Process Algebra) and ACP (Algebra of Communicating Processes) an equation system defines a contraction if and only if it is guarded, provided that there is more than one action.)

As an example we develop the third approximation $pproc_A(3,P(n,Gi,Gj))$ of the process $P(n,Gi,Gj)$. (Compare the actiontree and processgraph given in the introduction.)

$$T(f)(n,Gi,Gj) = (Gi!n)\cdot f(n+1,Gi,Gj)+(Gj!n+1)\cdot f(n,Gi,Gj)$$

$$\begin{aligned}T^2(f)(n,Gi,Gj)= {} & (Gi!n)[(Gi!n+1)\cdot f(n+2,Gi,Gj)+(Gj!n+2)\cdot f(n+1,Gi,Gj)]+\\ & +(Gj!n+1)[(Gi!n)\cdot f(n+1,Gi,Gj)+(Gj!n+1)\cdot f(n,Gi,Gj)]\end{aligned}$$

$$\begin{aligned}T^3(f)(n,Gi,Gj)= {} & (Gi!n)[(Gi!n+1)[(Gi!n+2)\cdot f(n+3,Gi,Gj)+(Gj!n+3)\cdot f(n+2,Gi,Gj)]+\\ & \quad +(Gj!n+2)[(Gi!n+1)\cdot f(n+2,Gi,Gj)+(Gj!n+2)\cdot f(n+1,Gi,Gj)]]+\\ & +(Gj!n+1)[(Gi!n)[(Gi!n+1)\cdot f(n+2,Gi,Gj)+(Gj!n+2)\cdot f(n+1,Gi,Gj)]+\\ & \quad +(Gj!n+1)[(Gi!n)\cdot f(n+1,Gi,Gj)+(Gj!n+1)\cdot f(n,Gi,Gj)]]\end{aligned}$$

$$\begin{aligned}pproc_A(3,T^3(f)(n,Gi,Gj)) = {} & (Gi!n)[(Gi!n+1)[(Gi!n+2)+(Gj!n+3)]+(Gj!n+2)[(Gi!n+1)+(Gj!n+2)]]+\\ & +(Gj!n+1)[(Gi!n)[(Gi!n+1)+(Gj!n+2)]+(Gj!n+1)[(Gi!n)+(Gj!n+1)]]\end{aligned}$$

Recursive process specifications RECSPEC⊇SPEC are yet very restrictive, for they allow only one equation for each process. What we actually need is compatibility of the enrichment with the completion of the initial algebras.

3.9 Definition (Continuous Enrichment) :

Given projection specifications SPEC=(S,OP,E) and SPEC1=(S,OP1,E1) with OP1⊇OP, E1⊇E, then SPEC1 is called continuous enrichment of SPEC if the complete initial projection-SPEC-algebra CT_{SPEC} is isomorphic to the SPEC-reduct of the complete initial projection-SPEC1-algebra CT_{SPEC1}, i.e. $CT_{SPEC} \cong (CT_{SPEC1})_{SPEC}$.

Continuous enrichment is in fact a generalization of recursive process specification, because if RECSPEC is contracting, then RECSPEC⊇SPEC is a continuous enrichment. This is based on the fact that $(CT_{RECSPEC})_{SPEC}=(CT_{SPEC},PROC1,...,PROCn)_{SPEC}=CT_{SPEC}$.

In the further development, it is intended to use any continuous enrichment SPEC1 of SPEC for process specifications, not only recursive process specifications RECSPEC.

4. CONCLUSION

Specification of processes means specification of infinite objects. In topological (resp. continuous algebra) models this infiniteness is defined relative to a metric induced by projections. So on the process sorts of a basic algebraic process specification, projections are defined as hidden functions, defining the (complete initial projection-algebra) semantics, but not meant as user operations. Complete projection-algebras with continuous operations contain solutions of recursive equation systems, provided that the associated operator T is a contraction. (In Bergstra/Klop's BPA,PA and ACP for example this condition holds for guarded equational systems, i.e. systems where each process variable in the RHS of an equation is guarded by an atomic prefix action (see /BK86/).) The fixed point of T can be obtained as limit of the sequence $(T^n(f_0))_{n\in \mathbf{N}}$.

The path to recursive process specifications RECSPEC starts with the combined specification SPEC0=**process(data)** with initial algebra semantics. This is extended to a projection specification with constraints CSPEC⊇SPEC⊇SPEC0 with a given correctness : SPEC⊇SPEC0 is conservative extension and $T_{SPEC} \cong T_{CSPEC}$ and a precise semantics : $CT_{SPEC} = (T_{CSPEC})^\infty = (T_{SPEC/\sim C})^\infty$.

The projection specification is then extended to a recursive process specification RECSPEC⊇SPEC , for which the correctness requires that RECSPEC be contracting and the semantics is given by $CT_{RECSPEC} = (CT_{SPEC}, PROC1,...,PROCn)$, where PROC=(PROC1,...,PROCn) is the unique fixed point of $T_{T_{CSPEC}}$.

The theory developed so far is still restricted to unparameterized combined data type and process specifications as the starting point for the recursive process specification. But the choice of appropriate constraints seems to fill this gap preserving the initiality of $T_{SPEC/\sim C}$ in Cat(CSPEC). Further recursive specifications shall be replaced by continuous enrichments and the whole theory shall be carried over to parameterized specifications (see /EM85/) and further to module specifications, that contain parameterized specifications as special case (see /BEP85/, /EFPB86/).

As an application we intend to specify kinds of process algebras in the sense of Bergstra et. al., corresponding to Milner's axioms for communicating processes. The concrete part without internal actions seems to cause no problems; it is still an open question however, whether there are topological (projection-algebra-) models for processes with abstraction τ. Graph models for processes with τ given by Bergstra/Klop in /BK86/ turned out not to satisfy the approximation induction principle **AIP**. But this condition is also intended to be dropped in our theory, when other conditions for the existence of unique limits can be given.

5. REFERENCES

/ADJ77/ J.A.Goguen, J.W.Thatcher, E.G.Wagner, J.B.Wright : Initial Algebra Semantics as Continuous Algebras, Journal ACM 24, 68-95, 1977

/ADJ78/ J.B.Wright, E.G.Wagner, J.W.Thatcher : A Uniform Approach to Inductive Posets and Inductive Closure, Theoretical Computer Science 7, 57-77, 1978

/AN80/ A.Arnold, M.Nivat : The metric space of infinite trees. Algebraic and topological properties , Societatis Mathematicae Polonae , Series IV:Fundamenta Informatica III,4 p. 445-476 , 1980

/BEP85/ E.K.Blum, H.Ehrig,F.Parisi-Presicce : Algebraic Specifications of Modules and Their Basic Interconnections, Journal of Computer and System Sciences Vol 34, April/June 1987

/BK83/ J.A. Bergstra, J.W. Klop, 1983 : The Algebra of recursively defined processes and the algebra of regular processes, Report IW 235/83, Math. Centrum, Amsterdam 1983

/BK86/ J.A. Bergstra, J.W. Klop: Algebra of Communicating Processes, in: CWI Monographs I Series, Proceedings of the CWI Symposium Mathematics and Computer Science, North-Holland, Amsterdam 1986, p. 89-138

/BS66/ M.N.Bleicher, H.Schneider : Completions of Partially Ordered Sets and Universal Algebras, Acta Math. Acad. Sci. Hung. Tomus 17 (3-4), 271-301, 1966

/BZa82/ J.W. De Bakker, J.I. Zucker : Denotational semantics of concurrency Proc. 14th. ACM Symp. on Theory of Computing, p.153-158, 1982

/BZb82/ J.W. De Bakker, J.I. Zucker : Processes and the denotational semantics of concurrency, Information and Control, Vol.54, No.1/2, p.70-120, 1982

/DEGR87/ C.Dimitrovici, H.Ehrig, M.Große-Rhode, C.Rieckhoff : Projektionsräume und Projektionsalgebren: Eine Algebraisierung von ultrametrischen Räumen , Technical Report No. 87-7, TU Berlin, 1987

/EFPB86/ H.Ehrig, W.Fey, F.Parisi-Presicce, E.K.Blum : Algebraic Theory of Module Specifications with Constraints, invited paper for MFCS'86, LNCS 233 (1986), 59-77

/EM85/ H.Ehrig, B.Mahr : Fundamentals of Algebraic Specifications 1 : Equations and Initial Semantics , Springer Verlag , Berlin-Heidelberg-New York-Tokyo 1985

/HM83/ M.Hennessy, R.Milner : Algebraic Laws for Nondeterminism and Concurrency, University of Edingburgh, Department of Computer Science, Internal Report CSR-133-83, June 1983

/Kra80/ E. Kranakis : Approximating the Projective Model, Report CS-R8607,Centre for Mathematics and Computer Science, Amsterdam 1980, 122-133,179-191

/Kra86/ E.Kranakis, Fixed point equations with parameters in the projective model, CWI Report CS-R8606, Amsterdam 1986, to be published in Information and Computation

/LOTOS83/ ISO-documents and draft proposals on the Specification Language LOTOS since 1983

/LOTOS86/ H.Ehrig, J.Buntrock, P.Boehm, K.P.Hasler, F.Nürnberg, C.Rieckhoff, J.deMeer : Towards an Algebraic Semantics of the ISO-Specification Language LOTOS, draft version, Technische Universität Berlin, May 1986

/LOTOS87/ Information processing systems-Open systems interconnection-LOTOS-A Formal Description Technique Based on the Temporal Ordering of Observational Behaviour,ISO DIS 8807 (ISO/TC97/SC21N), July 20, 1987

/Mil80/ R.Milner, A Calculus of Communicating Systems, Springer LNCS 92, 1980

/Mil85/ R.Milner, Lectures on a calculus for communicating systems, seminar on concurrency, Springer LNCS 197, 197-220, 1985

/MD86/ B.Möller, W.Dosch : On the Algebraic Specification of Domains, in Recent Trends in Data Type Specification (e.d. H.J.Kreowski), Informatik Fachberichte 116, Springer Verlag 1986, 178-195

/Möl82/ B.Möller : Unendliche Objekte und Geflechte, Fakultät für Mathematik und Informatik der TU München, Dissertation, TUM-18213, 1982

/Möl85/ B.Möller : On the Algebraic Specification of Objects - Ordered and Continuous Models of Algebraic Types, Acta Informatica 22, 537-578, 1985

/Niv75/ M.Nivat : On the Interpretation of Recursive Polyadic Program Schemes, Istituto Nazionale di Alta Mathematica XV, 255-281, Academic Press, London 1975

/TW86/ A.Tarlecki, M.Wirsing : Continuous abstract data types, Fundamenta Informaticae IX (1986) 95-126, North-Holland

STRUCTURING THEORIES ON CONSEQUENCE

José Fiadeiro and Amílcar Sernadas

INESC/IST
Rua Alves Redol, 9, 3º Esq, 1000 Lisboa, Portugal
uucp: mcvax!inesc!llf

Abstract - Building on the work of Goguen and Burstall on institutions and on Tarski's notion of deductive system, a categorial framework for manipulating theories in an arbitrary logic is presented. Its main contribution is the formalisation of the semantics of theory-building operations on top of a consequence relation. For that purpose, the notion of π-institution is proposed as an alternative to the notion of institution, replacing the notions of model and satisfaction by a primitive consequence operator in the definition of a logic. The resulting approach to the semantics of specification languages is intrinsically different from the original one in the sense that the ultimate denotation of a specification is taken herein to be a class of theories (sets of formulae closed for the consequence relation) and not a class of models of that logic. Adopting this point of view, the semantics of Clear-like specification building operations is analysed.

1. Introduction

Quoting from [Goguen and Burstall 86], "a specification is a finite text that should be readable at least by humans, and preferably by computers". The purpose of a specification language is to provide tools for writing specifications. In particular, and above all, to provide tools for putting together small specifications to build more complex ones. Defining (formally) the meaning, or *semantics*, of a specification text requires the adoption of a logical framework. The fact that much of the work of formalisation can (and should) be done independently of the chosen logic led Burstall and Goguen to introduce the notion of *institution* [eg, Goguen and Burstall 85, 86].

The institutional approach is based on abstract model theory [Barwise 74]: in simple terms, an institution defines a logical system by describing the allowed signatures and, for each signature, a set of formulae, a collection of models and a satisfaction relation between models and formulae. Although this provides a very abstract level for dealing with logics (see, for instance, [Tarlecki 86] for a discussion on the equivalence between the Craig interpolation theorem and the Robinson consistency theorem in institutions), there is neverthless a commitment to accept a dependency on the notions of model and satisfaction adopted for the logic. In the case of the semantics of specification languages, this means that one must be ready to accept that the ultimate semantics of specifications is to be given by signatures and classes of models of the logic [Sannella and Tarlecki 84]. That is to say, in institutions, the "*semantic unit*" is the model. Sometimes, this situation is not entirely satisfactory:

On one hand, one should have the possibility to define a logical system through a primitive notion of consequence. Defining a logic in this way may be a question of personal taste (which the authors happen to share) but with the advent of mechanical theorem provers this seems also to be the best approach that fits the future needs in terms of formal support to specification. Typically, consequence will be defined proof theoretically by giving axioms and inference rules, but not necessarily.

On the other hand, and in the same line of thought, it seems preferable to have the *theory* (as a pair of a signature and a set of formulae closed under a consequence relation) as the "semantic unit" that is used to define the semantics of specifications, in the same way that models are used in institutions. This is particularly so in the case of conceptual modelling where operations for structuring knowledge bases as theories are required. Of course, in institutions, it is possible not to go down to the level of models and stay at the *coarser level* of theories for dealing with specifications. But this level is generally not fine enough for supporting the expressive power required by some kinds of operations [Sannella and Tarlecki 84]. What is pretended is a formalism that supports the same expressive power as institutions but that adopts theories instead of models as the basic units of specification.

It should be recognised that these points of view agree with some schools of thought in computer science, namely in the program development area, where some authors [eg Maibaum et al 85, Maibaum 86] advocate that each layer of the specification refinement process should be based on a derivability relation and that the traditional notions concerning Abstract Data Types should be captured by syntactical concepts concerning "axiomatic theories". However, besides general frameworks such as LF [Harper et al 87] oriented towards proof checking and proof construction and specially designed for implementing systems of logic, no formalism has been proposed that gives the same kind of *abstract support* to specification building as institutions do (working only with first order logic like in [Maibaum et al 85] does not seem to be a good answer), while allowing the definition of a logic (and of operations on specifications) to be given on top of a primitive notion of consequence. The aim of this paper is to propose such a framework.

Hence, the answer to the question "what is a logic?" that is adopted herein assumes another approach, closer to some modern treatments of logic [Avron 87, Gabbay 81, Hacking 79, Scott 74] which take the notion of *consequence* as fundamental: the notion of *π-institution* is proposed as an alternative to the notion of institution, replacing the notions of model and satisfaction by a primitive consequence operator (à la Tarski). It should be stressed that the purpose herein is not to present a framework that is general enough to accomodate all notions of consequence that are relevant to computer science, or to characterise the simplest notion of consequence that serves our purposes in specification building. In particular, although the main motivation was approaching consequence through derivability, the proposed framework may not rule out a priori certain model-theoretic notions of consequence, but, again, this was not the aim. Rather, the main goal of the paper is to show how the semantics of specification languages can be given on top of a logic defined over a certain notion of consequence, stressing the distinction between approaches based on *consequence* and on *satisfaction*.

Indeed, this approach is believed to have more than a philosophical interest (if ever) and, consequently, π-institutions are not presented only per se. After the discussion on their definition and the presentation in Section 2 of an example (equational logic), the paper concentrates on the manipulation of theories towards the desired semantics of specification building. For that purpose, the notion of *interpretation* of a theory is introduced and a classification of interpretations is proposed. This classification is based on the notion of *conservativeness*, a core concept in the semantics of specifications, and on its relativisation to theory morphisms. A notion of model defined on top of consequence is also introduced, allowing to assess these constructions at the light of classical institutions.

Section 4 begins exactly by confronting the different levels of specification building distinguished by Sannella and Tarlecki with the distinction at the semantic level that results from the choice between building on consequence or on satisfaction. The discussion then proceeds with the semantics of data constraints and parameterisation.

With respect to program/software development, the paper (partially) addresses only what has been called *horizontal refinement*, ie, the process of structuring a specification in a fixed layer using the tools provided by a specification language. Vertical refinement, where the core concept is *implementation*, is not addressed. This and other topics that need further work are referred in the concluding remarks (Section 5).

As it happens with institutions, the theory of π-institutions builds heavily on category theory. Hence, the paper presupposes (some) familiarity with this subject, although only "simple" concepts and results are used, for which the tutorials in [Pitt et al 86] give an excellent introduction. Familiarity with the traditional institutional framework is also helpful. The basic reference with respect to the theory of institutions will be [Goguen and Burstall 85].

Space constraints have banned (almost) all proofs from the text. The reader interested in the missing proofs should consult the extended version of this paper [Fiadeiro and Sernadas 87]. This extended version also includes the analysis of clause logic as a π-institution and the development of the semantics of conceptual modelling in π-institutions.

Briefly, and to end up these introductory remarks, what this paper proposes is another step in the quest for abstraction and generality initiated by Goguen and Burstall with institutions. It is hoped that, with π-institutions, much of the work based on consequence rather than on satisfaction that has been done may be lifted to the same level of abstraction achieved with institutions, thus supporting much more computer science independently of the underlying logical systems. Using Goguen's and Burstall's arguments, this is essential to facilitate the transfer and comparison of results from one logical system to another, thus allowing to build upon the work of others, and to permit combining different logical systems when more than one is required for formalising some approach (eg, *object oriented approaches* [Sernadas et al 88]).

2. Π-Institutions

Even after having decided to adopt the notion of consequence as a primitive one for the definition of a logic, many approaches can still be followed. As argued in the introduction, it is not in the spirit of the paper to discuss on the nature of the consequence operator that should be given, or to characterise what minimal conditions it should satisfy (see [Avron 87] for an overview of consequence relations). Rather, it seemed better to choose an already studied definition of consequence, and to comment on its appropriateness. Hence, this section presents only one possible approach to consequence and some variations on that theme. These refer to alternative definitions of π-institutions, including definition via *proofs*.

First Definitions

The definition of π-institution proposed below generalises the notion of *deductive system* in the sense of Tarski [Tarski 30]. It relativises his primitive concepts of *proposition* and *consequence* subject to a given signature and defines the behaviour of these concepts subject to signature changes.

2.1 **Definition**: a *π-institution* is a triple $(\mathbf{Sign}, \Phi, \{Cn_\Sigma\}_{\Sigma:\,\mathbf{Sign}})$ consisting of

1. a category **Sign** (of signatures);
2. a functor Φ: **Sign** -> **Set** (giving the set of formulae over each signature);
3. for each object Σ of **Sign**, a *consequence operator* Cn_Σ defined in the power set of $\Phi(\Sigma)$ satisfying for each $A, B \subseteq \Phi(\Sigma)$ and $\mu: \Sigma \to \Sigma'$:

   (RQ1) $A \subseteq Cn_\Sigma(A)$ *(Extensiveness)*

   (RQ2) $Cn_\Sigma(Cn_\Sigma(A)) = Cn_\Sigma(A)$ *(Idempotence)*

   (RQ3) $Cn_\Sigma(A) = \bigcup_{B \subseteq A,\ B \text{ finite}} Cn_\Sigma(B)$ *(Compactness)*

   (RQ4) $\Phi(\mu)(Cn_\Sigma(A)) \subseteq Cn_{\Sigma'}(\Phi(\mu)(A))$ *(Structurality)* ◊

This definition is very similar in structure to the traditional definition of institution [Goguen and Burstall 85]. The characterisation of the "language" part of a logic is identical, given through a category of signatures and a functor giving the set of formulae over each signature. These sets can be restricted to recursive ones in order to enhance definability. In fact, the functor Φ could be defined over the category **Rec** of recursive sets and recursive total functions [Meseguer and Goguen 85]. Moreover, the sets of formulae are usually inductively defined through grammars, which can be implicitly associated to the functor in the definition.

Contrarily to what happens in institutions, the notion of *consequence* is considered to be primitive in π-institutions. The requirements (RQ1)-(RQ3) were taken directly from [Tarski 30]. These requirements are quite strong in the sense that they rule out many "non-classical" systems that are actually of practical interest. For instance, *monotonicity* if $A \subseteq B$ then $\mathbf{Cn}_\Sigma(A) \subseteq \mathbf{Cn}_\Sigma(B)$

is easily derived from the requirements above [ibid] thus ruling out, for instance, systems for non-monotonic reasoning. On the other hand, compactness (RQ3) rules out systems using infinitary inference rules as well as many "model-theoretic logics". Without this requirement, every institution would give rise to a π-institution by adopting the traditional model theoretic closure. Hence, these requirements should be weakened or strengthned in order to encompass more systems of logic or to rule out others. Neverthless, it should be said that (RQ3) can be safely replaced by monotonicity in the sequel, as no particular use of compactness is made. The only reason to have kept it in the definition is that is is part of Tarski's original definition [ibid] which was taken as a reference to the definition above. Dispensing monotonicity seems more problematic.

The fourth requirement is the counterpart to the satisfaction condition in institutions, ie, it expresses invariance of consequence under signature changes. This requirement is not usually referred in the literature because only the behaviour of theories with respect to changes in their axiomatisations has been studied. However, specifications may evolve both through modifications operated over their axioms and over their language. Hence the need to relativize the notion of consequence to signature and signature changes. The reader who is familiar with the classical institutional framework will have already recognized that (RQ4) corresponds to the well known closure lemma [Goguen and Burstall 85].

A fixed π-institution $(\mathbf{Sign}, \Phi, \{\mathbf{Cn}_\Sigma\}_{\Sigma:\,\mathbf{Sign}})$ is assumed throughout the paper.

2.2 **Remark**: It is interesting to note that a requirement quite similar to (RQ4) is introduced in [Blok and Pigozzi 86] for *substitutions* of formulae for (propositional) variables. In a sense, the notion of substitution seems to correspond to certain transformations on the sets of formulae over a signature induced by an endomorphism on that signature. In this way, (RQ4) enforces another requirement on the notion of consequence, *uniformity* [Avron 87], introduced in a rather vague way in [Gabbay 81]. ◊

2.3 **Notation**: For each signature Σ and set A of Σ-formulae, $\mathbf{Cn}_\Sigma(A)$ will be hereafter denoted by A° and, for every arrow μ in **Sign**, μ will also be taken to denote $\Phi(\mu)$. As usual, by $\mu^{-1}(A)$ it is meant the reverse image of the set A under μ (ie, under $\Phi(\mu)$). ◊

2.4 **Definition**: For every set of Σ-formulae A, the set A° is called the *closure* of A. A set of Σ-formulae A is said to be *closed* iff $A^\circ \subseteq A$. ◊

It results from (RQ1) that A is closed iff $A = A^\circ$. Notice that each consequence operator is a *closure operator* in the ordinary mathematical sense.

Some standard properties of such closure operators are captured in the following:

2.5 **Proposition**: Let Σ, Σ' : **Sign**, $A,B \subseteq \Phi(\Sigma)$, $A' \subseteq \Phi(\Sigma')$ and $\mu: \Sigma \to \Sigma'$:

a) If A and B are closed, so is $A \cap B$.

b) $(A \cup B)^\circ = (A^\circ \cup B)^\circ = (A \cup B^\circ)^\circ = (A^\circ \cup B^\circ)^\circ$

c) If A' is closed, so is $\mu^{-1}(A')$. ◊

There is an interesting "relativisation" of the consequence operator based on a generalisation of Tarski's relativisation theorem [Tarski 30]:

2.6 **Theorem**: Let Ψ: **Sign** -> **Set** be a functor together with a natural inclusion $\Psi \to \Phi$ (a natural transformation whose components are inclusions). Define $\mathbf{F}_\Sigma$ in the power set of $\Phi(\Sigma)$ by $\mathbf{F}_\Sigma(A) = \mathbf{Cn}_\Sigma(A) \cap \Psi(\Sigma)$. Then, for each object Σ, Σ': **Sign**, $A, B \subseteq \Phi(\Sigma)$ and $\mu: \Sigma \to \Sigma'$:

(FRQ1) $(A \cap \Psi(\Sigma)) \subseteq \mathbf{F}_\Sigma(A)$;

(FRQ2) $\mathbf{F}_\Sigma(A) = \mathbf{F}_\Sigma(\mathbf{F}_\Sigma(A))$;

(FRQ3) $\mathbf{F}_\Sigma(A) = \bigcup_{B \subseteq A,\ B \text{ finite}} \mathbf{F}_\Sigma(B)$;

(FRQ4) $\Phi(\mu)(\mathbf{F}_\Sigma(A)) \subseteq \mathbf{F}_{\Sigma'}(\Phi(\mu)(A))$. ◊

That is to say, (RQ2-4) hold when the operator $\mathbf{Cn}_\Sigma$ is replaced by $\mathbf{F}_\Sigma$. (FRQ1) requires additionally that the set of Σ-formulae A be contained in $\Psi(\Sigma)$ in order to satisfy the inclusion $A \subseteq \mathbf{F}_\Sigma(A)$. This leads to an interesting generalisation of π-institutions, hereafter called *non-extensive* because they may fail to satisfy (RQ1), where the consequence operator is defined sending sets of Σ-formulae to sets of formulae in $\Psi(\Sigma)$ and satisfying (FRQ1-4). This generalisation permits the restriction of the possible consequences of a set of formulae to formulae whose structure is given by the functor Ψ.

There are well known examples of such non-extensive π-institutions such as Horn clause logic with the consequence operator computing the Herbrand base B_P of a program P. Another example to be developed in Section 4 consists in the extension of π-institutions with data-constraints as formulae along the proposal of Burstall and Goguen for institutions: if there is no calculus to derive data-constraints, the consequence operator computes only formulae from the original π-institution.

Naturally, non-extensive π-institutions may fail to validate other properties of π-institutions. For instance, although the properties a) and c) in the proposition above are still valid for non-extensive π-institutions, b) is not necessarily valid. Indeed, in non-extensive π-institutions, the set of consequences of a set of formulae may contain less information than the original set of formulae. Therefore, comparing closures gives only a poor measure of the "expressive power" of the original sets of formulae. For instance, $\mathbf{F}_\Sigma(A) \subseteq \mathbf{F}_\Sigma(B)$ may fail to imply $\mathbf{F}_\Sigma(A \cup C) \subseteq \mathbf{F}_\Sigma(B \cup C)$.

There is an easy (and obvious) way of making a non-extensive π-institution a π-institution: extend the closure operator by setting $A^\varrho = A \cup \mathbf{F}_\Sigma(A)$. It is easy to check that (RQ1-4) are satisfied by this extended closure operator. Note that $A^\varrho \subseteq B^\varrho$ requires that $(A - \Psi(\Sigma)) \subseteq (B - \Psi(\Sigma))$, ie, it requires formulae in $\Phi(\Sigma) - \Psi(\Sigma)$ to be preserved by inclusion. This is quite intuitive because there is no way (at least, a priori) of manipulating such formulae.

2.7 **Remark**: This may seem to be too restrictive in some cases, at least in the case of Horn Clause Logic referred above. It seems worthwhile investigating another measure for "expressibility" giving equivalence between A and B iff their closures cannot be distinguished by adding them (finite sets of) formulae from a subset $\psi(\Sigma)$ (for another natural inclusion $\psi \to \Phi$). This measure is closer to the procedural interpretation of the consequence operator in the sense that, intuitively, it fails to distinguish between two sets of formulae *(programs)* that produce the same consequences *(output)* to the same extensions *(input)*. ◊

Alternative Formulations

(RQ4) is a requirement on structure that is usually captured by using functors in definitions. In the sequel, it is shown how a more categorial definition of π-institutions can be given by means of a "consequence" functor.

A preordering can be explicitly introduced for comparing sets of formulae over a given signature as discussed above:

2.8 **Definition**: Let Σ: **Sign** and $A, B \subseteq \Phi(\Sigma)$. Then, $A \leq_\Sigma B$ iff $A \subseteq \mathbf{Cn}_\Sigma(B)$. ◊

It is easy to check that a preordering is indeed obtained. It reduces to inclusion for closed sets of formulae. Notice that this relation does not define a preordering in the case of non-extensive π-institution because it fails to be reflexive.

2.9 **Notation**: $\leq_\Sigma$ will often be abbreviated to $\leq$ when the underlying signature is fixed. ◊

It is easy to prove that such a preordering satisfies the following properties:

2.10 **Proposition**: Let Σ: **Sign**, $A,B \subseteq \Phi(\Sigma)$ and $\mathbf{X} \subseteq 2^{\Phi(\Sigma)}$.

(≤1) if $A \subseteq B$ then $A \leq B$.

(≤2) if for every $X \in \mathbf{X}$, $X \leq A$, then $\cup\mathbf{X} \leq A$.

(≤3) $$A^\circ = \left(\bigcup_{B \leq A} B\right)$$

(≤4) Let $\mu: \Sigma \to \Sigma'$ for Σ': **Sign**. If $A \leq_\Sigma B$ then $\mu(A) \leq_{\Sigma'} \mu(B)$. ◊

Notice that considering the category **Pre** whose objects are preorderings and whose morphisms are order preserving mappings, the property (≤4) states that Φ induces a functor $\mathbf{X}$: **Sign** -> **Pre** where **Pre** is the category of preordered sets and monotone mappings. Moreover, this functor satisfies the equation $\mathbf{X};\mathbf{Y} = \Phi;\mathbf{2}$ where $\mathbf{2}$: **Set** -> **Set** is the "power" functor and $\mathbf{Y}$: **Pre** -> **Set** is the usual forgetful functor. It results that $\mathbf{X}(\Sigma)$ is a preordering $(2^{\Phi(\Sigma)}, \leq_\Sigma)$.

2.11 An *alternative definition* to 2.1 could therefore consist in a triple (**Sign**, Φ, $\mathbf{X}$) where **Sign** and Φ are as in 2.1, and the functor $\mathbf{X}$, defined as above, is such that each preordering $\mathbf{X}(\Sigma)$ satisfies ($\leq$1) and ($\leq$2). In these conditions, an operator defined through ($\leq$3) is easily shown to satisfy (RQ1), (RQ2) and (RQ4) together with monotonicity. ◊

2.12 **Remark**: The restriction of the preordering to pairs ({w},A) is usually called a *consequence relation* over Σ and $\{w\} \leq_\Sigma A$ is usually written $A \vdash_\Sigma w$. According to the classification introduced in [Gabbay 81], this is a *Tarski* consequence relation. Notice that although the full relation $\leq$ satisfies reflexivity and "cut", it does not correspond to the ordinary extension of deducibility to multi-conclusions as recalled, for instance, in [Hacking 79] (in particular it does not satisfy dilution on the right). However, as shown in [Gabbay 81], it is possible to define a *Scott consequence relation* from the consequence operator by extending consequence to multi-conclusions in the obvious way, ie, through $A \Vdash_\Sigma B$ iff $A^\circ \cap B \neq \emptyset$. As expected these consequence relations agree. As remarked earlier, the definition of π-institution could have been given through consequence relations instead of consequence operators. The choice that was made reflects the importance of the notion of closure and the associated preordering to the sequel. ◊

A Tarski consequence relation such as the one obtained above is usually defined through the notion of *Σ-proof* in terms of a *direct consequence relation* $\Rightarrow_\Sigma \subseteq 2^{\Phi(\Sigma)} \times \Phi(\Sigma)$:

2.13 **Definition**: Given Σ : **Sign**, $A \subseteq \Phi(\Sigma)$ and $w \in \Phi(\Sigma)$,

1. a Σ-proof of w from A is a sequence $w_1, \ldots, w_n$ of Σ-formulae such that
   a. $w_n = w$;
   b. for every $1 \leq i \leq n$, either $w_i \in A$ or $\emptyset \Rightarrow_\Sigma w_i$ or $w_{k1}, \ldots, w_{km} \Rightarrow_\Sigma w_i$ for some $1 \leq k1,\ldots,km \leq i-1$
2. $A \vdash_\Sigma w$ iff there is a Σ-proof of w from A. ◊

The closure of a set of formula A is thus the minimal set containing A that is closed with respect to the direct consequence relation. It is easy to prove that such a consequence operator satisfies (RQ1-3). Moreover, structurality is obtained if the direct consequence relation satisfies

$$\mu(A) \vdash_{\Sigma'} \mu(w) \quad \text{if} \quad A \Rightarrow_\Sigma w$$

2.14 **Remark**: The functor $\mathbf{X}$: **Sign** -> **Pre** introduced after 2.10 admits an interesting generalisation to a functor Π: **Sign** -> **Cat** which is obtained by generalising the preorderings $\mathbf{X}(\Sigma) = (2^{\Phi(\Sigma)}, \leq_\Sigma)$ to categories $\Pi(\Sigma)$ whose objects are sets of Σ-formulae and such that an arrow between two objects A and B is a proof of A from B. This is a generalisation of the alternative definition of π-institution (2.11) in the sense that $\Pi(\Sigma)$ collapses to $\mathbf{X}(\Sigma)$ in the ordinary way [MacLane 71], ie, by forgetting the different proofs between two sets of formulae and retaining merely the existence of a proof as a morphism between them. This is closer to Burstall and Goguen's suggestion of extending institutions through "sentence morphisms" [Goguen and Burstall 86]. However, this does not mean that π-institutions reduce to the extended notion of institutions because consequence is taken herein as primitive. ◊

Example: THE (MANY-SORTED) EQUATIONAL Π-INSTITUTION

It is now shown that equational logic yields a π-institution. See [Fiadeiro e Sernadas 87] for the case of clausal logic. Recalling from [Goguen and Burstall 85]:

2.15 **Definition**: An *equational signature* is a pair (S,Σ) where S is a set (of *sort* names) and Σ is an $S^* \times S$ indexed family of sets (of *operator* names). Σ will be often written instead of (S,Σ). σ in Σ_{us} is said to have *arity* u, *sort* s, and *rank* u,s which is often indicated by writing σ: u->s.

An *equational signature morphism* μ from a signature (S,Σ) to a signature (S',Σ') is a pair (f,g) consisting of a map f: S -> S' and an $S^* \times S$ indexed family of maps $g_{us}: \Sigma_{us} \to \Sigma'_{f^*(u)f(s)}$ of operator symbols where $f^*: S^* \to S'^*$ is the extension of f to strings. $\mu(s)$ will often be written for f(s), as well as $\mu(u)$ for $f^*(u)$, and $\mu(\sigma)$ or $\mu\sigma$ for $g_{us}(\sigma)$ when $\sigma \in \Sigma_{us}$. ◊

The category **Sig** has equational signatures as objects and equational signature morphisms as arrows.

For the rest of this section, an infinite set $\mathcal{X}$ of variable symbols is assumed. A *sort assignment* is a function X: $\mathcal{X}$ -> S where S is a set of sorts. X will also denote the S-indexed set defined by $X_s = \{x \in \mathcal{X} \mid X(x)=s\}$. For each such sort assignment X, there is a *free algebra* $T_\Sigma(X)$ with $|T_\Sigma(X)|_s$ consisting of all the *s-sorted terms* with variables from X.

2.16 **Definition**: A *Σ-equation* is a triple (X,t_1,t_2) where X is a sort assignment, S being the set of sorts of Σ, and where t_1 and t_2 are terms over X of the same sort s in S. Let $\mu: \Sigma \to \Sigma'$ be a signature morphism (f,g), X a sort assignment and X' the sort assignment X;f. Then, μ induces a function $\mu^\#$: $|T_\Sigma(X)| \to |T_{\Sigma'}(X')|$.

The functor **Eqn**: **Sig** -> **Set** takes each signature Σ to the set **Eqn**(Σ) of all Σ-equations, and takes each $\mu=(f,g)$: $\Sigma \to \Sigma'$ to the function **Eqn**(μ): **Eqn**(Σ) -> **Eqn**(Σ') defined by **Eqn**$(\mu)(X,t_1,t_2) = (X;f,\mu^\#(t_1),\mu^\#(t_2))$. ◊

The consequence relation is defined through the proof system GM discussed in [MacQueen and Sannella 85]. In the next definition, vars(t) denotes the set of variables occurring in the term t.

2.17 **Definition**: The direct consequence relation $\Rightarrow$ is defined as follows:

(REF) if X assigns sorts in Σ and t is a Σ-term with vars(t)$\subseteq$X, then $\emptyset \Rightarrow_\Sigma (X,t,t)$.

(SYM) $(X,t,t') \Rightarrow_\Sigma (X,t',t)$.

(TRA) $(X,t,t'),\ (X,t',t'') \Rightarrow_\Sigma (X,t,t'')$.

(SUB) if $x \in X_s$ and $u \in |T_\Sigma(Y)|_s$, then

$$(X,t,t'),\ (Y,u,u') \Rightarrow_\Sigma ((X-\{x:s\}) \cup Y, t[u/x], t'[u'/x])$$

where t[u/x] denotes the Σ-term obtained from t by replacing every occurrence of the variable x by the Σ-term u.

(ABS) if $x \notin X$ and s is a Σ-sort, then $(X,t,t') \Rightarrow_\Sigma (X \cup \{x:s\},t,t')$ ◊

2.18 **Proposition**: Structurality is satisfied by the consequence relation defined as above.
proof: Substitutivity is the only inference rule for which structurality may seem to be non-trivial. Assume that $(X,t,t'),\ (Y,u,u') \Rightarrow_\Sigma ((X\text{-}\{x:s\})\cup Y, t[u/x], t'[u'/x])$ with $x\in X_s$ and $u\in |T_\Sigma(Y)|_s$. Then, for every $\mu=(f,g):\Sigma\rightarrow\Sigma'$, one obtains $x\in (X;f)_{f(s)}$ and $\mu^\#(u)\in |T_{\Sigma'}(Y;f)|_{f(s)}$.
Because $\mu^\#(t[u/x])=\mu^\#(t)[\mu^\#(u)/x]$ and $((X\text{-}\{x:s\})\cup Y);f=(X;f\text{-}\{x:f(s)\})\cup Y;f$, it follows that $\mu(X,t,t'),\ \mu(Y,u,u') \Rightarrow_{\Sigma'} \mu((X\text{-}\{x:s\})\cup Y, t[u/x], t'[u'/x])$ ◊

3. Theories in Π-institutions

In this section, the notions of theory and its interpretations are developed. Since it is assumed that the main objective of a specification language is to provide tools for the definition and manipulation of theories, it is essential to establish and classify relationships between theories. Thus, theories will be manipulated in this section as objects, theory morphisms providing the necessary means for relating theories between themselves. In order to establish a "rich" set of structuring primitives, a π-institution must satisfy certain conditions. A typical example is the existence of pushouts of theories in order to support parameterisation. Other requirements will be investigated in this section, mainly for supporting data abstraction. For that purpose, the results concerning the existence of image factorisation systems for theories are of great importance for measuring the "expressive power" of a π-institution for specification building.

Theories and Classification of Theory Morphisms

Theories are defined below as in institutions. Presentations and axiomatisations of theories are also defined.

3.1 **Definition**:

1. The category **Pres** of *theory presentations* is defined as having pairs (Σ,A), where Σ is a signature and A is a set of Σ-formulae, for objects, and, as arrows $\mu: (\Sigma,A)\rightarrow(\Sigma',A')$ every signature morphism $\mu:\Sigma\rightarrow\Sigma'$ satisfying $\mu(A^\circ) \subseteq A'^\circ$.

2. The full subcategory of **Pres** whose objects are the theory presentations (Σ,A) such that A is closed, is the category **The** of *theories*. The consequence operator induces a functor sending each presentation (Σ,A) to the theory (Σ,A°) which is called the theory *presented* by (Σ,A). There is also a forgetful functor ϑ: **The** -> **Sign** that sends each theory (Σ,A) to the signature Σ and each theory morphism to the corresponding signature morphism [Goguen and Burstall 85].

3. The full subcategory of **Pres** whose objects are the theory presentations (Σ,A) such that A is finite (or recursive), is the category **Axo** of *theory axiomatisations*. Again, the

consequence operator induces a functor sending **Axo** to **The** but not vice-versa because a theory may fail to be axiomatisable. ◊

These definitions of (presentation, theory or axiomatisation) morphism essentially require that the properties introduced over the signature Σ through the set of formulae A be preserved when passing from the theory (Σ,A°) to another theory. There is an easier way of proving presentation morphisms [Goguen and Burstall 85]:

3.2 **Lemma** *(Presentation):* Let Σ, Σ': **Sign**, and μ: Σ→Σ'. Let (Σ,A) and (Σ',A') be presentations. Then, μ: (Σ,A)→(Σ',A') is a presentation morphism iff $\mu(A) \subseteq A'^{\circ}$ (ie, iff $\mu(A) \leq_{\Sigma'} A'$). ◊

Every theory morphism μ: (Σ,A)→(Σ',A') satisfies the inclusion

$$\mu^{-1}(\mu(A)) \subseteq \mu^{-1}(A')$$

which follows directly from definition 3.1 (recall -2.3- that μ also stands for Φ(μ) and μ^{-1} for $\Phi(\mu)^{-1}$). This inclusion is, in general, strict. Having the reverse inclusion,

$$\mu^{-1}(A') \subseteq \mu^{-1}(\mu(A))$$

and hence equality, is an interesting case because it means that if μ(w) is a theorem of A' then μ(w) belongs to μ(A) (ie, is an image of a theorem of A), that is to say, no new "properties" of the symbols in Σ, as given through A, can be derived using the additional knowledge given in A'. Note that this is weaker then requiring w to be a theorem of A which would be captured by the inclusion

$$\mu^{-1}(A') \subseteq A$$

Both requirements are equivalent in the case where μ (in **Set**, ie, Φ(μ)) is injective. Intuitively, they express that the original theory is somewhat preserved.

3.3 **Definition**: a theory morphism μ: (Σ,A)→(Σ',A') is called *true* iff $\mu^{-1}(A') \subseteq \mu^{-1}(\mu(A))$ and is called *conservative* iff $\mu^{-1}(A') \subseteq A$. If μ is a monic (in **Sign**), (Σ',A') is said to be an *extension* of (Σ,A). ◊

The definition of true morphisms was adapted from the one proposed in [Ehrich82] within the algebraic approach to ADTs. The alternative notion of conservative morphism is used instead by Tarlecki [Tarlecki 86]. Maibaum [Maibaum86] uses the notion of conservative extension meaning conservative inclusion. Notice that this classification is usually used for morphisms that induce injective mappings on formulae, in which case both notions coincide. However, it should be stressed that a signature monomorphism does not necessarily induce an injective mapping on formulae. This property depends on the nature of the functor Φ.

3.4 **Notation**: $\mu(T)$ will be often written instead of $\mu(A)$ when T is (Σ,A) for some Σ. ◊

Important properties of conservative theory morphisms are captured by the following lemmata:

3.5 **Lemma**: Let $\mu: T \to T'$ and $\sigma: T' \to T"$ be conservative theory morphisms. Then, $\mu;\sigma$ is also conservative. ◊

3.6 **Lemma**: Let $\mu: T \to T'$ and $\sigma: T' \to T"$ be theory morphisms such that $\mu;\sigma$ is conservative. Then, μ is conservative. ◊

3.7 **Lemma**: Let $\mu: T \to T'$ be a theory morphism such that $\vartheta(\mu)$ is an isomorphism. Then, μ is an isomorphism in **The** iff μ is conservative. ◊

From this lemma, it is easy to see that the property of being a monic in **The** is not very powerful because it is inherited from **Sign** and, thus, does not take into account the relationships between the sets of formulae of the theories. The "good" properties of being a monic are, in fact, recovered by conservative monics in **The**. Therefore, it is not surprising that "conservativeness" (or "trueness") has deserved so much attention in ADT specification [eg, Ehrich 82, Maibaum 86]. This point is better illustrated by examining image factorisation systems. This concept is recalled below, adapting from [Arbib and Manes 75]:

3.8 **Definition**: Given a category **C**, an image factorisation system for **C** is a pair (E,M) such that:

- E is a class of epimorphisms in **C** and M is a class of monomorphisms in **C**.
- E and M are closed under composition.
- E and M contain all isomorphisms in **C**.
- Every morphism f in **C** admits an (E,M)-factorisation that is unique up to isomorphism. That is to say, there exist $e \in E$ and $m \in M$ such that $f=e;m$ and if f admits another (E,M)-factorisation $f=e';m'$ then there is a isomorphism h such that $e;h=e'$ and $h;m'=m$.

An important property of factorisation systems is the following:

3.9 **Diagonal Fill-in Lemma**: Let (E,M) be an image factorisation system for a category **C**. Given a commutative square $e;g = f;m$ with $e \in E$ and $m \in M$, then there is a unique h such that $e;h=f$ and $h;m=g$. ◊

The following theorem shows how factorisation systems can be lifted from the category of signatures to the category of theories:

3.10 **Theorem**: Let (E,M) be an image factorisation system for **Sign**. Let ET be the class of all theory morphisms μ satisfying $\vartheta(\mu) \in E$. Let MT be the class of all conservative theory morphisms μ satisfying $\vartheta(\mu) \in M$. Then, (ET,MT) is an image factorisation system for **The**.

proof:

- ET is closed under composition because so is E. On the other hand, MT is also closed under composition because M is closed under composition and the product of two conservative morphisms is also conservative (Lemma 3.5).
- The condition on isomorphism of theories is a direct consequence of the condition on isomorphisms of signatures.
- Let μ: $(\Sigma,A)\rightarrow(\Sigma',A')$ be a theory morphism. As a signature morphism, μ admits an (E,M) factorisation μ=e;m where e: $\Sigma\rightarrow\Sigma^*$ belongs to E and m: $\Sigma^*\rightarrow\Sigma'$ belongs to M. To make it a factorisation in **The** it is necessary to define the centre theory through a closed set A^* of Σ^*-formulae satisfying $e(A)\subseteq A^*$ and $m(A^*)\subseteq A'$. Moreover, because m must be conservative, no choice is left but to take $m^{-1}(A')=A^*$. Note that this is a good definition because $m^{-1}(A')$ is closed (cf 2.5.c). On the other hand, $e(A)\subseteq m^{-1}(A')= A^*$ as required.

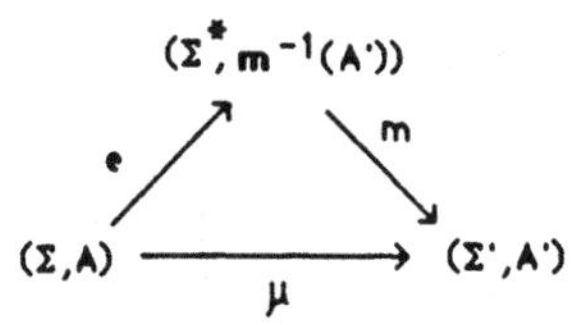

- It must still be shown that such a factorisation is unique up to isomorphism. But this is a mere consequence of the lemmata 3.6 and 3.7 above. ◊

3.11 **Corollary**: If **Sign** admits an image factorisation system, so does **The**. ◊

As it will become evident in the sequel, the existence of such image factorisation systems is one of the conditions that establish that a π-institution is "expressive" enough in order to support the semantics of a sufficiently "rich" set of specification building primitives, namely data-constraints. In a way, this condition is not surprising because in [Tarlecki 85] institutions were already required to support image factorisation of models in order to allow free constructions. Hence, the importance of this result: it provides an image factorisation system for **The** by merely requiring **Sign** to have one. That is to say, requirements for the existence of image factorisation of theories can be placed on the π-institution's category of signatures, ie on "syntax".

Interpretations, Nuclei and Canonical Interpretations

One of the most important of the envisaged concepts is that of interpretation of theories. Intuitively, interpretations of theories play the role of *semantic units* in π-institutions like models in institutions.

3.12 **Definition**: Given a theory T in **The**, a *T-interpretation* (or an interpretation of T) is a theory T' together with a morphism σ: T $\rightarrow$ T', called the *interpreter*, which says how the theory T is being interpreted in T'. Naturally, many interpretations of T in T' may exist each of which is characterised by its interpreter. Two interpretations (σ_1,T_1) and (σ_2,T_2) of a theory T are related to each other by the theory morphisms between T_1 and T_2 that make the diagram having T, T_1 and T_2 by vertices commute. The category $\iota(T)$ of T-interpretations is thus defined. ◊

The category $\iota(T)$ has a well known structure in Category Theory: it is the *comma category* (T↓**The**). Notice that a functor ι: **The** -> **Cat**^{op} can be defined sending each theory T to the category $\iota(T)$ and each theory morphism μ: T→T' to the functor $\iota(\mu)$: $\iota(T')$->$\iota(T)$ defined by $\iota(\mu)(\sigma,T")=(\mu;\sigma,T")$ and mapping each T'-interpretation morphism ϕ: $(\sigma_1,T"_1) \rightarrow (\sigma_2,T"_2)$ to "itself" as a morphism in $\iota(T)((\mu;\sigma_1,T"_1),(\mu;\sigma_2,T"_2))$.

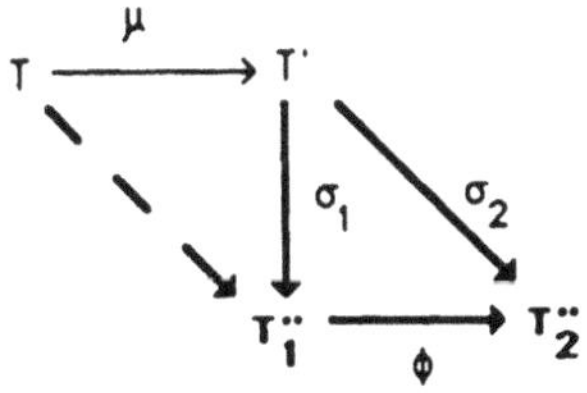

3.13 **Remark**: The use of the word *interpretation* may seem a little bit abusive. This term has been used in the literature [eg, Enderton 72, Maibaum 86] for what would be called herein a first-order signature morphism (see also [Barwise 74]). Other texts use it for what could be called a "semantics" for the logic. It is hoped that, after reading the rest of the present work, the use of this term will seem to be not so far from both "interpretations". ◊

Only some fragments of a T-interpretation are relevant to the interpretation itself in the sense that they are the image of the interpreter, ie the result of the interpretation. These parts identify the essence of the interpretation, enabling it to be classified and compared with respect to other interpretations. The notion of *nucleus* of an interpretation is therefore introduced. From the discussion above, the nucleus of a T-interpretation should be, in some way, minimal. On the other hand, every interpretation should be a conservative extension of its nucleus, ie, the nucleus should be a "faithful" image of the interpretation.

In order to insure the existence of such nuclei, it will be assumed in the sequel that the category **Sign** admits an image factorisation system (E,M). As shown in 3.10, an image factorisation system (ET,MT) for **The** is induced by (E,M), consisting of epis in E and of conservative monics in M.

3.14 **Definition**: Given an interpreter σ: T → T', the *nucleus* of (σ,T') is the interpretation $(e,T^{\bullet})$ where $T^{\bullet}$ is the centre theory for a (ET,MT) factorisation of σ with epi e. Recall (3.10) that if T is the theory (Σ,A) and T' is the theory (Σ',A'), then $T^{\bullet}$ is the theory $(\Sigma^{\bullet},m^{-1}(A'))$ where e: $\Sigma \rightarrow \Sigma^{\bullet}$ and m: $\Sigma^{\bullet} \rightarrow \Sigma'$ constitute a factorisation of $\vartheta(\sigma)$. ◊

The required conservative extension of the nucleus is given by m and the minimality of the nucleus is established by the following:

3.15 **Proposition**: The nucleus $(e,T^{\bullet})$ of an interpretation (μ,T') is minimal in the sense that every T-interpretation (σ,T") for which (μ,T') is a conservative extension (ie, such that T' is a conservative extension of T"), is itself a conservative extension of (e,T*). ◊

3.16 **Example**: Consider the theories **bool** and **squeezed_nat** presented in the equational π-institution by the following axiomatisations (an intuitive, minimal, Clear-like language will be used throughout the paper in an informal way):

```
bool:  sorts:  bool
       ops:    true, false: -> bool

squeezed_nat:
       sorts:  nat
       ops:    zero: -> nat
               suc: nat -> nat
       eqs:    x:nat,  x=suc(x)
```

An interpretation of **bool** in **squeezed_nat** is obtained by sending *true* and *false* to *zero*. In this case, the interpretation factorises into the nucleus

```
bool_in_squeezed_nat:
       sorts:  nat
       ops:    zero: -> nat
```

Notice that the interpreter of this nucleus is not a monic. Consider now the extension **squeezed_nat_with_one** of **squeezed_nat** presented as follows:

```
squeezed_nat_with_one:
       sorts:  nat
       ops:    zero, one: -> nat
               suc: nat -> nat
       eqs:    x:nat,  x=suc(x)
               one=suc(zero)
```

The nucleus of the interpretation of **bool** that sends *true* to *zero* and *false* to *one* has the following axiomatisation:

```
bool_in_squeezed_nat_with_one:
       sorts:  nat
       ops:    zero, one: -> nat
       eqs:    zero=one
```

Notice that although the interpreter of this nucleus is a monic, it is not conservative because the equation (true=false) which is not a theorem of **bool** is mapped to the axiom (zero=one). Finally, consider the theory **nat_with_one** presented by

```
nat_with_one:
       sorts:  nat
       ops:    zero, one: -> nat
               suc: nat -> nat
       eqs:    one=suc(zero)
```

The nucleus of the interpretation of **bool** that sends *true* to *zero* and *false* to *one* has the following axiomatisation:

```
bool_in_nat_with_one:
        sorts:  nat
        ops:    zero, one: -> nat
```

Notice that the interpreter of this nucleus is a conservative monic. ◊

Two important classes of interpretations can be identified according to their nuclei:

3.17 **Definition**: An interpretation (σ,T') of a theory T is said to be *canonical* iff its nucleus (e,T^{*}) yields an isomorphism e between T and T^{*}. A T-interpretation (σ,T') is said to be *minimal* iff it is isomorphic to its nucleus. ◊

Informally, an interpretation of T is canonical when it does not introduce new "knowledge" about the symbols in T. On the other hand, an interpretation is minimal when it does not introduce knowledge that is irrelevant to T ("junk" in the sense that this knowledge is *unreachable* from T). For instance, in the example above, neither of the interpretations is minimal. The interpretations of **bool** in **squeezed_nat** and in **squeezed_nat_with_one** are not canonical because both identify *true* and *false*. Finally, the interpretation of **bool** in **nat_with_one** is canonical.

These two classes are easily identified through the following

3.18 **Proposition**: An interpretation (σ,T') is canonical (resp. minimal) iff σ is a conservative monic (resp. an epi). ◊

3.19 This characterisation of minimal interpretations leads to a full functor $\rho_T: \iota(T)\text{->}\rho(T)$ (where $\rho(T)$ is the full subcategory of $\iota(T)$ whose interpreters are epis) sending each T-interpretation to its nucleus. On the other hand, each morphism $\varphi: (\sigma_1,T_1)\rightarrow(\sigma_2,T_2)$ is sent to the morphism $\phi: (e_1,T_1^{*})\rightarrow(e_2,T_2^{*})$ given by the diagonal fill-in lemma applied to the commutative diagram $e_1;(m_1;\varphi) = e_2;m_2$ where $\sigma_1= e_1;m_1$ and $\sigma_2= e_2;m_2$ are factorisations.

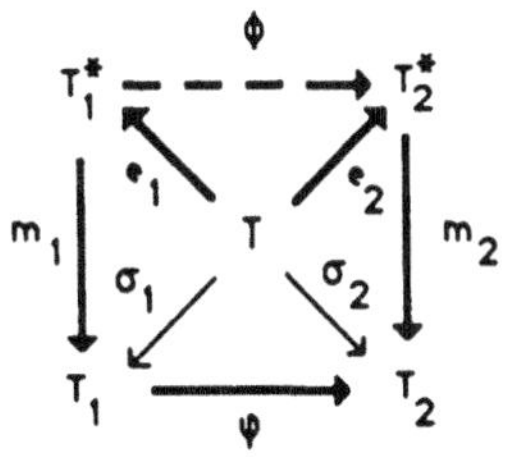

It results that there is at most one morphism between two minimal interpretations because their

interpreters are epis. Therefore, each category $\rho(T)$ is a preorder. The preordering relates any two interpretations that admit an interpretation morphism between them. ◊

3.20 This construction extends trivially to a natural transformation $\iota \text{->} \rho$ where ρ: **The**->**Cat**^{op} satisfies $\rho(\mu)=\varphi_{T'};\iota(\mu);\rho_T$ (where $\varphi_{T'}$: $\rho(T')\text{->}\iota(T')$ is the inclusion functor). Naturally, $\rho(\mu)$ for $\mu: T \to T'$ can be extended to a functor $\rho^*(\mu)$: $\iota(T')\text{->}\rho(T)$ given by $\rho^*(\mu)=\rho_{T'};\rho(\mu)$, ie, given a T'-interpretation (σ_1,T_1), $\rho^*(\mu)(\sigma_1,T_1)=\rho_T(\mu;\sigma_1,T_1)$. Hence, $\rho^*(\mu)$ sends each interpretation of T' to its nucleus as a T-interpretation. The interpretation of T that is obtained is called the <u>μ-nucleus</u> of the T'-interpretation. On the other hand, each morphism $\varphi:(\sigma_1,T_1)\to(\sigma_2,T_2)$ is sent to the morphism $\phi:(e_1,T_1^*)\to(e_2,T_2^*)$ given by the diagonal fill-in lemma applied to the commutative diagram $e_1;(m_1;\varphi)=e_2;m_2$ where $\mu;\sigma_1=e_1;m_1$ and $\mu;\sigma_2=e_2;m_2$ are factorisations.

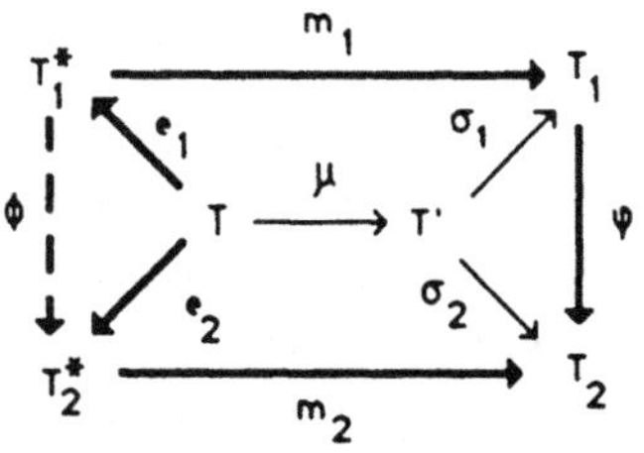

In the sequel, no distinction will be made between the functors ρ and ρ^*. ◊

μ-Free Translations and μ-Canonical Interpretations

It is now time to relativise the notion of canonicity of interpretations to theory morphisms. Basically, it corresponds to define the conditions under which an interpretation of a theory T' can be said to be "free" with respect to a morphism μ from another theory T to T'.

As pointed out by A. Poigné during the Workshop and, later on, by one of the referees, this relativisation falls under the standard structure of *indexed categories* (see the tutorials of A. Poigné in [Pitt et al 86] for a comprehensive introduction to this subject and for pointers to the relevant literature) and, in particular, under an abstract, categorial representation of bits of first-order logic in terms of subobjects, pullbacks and image factorisation. Herein, a dual version, in terms of pushouts and quotients, is taken. The following results are, therefore, standard categorial constructions in that setting (in a **The**-indexed category). What is important here is to give an intuitive account and show how these constructions are used in the context of theory interpretations in π-institutions.

The pushout construction has been widely used for describing how to apply parametric specifications to actual arguments [Ehrich82, Goguen and Burstall 85, Ehrig and Mahr 86] and how to put implementation steps together [Ehrich 82]. Intuitively, pushouts give a way to construct a new theory from two given theories by combining them in a "free" way while identifying certain parts of them. The construction of pushouts in **The** from pushouts in **Sign** is well known [eg, Goguen and Burstall 85] and is recalled in the following

3.21 **Proposition**: Assume that **Sign** admits pushouts. Let $\mu: (\Sigma, A^\circ) \rightarrow (\Sigma', A'^\circ)$ and $\sigma: (\Sigma, A^\circ) \rightarrow (\Sigma'', A''^\circ)$ be theory morphisms. Let $(\Sigma^\$, \mu^\$, \sigma^\$)$ be the pushout of (Σ, μ, σ) in **Sign** and $A^\$$ be the set $(\mu^\$(A'') \cup \sigma^\$(A'))$. Then, $((\Sigma^\$, A^{\$\circ}), \mu^\$, \sigma^\$)$ is a pushout in **The**. ◊

More general results, stating that the forgetful functor ϑ reflects colimits and that **The** is cocomplete if **Sign** is cocomplete, are easily derived as in [Goguen and Burstall 85]. Note that the proposition above also holds for **Axo**, the pushout of axiomatisations being an axiomatisation of the pushout of the respective theories.

3.22 **Remark**: Nuclei do not work as nicely on axiomatisations as pushouts do because, although $m^{-1}(A')^\circ \subseteq m^{-1}(A'^\circ)$, equality does not necessarily hold. However, since $m^{-1}(A'^\circ)$ is closed, proving $w \in m^{-1}(A'^\circ)$ amounts to proving $A' \vdash m(w)$, A' being recursive. Therefore, lacking an axiomatisation for the nucleus is not a problem as long as an axiomatisation for the interpretation is known. ◊

It is from now on assumed that the category **Sign** admits pushouts. This assumption may have implications on the consequence relations. For instance, it is somehow expected that a direct consequence relation in the pushout $\Sigma^\$$ of $\mu: \Sigma \rightarrow \Sigma'$ and $\sigma: \Sigma \rightarrow \Sigma''$ satisfies: if $A \Rightarrow_{\Sigma^\$} w$ then either $A \subseteq \sigma^\$(\Phi(\Sigma'))$ or $A \subseteq \mu^\$(\Phi(\Sigma''))$ or $A \cap (\Phi(\Sigma^\$) - (\sigma^\$(\Phi(\Sigma')) \cup \mu^\$(\Phi(\Sigma'')))) \neq \emptyset$. That is to say, an inference step in $\Sigma^\$$ either corresponds to an inference step in Σ' or an inference step in Σ'', or it involves hypotheses that do not come from either $\Phi(\Sigma')$ or $\Phi(\Sigma'')$. Further research is necessary on these conjectures.

3.23 **Definition**: Each theory morphism $\mu: T \rightarrow T'$ gives rise to a functor $\tau(\mu): \iota(T) \rightarrow \iota(T')$ satisfying

- $\tau(\mu)(\sigma_1, T_1)$ is $(\sigma_1^\$, T_1^\$)$ given by $(T_1^\$, \mu_1^\$, \sigma_1^\$)$, the pushout of (T, μ, σ_1).
- $\tau(\mu)(\phi)$, where $\phi: (\sigma_1, T_1) \rightarrow (\sigma_2, T_2)$, is the unique morphism φ in $\iota(T')$ sending $\tau(\mu)(\sigma_1, T_1)$ to $\tau(\mu)(\sigma_2, T_2)$ and satisfying $\mu_1^\$; \varphi = \phi; \mu_2^\$$ (existence and unicity result from the definition of pushout).

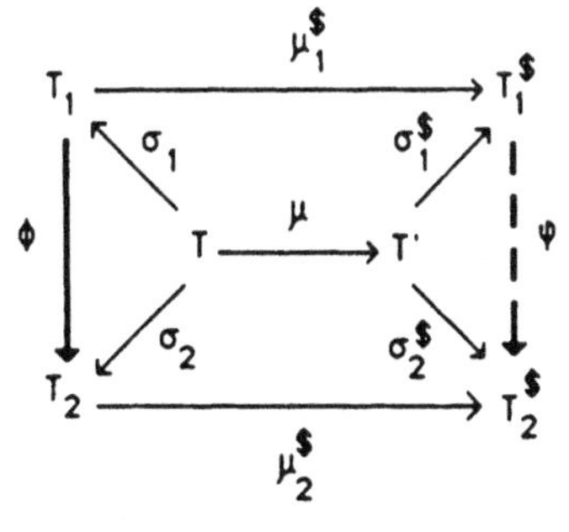

Intuitively, this functor tells, given a T-interpretation, how to translate it to a T'-interpretation that is, in a rough sense, minimal with respect to μ. The T-nucleus of this interpretation must be respected by the translation, which must "follow" μ. The remainder is to be translated "freely". Finally, in order to obtain a T'-interpretation, it is necessary to import those parts of T' that were not identified by μ. This is done in a "minimal" way in the sense that only the minimal interpretation of T' satisfying the referred translation is considered. The T'-interpretation obtained by applying the functor is called a *μ-free translation* of the T-interpretation.

3.24 **Remark**: Because the pushout of an epi is still an epi [MacLane 71], the μ-free translation of a minimal interpretation is still a minimal interpretation. This also means that $\tau(\mu)$ induces a functor $\rho(T)\text{->}\rho(T')$. ◊

Given a T'-interpretation $(\sigma,T")$, $\tau(\mu)(\rho(\mu)(\sigma,T"))$ is the free translation of the μ-nucleus of $(\sigma,T")$ (the T-interpretation $(e,T"^{*})$) to the T'-interpretation $(e^{\$},T"^{*\$})$ (cf picture below).

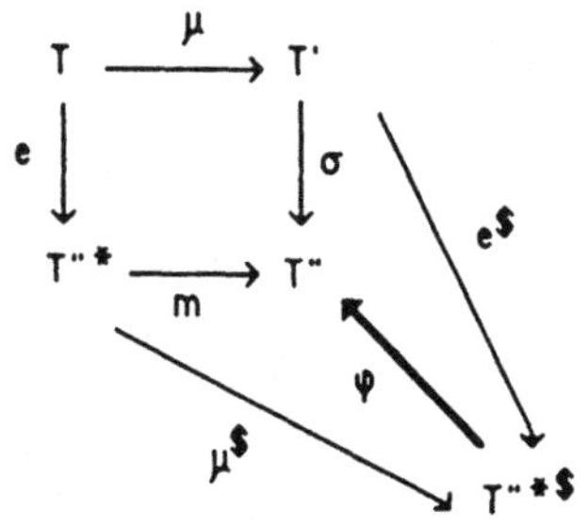

It provides a minimal interpretation (it is isomorphic to its nucleus) that identifies the free contribution of μ to $(\sigma,T")$. From the pushout construction, there is a unique $\iota(T')$-morphism φ: $\tau(\mu)(\rho(\mu)(\sigma,T")) \rightarrow (\sigma,T")$ (unicity is obtained because the interpreter is an epi) which tells us how that free contribution is interpreted in $(\sigma,T")$. An interesting case occurs when φ is a conservative monic because this tells us that the free contribution of μ to $(\sigma,T")$ is canonically interpreted.

3.25 **Definition**: Let $\mu: T \rightarrow T'$ be a theory morphism. A T'-interpretation $(\sigma,T")$ is said to be *μ-canonical* iff the only interpretation morphism $\varphi: \tau(\mu)(\rho(\mu)(\sigma,T")) \rightarrow (\sigma,T")$ is a conservative monic. ◊

3.26 **Remark**: In accordance to the remark 3.24, the restriction of $\tau(\mu)$ to $\rho(T)$ was used instead of $\tau(\mu)$. Moreover, following 3.20, the extension of $\rho(\mu)$ to $\iota(T')$ was also used above. This means that $\tau(\mu)(\rho(\mu)(\sigma,T"))$ has been (and will be) standing for $\tau(\mu)(\varphi_T(\rho(\mu)(\rho_{T'}(\sigma,T"))))$. ◊

3.27 **Example**: The following example is typical in conceptual modelling: the existence of an identification mechanism for entities (interpretations of the theory presented by **ents**) from a given theory of identifiers (an interpretation of **ids**). Let μ be the theory morphism (inclusion) between

ids and **ents**.

ids: $\xrightarrow{\mu}$ **ents**:

ids:

<u>sorts</u>: set
<u>ops</u>: any: -> set
another: set -> set

ents:

<u>sorts</u>: set,ent
<u>ops</u>: any: -> set
another: set -> set
map: set -> ent

Consider the **ents**-interpretation given through **clone** and the interpreter σ that sends *set* to *nat*, *ent* to *person*, *any* to *zero* and *another* to *suc* .

clone•:

<u>sorts</u>: nat
<u>ops</u>: zero: -> nat
suc: nat -> nat

clone:

<u>sorts</u>: nat, person
<u>ops</u>: zero: -> nat
suc: nat -> nat
one: -> nat
who: nat -> person
<u>eqs</u>: one = suc(zero)
who(one) = who(zero)

clone$^{\bullet\$}$:

<u>sorts</u>: nat, person
<u>ops</u>: zero: -> nat
suc: nat -> nat
who: nat -> person

It is easy to see that the interpretation morphism from the μ-free translation **clone**$^{\bullet\$}$ of the μ-nucleus **clone•** of **clone** is not a conservative monic. For instance, the reverse image of the theorem (who(one)=who(zero)) of **clone** is the equation (who(suc(zero))=who(zero)) which is not a theorem of **clone**$^{\bullet\$}$. Therefore, **clone** and σ <u>do not</u> yield a μ-canonical interpretation of **ents**. Intuitively, this says that the identification mechanism is not respected because there is a person that has two identifiers *(confusion)*.

Consider now the interpretation of **ents** given through **just-the-two-of-us**, and whose interpreter sends *set* to *nat*, *ent* to *person*, *any* to *zero* and *another* to *suc*.

just-the-two-of-us•:

<u>sorts</u>: nat
<u>ops</u>: zero: -> nat
suc: nat -> nat
<u>eqs</u>: x: nat, suc(suc(x)) = suc(x)

just-the-two-of-us:

<u>sorts</u>: nat, person
<u>ops</u>: zero: -> nat
suc: nat -> nat
one: -> nat
who: nat -> person
<u>eqs</u>: one=suc(zero)
x:nat, suc(suc(x))=suc(x)

just-the-two-of-us$^{\bullet\$}$:

<u>sorts</u>: nat, person
<u>ops</u>: zero: -> nat
suc: nat -> nat
who: nat -> person
<u>eqs</u>: x: nat, suc(suc(x)) = suc(x)

Its μ-nucleus (**just-the-two-of-us•**) includes the equation (x:nat,suc(suc(x))=suc(x)) as it belongs to the reverse image of **just-the-two-of-us**. Its μ-free translation is the theory **just-the-two-of-us**$^{\bullet\$}$ for which **just-the-two-of-us** is a conservative extension. Therefore, a μ-canonical interpretation of **ents** is obtained. Notice that, however, a canonical interpretation of **ents** is not obtained. Neverthless, the identification mechanism is respected because the subtheory of **ents** that is not canonically interpreted concerns only the theory of identifiers (there are only two possible identifiers !). ◊

This example also shows why isomorphism was not required in definition 3.25. Indeed, **just-the-two-of-us** and **just-the-two-of-us**$^{\bullet\$}$ are not isomorphic. However, it seems intuitive to ask for isomorphism with respect to the nucleus of the T'-interpretation (σ,T") because the nucleus is the minimal interpretation that admits (σ,T") as a conservative extension. Indeed, the following result is straightforward :

3.28 **Proposition**: Let μ: T→T' be a theory morphism. A T'-interpretation (σ,T") is μ-canonical iff $\tau(\mu)(\rho(\mu)(\sigma,T"))$ and $\rho_{T'}(\sigma,T")$ are isomorphic in $\iota(T')$. ◊

This proposition provides an alternative criterion for proving canonicity and has a more model theoretical flavour as it will become evident later on.

Proving that an interpretation is canonical with respect to a certain morphism is not always easy and, naturally, there are cases where one of the definitions is "better" than the other. For instance, a sufficient condition for an interpretation to be canonical with respect to a morphism is given by the following:

3.29 **Proposition**: Let μ: T → T' be a theory morphism. Then, a canonical T'-interpretation is also μ-canonical. ◊

Naturally, this is a very strong requirement because it does not take into account the contribution of μ which can be "forgotten" when asking for canonicity. Neverthless, it provides a useful criterion that can often be applied because a specification evolves mainly through conservative enrichments. Therefore, in general, only local requirements for canonicity have to be carefully checked.

In the same direction, it can be proved that the property of being canonical with respect to a morphism is preserved by conservative extensions of the nuclei:

3.30 **Proposition**: Let μ: T → T' be a theory morphism, (σ_1,T_1) a μ-canonical interpretation of T' and ϕ: (σ_1,T_1) → (σ_2,T_2) an interpretation morphism. Then, (σ_2,T_2) is μ-canonical if m;ϕ (where m is the monic factor of a factorisation of σ_1) is a conservative monic. ◊

This proposition provides a sharper criterion because it does not require σ_1;ϕ to be a conservative monic, taking advantage from the fact that (σ_1,T_1) is μ-canonical. Moreover, ϕ does not need to be a conservative monic either, although this is an obvious sufficient condition.

Models and Institutions

A correspondence between π-institutions and institutions is now established, allowing to "interpret" the concepts introduced above in institutional terms. Because the rest of this section requires knowledge on the theory of institutions, its main concepts are briefly recalled below. The following definition is adapted from [Goguen and Burstall 85]:

3.31 **Definition**:

1. An *institution* is a quadruple $(\mathbf{Sign}, \Phi, \mathbf{Mod}, \{\vdash_\Sigma\}_{\Sigma:\mathbf{Sign}})$ where
   - **Sign** (a category) and Φ: **Sign** -> **Set** (a functor) play the same role as in definition 2.1 (ie they define the signatures and the formulae over each signature).
   - **Mod**: **Sign** -> $\mathbf{Cat}^{op}$ is a functor giving models over each signature.
   - each $\vdash_\Sigma \subseteq |\mathbf{Mod}(\Sigma)| \times \Phi(\Sigma)$ is called a satisfaction relation and is required to satisfy for each μ: $\mathbf{Sign}(\Sigma,\Sigma')$, $w \in \Phi(\Sigma)$ and m':$\mathbf{Mod}(\Sigma')$

     $m' \vdash_{\Sigma'} \Phi(\mu)(w)$ iff $\mathbf{Mod}(\mu)(m') \vdash_\Sigma w$ *(satisfaction condition)*

2. For every signature Σ, every set A of Σ-formulae and every set M of Σ-models:
   - a Σ-model *satisfies* A iff it satisfies every formula in A.
   - A^* is the collection of all Σ-models that satisfy A. (A^* is sometimes regarded as the full subcategory of $\mathbf{Mod}(\Sigma)$ whose objects satisfy A).
   - M^* is the collection of all Σ-formulae that are satisfied by each model in M.
   - The closure of A is the set A^{**}.
   - A pair (Σ,A) such that $A=A^{**}$ is called a theory. A theory morphism μ: $(\Sigma,A)\to(\Sigma',A')$ between two theories is a signature morphism $\mu: \Sigma\to\Sigma'$ such that $\Phi(\mu)(A)\subseteq A'$. Each theory morphism μ: $(\Sigma,A)\to(\Sigma',A')$ defines a forgetful functor μ^*: A'^*->A^*.

3. An institution is called *liberal* if for every theory morphism μ:$(\Sigma,A)\to(\Sigma',A')$ the forgetful functor μ^* admits a left adjoint $\mu^\$$. Then, a model m': A'^* is *μ-free* if the counit morphism $\mu^\$(\mu^*(m'))\to m'$ is an isomorphism. ◊

Models in π-institutions are now introduced, allowing to define for each π-institution a corresponding institution. The proposed notion of model is very trivial but allows to establish a relation between canonicity of interpretations and freeness of models. Its interest from the point of view of specification language semantics is discussed in the next section.

3.32 **Proposition**: The forgetful functor ϑ: **The**-> **Sign** admits a left adjoint Γ such that $\Gamma(\Sigma)=(\Sigma,\emptyset^\circ)$. ◊

3.33 **Definition**: A *Σ-model* is a pair (σ,T) where T is a theory and σ: $\Gamma(\Sigma)\to T$ is a theory epimorphism. The functor **Mod**: **Sign**->$\mathbf{Cat}^{op}$ that gives models and morphisms between models over the underlying π-institution is the composition $(\Gamma;\rho)$ where ρ was defined in 3.20. ◊

A satisfaction relation can be defined over this notion of model as follows:

3.34 Definition: For every signature Σ in **Sign**, let $\models_\Sigma \subseteq |\mathbf{Mod}(\Sigma)| \times \Phi(\Sigma)$ be defined by $(\sigma,T) \models_\Sigma w$ iff $T \vdash_\Sigma \Phi(\sigma)(w)$ (where $(\Sigma,A) \vdash_\Sigma w$ iff $A \vdash_\Sigma w$ iff $w \in A^\circ$). ◊

3.35 Proposition: For every signature morphism $\mu: \Sigma \to \Sigma'$, Σ'-model m and Σ-formula w, $\mathbf{Mod}(\mu)(m) \models_\Sigma w$ iff $m \models_{\Sigma'} \Phi(\mu)(w)$. ◊

That is to say, the *Satisfaction Condition* is verified. The next theorem follows trivially from these results:

3.36 Theorem: Let π=(**Sign**,Φ,$\{Cn_\Sigma\}_{\Sigma:\mathbf{Sign}}$) be a π-institution such that **Sign** admits an image factorisation system. Then, (**Sign**,Φ,**Mod**,$\{\models_\Sigma\}_{\Sigma:\mathbf{Sign}}$) with **Mod** and $\models_\Sigma$ defined as in 3.33 and 3.34 is an institution. ◊

This relationship can be given a more functorial flavour by defining the category of π-institutions (cf. [Fiadeiro and Sernadas 87]).

The Galois connection over this institution is (trivially) established as follows:

3.37 Proposition: For every set A of Σ-formulae, the category $A^\bullet$ of the models that satisfy A is the category $\rho(\Sigma,A^\circ)$ of minimal (Σ,A°)-interpretations. For every collection M of Σ-models, the set $M^\bullet$ of the formulae satisfied by every model in M is given by $M^\bullet = \bigcap_{(\sigma,(\Sigma',A')) \in M} \sigma^{-1}(A')$. ◊

The expected relation between closure in the π-institution and in the corresponding institution is also trivially established:

3.38 Theorem: For every $A \subseteq \Phi(\Sigma)$, $A^{\bullet\bullet} = A^\circ$ ie, the two notions of closure coincide. ◊

The notion of free-model is now investigated.

3.39 Proposition: Given a theory morphism $\mu: T \to T'$, the forgetful functor $\mu^\bullet: T'^\bullet \to T^\bullet$ is the functor $\rho(\mu)$ defined in 3.20. ◊

3.40 Theorem: The restriction of $\tau(\mu)$ to $\rho(T)$ (3.24) is a left adjoint to $\rho(\mu)$. ◊

The following results are now trivial to prove:

3.41 Theorem: A π-institution induces a *liberal* institution through 3.36 if its category of signatures admits pushouts and an image factorisation system. ◊

And, finally, the connection between freeness of models and canonicity of interpretations:

3.42 **Theorem**: Given a theory morphism $\mu: T \to T'$, a Σ-model (σ,T'') of T' is μ-free iff (σ,T'') is a μ-canonical interpretation of T'. ◊

That is to say, the notion of μ-canonical interpretation of a theory T' coincides with the notion of μ-free model of T' in the institution where models of theories are taken to be their minimal interpretations. The reason for adopting this notion of model will become evident in the next section: basically, it was motivated by the idea that the purpose of a specification is to denote a class of theories. Restricting models to epi-interpretations is not a problem: full interpretations can be dealt with through their nuclei.

4. Semantics of Specification Building

The semantics of specifications in an arbitrary institution was analysed in [Sannella and Tarlecki 84] where three levels (besides the textual level) were distinguished for dealing with specifications:

- The *axiomatisation* level (usually called *presentation* level): a specification denotes an axiomatisation of a theory, ie a signature and a (recursive) set of formulae over that signature.
- The *theory* level: a specification denotes a theory of the underlying institution.
- The *model* level: a specification denotes a signature and a class of models over that signature.

There are "natural" mappings from some levels to the others, namely the axiomatisation level maps to the theory level by taking closures and the theory level maps to the model level by taking the class of models that satisfy a theory. However, not every theory admits an axiomatisation and not every class of models is the class of models of a theory. Hence, models provide the finest grain of specification.

Not every specification building operation has a semantics at the axiomatisation or at the theory levels. For instance, the operation of *deriving* a specification from another [Burstall and Goguen 81] does not have a semantics at the axiomatisation level and data constraints [Burstall and Goguen 81] do not have a semantics at the theory level. Hence, the ultimate semantics of specification building in institutions requires the model level [Sannella and Tarlecki 84].

The π-institution concept aims at providing the possibility of giving a semantics for specification languages, as *clear* as model theoretic semantics in institutions, but relying upon a consequence relation rather than on a satisfaction relation. Obviously, it may happen that the chosen consequence relation is model-theoretic but, recalling what was said in the introduction, the emphasis herein is put on the distinction between approaches based on satisfaction (that intrinsically manipulate models) and on consequence. The ultimate semantics of a specification in this case is given through the manipulation of theories of the logic. Stressing the point, this means that even if a model-theoretic consequence relation is chosen, the semantics of specifications at the model level in institutions and in π-institutions will be radically different.

For instance, consider the operation of defining a basic specification through an axiomatisation. In institutions, such a specification is taken to denote the class of all models that satisfy the axiomatisation [Sannella and Tarlecki 84]. In π-institutions, such a specification is taken to denote the class of interpretations of the axiomatisation. This means that an equational axiomatisation of booleans is taken to denote the class of its equational interpretations, among which are the interpretations of example 3.16. Restricting these interpretations to the canonical ones is another decision that can be made by the specifier.

Hence, it remains to show how specification building operations have a semantics in π-institutions. From the discussion on models held at the end of Section 3, it should be obvious that the three levels of specification distinguished in the traditional institutional framework are maintained when using π-institutions. All the operations that have a semantics at the theory level in institutions also have a semantics at the theory level in π-institutions. Indeed, this semantics corresponds to replacing model-theoretic closure in the underlying institution by the primitive closure operator of the chosen π-institution. Hence, the Clear like operations such as combining, enriching and deriving specifications from others [Burstall and Goguen 81], have a "natural" and obvious semantics in π-institutions.

Only the operations that do not have a semantics at the theory level in institutions raise problems because they depend on the notion of model that is adopted for the underlying logic. However, choosing models as in the preceding section gives a "natural" semantics for this kind of operations by taking the usual institutional semantics over the institution induced by the chosen π-institution (cf 3.45). As already argued, this corresponds to consider that **specifications denote classes of interpretations of theories**. Naturally, it is essential to characterise what this semantics is in terms of operations on interpretations. This will be done below for the semantics of data constraints as defined in [Goguen and Burstall 85]. The semantics of other operations on specifications that do not have a semantics at the theory level such has behavioural abstraction [Sannella and Tarlecki 84] have not been analysed yet. The semantics of "derive" à la ASL [ibid] is also quite straightforward: deriving a specification under a signature morphism μ corresponds to applying the functor $\rho(\mu)$ to the models of the specification which, as in [ibid], does not cover the class of the models (minimal interpretations) of the theory derived à la Clear in the case where the semantics of the specification can be given at the theory level.

Data constraints were introduced in [Burstall and Goguen 80], generalising and relativising the initial algebra approach to abstract data types introduced by the ADJ group [Goguen et al 75]. Briefly, a data constraint requires that some parts of a theory have a "standard" interpretation relative to other parts. The following definition is adapted from [Goguen and Burstall 85].

4.1 **Definition**: Given an institution and a signature Σ, a *Σ-constraint* is a pair $<\mu:T\rightarrow T', \theta:$

$\vartheta(T') \rightarrow \Sigma>$ consisting of a theory morphism and a signature morphism (where ϑ is the forgetful functor sending theories to their signatures). A Σ-model m satisfies the Σ-constraint $<\mu: T \rightarrow T', \theta: \vartheta(T') \rightarrow \Sigma>$ iff $\theta^*(m)$ satisfies T' and is μ-free (assuming that the institution is liberal). ◊

Taking into account this definition, theorem 3.42 can be rewritten as follows:

4.2 **Theorem**: Given a π-institution $\star$ for which the category of signatures **Sign** admits pushouts and an image factorisation system, and Σ: **Sign**, a Σ-model (σ, T'') satisfies the Σ-constraint $<\mu: T \rightarrow T', \theta: \vartheta(T') \rightarrow \Sigma>$ in the institution defined by $\star$ (cf 3.36) iff $(\theta; \sigma, T'')$ is a μ-canonical interpretation of T'. ◊

Hence, as already hinted in the previous section, the semantics of data-constraints in π-institutions is given through canonicity of interpretations. Notice that this semantics is given at the model level.

Goguen and Burstall have shown [Goguen and Burstall 85] that it is possible to keep the semantics of data-constraints at the theory level by shifting to another institution. Basically, it amounts to extending the set of formulae over a signature with constraints over that signature and to extend satisfaction as defined in 4.1. This technique can be applied to π-institutions, defining for each π-institution $\star$ another π-institution D($\star$), by extending consequence as follows: given a set of formulae $F = A \cup C$ where A is a set of formulae from $\star$ and C a set of constraints, define the closure of F in D($\star$) to be the closure of A in $\star$. This defines a non-extensive π-institution (2.6) which can be transformed into a π-institution by defining $F^{\circ} = A^{\circ} \cup C$, where A° is the closure of A taken in $\star$. This means that there is no calculus of constraints nor any effect of constraints on the original notion of consequence. Indeed, it is just a way of keeping the semantics of data-constraints at the theory level, the resulting π-institution being of no particular interest unless there is such a calculus of constraints that allows, for instance, as hinted in [Goguen and Burstall 85], to derive induction principles ("namability axioms" as used in [Maibaum et al 85] might be an example of consequences in the original signature derived from certain data constraints).

Even so, notice that although the semantics of data abstraction can be given at the theory level in D($\star$), its semantics at the model level should be given in $\star$ because the notion of model that results from 3.33 applied to D($\star$) is of no particular interest. Therefore, this technique should be considered only as a way to implicitly manipulate classes of models through extended theories (as it was already considered in institutions).

Finally, a word about the semantics of parameterisation at the theory level. Given a theory morphism $\mu: AT \rightarrow TT$, the functor $\tau(\mu): \iota(AT) \rightarrow \iota(TT)$ can be seen as the denotation of the parameterised theory μ. In this case, $\iota(AT)$ can be considered to be the category of fittings into AT as the application of the parameterised theory to an argument theory requires a fitting to the formal parameter AT. The application of the functor returns an interpretation of TT. In general, only the theory part of the result is wanted. However, the theory morphism (interpreter) can be quite useful as shown in [Fiadeiro and Sernadas 87] for the semantics of conceptual modelling. Notice that when specifications are being dealt with at the model level, this is a restricted case of parameterised specifications. In this case, application is done pointwise on the models of the argument theory (recall - 3.24 - that $\tau(\mu)$ sends models of AT to models of TT).

5. Concluding Remarks

A categorial formalism was presented for the abstract definition of logics. This formalism differs from the institutional one in that the definition of a logic in a π-institution takes consequence as a primitive concept. This alternative was also analysed from a pragmatic point of view: in π-institutions, the semantics of specifications is defined over operations which take interpretations of theories as *units*, while the corresponding semantics in institutions is based on the manipulation of models. The semantics of the traditional Clear-like operations was analysed in this framework, with special emphasis to data constraints. For this purpose, several operations on theories and on their interpretations were defined. In particular, the role played by conservative interpretations was highlighted and conservativeness was relativised to theory morphisms in order to capture the semantics of data constraints (canonicity requirements on interpretations). These results were compared to those previously obtained in institutions by establishing a correspondence between the two frameworks. Further work is needed to analyse the semantics of other specification building operations that have been characterised from the institutional point of view, such as behavioural abstraction [Sannella and Tarlecki 84].

Further work is also needed in order to define *implementations* of specifications within the proposed framework. This is a subject that has been intensively studied in algebraic frameworks [eg, Ehrich 82] and in institutions [Sannella and Tarlecki 87]. A notion of implementation that seems to be closer to the formalism developed herein is presented in [Maibaum et al 85, Maibaum 86] based on the notion of interpretation of first order theories. It seems worthwhile combining it with the notions of interpretation and of morphism of π-institutions proposed in [Fiadeiro and Sernadas 87], so that the change of π-institutions during vertical refinement of specifications can be supported. In particular, Maibaum raises a number of requirements on the underlying logic (namely what he calls the modularisation property) that seem to deserve investigating from the more abstract point of view of π-institutions.

As often said in the paper, a particular notion of consequence, à la Tarski, was adopted without concern to generality or minimality. The results that were obtained are thus valid only for what could be called Tarskian π-institutions. Working with other notions of consequence and analysing their adequacy for the semantics of specification building seems interesting. For this purpose, [Avron 87] would be a rich source of inspiration.

Also, it seems interesting to investigate connections with Edinburgh LF [Harper et al 87]: a system designed for implementing systems of logic, mainly oriented to interactive proof checking and proof construction, thus capable to provide an effective support to specification building.

Acknowledgments

The authors wish to thank the referees for many suggestions and, most of all, for the numerous questions raised. Special thanks to Luís Monteiro for his comments on an earlier version of this work. The authors also thank Cristina Sernadas for many useful discussions concerning the algebraic semantics of conceptual modelling, as well as José Carmo, Laurence Cholvy and Samit Khosla for many fruitful discussions concerning logic in general (and the universe in particular). This work was partially supported by ESPRIT Project 1542 (Indoc) and COST13 Project on Artificial Intelligence and Non-Standard Logics (Evolution of Knowledge Bases).

References

[Arbib and Manes 75] M.Arbib and E.Manes, Arrows, Structures, and Functors, Academic Press 1975

[Avron 87] A.Avron, "Simple Consequence Relations", Report ECS-LFCS-87-30, Edinburgh, June 1987

[Barwise 74] J.Barwise, "Axioms for Abstract Model Theory", Annals of Mathematical Logic 7, 1974

[Blok and Pigozzi 86] W.Blok and D.Pigozzi, "A Characterization of Algebraizable Logics", Internal Report, Univ. Illinois at Chicago, January 1986

[Burstall and Goguen 80] R.Burstall and J.Goguen, "The Semantics of Clear, a Specification Language", in LNCS 86, Proc. 1979 Copenhagen Winter School on Abstract Software Specification, Springer-Verlag 1980, 292-332

[Burstall and Goguen 81] R.Burstall and J.Goguen, "An Informal Introduction to Specifications using Clear", in The Correctness Problem in Computer Science, R. Boyer and J. Moore (eds), Academic Press 1981, 185-213

[Ehrich 82] H.-D.Ehrich, "On the Teory of Specification, Implementation and Parametrization of Abstract Data Types", Journal of the ACM, 29(1), January 1982, 206-227

[Ehrig and Mahr 85] H.Ehrig e B.Mahr, Fundamentals of Algebraic Specifications 1, EATCS Monographs on Computer Science, Springer-Verlag 1985

[Enderton 72] H.Enderton, A Mathematical Introduction to Logic, Academic Press 1972

[Fiadeiro and Sernadas 87] J.Fiadeiro and A.Sernadas, "Structuring Theories on Consequence" - extended version, INESC, 1987

[Gabbay 81] D.Gabbay, Semantical Investigations in Heyting's Intuitionistic Logic, Reidel, 1981

[Goguen and Burstall 85] J.Goguen and R.Burstall, "Institutions: Abstract Model Theory for Computer Science", CSLI - 85-30, Stanford University, 1985 (preliminary version in LNCS 164, Proc. Logics of Programming Workshop, E. Clarke and D. Kozen (eds), Springer-Verlag 1984, 221-256)

[Goguen and Burstall 86] J.Goguen and R.Burstall, "A Study in the Foundations of Programming Methodology: Specifications, Institutions, Charters and Parchments", in LNCS 240, Proc. Conference on Computer Science and Category Theory, D. Pitt et al (eds), Springer-Verlag 1986, 313-333

[Goguen et al 75] J.Goguen, J.Thatcher, E.Wagner and J.Wright, "Abstract Data Types as Initial Algebras and the Correctness of Data Representations", in Computer Graphics, Pattern Recognition and Data Structures, IEEE 1975, 89-93

[Hacking 79] I.Hacking, "What is Logic?", The Journal of Philosophy 76, 1979, 285-318

[Harper et al 87] R.Harper, F.Honsell and G.Plotkin, "A Framework for Defining Logics", Proc. 2nd Annual Conference on Logic in Computer Science, Ithaca, NY, June 1987

[MacLane 71] S.MacLane, Categories for the Working Mathematician, Springer Verlag 1971

[MacQueen and Sannella 85] D.MacQueen and D.Sannella, "Completeness of Proof Systems for Equational Specifications", IEEE Transactions on Software Engineering 11, 1985, 454-461

[Maibaum et al 85] T.Maibaum, P.Veloso and M.Sadler, "A Theory of Abstract Data Types for Program Development: Bridging the Gap?", in LNCS 186, Mathematical Foundations of Software Development, vol 2, Springer-Verlag 1985, 214-230

[Maibaum 86] T.Maibaum, "Role of Abstraction in Program Development", in Information Processing 86, H.-J. Kugler (ed), North-Holand 1986, 135-142

[Meseguer and Goguen 85] J.Meseguer and J.Goguen, "Initiality, Induction and Computability", in Algebraic Methods in Semantics, M. Nivat and J. Reynolds (eds), Cambridge University Press 1985, 459-540

[Pitt et al 86] D.Pitt, S.Abramski, A.Poigné and D.Rydeheard (eds), Category Theory and Computer Programming, LNCS 240, Springer Verlag, 1986

[Sannella and Tarlecki 84] D. Sannella and A. Tarlecki, "Specifications in an Arbitrary Institution", in LNCS 173, Proc. Int. Symposium on Semantics of Data Types, Springer-Verlag 1984, 337-356

[Sannella and Tarlecki 87] D.Sannella and A.Tarlecki, "Toward Formal Development of Programs From Algebraic Specifications: Implementations Revisited", in LNCS 249, Proc. TAPSOFT '87, vol 1, Springer-Verlag 1987, 96-110 (an extended version will appear in Acta Informatica)

[Scott 74] D. Scott, "Rules and Derived Rules", in Logical Theory and Semantical Analysis, S. Stenlund (ed), Reidel, Dordrecht, 1974, 147-161

[Sernadas et al 88] A.Sernadas, J.Fiadeiro, C.Sernadas and H.-D.Ehrich, "Abstract Object Types: A Temporal Perspective", Colloquium on Temporal Logic and Specification, A.Pnueli et al (eds), Springer-Verlag 1988

[Tarlecki 85] A.Tarlecki, "On the Existence of Free Models in Abstract Algebraic Institutions", Theoretical Computer Science, 37(3), 1985, 269-304

[Tarlecki 86] A.Tarlecki, "Bits and Pieces of the Theory of Institutions", in [Pitt et al 86], 334-363

[Tarski 30] A.Tarski, "Fundamentale Begriffe der Methodologie der Deduktiven Wissenschaften" French translation in Logique, Sémantique, Métamathématique, vol 1, Armand Colin 1972, 67-116

Completion with History-Dependent Complexities for Generated Equations*

Harald Ganzinger
Fachbereich Informatik, Universität Dortmund
D-4600 Dortmund 50, W. Germany
uucp, bitnet: hg@unido

The paper presents a new system of inference rules for the completion of conditional equations. Conditional equations that are generated during completion can either be eliminated, oriented into reductive rewrite rules or considered as nonoperational. Rewrite rules are, as usual, subject to critical pair computation. Nonoperational equations are superposed by the rewrite rules on one of their conditions. A conditional equation can be eliminated if there is also a proof of the equation which is simpler than the equation itself. The purpose of this paper is to present a technique in which the origin of an equation defines the complexity bound which alternative proofs must respect. This technique is shown to be particularly useful in the conditional case, making the completion process terminate on a number of nontrivial specifications which it would fail to terminate otherwise.

1 Introduction

Completion procedures for conditional equations must provide techniques for handling nonreductive equations which are either initially given or generated during completion.

In [Gan87], improving earlier work including [Kap84b], [JW86], [KaR87], and stimulated by [KR87], nonreductive equations are superposed by the reductive rewrite rules on one of their conditions. This process enumerates the solutions of the conditions of a clause. Different classes of solutions are represented as different instances of the original clause. The completion procedure can then treat these instances independently of each other. Some instances may be trivial, others may become a reductive rule, again others may be nonreductive themselves. In the latter case, the process can become nonterminating. As with narrowing, nontrivial techniques for detecting and short-cutting loops are required in practise.

Completion means according to [Bac87] and [BDH86] to produce sufficiently many rewrite rules such that in particular any application of an equation in a proof within the equational theory can be transformed into a rewrite proof. Hence, an equation can be eliminated during completion, if there is already a rewrite proof for it, or, more generally, if there is a "simpler" proof of the same equation which we know will become a rewrite proof eventually. In the unconditional case the idea of constructing some simpler proof, not necessarily of rewrite proof type, is reflected by various techniques, called critical pair criteria in [Bac87], [BD86]. These techniques may considerably speed-up completion, however, they do not seem to be relevant for achieving termination per se. Quite differently so in the conditional case. The narrowing-like process of producing instances of nonreductive conditional equations almost never terminates if one, in order to eliminate an equation, only attempts to construct a rewrite proof for it. It is required that one also makes use of other existing *equations*. If a candidate for an alternative proof of an equation has been found, one then

*This work is partially supported by the ESPRIT-project PROSPECTRA, ref#390.

actually must prove that it is in fact simpler than the equation itself. This will succeed more often if the equation for which the simpler proof is being constructed can be considered sufficiently complex.

In this paper we describe on the rather abstract level of completion inference rules a technique that allows to give an equation a complexity originating from the proof (critical pair peak, narrowing derivation) that has caused its generation. It is these forbidden proof patterns, and not the applications of the generated equation, which ought to be simplified during completion. For user equations, the user may choose any complexity, provided it satisfies some general restrictions. The complexity of an application of an equation in an equational proof will be induced by the complexity of the equation. We will show by means of a detailed example that the power of eliminating equations during completion is substantially increased. The completion process terminates very often where it would fail to terminate when using standard subsumption techniques as described in [KR87] and [Rus87]. Subsumption is a special case of our techniques. Our approach also subsumes the concept of subconnectedness [WB83] and weak connectivity [Kue85,86] in the unconditional case.

For many of the details in the proofs of the theorems we refer to our earlier paper [Gan87].

2 Basic Notions and Notations

We consider terms over many-sorted signatures. A signature $\Sigma = (S, \Omega)$ consists of a set of sorts S and a family Ω of sets of operator symbols with arity in S^*. T_Σ denotes the set of all Σ-terms, $(T_\Sigma)_s$ is the set of terms of sort $s \in S$. By X we denote a fixed set of sorted variables containing denumerably infinitely many variables for each sort. $T_\Sigma(X)$ is the set of all terms that may contain variables from X. Given a term or formula t, $var(t)$ denotes the set of variables occurring in t.

Substitutions are denoted by σ, σ', etc. and their application to a term t by $t\sigma$. Substitutions σ with domain $x_1, ..., x_n$ are also written as $[x_1\sigma/x_1, ..., x_n\sigma/x_n]$. If o is an occurrence in t, then t/o denotes the subterm of t at o and $t[o \leftarrow t']$ denotes the result of subterm replacement at o using t'. $t[o_1 \leftarrow t_1, ..., o_n \leftarrow t_n]$, for independent occurrences o_i in t, is a shorthand for $t[o_1 \leftarrow t_1]...[o_n \leftarrow t_n]$.

If $t \in T_\Sigma(X)$, by $\bar{t}$ we denote the term obtained from t by considering the variables as constants. For that purpose we assume the variables to be distinct from any operator symbol.

We assume a reduction ordering $>$ on $T_\Sigma(X)$ to be given. A reduction ordering is a well-founded ordering which is compatible with operators and stable under substitutions. If $>$ is a reduction ordering and st is the strict subterm ordering, then the transitive closure $>_{st}$ of $(> \cup st)$ is a noetherian order on $T_\Sigma(X)$ which is stable under substitutions and satisfies the subterm property, i.e. terms are greater than any of their proper subterms.

We also assume that (for each sort) we have an auxiliary constant [] in Σ such that [] is smaller than any other nonvariable term in $T_\Sigma(X)$ wrt. the given reduction ordering. A *context* N is a term with exactly one occurrence of [], indicating a hole into which other terms can be inserted. $N[s]$ denotes the replacement of the hole in N by s. The distance of the hole from the root is called the depth of a context. Contexts of depth 0 simply consist of a hole. These are also called *empty contexts*.

A conditional equation over Σ is a formula of form

$$t_1 = t_1' \wedge ... \wedge t_n = t_n' \;\Rightarrow\; t_0 = t_0'$$

where $n \geq 0$ and $t_i, t_i' \in T_\Sigma(X)_{s_i}$. A conditional equation in which the order of terms in the conclusion is relevant is called a conditional rewrite rule. We will use the arrow $\rightarrow$ to explicitly distinguish rules from equations. For conditional rewrite rules, an additional requirement is $var(t_0') \subset var(t_0)$ and, for $i > 0$, $var(t_i) \subset var(t_0)$ and $var(t_i') \subset var(t_0)$, i.e. each variable that occurs in the rule must already occur in the left side of the conclusion.

In this paper, we assume the reader to be familiar with the basic properties of reduction orderings and in particular the recursive path ordering. A recursive path ordering of terms is obtained by lifting a well-founded ordering $>$ on the (possibly infinite) set of operators of the given signature to paths in terms. The reader may consult [DM79], [HO80], [Der85] for definitions and basic results. We briefly repeat some of the basic properties needed below.

Recursive path orderings $>$ are simplification orderings. That is they are compatible with operators, stable under substitutions, and satisfy the subterm property. Such orderings are in particular well-founded. In this paper we will make use of the following fact about recursive path orderings: Suppose to be given two terms s and t such that there is a subterm s' of s for which $var(t) \subset var(s')$ and $s'(\varepsilon) > t(o)$, for each nonvariable occurrence o in t. Then, $s > t$. ($s'(\varepsilon)$ is the root operator in s', $t(o)$ is the operator at o in t.) This property about operator precedences is not preserved under substitutions. Nevertheless, $s\sigma > t\sigma$ will follow from the stability of the recursive path ordering under substitutions.

The operators in proof terms will be ordered by multiset orderings, cf. [DM79] for details. For multisets we have $M > N$, if N can be obtained by replacing one or more elements in M by any finite number of smaller elements. The multiset ordering is noetherian on finite multisets, provided the ordering on elements is.

Kaplan's concept of conditional rewriting introduces the notion of a simplifying rewrite rule. It has been generalized to the notion of reductive rewrite rules by Jouannaud and Waldmann [JW86]. A rule is reductive, if $t_0 > t'_0$ and, for $i > 0$, $t_0 > t_i$ and $t_0 > t'_i$, i.e. if the term on the right side and each term that occurs in the condition is be smaller than the left side of the equation.

Let R be a set of Σ-rules and $t, t' \in T_\Sigma(X)$. The rewrite relation $t \rightarrow_R t'$ is given as the least fixpoint of the following recursive definition: $t \rightarrow_R t'$ iff there exists a rule

$$t_1 = t'_1 \wedge \ldots \wedge t_n = t'_n \;\Rightarrow\; l \rightarrow r$$

in R, an occurrence u in t, a substitution $\sigma : X \rightarrow T_\Sigma(X)$ such that $t/u = l\sigma$, $t' = t[u \leftarrow r\sigma]$, and for each $i \leq n$ there exists a term s_i such that $t_i\sigma \rightarrow_R^* s_i$ and $t'_i\sigma \rightarrow_R^* s_i$. (We will subsequently write $t_i\sigma \downarrow_R t'_i\sigma$ to denote this converging of t_i and t'_i under R.)

In [Kap84b] and [JW86] it is shown that in the case of finite and reductive $R \rightarrow_R$ is decidable and finitely terminating. (This is proved mainly by the observation that $N[l\sigma] >_{st} t_i\sigma$ and $N[l\sigma] >_{st} t'_i\sigma$, for any context N and substitution σ.) Moreover, in this case, local confluence is equivalent to global confluence and, then, $\equiv_R = \downarrow_R$. In this paper, conditional rewrite rules are always assumed to be reductive. A conditional equation, however, may have conditions of arbitrary complexity.

3 Proof Terms for Conditional Equational Logic

3.1 The Signature of Proofs

Proofs are terms in which the operators represent applications of logical inference rules. By the "propositions-as-types" paradigm, the sort of a proof term is the proved theorem. Hence, for equational logic, the sorts of proof terms are unconditional Σ-equations

$$u = v, \quad \text{for} \quad u, v \in T_\Sigma(X)_s, \; s \in S.$$

Given sets E and R of conditional equations and conditional rewrite rules respectively, the following set of operators (inference rules) is complete for $\equiv_{E \cup R}$:

a) Applications and reverse applications of rules and equations:

$$apply_{\eta,\sigma} \;:\; c_1\sigma \times \ldots \times c_k\sigma \;\rightarrow\; s\sigma = t\sigma,$$

and

$$applyR_{\eta,\sigma} \;:\; c_1\sigma \times \ldots \times c_k\sigma \;\rightarrow\; t\sigma = s\sigma,$$

for $\eta = C \Rightarrow s \rightarrow t \in R$ and $\eta = C \Rightarrow s = t \in E$, where $C = c_1 \wedge \ldots \wedge c_k$, $k \geq 0$. Hence, $apply_{\eta,\sigma}$ and $applyR_{\eta,\sigma}$ are k-ary operators that map proofs for the condition instances $c_i\sigma$ to a proof for $s\sigma = t\sigma$

and $t\sigma = s\sigma$, respectively. The signature of proof terms has a particular operator for each *(head) application and reverse application* of a rule or equation. The signature of proof terms is infinite, even if the set of rules and equations is finite. We will also use the notation

$$\frac{P_1 \ldots P_k}{s\sigma \rightarrow t\sigma} \text{ for } apply_{C \Rightarrow s \rightarrow t, \sigma}(P_1, \ldots, P_k),$$

$$\frac{P_1 \ldots P_k}{t\sigma \leftarrow s\sigma} \text{ for } applyR_{C \Rightarrow s \rightarrow t, \sigma}(P_1, \ldots, P_k),$$

$$\frac{P_1 \ldots P_k}{s\sigma \leftrightarrow t\sigma} \text{ for } apply_{C \Rightarrow s = t, \sigma}(P_1, \ldots, P_k), \text{ and}$$

$$\frac{P_1 \ldots P_k}{t\sigma \leftrightarrow s\sigma} \text{ for } applyR_{C \Rightarrow s = t, \sigma}(P_1, \ldots, P_k).$$

This notation obviously abstracts from the details about the used rule or equation and substitution, and hence will not always be sufficiently precise. Where needed we will provide additional information separately, e.g., attach the rules or equations as subscripts. In the case of an empty condition we will simply write $s\sigma\, \rho\, t\sigma$, for $\rho \in \{\rightarrow, \leftarrow, \leftrightarrow\}$.

b) Reflexivity and Transitivity:

$$\_;\ldots;\_ \;:\; s_0 = s_1 \times s_1 = s_2 \times \ldots \times s_{n-1} = s_n \;\rightarrow\; s_0 = s_n, \quad n \geq 2, \text{ or } n = 0.$$

This operator allows to form sequences of proofs. We have chosen a variadic operator to abstract from the obvious associativity property of the binary ";". The case $n = 0$ represents the reflexivity axioms $s_0 = s_0$. We will also use the notation

$$\frac{P_{11} \ldots P_{1k_1}\; P_{21} \ldots P_{2k_2}\; \ldots \;\ldots\; P_{n1} \ldots P_{nk_n}}{s_1\, \rho_1\, s_2\, \rho_2\, s_3\, \ldots\, s_{n-1}\, \rho_{n-1}\, s_n}, \text{ for } \frac{P_{11} \ldots P_{1k_1}}{s_1\, \rho_1\, s_2}; \frac{P_{21} \ldots P_{2k_2}}{s_2\, \rho_2\, s_3}; \ldots; \frac{P_{n1} \ldots P_{nk_n}}{s_{n-1}\, \rho_{n-1}\, s_n},$$

where $\rho_i \in \{\rightarrow, \leftarrow, \leftrightarrow\}$. Another notation is

$$\frac{Q_1 \ldots Q_k}{s_0 \rho^* s_n} \text{ for } \frac{Q_1 \ldots Q_k}{s_0\, \rho\, s_1\, \rho\, \ldots\, \rho\, s_n}, n \geq 0, \rho \in \{\rightarrow, \leftarrow, \leftrightarrow\}.$$

c) Compatibility with contexts:
Contexts N *of depth* 1 take proofs for $s = t$ into proofs of $N[s] = N[t]$:

$$N[\_] \;:\; s = t \;\rightarrow\; N[s] = N[t].$$

We will write

$$\frac{P_1 \ldots P_k}{N[s_1]\, \rho_1\, N[s_2]\, \rho_2\, \ldots\, \rho_{n-1}\, N[s_n]} \text{ for } N[\frac{P_1 \ldots P_k}{s_1\, \rho_1\, s_2\, \rho_2\, \ldots\, \rho_{n-1}\, s_n}].$$

Formally, contexts of depth > 1 have to be represented as nested applications of contexts of depth 1.

d) Symmetry:

$$i_{s,t} \;:\; s = t \;\rightarrow\; t = s$$

Given E and R, we will denote by $\mathcal{E}(E, R)$ this signature of proof rules of the equational calculus.

As we have operators for applying rules and equations both ways, the operator for the symmetry of equality is redundant. It will be used as an auxiliary operator for defining transformations of proof terms. We also could have avoided the introduction of context operators if we had extended the notion of rule and equation application to applications in context. This is done in [BDH86], [Bac87], and [Kue86]. In these papers, moreover, proofs P and inverse proofs $i_{s,t}(P)$ are identified. Hence, there is no need for the i-operators at all. We have felt that our slightly more complex notion of proof orderings to be developed later justifies our slightly more redundant signature of proof terms. The redundancies will be removed by proof normalization rules to be given below. Proof normalization will provide a formalism for estimating the complexity bounds for proofs of form $i_{s,t}(P)$ and $N[P]$.

For an example, suppose we have the following set E of equations

```
1    (0 <s0) = tt
2    (0 < 0) = ff
3    (sx< y) = (x <py)
4    (px< y) = (x <sy)
5    (0 < x) = ff =>  (0 <px) = ff
```

and the set R of rules

```
6    (0 < x) = tt =>  (0 < sx) -> tt
7    spx -> x
8    psx -> x
```

In this case,

$$\frac{\dfrac{(0 < s0) \leftrightarrow_1 tt}{(0 < ss0) \to_6 tt}}{(p0 < sssp0) \to_7 (p0 < ss0) \leftrightarrow_4 (0 < sss0) \to_6 tt}$$

is proof for $(p0 < s\,s\,s\,p0) \;=\; tt$, in which we have explicitly indicated the used equations and rules. The inference rule notation of proof terms also abstracts from the precise interleaving between the context operators and the other proof operators. For normalized proof terms there is always one unique way of inferring this interleaving:

Definition 3.1 *A proof term is said to be normalized if it is in normal form with respect to the following proof transformations (we use the arrow* $\longrightarrow$ *to distinguish the rewriting of proof terms from the rewriting* $\to$ *of object terms;* π *and* π_i *are variables for proofs):*

$$\begin{array}{rcl} i(K[\pi]) & \longrightarrow & K[i(\pi)] \\ K[\pi_1;\pi_2;\ldots;\pi_n] & \longrightarrow & K[\pi_1];K[\pi_2];\ldots;K[\pi_n] \\ i(\pi_1;\pi_2;\ldots;\pi_n) & \longrightarrow & i(\pi_n);\ldots;i(\pi_2);i(\pi_1) \\ i(apply(\pi_1,\ldots,\pi_n)) & \longrightarrow & applyR(\pi_1,\ldots,\pi_n) \\ i(applyR(\pi_1,\ldots,\pi_n)) & \longrightarrow & apply(\pi_1,\ldots,\pi_n) \\ i(i(\pi)) & \longrightarrow & \pi \end{array}$$

Normalization removes patterns of form $i(P)$, for a nonvariable term P, and distributes contexts over sequences of rule and equation applications. The proof normalization rules are confluent and terminating.

Definition 3.2 *A (normalized) proof term is a rewrite proof if it has the form*

$$\frac{P_1 \ldots P_n}{s \to^* u \leftarrow^* t},$$

with rewrite proofs P_i, $1 \leq i \leq n$, $n \geq 0$.

Hence, rewrite proofs contain no applications of equations and no peaks $\leftarrow\to$ in rewrite rule applications. If $s \to_R t$, this step of conditional rewriting is represented by a proof term of form $\dfrac{P_1 \ldots P_n}{s \to t}$ over $\mathcal{E}(E,R)$, with a tuple P_i of rewrite proofs for the appropriately substituted conditions of the used rule.

3.2 Complexity of Proofs

In order to define a well-founded ordering on proof terms, we will now introduce a complexity measure c on the proof operators. We will then, for any two proof operators F and G, define $F > G$ iff $c(F) > c(G)$. This precedence of operators will be well-founded. Therefore, the lifting of $>$ on operators to a recursive path ordering $>_{\mathcal{P}}$ on the proof terms will yield a simplification ordering on proof terms with variables, i.e. on $T_{\mathcal{E}}(X)$.

We have assumed to be given a reduction ordering $>$ on $T_\Sigma(X)$. Moreover, let *min* be an element smaller than any term in $T_\Sigma(X)$ (including holes []). If C is a set of unconditional equations, by *terms*(C) we denote the multiset of terms on the left and right sides of the equations in C. By $\cup$ we denote the union of multisets.

In contrast to [Gan87] the complexity of an application of an equation will crucially depend on a complexity explicitly associated with the particular equation. This complexity will itself depend on the origin of the equation during completion. The completion inference rules below will precisely define this association. For the moment it suffices to assume that complexities are given as terms over an enriched signature $\Sigma C \supset \Sigma$. To represent the complexity of rewriting, we assume that ΣC has (for each sort vector) a distinguished operator ρ. The reduction ordering on $T_\Sigma(X)$ is assumed to be extended to a reduction ordering on $T_{\Sigma C}(X)$. This extension is required to satisfy $\rho(t_1, ..., t_k) > \rho(s_1, ..., s_n)$, iff $\{t_1, ..., t_k\} > \{s_1, ..., s_n\}$, using the lifting of $>$ on $T_{\Sigma C}(X)$ to multisets of terms.[1] For any complexity γ associated with an equation η we require that $\gamma \geq_{st} \rho(\vec{\eta})$, if $\vec{\eta}$ denotes the list of terms which occur in η. (Intuitively, $\rho(t)$ will roughly represent the complexity of any rewriting with redex t. Requiring the complexity of an equation to not go below $\rho(\vec{\eta})$, will make the reduction of an equation by rewriting less complex than the application of the equation.)

Definition 3.3 *We define*

$$\begin{aligned} c(apply_{C\Rightarrow s\to t,\sigma}) = c(applyR_{C\Rightarrow s\to t,\sigma}) &= (\rho(s)\sigma,\ \rho(s)\sigma,\ \{s\},\ terms(C)\cup\{t\}),\\ c(apply_{C\Rightarrow s=t,\sigma}) = c(applyR_{C\Rightarrow s=t,\sigma}) &= (\gamma\sigma,\ \rho(\vec{C},s,t)\sigma,\ terms(C)\cup\{s,t\},\ \emptyset), \end{aligned}$$

where γ is the complexity currently associated with $C \Rightarrow s = t$,

$$\begin{aligned} c(K[\_]) &= (min,\ \emptyset,\ \emptyset,\ \{K\}),\\ c(\_;\ldots;\_) &= (min,\ \emptyset,\ \emptyset,\ \emptyset),\\ c(i_{s,t}) &= (min,\ \{min\},\ \emptyset,\ \emptyset). \end{aligned}$$

These quadruples are compared lexicographically, using $>_{st}$ on $T_{\Sigma C}(X)$-terms for the first two components, the lifting of the subsumption ordering $>>$ on terms to multisets of terms for the third component and the ordering of the multiset of terms induced by $>_{st}$ for the fourth component.

For an equation η, $\gamma \geq_{st} \rho(\vec{\eta})$ is required. If $\gamma >_{st} \rho(\vec{\eta})$, the assigned complexity γ is the dominating component of the complexity of any application of the equation in a proof.

Note that there is a difference between the complexity associated with an equation and the complexity of any of its applications. For the latter, the corresponding substitution is taken into account, as well as other syntactic properties of the equation. In the following, if η is a conditional equation or rule, $c(\eta)$ will always denote the complexity $c(apply_{\eta,[]})$ of an *application* of η under the identity substitution []. To indicate the complexity γ that is currently associated with an equation $C \Rightarrow s = t$ we use the notation $\gamma \diamond C \Rightarrow s = t$.

Note that normalization of proof terms simplifies these wrt. $>_{\mathcal{P}}$. Any of the normalization rules $L \longrightarrow R$ satisfies $L >_{\mathcal{P}} R$.

[1] If the operators ρ are the only additional operators in ΣC, this restriction can be taken as the definition of the extension of $>$ to $T_{\Sigma C}(X)$ which will always work out. Further auxiliary operators are not necessarily needed. To have an auxiliary operator for each initial user-given equation may, however, improve the termination behaviour of the completion process, cf. example in section 5.

3.3 Proofs of Conditional Equations

Proofs of conditional equations can be written as proof terms with variables to represent the "assumed proofs" for the conditions. We denote by X_C, for any given set C of unconditional equations, a C-sorted family of sets of proof variables. Proof variables π of sort $s = t$ are also written as $\pi : s = t$. This representation of proofs for conditional equations is complete as $C \Rightarrow s = t$ is valid in $T_\Sigma(X)_{\equiv_{E \cup R}}$ iff $\tilde{s} \equiv_{E \cup R \cup \tilde{C}} \tilde{t}$. For proof terms $P \in T_{\mathcal{E}(E,R)}(\{\pi_1 : e_1, \ldots, \pi_n : e_n\})_e$ we will also use the sequent-like notation

$$\pi_1 : e_1, \ldots, \pi_n : e_n \vdash P : e$$

and abbreviate $\pi_i : e_i$ simply by e_i, where the names of the variables do not matter. As an example,

$$(0 < sx) = tt \vdash (p0 < x) \leftrightarrow_4 (0 < sx) = tt$$

represents a proof of $(0 < sx) = tt \Rightarrow (p0 < x) = tt$.

We will later have to transform proofs for conditional equations into proofs for substituted equations. Let σ be a Σ-substitution. If Q is a proof, by $\sigma(Q)$ we denote the proof obtained from P by the following rules:

$$\begin{aligned}
\sigma(N[P]) &= N\sigma[\sigma(P)] \\
\sigma(apply[R]_{D \Rightarrow l\, \rho\, r, \sigma'}(P_1, \ldots, P_k)) &= apply[R]_{D \Rightarrow l\, \rho\, r, \sigma'\sigma}(\sigma(P_1), \ldots, \sigma(P_k)) \\
\sigma(i_{s,t}(P)) &= i_{s\sigma, t\sigma}(\sigma(P)) \\
\sigma(P_1; \ldots; P_k) &= \sigma(P_1); \ldots; \sigma(P_k) \\
\sigma(\pi : s = t) &= \pi : s\sigma = t\sigma, \text{ for any proof variable } \pi.
\end{aligned}$$

Hence, if $\pi_1 : e_1, \ldots, \pi_n : e_n \vdash Q$ is a proof of $e_1 \wedge \ldots \wedge e_n \Rightarrow s = t$, $\sigma(\pi_1 : e_1, \ldots, \pi_n : e_n \vdash Q)$ represents a proof of $C\sigma \Rightarrow s\sigma = t\sigma$. $\sigma(Q)$ can be viewed as the result of applying an $\mathcal{E}(E,R)$-signature morphism induced by σ to Q. It should not be mixed up with applications of substitutions τ of proofs for proof variables to a proof P. The latter would be written as $P\tau$.

When, during completion, one wants to eliminate a conditional equation, one is obliged to construct a proof of the equation which has a *bounded complexity*. Our concept of boundedness will be quite general. In the unconditional equational case, it includes the notion of subconnectedness of a proof [WB83] and Küchlin's generalisation to weak connectivity [Kue85]. An equation that is generated from a peak will have the complexity of the superposition term of the peak associated with it, and hence will allow any proof below the superposition term for its elimination.

A proof $P \in T_{\mathcal{E}(E,R)}(X_C)_{s=t}$ is said to be η*-bounded*, η a conditional equation, if for any operator F in P it is $c(\eta) > c(F)$. Hence, a proof for $C \Rightarrow s = t$ which is bounded by $\gamma \diamond C \Rightarrow s = t$ is in particular simpler than the proof that just applies $\gamma \diamond C \Rightarrow s = t$ under the identity substitution. The complexities are generally such that rewriting a term in an equation $\gamma \diamond C \Rightarrow s = t$ is always a proof that is $\gamma \diamond C \Rightarrow s = t$-bounded.

Let us emphasize that depending on the complexity γ associated with an equation η, bounded proofs can be of quite different nature. If γ is big, then the set of η-bounded proofs becomes larger. On the other hand, a big γ increases the complexity of any proof that uses η, possibly causing that proof to violate some other complexity bound which one might want to respect. There is some trade-off here, the nature of which we have not investigated yet.

The comparison of the first two components of our complexity quadruples is stable under substitutions. The two last components do not depend on the substitution with which an equation or rule is applied. Therefore, if $Q \in T_{\mathcal{E}(E,R)}(X_C)_{s=t}$ is bounded by η then, for any σ, $\sigma(Q)$ is bounded by $\eta\sigma$.

4 Inference Rules for Completion

The set of inference rules which we give here is different from the one given in [Gan87]. Here we explicitly keep a third set of axioms, the set N of nonoperational equations. Also, reduction of rules and equations is restricted to conditional rewriting using the conditions as additional rules. The more general formulation in [Gan87] is of no importance here. The present set of inference rules closely corresponds to what we have implemented in the CEC-system [BGS88].

The completion procedure transforms states consisting of three sets of axioms, namely rules, equations and nonoperational equations. Rules are always reductive. Equations are axioms which eventually may be eliminated, or else oriented into a rule or, alternatively, be considered nonoperational. Rules are subject to critical pair computation:

Definition 4.1 *Let two conditional rules $C \Rightarrow u \to v$ and $D \Rightarrow l \to r$ be given and assume that their variables have been renamed such that they do not have any common variables. Assume moreover that o is a nonvariable occurrence in u such that u/o and l can be unified with a mgu σ. Then, $(C \wedge D)\sigma \Rightarrow u[o \leftarrow r]\sigma = v\sigma$ is a contextual critical pair with superposition term $u\sigma$.*

Operational aspects of what we call nonoperational equations have to be extracted by overlapping all rewrite rules on a selected condition of the equation. The result is a one-step narrowing derivate of the equation which we call a superposition instance of the equation. For any equation, superposition can be restricted to just one condition. In the formal treatment below we assume that the selected condition for superposition is the last one. In our actual implementation we allow the user to select an arbitrary condition.

Definition 4.2 *Let a conditional equation $C \wedge u = v \Rightarrow s = t$ and a conditional rule $D \Rightarrow l \to r$ be given and assume that the variables in the rule and the equation have been renamed such that no common variables occur. Let o be a nonvariable occurrence in $u = v$ such that $(u = v)/o$ and l can be unified with a mgu σ. Moreover, if $u\sigma > v\sigma$, then o is inside u, and if $v\sigma > u\sigma$, then o is inside v. With these assumptions, $(D \wedge C \wedge (u = v)[o \leftarrow r])\sigma \Rightarrow s\sigma = t\sigma$ is called a superposition instance from superposing $D \Rightarrow l \to r$ on $u = v$ in $C \wedge u = v \Rightarrow s = t$.*

The completion procedure adds the superposition instances of a nonoperational equation to the current set of equations. Hence, an equation derived from a "nonoperational" equation may itself be operational and become a rewrite rule eventually. As in [Rus87], superposition can be restricted to occurrences inside the larger term of the selected condition.

Reducing an equation or rule in the unconditional case means to apply a rewrite rule. In the conditional case, increased reduction power can be obtained by also rewriting with those (skolemized) conditions which can be oriented according to the given reduction ordering. For that purpose, if C is a set of unconditional equations, by $C_{\mathcal{R}}$ we denote the (oriented) subset of those equations of C which can be oriented according to the given reduction ordering.

We define the complexity of an equation which is created during completion specifically depending on how the equation has been generated. A generated equation is a consequence of the original equations. It may represent a peak in rewriting or a superposition instance of a conditional equation. These proof pattern are not allowed inside rewrite proofs. Proofs of this kind must eventually be replaced by simpler proofs. Hence, the corresponding equation must eventually be reduced, eliminated, or turned into a rewrite rule. The equation can be eliminated, if there is a proof which is simpler than the proof which leads to the generation of the equation. In order to record the complexity of the proof pattern, its complexity will be associated with the generated equation. (Remember, we will use the notation $\gamma \diamond \eta$ to indicate that γ is the complexity associated with η.) It may be the case that the same equation occurs twice within the current set of equations, however with different complexities attached.

We are now prepared to give the inference rules for conditional completion CC. In the following, R, E, and N denote the current set of rules, equations, and nonoperational equations, respectively.

(O) Orienting an equation

$$\frac{N,\ E \cup \{\gamma \diamond \ldots u = v \ldots \Rightarrow s = t\},\ R}{N,\ E,\ R \cup \{\ldots u = v \ldots \Rightarrow s \to t\}}, \quad \text{if } \{s\} > \{\ldots, u, v, \ldots, t\}.$$

We may orient an equation, if one side is greater than each term in the condition as well as the term on the right side wrt. the given reduction ordering.

(NOP) Considering an equation as nonoperational

$$\frac{N,\ E \cup \{\gamma \diamond \eta\},\ R}{N \cup \{\gamma' \diamond \eta\},\ E,\ R}, \quad \text{if } \gamma \geq_{st} \gamma' \geq_{st} \rho(\vec{\eta}).$$

With the side condition about the complexity association, old proofs have the same or a lower complexity in the new system.

(NOP) allows to decrease the complexity of an equation upon considering it nonoperational. This decreases the chances of finding a simpler proof for the equation later in the process. At the same time it, however, increases the chance that the equation itself be used to simplify other equations. As said before, there is some trade-off here. The complexity of an equation can always safely be decreased. We have combined this into the (NOP)-rule to mirror the conceptual difference between the two classes of equations that we see. Equations in E are in the first place sought to be eliminated. For that purpose it is of advantage if their complexities are as high as possible. If an equation cannot be eliminated it must either be oriented or considered nonoperational. In the latter case, it is important to be able to use the equation to eliminate other equations, in particular those that are generated from itself by narrowing. Loops in the narrowing process can be cut this way. Hence one may want to define its complexity as low as possible.

In our actual implementation, we set $\gamma' = \gamma$ if a user equation is considered nonoperational. In all other cases, we reduce γ' to its minimum $\rho(\vec{\eta})$.

(ACP) Adding a critical pair

$$\frac{N,\ E,\ R}{N,\ E \cup \{\rho(u) \diamond \eta\},\ R},$$

if η is a critical pair between two rules in R with superposition term u.

Here, the superposition term of the overlap that leads to the critical pair equation defines its complexity. $\rho(u) >_{st} \rho(\vec{\eta})$ follows from the reductivity of the rewrite rules which create the peak.

(ASI) Adding a superposition instance of a nonoperational equation

$$\frac{N,\ E,\ R}{N,\ E \cup \{\gamma\sigma \diamond \eta\},\ R},$$

if η is a superposition instance of a nonoperational equation $\gamma \diamond \eta' \in N$ by a rule in $R \cup \{x = x \rightarrow true\}$[2] with σ the associated mgu.

The complexity of the new equation η is the complexity of the instance of the equation on which the superposition is performed. Note that any term in the new equation is equal to or smaller than some term in the σ-instance of η', with at least one term being smaller or eliminated. This follows from the reductivity of the rewrite rules as one step of rewriting is applied to the instance $\eta'\sigma$ of the selected condition in η'. Hence, $\gamma\sigma \geq_{st} \rho(\vec{\eta'})\sigma >_{st} \rho(\vec{\eta})$. $\gamma \geq_{st} \rho(\vec{\eta'})$ is guaranteed upon creation of η'.

(SE) Simplifying an equation

$$\frac{N,\ E \cup \{\gamma \diamond C \Rightarrow s = t\},\ R}{N,\ E \cup \{\gamma \diamond C \Rightarrow u = t\},\ R}, \quad \text{if } \tilde{s} \rightarrow_{R \cup \widetilde{C_R}} \tilde{u}.$$

$$\frac{N \cup \{\gamma \diamond C \Rightarrow s = t\},\ E,\ R}{N,\ E \cup \{\gamma \diamond C \Rightarrow u = t\},\ R}, \quad \text{if } \tilde{s} \rightarrow_{R \cup \widetilde{C_R}} \tilde{u}.$$

[2] After superposition with $x = x \rightarrow true$ we delete *true* from the condition. The meta-operator $=$ is assumed not to be contained in the given signature Σ.

We may rewrite the conclusion of a conditional equation, assuming the conditions as additional rules. Note that $\widetilde{C_{\mathcal{R}}}$ means that a condition equation is first oriented in a way compatible with the given termination ordering, if at all possible, and then skolemized. To first skolemize and then orient is not allowed as otherwise u may become greater than s.

The same rule is assumed to exist for the symmetric case in which t is simplified. If a nonoperational equation is simplified it is turned back into an equation.

(D) Deleting a trivial equation

$$\frac{N,\ E \cup \{\gamma \diamond C \Rightarrow s = t\},\ R}{N,\ E,\ R}, \quad \text{if } \exists P \in T_{\mathcal{E}(N \cup E, R)}(X_C)_{s=t} \text{ bounded by } \gamma \diamond C \Rightarrow s = t.$$

$$\frac{N \cup \{\gamma \diamond C \Rightarrow s = t\},\ E,\ R}{N,\ E,\ R}, \quad \text{if } \exists P \in T_{\mathcal{E}(N \cup E, R)}(X_C)_{s=t} \text{ bounded by } \gamma \diamond C \Rightarrow s = t.$$

An equation may be deleted, if there is a simpler proof for it than the equation itself. The complexity of the equation is the main component of the bound which the proof must stay below. Particularly simple cases of this rule are obtained for $s \equiv t$ or $s = t \in C$. In the first case, ';' (the 0-ary variant), in the second case $\pi : s = t \vdash \pi$, is a $\gamma \diamond C \Rightarrow s = t$-bounded proof. Another special case is subsumption, if there exists an equation $\gamma' \diamond \eta' \in E \cup N$ such that $\eta'\sigma = C \Rightarrow s = t$ and $\gamma >_{st} \gamma'\sigma$, for some substitution σ.

(SC) Simplifying a condition

$$\frac{N,\ E \cup \{\gamma \diamond C \wedge u = v \Rightarrow s = t\},\ R}{N,\ E \cup \{\gamma \diamond C \wedge w = v \Rightarrow s = t\},\ R}, \quad \text{if } \tilde{u} \rightarrow_{R \cup \widetilde{C_{\mathcal{R}}}} \tilde{w}.$$

$$\frac{N \cup \{\gamma \diamond C \wedge u = v \Rightarrow s = t\},\ E,\ R}{N,\ E \cup \{\gamma \diamond C \wedge w = v \Rightarrow s = t\},\ R}, \quad \text{if } \tilde{u} \rightarrow_{R \cup \widetilde{C_{\mathcal{R}}}} \tilde{w}.$$

A condition equation may be simplified under the assumption that the remaining condition equations hold true. The symmetric case, in which v is rewritten, is assumed to be also covered by this rule. As for (SE), a simplified nonoperational equation becomes a regular equation.

(DC) Deleting a trivial condition

$$\frac{N,\ E \cup \{\gamma \diamond C \wedge u = u \Rightarrow s = t\},\ R}{N,\ E \cup \{\gamma \diamond C \Rightarrow s = t\},\ R}$$

The same inference rule is assumed to exist for the elimination of trivial conditions of nonoperational equations or rewrite rules. In the former case, the nonoperational equation becomes a regular one.

(SRL) Simplifying the left side of a rule

$$\frac{N,\ E,\ R \cup \{C \Rightarrow s \rightarrow t\}}{N,\ E \cup \{\rho(s) \diamond C \Rightarrow u = t\},\ R}, \quad \text{if } \tilde{s} \rightarrow_{R \cup \widetilde{C_{\mathcal{R}}}} \tilde{u}.$$

The application of this inference rule is further restricted to cases, in which the redex of the rewriting is a proper subterm of s, or s is properly subsumed by the left side of the applied rule.

(SRR) Simplifying the right side of a rule

$$\frac{N,\ E,\ R \cup \{C \Rightarrow s \rightarrow t\}}{N,\ E,\ R \cup \{C \Rightarrow s \rightarrow u\}}, \quad \text{if } \tilde{t} \rightarrow_{R \cup \widetilde{C_{\mathcal{R}}}} \tilde{u}.$$

It is obvious that any of the above inference rules leaves the congruence $=_{N \cup E \cup R}$ invariant. Proof terms become less complex in proof signatures that are obtained by inference rule application:

Theorem 4.3 *The ordering $>_{\mathcal{P}}$ is a proof ordering for conditional completion CC, i.e. for any inference $(N,E,R) \vdash_{CC} (N',E',R')$ and any proof $P \in (T_{\mathcal{E}(N\cup E,R)})_{u=v}$ we have $P \in (T_{\mathcal{E}(N'\cup E',R')})_{u=v}$, i.e. P is also a proof of $u = v$ in the new system, or there exists a proof $P' \in (T_{\mathcal{E}(N'\cup E',R')})_{u=v}$ of $u = v$ in the new system which is less complex, i.e. $P >_{\mathcal{P}} P'$.*

Proof: The proof is a straightforward extension of proofs given for the completion inference rules in [Gan87]. To demonstrate this, we look at inference rule (SC) in detail. The rewriting $\tilde{u} \to_{R\cup\widetilde{C_R}} \tilde{w}$ corresponds to a proof P of $C \Rightarrow u = w$ of the form

$$(\pi_1 : e_1, \ldots, \pi_n : e_n \vdash Q : u = w)[P_i/\pi_i; 1 \leq i \leq n],$$

with $P_i = l_i \to r_i$, if the i-th equation e_i in C can be oriented into $l_i \to r_i$, and $P_i = \pi_i$, otherwise. (Note that the variables π_i of the latter kind do not occur in Q.) Consider the following proof transformation rules[3] in which π is a (new) proof variable of sort $u\sigma = v\sigma$:

$$\frac{\pi_1 : e_1\sigma, \ldots, \pi_n : e_n\sigma, \pi}{s\sigma =_{C\wedge u=v\Rightarrow s=t} t\sigma} \longrightarrow \frac{\pi_1 : e_1\sigma, \ldots, \pi_n : e_n\sigma, (i(\sigma(Q)); \pi)}{s\sigma =_{C\wedge w=v\Rightarrow s=t} t\sigma}$$

$$\frac{\pi_1 : e_1\sigma, \ldots, \pi_n : e_n\sigma, \pi}{t\sigma =_{C\wedge u=v\Rightarrow s=t} s\sigma} \longrightarrow \frac{\pi_1 : e_1\sigma, \ldots, \pi_n : e_n\sigma, (i(\sigma(Q)); \pi)}{t\sigma =_{C\wedge w=v\Rightarrow s=t} s\sigma}$$

As Q is a proof for $u = w$, $i(\sigma(Q)); \pi$ proves $w\sigma = v\sigma$. The monotonicity (wrt. $>_{\mathcal{P}}$) of these proof rewrite rules follows easily. The reduced equation is smaller than the original one. This decreases the second component in the complexity of any of its applications. P is a rewrite proof. Except for contexts and the proof variables π_i, Q contains only applications and reverse applications of rewrite rules. It contains no application of an equation. Moreover, the redex l of any rewrite step in Q is a term smaller than or equal to $u\sigma$. This is a consequence of the reductivity of rules. For any such rule application we obtain the complexity $(\rho(l),\ \rho(l),\ \ldots,\ \ldots)$, which is smaller than $(\gamma\sigma,\ \rho(\vec{C},u,v,s,t)\sigma,\ \ldots,\ \ldots)$. The latter follows as $terms(C\sigma) \cup \{u\sigma, v\sigma, s\sigma, t\sigma\} > \{l\}$, hence $\gamma\sigma \geq_{st} \rho(l)$ and $\rho(\vec{C},u,v,s,t)\sigma >_{st} \rho(l)$. Altogether, any proof operator on the right side of the proof transformation rules is smaller than the application of the original equation on the left side. □

This proof clearly shows that complexities of equations η must not go below the bound $\rho(\vec{\eta})$ to make inference rules like (SC) work as desired.

The following two theorems are the basic fundaments of conditional completion:

Theorem 4.4 *Let R be reductive. If $s \leftarrow_R w \to_R t$, then there is also a simpler proof Q of $s = t$ or there exists a contextual critical pair $C \Rightarrow c = d$ between two rules in R such that $s = N[c\sigma]$, $t = N[d\sigma]$ and $C\sigma \subset\downarrow_R$. Moreover, Q does not contain any application of an equation. In particular, Q is a rewrite proof in the case of unconditional rewriting of w.*

The proof of 4.4 is exactly as in [Gan87]. If a critical pair equation $C \Rightarrow c = d$ is added to E, the new system allows for a simpler proof for the peak $c \leftarrow u \to d$, with u the superposition term of the critical pair. In one of the rewrite steps, say in $u \to d$, the superposition term u is the redex. This rule application has the complexity $(\rho(u),\ \rho(u),\ \ldots,\ \ldots)$. For the critical pair we have $c(C \Rightarrow c = d) = (\rho(u), \rho(\vec{C},c,d),\ \ldots,\ \ldots)$. From the reductivity of the rewrite rules which create the peak it follows that $\rho(u) >_{st} \rho(\vec{C},c,d)$, hence the rewrite step is more complex than the equation application.

Theorem 4.5 *Assume E, N, and R to be given sets of equations, nonoperational equations, and rules, respectively. Let $\gamma \diamond C \wedge u = v \Rightarrow s = t$ be an equation in N. Moreover assume that*

[3] These rules are, as usually, meant as rule schemes in which arbitrary proof terms (with or without variables) may be substituted for the variables π and π_i.

E contains all instances of the equation generated by applying inference rule (ASI) with rules in $R \cup \{x = x \to true\}$ by superposing on the condition $u = v$ in the given equation. If

$$P = \frac{Q_1 \ldots Q_k}{s\sigma =_{C \wedge u=v \Rightarrow s=t} t\sigma}$$

is a proof in $T_{\mathcal{E}(N \cup E,R)}$ with Q_i a tuple of rewrite proofs for the condition equations in $(C \wedge u = v)\sigma$, then $T_{\mathcal{E}(N \cup E,R)}$ also contains a proof of $s\sigma = t\sigma$ which is simpler than P.

Again the proof proceeds along the lines of the proof of the same theorem in [Gan87].

These theorems say that if inference rules (ACP) and (ASI) are applied sufficiently often, completion will produce a canonical set of rules generating the same equational theory as the initial set of equations. This fairness constraint is made more precise in the next definition. By CP_i we denote the set of critical pairs between any two rules in R_i with the superposition terms attached as complexities, cf. (ACP). By SP_i we denote the set of superposition instances of an equation in N_i by all rules in $R_i \cup \{x = x \to true\}$ on one selected condition of the equation, with complexities attached as specified by (ASI).

Definition 4.6 *A CC-derivation $(N_0, E_0, R_0), (N_1, E_1, R_1), \ldots$ is called fair,* iff:

1. $\cap_{j>i} E_j = \emptyset$, for all i.

2. If $\gamma \diamond C \Rightarrow s = t \in \cap_{j \geq i} CP_j$ for some i, then there exists an index i' such that $\gamma \diamond C \Rightarrow s = t \in E_{i'}$.

3. If $\gamma \diamond C \Rightarrow s = t \in \cap_{j \geq i} SP_j$ for some i, then there exists an index i' such that $\gamma \diamond C \Rightarrow s = t \in E_{i'}$.

In other words, each equation in E must be eventually eliminated, oriented into a rule or considered nonoperational. All critical pairs between final rules must be computed, as well as all superposition instances of final rules on final nonoperational equations. The latter two requirements can be relaxed, in particular superpositions with rules that are reduced on their right side or on their condition need not be recomputed. Other critical pair criteria [BD86] can be applied as well.

Theorem 4.7 *Let $(N_0, E_0, R_0), (N_1, E_1, R_1), \ldots$ be a fair CC-derivation and P be a normalized proof in $(T_{\mathcal{E}(N_i \cup E_i, R_i)})_{u=v}$ for some equation $u = v$. If P is not a rewrite proof, then there is, for some $k \geq i$, a proof $P' \in (T_{\mathcal{E}(N_k \cup E_k, R_k)})_{u=v}$ such that $P >_{\mathcal{P}} P'$.*

Hence, if the completion procedure is started on input $E_0 = E$, with any admissible complexities for the equations, and on $N_0 = \emptyset$, $R_0 = \emptyset$ and $>$, and if it does not *fail*, i.e. generates a fair *CC*-derivation, for any equality $u \equiv_E v$ there exists an index k such that $u \downarrow_{R_k} v$. In particular, the limit $R_\infty = \cup_i \cap_{j>i} R_j$ is canonical and $\equiv_{R_\infty} = \equiv_E$. In this case, the equational theory can be decided by rewriting. Equations in $N_\infty = \cup_i \cap_{j>i} N_j$ are irrelevant for $\equiv$, hence in fact nonoperational.

5 Examples

In this section we present some examples. The first example will be looked at in more detail to illustrate the effectiveness of associating complexities with equations. The other examples are meant to give further evidence of the practical relevance of the completion procedure in CEC.

5.1 Integers with Transitivity Axiom

Initial Equations:

```
1    x<x = ff
2    x<s(x) = tt
3    s(x)<y = x<p(y)
4    p(x)<y = x<s(y)
5    y<x = tt => y<s(x) = tt
6    y<x = ff => y<p(x) = ff
7    s(p(x)) = x
8    p(s(x)) = x
9    x<y = tt and y<z = tt => x<z = tt
```

Equation 9, the transitivity of $<$, is clearly nonreductive. As a user equation it may be given any admissible complexity. For that purpose, we add an additional auxiliary operator τ into ΣC. On the initial signature we assume the precedence ordering of [KNS85], established by the operator precedences "$<$">"p", "$<$">"s" with lr-status for "$<$". This ordering can be extended to $T_{\Sigma C}(X)$ by the additional precedences $\tau > \rho >$ "$<$", with multiset status for ρ and lr-status for τ. With this we may assign the complexity $\tau(x < z, tt, x < y, tt, y < z, tt)$ to the transitivity axiom $x < y = tt$ and $y < z = tt \Rightarrow x < z = tt$. Note that we have rearranged the terms in this axiom into the order "conclusion–1st condition–2nd condition", which, together with the lr-status of τ, will turn out favorable later. In our system, we in fact allow the user to specify such an order by hand. With this ordering, each equation, except for 9, becomes a rule by orienting it from left to right. Equation 9 is considered nonoperational.

Termination problems in the completion of this example arise from the superpositions issued from 9. As a nonoperational equation, it will be overlapped on its first condition by rule 3, among others, generating the equation

$$x < p(y1) = tt \text{ and } y1 < z = tt \;\Rightarrow\; s(x) < z = tt$$

which is reduced to

(13) $$x < p(y1) = tt \text{ and } y1 < z = tt \;\Rightarrow\; x < p(z) = tt.$$

According to (ASI) this equation will be associated the complexity

$$\tau(\, s(x) < z, tt, s(x) < y1, tt, y1 < z, tt),$$

as

$$s(x) < y1 = tt \text{ and } y1 < z = tt \;\Rightarrow\; s(x) < z = tt$$

is the substitution instance of 9 which gets superposed on the first condition by rule 3. The following proof is bounded by 13.

$$x < p(y1) = tt, y1 < z = tt \vdash \frac{x < p(y1) = tt,\;\; p(y1) < p(z) \rightarrow_4 y1 < s(p(z)) \rightarrow_7 y1 < z = tt}{x < p(z) \leftrightarrow_9 tt}$$

To conclude that this proof is in fact bounded by (13), let us take a look at the complexities of the applications of the rules 4 and 7 and equation 9. The first component in the complexity of the application of the transitivity axiom 9 is

$$\tau(x < p(z), tt, x < p(y1), tt, p(y1) < p(z), tt).$$

From the lr-status of "$<$" we have $(s(x) < z) > (x < p(z))$, hence, from the lr-status of τ,

$$\tau(s(x) < z, tt, s(x) < y1, tt, y1 < z, tt) > \tau(x < p(z), tt, x < p(y1), tt, p(y1) < p(z), tt).$$

As $\tau > \rho$, any rewriting is less complex than any application of 13. Therefore, equation 13 can be eliminated by (D). If equation 13 had been assigned the complexity

$$\tau(x < p(z), tt, x < p(y1), tt, y1 < z, tt),$$

which would be the case in our earlier paper [Gan87], the use of 9 in the above proof would have been too complex for a bounded proof. Also, if we had not allowed the introduction of auxiliary operators for representing the complexity of user equations, we could not have given τ lr-status and precedence over rewriting, two properties which are substantial to be able to eliminate 13. If 13 cannot be eliminated, it will generate further equations of similar kind, causing the nontermination of the completion process.

A second nontrivial situation occurs from superposing 9 by rule 5. The substitution instance of 9 is then

$$x < s(y) = tt \text{ and } s(y) < z = tt \Rightarrow x < z = tt,$$

the narrowing step with 5 yields

$$x < y = tt \text{ and } tt = tt \text{ and } s(y) < z = tt \Rightarrow x < z = tt,$$

which can be reduced to the equation

$$x < y = tt \text{ and } y < p(z) = tt \Rightarrow x < z = tt. \tag{17}$$

The complexity of 17 is

$$\tau(x < z, tt, x < s(y), tt, s(y) < z, tt).$$

At the time when this equation is generated, the system also has the nonoperational equation

$$y < p(z) = tt \Rightarrow y < z = tt, \tag{N2}$$

which has been generated from superposing the transitivity axiom by rule 2. Not a user equation, it will be given the lowest possible complexity, which is $\rho(y < z, tt, y < p(z), tt)$, upon considering it nonoperational. An alternative proof of 17, bounded by 17, is the following:

$$(x < y) = tt, (y < p(z)) = tt \vdash \quad \cfrac{(x < y) = tt, \quad \cfrac{(y < p(z)) = tt}{(y < z) \leftrightarrow_{N2} tt}}{(x < z) \leftrightarrow_9 tt}$$

Its boundedness follows from

$$\tau(x < z, tt, x < s(y), tt, s(y) < z, tt) \quad >_{st} \quad \rho(y < z, tt, y < p(z), tt),$$

for the application of N2, and

$$\tau(x < z, tt, x < s(y), tt, s(y) < z, tt) \quad >_{st} \quad \tau(x < z, tt, x < y, tt, y < z, tt),$$

for the application of 9.

The final system is the following:

```
No equations
Rules
1    x<x -> ff
2    x<s(x) -> tt
3    s(x)<y -> x<p(y)
4    p(x)<y -> x<s(y)
5    y<x = tt => y<s(x) -> tt
6    y<x = ff => y<p(x) -> ff
7    s(p(x)) -> x
```

```
8    p(s(x)) -> x
Nonoperational equations
1    x<y = tt and y<z = tt => x<z = tt
2    y<p(z) = tt => y<z = tt
3    y<s(x) = ff => y<x = ff
```

The CEC-system has hence proved that this set of rules is canonical, in particular confluent on all terms (not just on ground terms as in [KR87]), with the considerably more complex situation that is obtained when including the transitivity axiom. It has also been proved by an automated procedure that adding the transitivity axiom does not enrich the equational theory. This example is somewhat special as there is no real transformation of the system during completion. In the following we give a few more examples which have been completed using the techniques as described in this paper. In these examples the superposition processes (ACP) and (ASI) have created new rules from the initially given axioms.

5.2 Smolka's Example

This example is the result of translating an order-sorted specification into an equivalent many-sorted one using injections between subsorts. The example is due to Smolka and shows the incompleteness of order-sorted replacement of equals by equals, cf. [Smo87] or [KKM88].

```
Initial Equations
1    i(a) = d
2    i(b) = d
3    i(x) = i(y)  => x = y
```

where $a : s1$, $b : s1$, and $d : s2$ are constants and where $i : s1 \rightarrow s2$. Axiom 3 is the injectivity property of i which is clearly nonreductive. Orienting 1 and 2 from left to right creates the following final system:

```
No equations
Rules
2    i(a) -> d
3    b -> a
Nonoperational equations
1    i(x) = i(y)  => x = y
2    d = i(y) => a = y
```

The nonoperational equation 2 is generated from superposing rule 1 (which is later deleted) on the condition of the injectivity axiom. After this, the nonoperational equation 2 generates rule 3 from superposition with $i(b) \rightarrow d$. In the transformed system, the injectivity axiom has become irrelevant whereas in the initial system it affects the equational theory.

5.3 A Single-Sorted Specification with Type Predicates

The following example is the result of a different kind of translating an order-sorted specification into an equivalent many-sorted one. Sorts are represented by predicates, i.e. functions of sort *bool*. Each sort is subtype of one single universe named *d*. As subtypes of *d* we have the integers *int*, the natural numbers *nat*, the non-zero natural numbers *nzNat*, the non-zero integers *nzInt*, and the boolean values (*boolean*). This kind of translation corresponds to the semantics of order-sorted specifications as given in [Smo87], whereas the one using injections corresponds to the semantics given in [KKM88].

```
Signature
% sort predicates
```

```
op nzNat :  d -> bool.
op nat :  d -> bool.
op int :  d -> bool.
op nzInt :  d -> bool.
op boolean :  d -> bool.
% operations on integers as partial functions on the universe d
op 0 :  d.
op s :  d -> d.
op '-' :  d -> d.
op < :  d,d -> d.
% boolean values
op tt :  d.
op ff :  d.
Equations
% inclusion properties between types
1     nzNat(d) = true =>   nat(d)=true.
2     nat(d) = true =>  int(d)=true.
3     nzNat(d) = true =>  nzInt(d)=true.
4     nzInt(d) = true =>  int(d)=true.
% type properties of operators
5     nat(0) = true.
6     nat(d)=true => nzNat(s(d))=true.
7     nat(d)=true => int(-d)=true.
8     nzNat(d)=true => nzInt(-d)=true.
9     int(d)=true => int(-d)=true.
10    nzInt(d)=true => nzInt(-d)=true.
11    int(d1)=true and int(d2)=true => boolean(d1 < d2)=true.
12    boolean(tt)=true.
13    boolean(ff)=true.
% definition of operators depending on the types of the arguments
14    -(0) = 0.
15    int(i)=true => -(-i) = i.
16    nzNat(n)=true => 0 < n = tt.
17    nzNat(n)=true and nat(m)=true => -m < n = tt.
18    nat(k)=true and nat(m)=true => m < -k = ff.
19    nat(k)=true and nat(m)=true => s(m) < s(k) = m < k.
20    nat(k)=true and nat(m)=true => m<k = -k < -m.
```

Final system after completion:

```
No equations
Rules
% inclusion properties between types
1     nzNat(d) = true => nat(d) -> true
2     nat(d) = true => int(d) -> true
3     nzNat(d) = true => nzInt(d) -> true
4     nzInt(d) = true => int(d) -> true
% type properties of operators
5     nat(0) -> true
6     nat(d) = true => nzNat(s(d)) -> true
9     int(d) = true => int(-d) -> true
10    nzInt(d) = true => nzInt(-d) -> true
11    int(d1) = true and int(d2) = true => boolean(d1<d2) -> true
12    boolean(ff) -> true
13    boolean(tt) -> true
% definition of operators depending on the types of the arguments
14    -(0) -> 0
15    int(i) = true => - (-i) -> i
16    nzNat(n) = true => 0<n -> tt
17    nzNat(n) = true and nat(m) = true => -m<n -> tt
18    nat(k) = true and nat(m) = true => m< -k -> ff
19    nat(k) = true and nat(m) = true => s(m)<s(k) -> m<k
```

```
20    nat(k) = true and nat(m) = true => -k< -m -> m<k
21    nat(m) = true => m<0 -> ff
22    nat(k) = true => -k<0 -> 0<k
Nonoperational equations
1     nzInt(-i) = true and int(i) = true => nzInt(i) = true
2     nzNat(0) = true => tt = ff
3     nat(-i) = true and int(i) = true and nat(m) = true => m<i = ff
4     nat(-i) = true and int(i) = true and nzNat(n) = true => i<n = tt
5     nzNat(-k) = true and nat(k) = true => tt = ff
6     nat(-i) = true and int(i) = true => 0< -i = i<0
7     nat(-i) = true and int(i) = true and nat(k) = true => -k<i = -i<k
8     nat(-i) = true and int(i) = true and nat(m) = true => i< -m = m< -i
9     nat(-i) = true and nzNat(i) = true => tt = ff
10    nzNat(-i) = true and int(i) = true => nzInt(i) = true
11    nzNat(-i) = true and nzNat(n) = true and nzInt(i) = true => i<n = tt
12    nzNat(-i) = true and nat(m) = true and nzInt(i) = true => m<i = ff
13    nzNat(-i) = true and nzInt(i) = true => i<0 = tt
14    nzNat(-i) = true and int(i) = true and nat(m) = true => i< -m = m< -i
15    nzNat(-i) = true and int(i) = true and nat(k) = true => -k<i = -i<k
```

Axioms 7 and 8 have been eliminated, the rules 21 and 22 have been created during completion. The complexity of this example is indicated by the large number of nonoperational equations which are generated during completion. Note that many of the nonoperational equations could have been oriented into a reductive rewrite rule. It is important to apply the inference rules (O) and (NOP) flexibly. The example seems to suggest that our completion procedure is sufficiently powerful to also support more advanced type concepts in algebraic specification languages.

6 Conclusions

We have presented a completion technique for conditional equations in which with equations that are generated during completion complexities are associated which reflect the history of their creation. We have argued and illustrated by means of an example that this technique may allow to detect loops in the narrowing-like process of deriving equations from nonoperational equations. Hence, completion employing this technique may terminate where previously described techniques [Gan87], [KR87], [Rus87] fail to terminate. We have described, by means of inference rules, and proved correct a completion procedure which attaches complexities with equations upon their creation from a peak or from a superposition of a nonoperational equation. User equations may have any (admissible) complexity. This increases the power of the system to handle user-given nonreductive equations.

The main part of our procedure in CEC which has not been described in this paper is its way of applying inference rule (D), i.e. its technique of finding simpler proofs to a given equation. Theoretically, any complete proof mechanism, e.g. the one described in [KR87], which is extended by checking the complexity bounds wrt. $>_{\mathcal{P}}$ is conceivable. In practise, however, this can be very time consuming. In our implementation we have sacrificed completeness for increased efficiency. Further insight seems to be needed here. Also, it should be useful to incorporate other techniques from narrowing [Ret88].

Also it has turned out that equations can be generated which can easily be oriented into a reductive rule (with satisfiable condition), yet should be considered nonoperational in order to achieve termination of the completion process. In other words, if one always selects a maximal literal for superposition, as proposed by the "extended superposition rule" in [KR87] and [Rus87], one may loose termination. Again, more experience is needed to come to conclusions for this problem.

Acknowledgements. The author is grateful to H. Bertling for many discussions on the subject of this paper.

7 References

[Bac87] Bachmair, L.: Proof methods for equational theories. PhD-Thesis, U. of Illinois, Urbana Champaign, 1987.

[BD86] Bachmair, L. and Dershowitz, N.: Critical pair criteria for the Knuth-Bendix completion procedure. Proc. ACM Symp. on Symbolic and Alg. Computation, 1986, 215-217.

[BDH86] Bachmair, L., Dershowitz, N. and Hsiang, J.: Proof orderings for equational proofs. Proc. LICS 86, 346-357.

[BGS88] Bertling, H., Ganzinger, H. and Schäfers, R.: CEC: A system for conditional equational completion. User Manual Version 1.0, PROSPECTRA-Report M.1.3-R-7.0, U. Dortmund, 1988.

[Der85] Dershowitz, N.: Termination. Proc. RTA 1985, LNCS 202, 1985, 180-224.

[DM79] Dershowitz, N. and Manna, Z.: Proving termination with multiset orderings. CACM 22 (1979), 465-476.

[Gan87] Ganzinger, H.: A Completion procedure for conditional equations. Report 234, U. Dortmund, 1987 (revised version to appear in J. Symb. Computation).

[HO80] Huet, G. and Oppen, D.C.: Equations and Rewrite Rules. A Survey. In: R. Book (ed): Formal Languages: Perspectives and open Problems. Academic Press, New York, 1980, 349-405.

[JW86] Jouannaud, J.P. and Waldmann, B.: Reductive conditional term rewriting systems. Proc. 3rd TC2 Working Conference on the Formal Description of Prog. Concepts, Ebberup, Denmark, Aug. 1986, North-Holland.

[Kap84a] Kaplan, St.: Conditional rewrite rules. TCS 33 (1984), 175-193.

[Kap84b] Kaplan, St.: Fair conditional term rewrite systems: unification, termination and confluence. Report 194, U. de Paris-Sud, Centre d'Orsay, Nov. 1984.

[KaR87] Kaplan, St. and Remy J.-L.: Completion algorithms for conditional rewriting systems. MCC Workshop on Resolution of Equations in Algebraic Structures, Austin, May 1987.

[KKM88] Kirchner, C, Kirchner, H., and Meseguer, J.: Operational semantics of OBJ3. Proc. ICALP 88, 1988, to appear.

[KNS85] Kapur, D., Narendran, P., and Sivakumar, G.: A path ordering for proving termination of term rewrite systems. LNCS 186, 1985, 173-187.

[KR87] Kounalis, E. and Rusinowitch, M.: On word problems in Horn logic. Proc. 1st Int'l Workshop on Conditional Term Rewriting, Orsay, 1987, to appear in LNCS.

[Kue85] Küchlin, W.: A confluence criterion based on the generalised Newman lemma. Proc. Eurocal 1985, LNCS 204, 1985, 390-399.

[Kue86] Küchlin, W.: Equational completion by proof transformation. Ph.D. thesis, Dep't. of Mathematics, ETH Zürich, 1986.

[Ret88] Réty, P.: Méthodes d'unification par surréduction. Thesis, U. de Nancy 1, 1988.

[Rus87] Rusinowitch, M.: Theorem-proving with resolution and superposition: an extension of Knuth and Bendix procedure as a complete set of inference rules. Report 87-R-128, CRIN, Nancy, 1987.

[Smo87] Smolka, G., Nutt, W., Goguen, J.A. and Meseguer, J.: Order-sorted equational computation. SEKI Report SR-87-14, U. Kaiserslautern, 1987.

[WB83] Winkler, F. and Buchberger, B.: A criterion for eliminating unnecessary reductions in the Knuth-Bendix algorithm. Coll. on Algebra, Combinatorics and Logic in Comp. Sci., Györ, 1983.

JUNGLE EVALUATION

Annegret Habel, Hans-Jörg Kreowski, and Detlef Plump*
Fachbereich Mathematik und Informatik
Universität Bremen
D-2800 Bremen 33

Abstract

Jungle evaluation is proposed as a new graph rewriting approach to the evaluation of functional expressions and, in particular, of algebraically specified operations. Jungles - being intuitively forests of coalesced trees with shared substructures - are certain acyclic hypergraphs (or equivalently, bipartite graphs) the nodes and edges of which are labeled with the sorts and operation symbols of a signature. Jungles are manipulated and evaluated by the application of jungle rewrite rules, which generalize equations or, more exactly, term rewrite rules. Indeed, jungle evaluation turns out to be a compromise between term rewriting and graph rewriting displaying some favorable properties: the inefficiency of term rewriting is partly avoided while the possibility of structural induction is maintained, and a good part of the existing graph grammar theory is applicable so that there is some hope that the rich theory of term rewriting is not lost forever without a substitute.

1 Introduction

Whenever an algebraic specification is meant to be a design specification and as such to solve a data-processing problem, it must be executable. The demand of executability distinguishes a solution from the problem, a design specification from the requirement definition. Hence, the issue of operational semantics has been of great interest for more than ten years within the algebraic approach to software development. Algebraic specifications with operational semantics are meaningful in the following respects:

(1) Interpreters can be built as tools supporting the process of software development.

(2) Tests can be run at a comparatively early stage of software development.

(3) Algebraic specifications can be used as prototypes of software systems.

(4) Algebraic specifications can be considered as programs in an algebraic programming language.

(5) Algebraic specifications may be employed as rule-based systems within expert systems.

The favorite approach to equip algebraic, particularly equational specifications with operational semantics is term rewriting. This is not surprising because equations as the key concept of the algebraic-specification technique consist of terms and may be seen as left-to-right term rewrite rules. Moreover, the theoretical foundations of and practical experience with term rewriting are tremendous and a lot of knowledge is available how termination, confluence and related concepts work.

Nevertheless, there are reasons for concern: among them we would like to point at the possible inefficiency of term rewriting. The execution of algebraic specifications may be extremely slow compared with the evaluation of functional or logical programs. If the solved problems are hard, nothing can be done. But what if the framework must be blamed?

*Work of this author is partially supported by the ESPRIT-project PROSPECTRA, ref. # 390.

Consider, for example, the specification of a function generating a totally balanced binary tree (without labels) of height n if n is the input.

generate = **nat** + **bintree**+
opns : $GEN : nat \to bintree$
eqns : $GEN(0) = BIN(EMPTY, EMPTY)$
$GEN(SUCC(N)) = BIN(GEN(N), GEN(N))$

Concerning the imported specifications we assume that **nat** provides a sort *nat*, a constant(symbol) 0 and a unary operation(symbol) $SUCC$ at least and that **bintree** provides a sort *bintree*, a constant(symbol) $EMPTY$ and a binary operation(symbol) BIN at least. Now, the evaluation of the term $GEN(SUCC^n(0))$ for some $n \geq 0$ within the framework of term rewriting (or, likewise, of tree rewriting) consumes time and space or a number of processors exponential in n.

This unfortunate behavior is easily avoided as long as the two identical subterms of the right-hand side of the second equation do not cause a duplication of computation.

The recipe is clear: Represent functional expressions by structures with shared substructures rather than by terms or trees. This is the basic idea of graph grammar approaches to the evaluation of functional expressions as studied by Ehrig, Padawitz, Rosen, Staples and – most recently – by Barendregt, van Eekelen, Glauert, Kennaway, Plasmeijer, and Sleep (see [ER 76], [St 80], [Pa 82], [BEGKPS 87]). Unfortunately, these approaches have some drawbacks. The types of graphs and graph rewrite rules introduced and used are exotic in the sense that the major body of graph grammar theory is not applicable. Moreover, there is no structural induction available which has been proved so extremely helpful in term and tree rewriting.

Therefore, we feel encouraged to introduce a new and alternative graph grammar approach to the evaluation of functional expressions and, in particular, of algebraically specified operations. We propose jungle evaluation the characteristics of which are the following:

(1) If the reader understands the intuition behind the notions of a *tree* and a *forest* in the sense of graph theory or computer science, he or she may think of a *jungle* as a forest of "coalesced trees" with shared substructures.

(2) Formally, jungles are recursively generated acyclic (hyper-)graphs so that structural induction is available.

(3) Jungle evaluation is intentionally related to the evaluation of algebraic specifications.

(4) Jungle evaluation can be seen as graph rewriting in the sense of the "Berlin-approach" so that various known results on graph grammar derivations can be applied (see, e.g., [Eh 79] and [Kr 87]).

(5) Especially, jungle evaluation comprises modes of non-sequential rewriting.

The paper is organized in the following way. In section 2, jungles are defined, and some of their basic properties are established while their relationship to terms is considered in section 3. Jungle rewriting is the topic of section 4 including the main result of the paper which presents sufficient conditions on (hyper-)graph rewriting rules so that their application to jungles yields jungles again. In section 5, some first evidence is presented that jungle evaluation can simulate term evaluation in a meaningful and efficient way. Section 6 contains a short concluding discussion. Finally, the basic notions on (hyper-)graphs and (hyper-)graph rewriting are recalled in the appendix as far as they are needed in this paper.

2 Jungles

In this section we define jungles as special hypergraphs that reflect the typing of a given signature. Intuitively, jungles are forests with interwoven trees. This structure ensures that each node in a jungle represents a unique term (cf. section 3). Moreover, it is possible to characterize jungles by a set of generating rules. As a consequence, a structural induction principle and efficient syntax analysis for jungles are available.

2.1 General Assumption
In the following we consider hypergraphs over an arbitrary, but fixed signature $SIG = (S, OP)$, i.e., nodes are labeled by sorts from S and hyperedges are labeled by operation symbols from OP. □

2.2 Definition (Jungle)
A hypergraph G is a *jungle* (*over SIG*) if

1. G is acyclic,[1]
2. $outdegree_G(v) \leq 1$ for each $v \in V_G$,[2]
3. the labeling of G is *compatible* with SIG, i.e., for each $e \in E_G$, $m_G(e) = op : s_1 \dots s_n \rightarrow s$ implies $l_G^*(s_G(e)) = s$ and $l_G^*(t_G(e)) = s_1 \dots s_n$.

Remarks
1. Trees and forests over SIG are special jungles where the indegree of each node is at most one.
2. For each hyperedge in a jungle labeled by an operation symbol $op : s_1 \dots s_n \rightarrow s$ there is a unique source node labeled by s and a sequence of n (not necessarily distinct) target nodes labeled by $s_1, \dots, s_n$. The sequence of target nodes is empty if op is a constant symbol.
3. Each subhypergraph of a jungle is a jungle, too. Such a subhypergraph is called a *subjungle*. □

2.3 Example
The following hypergraph is a jungle over the signature of the specification **generate** (where "bin" stands for "*bintree*").

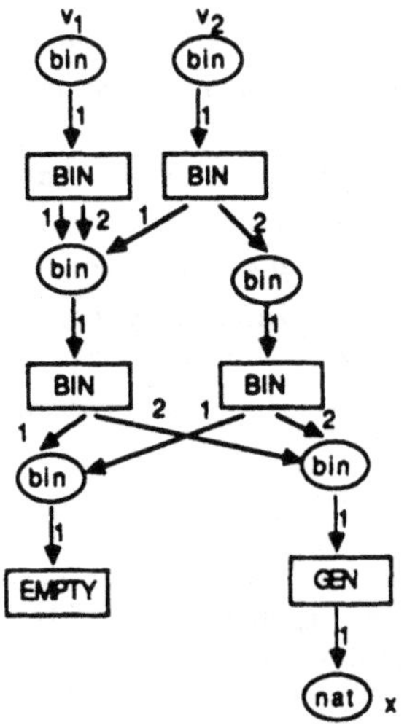

Figure 2.1: A Jungle

□

[1] A hypergraph G is said to be acyclic if the underlying bipartite graph $U(G)$ is acyclic.

[2] For a hypergraph G and a node $v \in V_G$, $indegree_G(v)$ denotes the number of "tentacles" incoming in v and $outdegree_G(v)$ denotes the number of "tentacles" outgoing from v, i.e., $indegree_G(v) = \sum_{e \in E_G} \#(v, t_G(e))$ and $outdegree_G(v) = \sum_{e \in E_G} \#(v, s_G(e))$, where $\#(a, w)$ denotes the number of occurrences of an element a in a sequence w.

Beside the graph-theoretic description given in Definition 2.2 jungles can be characterized by three kinds of jungle generating rules. Theorem 2.5 shows that each jungle is generated from the empty hypergraph $\emptyset$ (which is a jungle) by repeated application of these rules. (Note that general hypergraph rules and their application are discussed in the appendix.)

2.4 Definition (Jungle Generating Rules)
The set GEN of *jungle generating rules* consists of the following rules:

(Variable Generation)[3]

$$< s > = \left(\emptyset \supseteq \emptyset \subseteq \boxed{\text{s}} \right) \quad \text{for each sort } s \in S,$$

(Constant Generation)

$$< c : \to s > = \left(\emptyset \supseteq \emptyset \subseteq \; \substack{\text{s} \\ | \\ \text{c}} \right) \quad \text{for each constant symbol } c : \to s,$$

(Operation Application)

$$< op : s_1 \ldots s_n \to s > = \left(\; \substack{\text{s}_1} \ldots \substack{\text{s}_n} \supseteq \substack{\text{s}_1} \ldots \substack{\text{s}_n} \subseteq \substack{\text{s}_1} \ldots \substack{\text{s}_n} \; \right) \quad \begin{array}{l}\text{for each operation symbol } op : s_1 \ldots s_n \to s.\end{array}$$

$\square$

Figure 2.2 (see next page) shows how the jungle of Figure 2.1 can be generated. It turns out that the set of all hypergraphs derivable from the empty hypergraph by GEN and the set of all jungles are equal.

2.5 Theorem (Characterization of Jungles)
A hypergraph G is a jungle if and only if $\emptyset \stackrel{*}{\underset{GEN}{\Longrightarrow}} G$.

Proof
It is simple to check that each of the rules, when applied to a jungle, preserves the conditions of Definition 2.2. Hence each derivation with these rules starting from the empty jungle yields a jungle.

Now let G be a jungle. We show $\emptyset \stackrel{*}{\underset{GEN}{\Longrightarrow}} G$ by induction on the number n of nodes in G. Obviously the proposition holds for $n = 0$ since then G is the empty jungle. Let therefore $n \geq 1$ and assume $\emptyset \stackrel{*}{\underset{GEN}{\Longrightarrow}} \overline{G}$ for each jungle $\overline{G}$ with less than n nodes. Because G is non-empty and acyclic, there is a node v in G with $indegree_G(v) = 0$. Let $\overline{G}$ be the subjungle of G induced by $V_G - \{v\}$. The following case analysis shows that $\overline{G} \underset{GEN}{\Longrightarrow} G$ which by the induction hypothesis implies $\emptyset \stackrel{*}{\underset{GEN}{\Longrightarrow}} G$.

Case 1: $outdegree_G(v) = 0$. Then $\overline{G} \underset{<s>}{\Longrightarrow} G$, where s is the label of v.

Case 2: $outdegree_G(v) = 1$. Let e be the unique hyperedge in G with $s_G(e) = v$. By construction of $\overline{G}$ we have $E_{\overline{G}} = E_G - \{e\}$.

Case 2.1: $m_G(e)$ is a constant symbol $c :\to s$. Then $l_G^*(s_G(e)) = s$ and $t_G(e) = \lambda$ imply $\overline{G} \underset{<c:\to s>}{\Longrightarrow} G$.

Case 2.2: $m_G(e)$ is an operation symbol $op : s_1 \ldots s_n \to s$. Then all nodes in $t_G(e)$ belong to $\overline{G}$. Consequently $l_G^*(t_G(e)) = s_1 \ldots s_n$ implies that the target nodes of e constitute an occurrence of the left-hand side of $< op : s_1 \ldots s_n \to s >$ in $\overline{G}$. Further $l_G^*(s_G(e)) = s$ holds, so $\overline{G} \underset{<op:s_1 \ldots s_n \to s>}{\Longrightarrow} G$. $\square$

---

[3]The notation refers to the relation between jungles and terms with variables which is discussed in section 3.

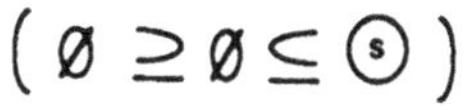

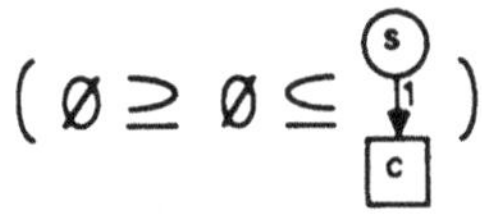

2.6 Example

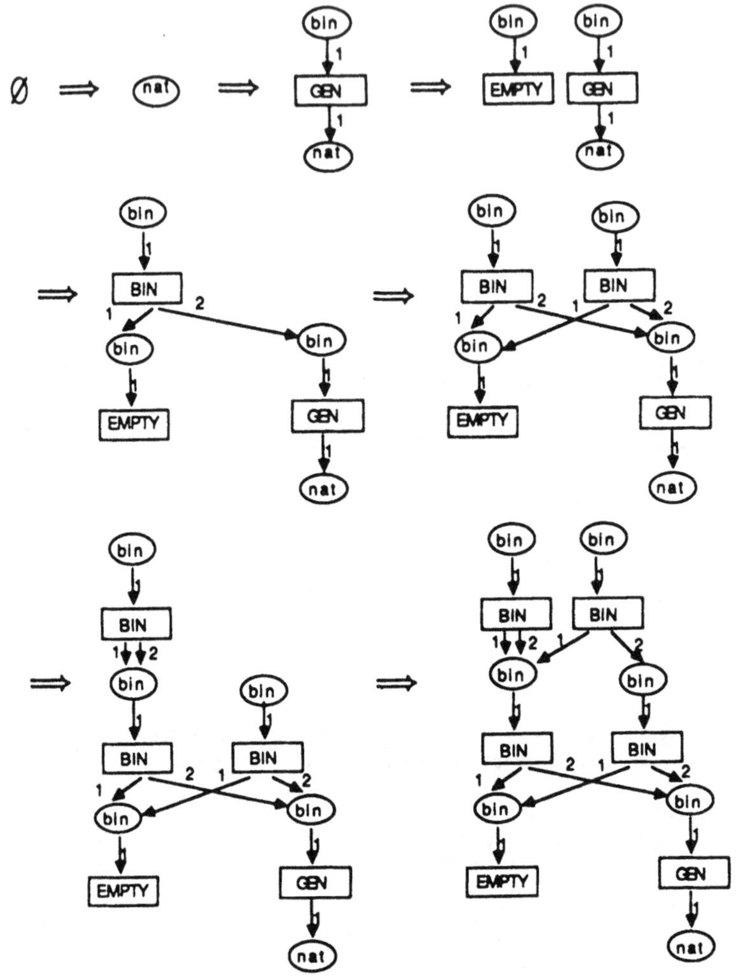

Figure 2.2: Generation of a Jungle

□

Theorem 2.5 establishes a structural induction principle.

2.7 Corollary (Structural Induction)
A property P holds for all jungles provided that

1. P holds for the empty jungle, and

2. for all jungles G and H, if P holds for G and $G \underset{GEN}{\Longrightarrow} H$, then P holds for H also.

Proof
By Theorem 2.5 for all non-empty jungles G there are derivation sequences of the form $\emptyset \underset{GEN}{\Longrightarrow} G_1 \underset{GEN}{\Longrightarrow} \dots \underset{GEN}{\Longrightarrow} G_n = G$. Induction on the lengths of these sequences yields the desired result. □

For testing whether or not a given hypergraph is a jungle one may check acyclicity, the outdegree condition, and the labeling condition given in Definition 2.2. By Theorem 2.5 there is a more efficient method based on the set GEN^{-1} of all inverse rules of jungle generating rules.

2.8 Corollary (Syntax Analysis)
If *SIG* is finite,[4] the algorithm

apply rules from GEN^{-1} *as long as possible*

reduces a given hypergraph G to the empty hypergraph if and only if G is a jungle.

The algorithm consumes linear time provided that hypergraphs are represented in such a way that the applicability of each rule in GEN^{-1} can be tested in constant time.

Proof
If *SIG* is finite, GEN^{-1} contains a fixed number of rules. Since the applicability of each rule can be checked in constant time, the test whether any of the rules is applicable to a given hypergraph can be performed in constant time, too. Furthermore, each application of a rule removes a node, so each derivation stops after at most n steps, where n is the number of nodes in the given hypergraph. Hence the above algorithm terminates in linear time.

To show that the algorithm is correct, let G, H be hypergraphs and $G \overset{*}{\underset{GEN^{-1}}{\Longrightarrow}} H$ be a derivation such that no rule in GEN^{-1} can be applied to H. Then $H \overset{*}{\underset{GEN}{\Longrightarrow}} G$ implies that G is a jungle in case $H = \emptyset$. If H is non-empty, there is no derivation of the form $H \overset{*}{\underset{GEN^{-1}}{\Longrightarrow}} \emptyset$ and consequently no derivation $\emptyset \overset{*}{\underset{GEN}{\Longrightarrow}} H$. Thus H is not a jungle by Theorem 2.5. □

3 Relating Terms and Jungles

The jungles introduced and investigated in the previous section are closely related to terms. On one hand, each node of a jungle represents uniquely a term. On the other hand, there are several possibilities for representing a term as a jungle. A natural and simple representation is by a "variable–collapsed" tree. Another distinguished, useful representation (exploiting the possibility of structure sharing exhaustively) is by a "fully collapsed" tree. Beside these presentations of terms there are lots of other jungles representing a given term. When translating term rewrite rules into jungle rules we make use of the different term presentations (compare Section 5).

Jungles over a signature *SIG* are special hypergraphs the nodes and hyperedges of which are labeled by sorts and operation symbols, respectively. Fixing a node in a jungle, a term may be extracted from the jungle by (a) taking the label of the only outgoing hyperedge and gathering the terms of the target nodes (of the hyperedge) and (b) taking the node as a variable provided that there is no outgoing hyperedge. In this way, each node of a jungle represents a term. Given a jungle G, the nodes without outgoing hyperedges play a specific role: with respect to terms they represent variables. To indicate this role, they are called *variable nodes*. The set of these nodes is denoted by VAR_G.

3.1 Theorem (Terms Represented by a Jungle)
Let G be a jungle. Then for each node $v \in V_G$ the following construction yields a unique term from $T_{SIG}(VAR_G)$, denoted by $term_G(v)$:

- $term_G(v) = v$ if $v \in VAR_G$, i.e., there is no $e \in E_G$ with $s_G(e) = v$,
- $term_G(v) = c$ if there is $e \in E_G$ with $s_G(e) = v$, $t_G(e) = \lambda$, and $m_G(e) = c$,
- $term_G(v) = op(term_G(v_1), \ldots, term_G(v_n))$ if there is $e \in E_G$ with $s_G(e) = v$, $t_G(e) = v_1 \ldots v_n$, and $m_G(e) = op$.

[4] $SIG = (S, OP)$ is said to be finite if both S and OP are finite sets.

Moreover, $l_G(v)$ is the sort of $term_G(v)$.

Remarks

1. By jungle properties, the construction yields a *unique* term: The outdegree property (the outdegree of each node in a jungle is at most one) as well as the cycle-freeness property (each jungle is acyclic) are essential.

2. By Theorem 3.1 each node of a jungle refers to a term which may contain variables. In particular, each node without outgoing hyperedges represents a variable. Thus, these nodes are called variable nodes. □

3.2 Example

Considering the jungle given in Figure 2.1, the nodes v_1 and v_2 both represent the term
$BIN(BIN(EMPTY, GEN(x)), BIN(EMPTY, GEN(x)))$. □

According to Theorem 3.1 , each jungle represents a collection of terms; each node of a jungle represents *one* term. Vice versa, we want to represent terms by jungles. For this purpose we consider special jungles, called *variable-collapsed trees* and *fully collapsed trees.* These jungles possess exactly one node without incoming hyperedges which is called *root.* It turns out that each term can be represented by a variable-collapsed tree and by a fully collapsed tree the root of which represents the term.

3.3 Definition (Variable–Collapsed Tree)

A jungle T is called a *variable-collapsed tree* if there is exactly one node in T, denoted by $root_T$, with $indegree_T(root_T) = 0$ and $indegree_T(v) = 1$ for each $v \in V_T - (VAR_T \cup \{root_T\})$.

Remark

In variable–collapsed trees, non-variable nodes are required to satisfy a restrictive indegree condition (like the indegree condition for trees) while variable nodes are not required to satisfy this condition. In this sense, a variable–collapsed tree may be seen as a tree in which some of the leaves are collapsed. This is depicted as follows:

□

3.4 Theorem (Representation of Terms)

For each term t, there is a (up to isomorphism) unique variable–collapsed tree T satisfying
$term_T(root_T) = t$.

Sketch of Proof

Given a term t with n operation symbols, a variable–collapsed tree T satisfying $term_T(root_T) = t$ may be constructed according to the following rules:

(1) For each variable of sort s, a variable node with label s is generated. Let $jungle_0(t)$ be the obtained jungle. Then it represents the set of all variables of t.

(2) Suppose $jungle_k(t)$ is already constructed representing the set of all variables as well as the multi-set of all occurrences of subterms with at most k (but at least one) operation symbols. If $k = n$, choose T as $jungle_k(t)$. Otherwise we construct a jungle, denoted by $jungle_{k+1}(t)$, which represents the set of all variables and the multi-set of all subterms with at most $k+1$ (but at least one) operation symbols. This may be done as follows: Let t_0 be a subterm of t with $k+1$ operation symbols. Then t_0 is of the form

$op(t_1, \ldots, t_n)$ where $t_1, \ldots, t_n$ possess at most k operation symbols. Since $t_1, \ldots, t_n$ are subterms of t, there are nodes $v_1, \ldots, v_n$ in $jungle_k(t)$ representing $t_1, \ldots, t_n$, respectively. Suitable application of the jungle generating rule $< op : s_1 \ldots s_n \rightarrow s >$ to $jungle_k(t)$ yields a jungle with a node v representing the term $t_0 = op(t_1, \ldots, t_n)$.

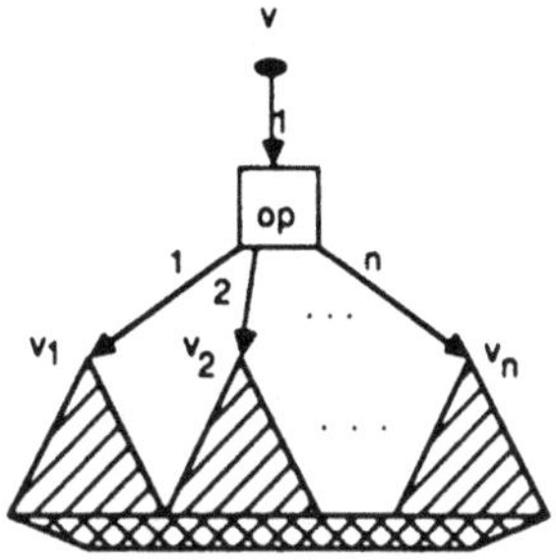

Analogously, all (occurrences of) subterms with $k + 1$ operation symbols may be handled.

Notation
The variable–collapsed tree T corresponding to t is denoted by $jungle(t)$. □

3.5 Definition (Fully Collapsed Jungle and Fully Collapsed Tree)

1. A jungle T is said to be *fully collapsed* if for all $v, v' \in V_T$, $term_T(v) = term_T(v')$ implies $v = v'$.
2. A fully collapsed jungle T is called a *fully collapsed tree* if there is exactly one node in T, denoted by $root_T$, with $indegree_T(root_T) = 0$. □

3.6 Theorem (Representation of Terms)
For each term t there is a (up to isomorphism) unique fully collapsed tree T with $term_T(root_T) = t$.

Sketch of Proof
Let $SUB(t)$ be the set of all subterms of t. Choose $V_T = SUB(t)$ and $E_T = SUB(t) - VAR(t)$.[5] For each $e = op(t_1, \ldots, t_n) \in E_T$ define $s_T(e) = e$, $t_T(e) = t_1 \ldots t_n$, and $m_T(e) = op$. Further let l_T map each subterm of t to its sort. Then $T = (V_T, E_T, s_T, t_T, l_T, m_T)$ is a fully collapsed tree with $root_T = t$ and $term_T(root_T) = t$. Moreover, for any fully collapsed tree T' with $term_{T'}(root_{T'}) = t$ an isomorphism $g : T' \rightarrow T$ is defined for all $v \in V_{T'}$ and all $e \in E_{T'}$ by $g_V(v) = term_{T'}(v)$ and $g_E(e) = term_{T'}(s_{T'}(e))$.

Notation
The fully collapsed tree T corresponding to t is denoted by $JUNGLE(t)$. □

Beside the variable–collapsed tree $jungle(t)$ and the fully collapsed tree $JUNGLE(t)$ there are several other jungles (with one root) which represent the term t. These may be obtained from $jungle(t)$ by "folding" and from $JUNGLE(t)$ by "unfolding". Among all jungles representing t, $JUNGLE(t)$ is the most efficient representation of t: equal subterms are represented only once. Jungles may be folded by the application of rules called *folding* rules. These rules make use of auxiliary operation symbols indicating the equality of terms.

3.7 Definition (Folding and Unfolding Rules)
Let $SIG = (S, OP)$ be extended to the signature $SIG' = (S, OP')$ where OP' contains OP and an operation symbol $id_s : s \rightarrow s$ for each sort $s \in S$.

1. The set *FOLD* of *folding rules* consists of the following rules:

[5] $VAR(t)$ denotes the set of all variables in t.

(Constant Identification)

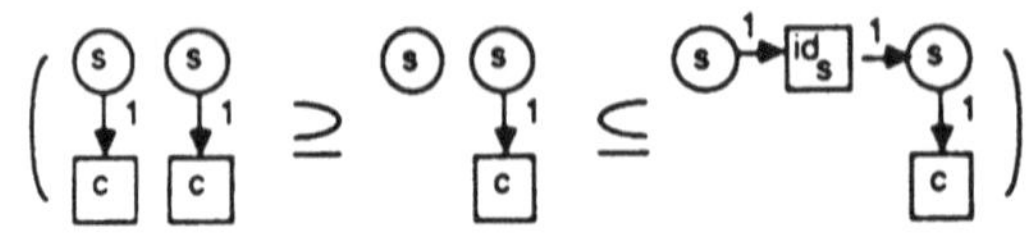

for each constant symbol $c : \rightarrow s$,

(Operation Identification)

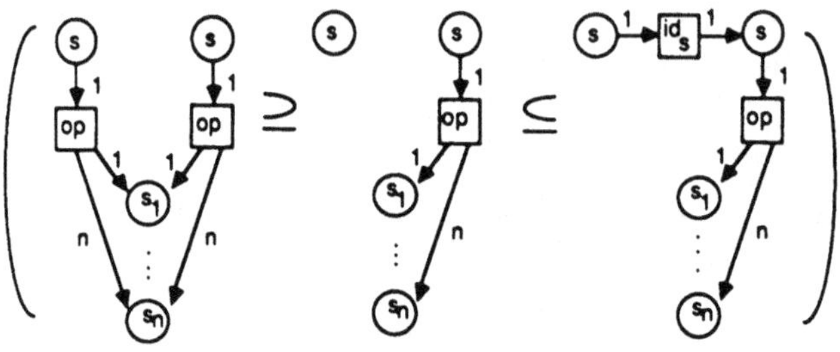

for each operation symbol $op : s_1 \ldots s_n \rightarrow s$,

(Id–Bridging)

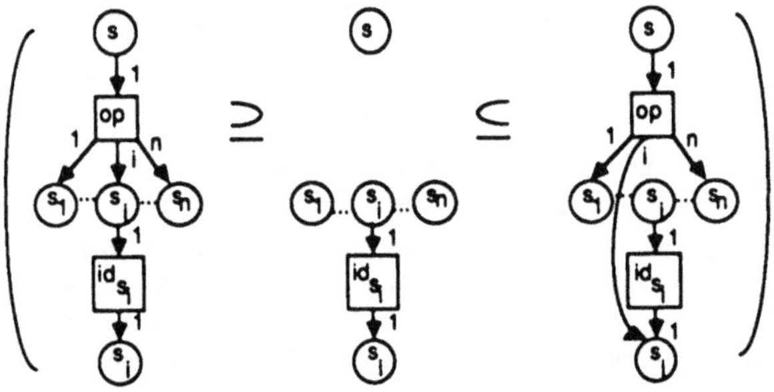

for each operation symbol $op : s_1 \ldots s_n \rightarrow s$ and each $i \in \{1, \ldots, n\}$,

(Id–Elimination)

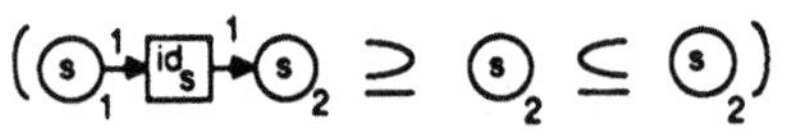

for each sort $s \in S$.

2. The set *UNFOLD* of *unfolding rules* consists of the inverse rules of *FOLD*.

Remark
Folding rules as well as unfolding rules are jungle rules in the sense of Definition 4.2. By the Jungle Preservation Theorem given in 4.3, the application of these rules to jungles yields jungles again. □

3.8 Theorem (Jungle Variation)
Let $\mathcal{J}_{SIG}$ denote the set of all jungles with one root over the signature *SIG*. Let t be a term over *SIG* and $\mathcal{J}(t)$ be the set of all jungles in $\mathcal{J}_{SIG}$ representing t. Then

$$\begin{aligned} \mathcal{J}(t) &= \{J \in \mathcal{J}_{SIG} \mid jungle(t) \underset{FOLD}{\overset{\bullet}{\Longrightarrow}} J\} \\ &= \{J \in \mathcal{J}_{SIG} \mid J \underset{FOLD}{\overset{\bullet}{\Longrightarrow}} JUNGLE(t)\} \\ &= \{J \in \mathcal{J}_{SIG} \mid JUNGLE(t) \underset{UNFOLD}{\overset{\bullet}{\Longrightarrow}} J\}. \end{aligned}$$

Sketch of Proof
Let $|G|$ denote the number of nodes and edges in a jungle G. Then we have $|jungle(t)| \geq |J| \geq |JUNGLE(t)|$ for each $J \in \mathcal{J}(t)$. Moreover, $jungle(t)$ and $JUNGLE(t)$ are uniquely determined, i.e., for all J_{max} and all J_{min} in $\mathcal{J}(t)$, $|J_{max}| = |jungle(t)|$ and $|J_{min}| = |JUNGLE(t)|$ implies $J_{max} \cong jungle(t)$ and $J_{min} \cong JUNGLE(t)$. Now, given $J \in \mathcal{J}(t)$ with $|jungle(t)| > |J|$ one can show that there is $J' \in \mathcal{J}(t)$ such that $|J'| > |J|$ and $J' \underset{FOLD}{\overset{*}{\Longrightarrow}} J$. This proves that each jungle in $\mathcal{J}(t)$ can be obtained from $jungle(t)$ by folding. Furthermore, for each $J \in \mathcal{J}(t)$ with $|J| > |JUNGLE(t)|$ there is $J' \in \mathcal{J}(t)$ such that $|J| > |J'|$ and $J \underset{FOLD}{\overset{*}{\Longrightarrow}} J'$. So each jungle in $\mathcal{J}(t)$ can be reduced to $JUNGLE(t)$ by folding. The rest follows from the fact that the *UNFOLD* rules are the inverses of the *FOLD* rules. □

4 Jungle Preservation

From an implementation point of view, a jungle can be regarded as a record structure (where a hyperedge corresponds to a list of pointers). Therefore, beside function evaluation, tasks like garbage collection or handling of indirect pointers should be implementable by transformations on jungles. To provide rule–based descriptions of such transformations it is desirable to have a wide spectrum of jungle manipulating rules. However, in 4.1 it is shown that the class of all jungles is not closed under applications of arbitrary hypergraph rules the components of which are jungles. In Definition 4.2 we require two weak conditions for such rules to be *jungle rules*. Theorem 4.3 states that derivations through jungle rules preserve jungles.

4.1 Preliminary Considerations
Consider the hypergraph rules

$r_1 =$ 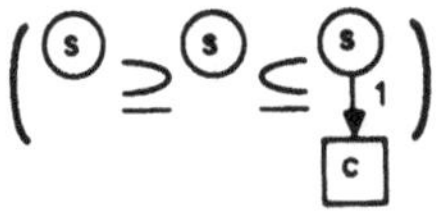 and $r_2 =$ 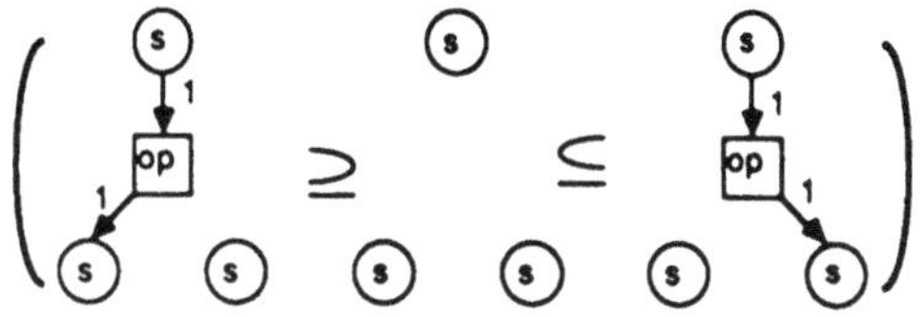

the components of which are jungles. Unfortunately, we cannot be sure that the application of these rules to a jungle yields a jungle again. Application of rule r_1 to the jungle given in Figure 4.1(1) yields a hypergraph in which the outdegree condition required for jungles is violated. Application of rule r_2 to the jungle in Figure 4.1(2) yields a hypergraph in which the cycle–freeness condition is violated.

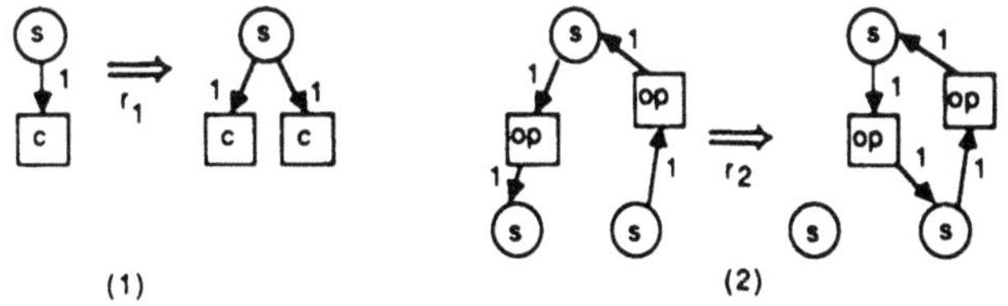

Figure 4.1: Derivations from Jungles to Hypergraphs which are not Jungles

What are the reasons?

(1) Rule r_1 appends a hyperedge to a variable node. Applying this rule to a node with an outgoing hyperedge, the outdegree condition is violated. Hence we have to forbid this kind of rule.

(2) The right–hand side of rule r_2 contains a path[6] from a gluing node v to a gluing node x without outgoing hyperedges while the left–hand side does not possess a path between these nodes. By applying

[6] Let v_1, v_2 be two nodes in a hypergraph G. Then there is a *path* from v_1 to v_2 in G if there is a path from v_1 to v_2 in the underlying bipartite graph $U(G)$.

the rule to a jungle containing a path from the image of x to the image of v, one gets a cycle. Requiring that whenever there is a path from a gluing node v to a gluing node x without outgoing hyperedges in the right-hand side there must be a path from v to x already in the left-hand side, the application of the rule cannot generate a cycle in the given jungle. □

4.2 Definition (Jungle Rule)
A rule $r = (L \supseteq K \subseteq R)$ with jungles L, K, and R is called a *jungle rule* if the following conditions are satisfied:

1. For each $x \in V_K$, $x \in VAR_L$ implies $x \in VAR_R$.
2. For each $v \in V_K$ and each $x \in V_K \cap VAR_L$, $v >_R x$ implies $v >_L x$.[7]

Examples and Remarks

1. All jungle generating rules shown in 2.4 and their inverse rules are jungle rules in the sense of Definition 4.2.
2. The folding and unfolding rules given in 3.7 are jungle rules.
3. The following rule is a jungle rule:

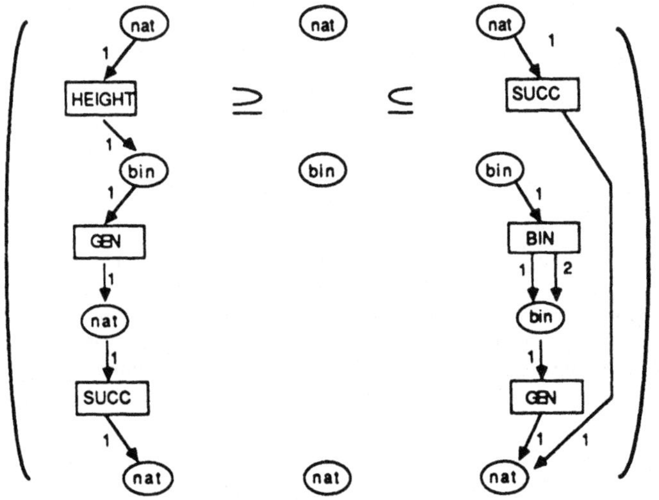

Figure 4.2: A Jungle Rule

4. Further jungle rules are shown in 5.4.
5. Note that the above definition is not symmetric, i.e., in general the inverse rule of a jungle rule is not a jungle rule.
6. The conditions of Definition 4.2 are necessary for jungle preservation in the following sense:
Let $r = (L \supseteq K \subseteq R)$ be a rule with jungles L, K, and R such that 4.2.1 or 4.2.2 is not satisfied. Then one can construct a jungle L' by adding one hyperedge to L (and extending *SIG* by one operation if necessary) such that $L' \underset{r}{\Rightarrow} R'$, where R' is not a jungle. □

[7] The relation $>_G$ on the nodes of a hypergraph G is defined for all $v_1, v_2 \in V_G$ by: $v_1 >_G v_2$ if and only if there is a non-empty path from v_1 to v_2. We write $v_1 \geq_G v_2$ if $v_1 >_G v_2$ or $v_1 = v_2$.

4.3 Jungle Preservation Theorem
Applying a jungle rule to a jungle yields a jungle.

Proof
Let G be a jungle, $r = (L \supseteq K \subseteq R)$ be a jungle rule, and $G \Rightarrow H$ be a direct derivation, given by the diagram

$$\begin{array}{ccccc} L & \supseteq & K & \subseteq & R \\ {\scriptstyle g}\downarrow & & {\scriptstyle d}\downarrow & & {\scriptstyle h}\downarrow \\ G & \supseteq & REM & \subseteq & GLUE \cong H \end{array}$$

It is sufficient to show that $GLUE$ is a jungle. Since REM and R are jungles, $GLUE$ satisfies condition 2.2.3 by construction. To show that the outdegree of each node in $GLUE$ is at most one, let $e_1, e_2 \in E_{GLUE}$ and $v \in V_{GLUE}$ such that $s_{GLUE}(e_1) = v = s_{GLUE}(e_2)$. For $v \in V_{REM} - V_{d(K)}$ we have $e_1, e_2 \in E_{REM}$, so $outdegree_{REM}(v) \leq 1$ implies $e_1 = e_2$. Analogously $v \in V_R - V_K$ implies $e_1, e_2 \in E_R$ and consequently $e_1 = e_2$ since $outdegree_R(v) \leq 1$. Assume therefore $v \in V_{d(K)}$.

Case 1: $e_1, e_2 \in E_R - E_K$. Let $v_1 = s_R(e_1)$ and $v_2 = s_R(e_2)$. Then $h_V(v_1) = v = h_V(v_2)$ so $v_1, v_2 \in V_K$. Since $v_1, v_2 \notin VAR_R$ there are $\overline{e_1}, \overline{e_2} \in E_L$ with $s_L(\overline{e_1}) = v_1$ and $s_L(\overline{e_2}) = v_2$, according to the definition of jungle rule. Further $\overline{e_1}$ and $\overline{e_2}$ must belong to $E_L - E_K$ as otherwise the outdegree of v_1 and v_2 in R would be greater than one. Now $s_G(g_E(\overline{e_1})) = g_V(v_1) = h_V(v_1) = v = h_V(v_2) = g_V(v_2) = s_G(g_E(\overline{e_2}))$ together with $outdegree_G(v) \leq 1$ implies $g_E(\overline{e_1}) = g_E(\overline{e_2})$. With the identification condition we conclude $\overline{e_1} = \overline{e_2}$. Hence $v_1 = v_2$ and, because $outdegree_R(v_1) \leq 1, e_1 = e_2$.

Case 2: $e_1 \in E_R - E_K$, $e_2 \in E_{REM}$. Analogously to the first case one shows that there is $\overline{e_1} \in E_L - E_K$ with $s_G(g_E(\overline{e_1})) = v$. But then $g_E(\overline{e_1}) \in E_{g(L)} - E_{g(K)}$ and $s_G(e_2) = v$ imply $outdegree_G(v) \geq 2$, contradicting the precondition that G is a jungle.

Case 3: $e_1, e_2 \in E_{REM}$. Then $s_{REM}(e_1) = s_{REM}(e_2)$ implies $e_1 = e_2$ since REM is a jungle.

Thus we have $outdegree_{GLUE}(v) \leq 1$ for all $v \in V_{GLUE}$.

It remains to show that $GLUE$ is acyclic. Suppose that $e_1, \ldots, e_n$ is a cycle in $GLUE$. Then some of these edges belong to $E_R - E_K$ since REM is acyclic. Further, because R is acyclic, at least one edge in the cycle has its source node in $V_{d(K)}$. Let a be an edge in $\{e_1, \ldots, e_n\} \cap (E_R - E_K)$. Since $outdegree_{GLUE}(s_{GLUE}(e_i)) = 1$ for $i = 1, \ldots, n$, a belongs to a path $a_1, \ldots, a_k$ in R from some $v \in V_K$ to some $x \in V_K \cap VAR_R$ such that $h_E(a_1), \ldots, h_E(a_k)$ is a subpath of $e_1, \ldots, e_n$. Therefore one can find pairs of nodes $(v_1, x_1), \ldots, (v_m, x_m)$ such that

(i) $v_i \in V_K$, $x_i \in VAR_R \cap V_K$, and $v_i >_R x_i$ for $i = 1, \ldots, m$,
(ii) $h_V(x_i) \geq_{REM} h_V(v_{i+1})$ for $i = 1, \ldots, m-1$ and $h_V(x_m) \geq_{REM} h_V(v_1)$.

We want to show $x_i \in VAR_L$ for $i = 1, \ldots, m$. Consider some $x \in \{x_1, \ldots, x_m\}$. $x \in VAR_R$ implies $outdegree_K(x) = 0$. Suppose that there is $e \in E_L - E_K$ with $s_L(e) = x$. By (i) and (ii) there is an edge in $GLUE$ with source $h_V(x)$. This edge cannot belong to REM as otherwise $s_G(g_E(e)) = g_V(x) = h_V(x)$ would imply $outdegree_G(g_V(x)) \geq 2$. Hence there is $e' \in E_R - E_K$ with $h_V(s_R(e')) = h_V(x)$. The definition of jungle rule implies that there is $\overline{e} \in E_L - E_K$ with $s_L(\overline{e}) = s_R(e')$. Consequently we have $s_G(g_E(e)) = h_V(x) = h_V(s_R(e')) = h_V(s_L(\overline{e})) = g_V(s_L(\overline{e})) = s_G(g_E(\overline{e}))$. Furthermore, e and $\overline{e}$ are different edges since $x \in VAR_R$ implies $s_L(e) = x \neq s_R(e') = s_L(\overline{e})$. With the identification condition we conclude $g_E(e) \neq g_E(\overline{e})$. Hence $outdegree_G(s_G(g_E(e))) \geq 2$, contradicting the assumption that G is a jungle.

Thus $x_1, \ldots, x_m \in VAR_L$ and we can rewrite (i) and (ii) to

(i') $v_i \in V_K$, $x_i \in VAR_L \cap V_K$, and $v_i >_R x_i$ for $i = 1, \ldots, m$,
(ii') $g_V(x_i) \geq_G g_V(v_{i+1})$ for $i = 1, \ldots, m-1$ and $g_V(x_m) \geq_G g_V(v_1)$.

Since r is a jungle rule, (i') implies $v_i >_L x_i$ for $i = 1, \ldots, m$. But then

$$g_V(v_1) >_G g_V(x_1) \geq_G g_V(v_2) >_G \cdots \geq_G g_V(v_m) >_G g_V(x_m) \geq_G g_V(v_1)$$

which contradicts the fact that G is acyclic.

□

5 Relating Term Rewriting and Jungle Evaluation

Jungle rules as introduced in the last section are general means for deriving jungles from jungles. In this section we define *evaluation rules* as special jungle rules which perform term rewriting on the terms of a given jungle. In general, the application of an evaluation rule to a jungle corresponds to a set of sequences of rewrite steps, performed on certain terms in that jungle.

We assume familiarity with the notion of term rewriting as defined, for example, by Huet and Oppen [HO 80] or Klop [Kl 87].

5.1 General Assumption
Let TR be a term rewriting system in which each rewrite rule $l \rightarrow r$ consists of two terms l, r of equal sort such that l is not a variable and the variables in r occur already in l. Moreover, we assume that r is not a variable.

Notation
The rewrite relation associated with TR is denoted by $\rightarrow$. We write $\xrightarrow{*}$ and $\xrightarrow{n}$ for the reflexive transitive closure and the n-fold composition of $\rightarrow$, respectively. □

5.2 Preliminary Considerations
Given a rewrite rule $l \rightarrow r$, we are searching for jungle rules corresponding to the rewrite rule. For handling this problem, one may argue as follows.

(1) Choose $jungle(l)$ as the left-hand side of the rule. $jungle(l)$ (more precisely, the root of $jungle(l)$) represents the term l. Moreover, among all l-representing jungles with one root, $jungle(l)$ is "largest", i.e., for each jungle J with one root representing l there is a surjective hypergraph morphism $fold : jungle(l) \rightarrow J$. Whenever J has an occurrence in a jungle G, $jungle(l)$ has an occurrence, too. The converse is not true. Thus, $jungle(l)$ is the most attractive candidate.

(2) Choose $JUNGLE(r)$ as the right-hand side of the rule. $JUNGLE(r)$ (more precisely, the root of $JUNGLE(r)$) represents the term r. Moreover, among all r-representing jungles (with one root) $JUNGLE(r)$ is the most efficient representation.

(3) Finally, we have to choose a gluing jungle. For this we may choose the root of $jungle(l)$ which corresponds to the root of $JUNGLE(r)$ as well as the variable nodes of $JUNGLE(r)$. (Note that by Assumption 5.1 $VAR(r) \subseteq VAR(l)$ and hence the variable nodes of $JUNGLE(r)$ are contained in $jungle(l)$).

In this way, one gets a rule corresponding to the given rewrite rule which - unfortunately - does not yet work well. Where is the problem?

Let $l \rightarrow r$ be a rewrite rule and t be a term. Let $p = (L \supseteq K \subseteq R)$ be the corresponding rule constructed according to (1) - (3) and T be an arbitrary jungle representing t. Since in jungles the indegree of a node is not bounded by 1, $l \rightarrow r$ may be applicable to t while the corresponding rule p is not applicable to T (because the contact condition may not hold).

To avoid this problem as far as possible we proceed as follows: We choose L as described in (1). In contrast to (2) and (3) we do not delete the jungle L (up to the root and some variable nodes), but preserve $L - \{e\}$ where e denotes the hyperedge outcoming from the root of L. Thus, in the new rule all nodes of L remain preserved by an application of the rule. □

5.3 Definition (Evaluation Rule and Evaluation Step)
1. Let $l \rightarrow r$ be a rewrite rule in TR. A jungle rule $p = (L \supseteq K \subseteq R)$ is called an *evaluation rule for* $l \rightarrow r$ if the following conditions are satisfied:

1. L is the variable-collapsed tree $jungle(l)$,
2. $K = L - \{e\}$ [8] where e denotes the hyperedge outgoing from $root_L$,

[8] For a hypergraph L and a hyperedge $e \in E_L$, $L - \{e\}$ denotes the subhypergraph X with $V_X = V_L$ and $E_X = E_L - \{e\}$.

3. R is a jungle containing K such that $term_R(root_L) = r$.

$l \rightarrow r$ is said to be the *underlying rewrite rule* of p.

2. A direct derivation $G \Rightarrow H$ through an evaluation rule is called an *evaluation step* provided that G (and thus H) is a jungle. □

5.4 Remarks, Illustrations, and Examples

1. There is a (non-empty) set of evaluation rules for each rewrite rule $l \rightarrow r$:
By assumption, l possesses at least one operation symbol. Thus, there is a unique hyperedge e in $L = jungle(l)$ outgoing from the root and corresponding to the leftmost operation symbol in l. Only this hyperedge does not occur in the gluing jungle $K = jungle(l) - \{e\}$. The requirement for the right-hand side R is more liberal then that for L and K. There are several (non-isomorphic) jungles which may be chosen as right-hand side of the rule. For instance, $JUNGLE(r)$ combined with the gluing jungle K is a candidate. The obtained rule may be depicted as follows.

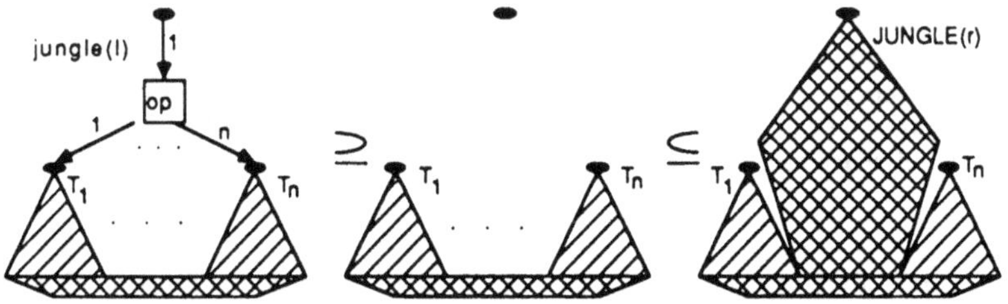

The rule ($L \supseteq K \subseteq R$) turns out to be a jungle rule in the sense of Definition 4.2 because (1) $VAR_L = VAR_R$ and (2) $root_L >_L x$ for all $x \in VAR_L$ and, for all $v \in V_K - \{root_L\}$ and all $x \in VAR_L$, $v >_R x$ if and only if $v >_L x$.

2. Consider the rewrite rules of the **generate** specification (given in the introduction):
$GEN(0) \rightarrow BIN(EMPTY, EMPTY)$ and $GEN(SUCC(N)) \rightarrow BIN(GEN(N), GEN(N))$. Corresponding evaluation rules are shown in Figure 5.1.

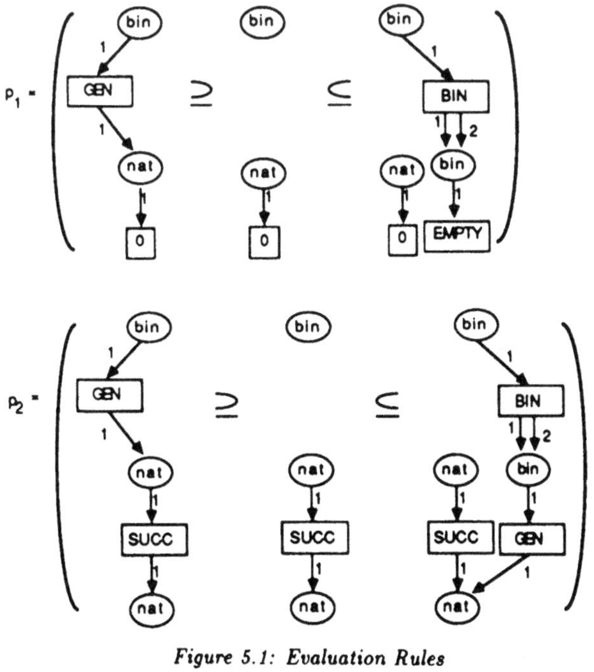

Figure 5.1: Evaluation Rules

3. Evaluation rules as defined in 5.3 do not remove nodes. Thus, for each evaluation step $G \Rightarrow H$, the nodes of G are contained in H up to renaming. For notational convenience we will ignore the renaming and assume that $V_G \subseteq V_H$. □

In order to check the applicability of an evaluation rule to a given jungle one just has to find an occurrence of the left-hand side in that jungle.

5.5 Lemma (Applicability of Evaluation Rules)
Let $p = (L \supseteq K \subseteq R)$ be an evaluation rule and let G be a jungle. Then p is applicable to G (i.e., there is an evaluation step $G \underset{p}{\Rightarrow} H$) if and only if there is a hypergraph morphism $g : L \to G$.

Proof
By the definition of direct derivation, $G \underset{p}{\Rightarrow} H$ implies that there is a hypergraph morphism from L to G. Conversely, let $g : L \to G$ be a hypergraph morphism. The contact condition is satisfied since $V_K = V_L$. To show that g satisfies also the identification condition, let e be the unique hyperedge with $s_L(e) = root_L$ and let e' be any hyperedge in L different from e. Then $s_L(e) >_L s_L(e')$ by the structure of L so $g_V(s_L(e)) >_G g_V(s_L(e'))$. Hence $g_V(s_L(e)) \neq g_V(s_L(e'))$ according to the acyclicity of G. Consequently we have $g_E(e) \neq g_E(e')$, i.e., g satisfies the identification condition because each two other items belong to the gluing part and hence may be identified. Thus there is a direct derivation $G \underset{p}{\Rightarrow} H$ based on g. □

Remark
By Lemma 5.5, an evaluation rule $(L \supseteq K \subseteq R)$ is applicable to a jungle G whenever L has an occurrence in G. Nevertheless, the problem mentioned in 5.2 is not solved completely. Let us explain this in more detail. A nice result would be the following:

Let $l \to r$ be an arbitrary rewrite rule and t be a term. Moreover, let p be an evaluation rule for $l \to r$ and T be a jungle representing t. Then p is applicable to T provided that $l \to r$ is applicable to t.

Unfortunately, in the case that l is a term in which a variable occurs several times this is not true for all jungles T representing t. Consider, for example, the rewrite rule $f(x,x) \to g(x)$ which is applicable to $f(c,c)$. Then the evaluation rule

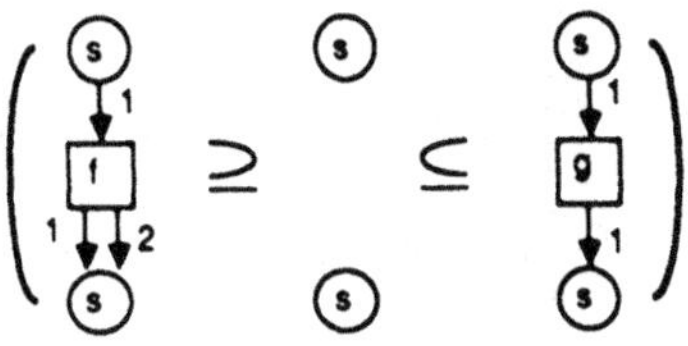

is not applicable to

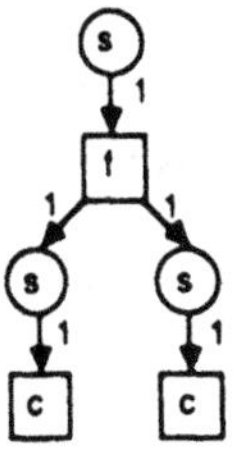

On the other hand, it is applicable to the fully collapsed jungle $JUNGLE(f(c,c))$. What is to be done?

(1) If all rewrite rules are *left-linear*, i.e., in the left-hand side of the rule each variable occurs only once, the problem does not occur. But left-linear term rewriting systems seem to be too restrictive.

(2) If the considered jungles are "folded" (i.e. suitably collapsed) the problem does not occur. Thus, our proposal for handling the problem is to use the folding rules introduced in Section 3 to compress jungles (if necessary) before applying evaluation rules. □

5.6 Example
The evaluation rule p_2 given in Figure 5.1 can be applied to the jungle G yielding the jungle H given in

Figure 5.2.

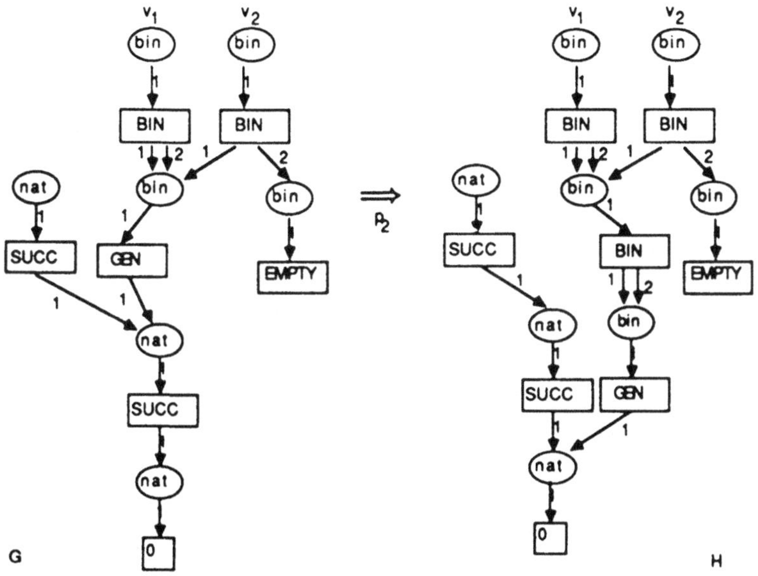

Figure 5.2: Application of an Evaluation Rule

The jungle G represents a collection of terms, for example
$term_G(v_1) = BIN(GEN(SUCC(0)), GEN(SUCC(0)))$ and
$term_G(v_2) = BIN(GEN(SUCC(0)), EMPTY)$.
Concerning these nodes, the evaluation step through the evaluation rule p_2 performs the rewriting steps
$BIN(GEN(SUCC(0)), GEN(SUCC(0))) \xrightarrow{2} BIN(BIN(GEN(0), GEN(0)), BIN(GEN(0), GEN(0)))$ and
$BIN(GEN(SUCC(0)), EMPTY) \xrightarrow{1} BIN(BIN(GEN(0), GEN(0)), EMPTY)$. □

The application of an evaluation rule to a jungle rewrites the term represented by the root of the occurrence of the left-hand side. Simultaneously, the terms of all nodes from which there is a path to this root are rewritten, too. Moreover, the existence of several distinct paths leads to a sequence of rewrite steps.

5.7 Theorem (Evaluation Steps Perform Term Rewriting)
Let $G \Rightarrow H$ be an evaluation step through an evaluation rule $(L \supseteq K \subseteq R)$ with an occurrence $g : L \rightarrow G$. Then for each $v \in V_G$, $term_G(v) \xrightarrow{n} term_H(v)$ where n is the number of paths from v to $g_V(root_L)$.

Sketch of Proof
The occurrence g induces a substitution $\sigma : T_{SIG}(VAR_L) \rightarrow T_{SIG}(VAR_G)$ satisfying $term_G(g_V(v)) = \sigma(term_L(v))$ for each $v \in V_L$. In particular we have $term_G(g_V(root_L)) = \sigma(term_L(root_L)) = \sigma(l)$ for the left-hand side l of the underlying rewrite rule $l \rightarrow r$. By the definition of evaluation rule one gets $term_H(g_V(root_L)) = \sigma(term_R(root_L)) = \sigma(r)$ so $term_G(g_V(root_L)) \rightarrow term_H(g_v(root_L))$. Now let $v \in V_G$ such that there are n paths from v to $g_V(root_L)$ for some $n \geq 1$. Then there are n distinct occurrences of the subterm $\sigma(l)$ in $term_G(v)$ which are simultaneous rewritten to $\sigma(r)$ by the evaluation step, so $term_G(v) \xrightarrow{n} term_H(v)$ holds. Finally we have $term_G(v) \xrightarrow{0} term_H(v)$ for all nodes v in G from which there is no path to $g_V(root_L)$, since these nodes represent in H the same terms as in G. □

The situation described in Theorem 5.7 may be depicted as follows:

$$\begin{array}{ccccc} & G & \underset{EVAL}{\Longrightarrow} & H & \\ \text{REPRESENTS} & \downarrow & & \downarrow & \text{REPRESENTS} \\ & t & \underset{TR}{\overset{*}{\longrightarrow}} & u & \end{array}$$

where $EVAL$ denotes a set of evaluation rules for TR.

In general, one evaluation step corresponds to a set of sequences of rewrite steps as stated in Theorem 5.7. Nevertheless, each single rewrite step can be simulated by an evaluation step if an appropriate jungle is chosen for representing the term to be rewritten.

5.8 Theorem (Simulation of Rewrite Steps)
Let $t \to u$ be a rewrite step. Then there is an evaluation step $G \Rightarrow H$ where G contains a node v_0 satisfying $term_G(v_0) = t$ and $term_H(v_0) = u$.

Proof
Let $l \to r$ and σ be the rewrite rule and the substitution associated with the rewrite step $t \to u$. Let T be the fully collapsed tree with $term_T(root_T) = \sigma(l)$. By a derivation $T \overset{*}{\underset{GEN}{\Longrightarrow}} G$ one can construct a jungle G containing T and a node v_0 such that $term_G(v_0) = t$ and

(*) changing $term_G(root_T)$ from $\sigma(l)$ to $\sigma(r)$ yields $term_G(v_0) = u$.[9]

Now let $p = (L \supseteq K \subseteq R)$ be an evaluation rule for $l \to r$. Then for each $v \in V_L$ there is exactly one $v' \in V_T$ with $term_G(v') = \sigma(term_L(v))$. This correspondence uniquely extends to a hypergraph morphism $g : L \to G$ satisfying $term_G(g_V(v)) = \sigma(term_L(v))$ for each $v \in V_L$. Hence there is an evaluation step $G \underset{p}{\Longrightarrow} H$ based on g, according to Lemma 5.5. Further $g_V(root_L) = root_T$ holds, so $term_H(root_T) = \sigma(r)$ by the definition of evaluation rule. Now (*) implies $term_H(v_0) = u$. □

The situation described in Theorem 5.8 may be depicted as follows.

$$\begin{array}{ccccc} & t & \underset{TR}{\longrightarrow} & u & \\ \text{REPRESENTS} & \uparrow & & \uparrow & \text{REPRESENTS} \\ & G & \underset{EVAL}{\Longrightarrow} & H & \end{array}$$

Moreover, if PRE denotes the set of folding and unfolding rules given in 3.7, one gets that for each rewrite step $t \to u$ and each jungle $\overline{G}$ representing t there are derivations $\overline{G} \overset{*}{\underset{PRE}{\Longrightarrow}} G$ and $G \underset{EVAL}{\Longrightarrow} H$ such that H represents u. In this sense, term rewriting may be simulated by jungle evaluation.

6 Discussion

Based on the fundamental study in [Pl 86], we have introduced jungle evaluation as a certain type of graph rewriting in this paper. As jungles are inductively structured and each one represents a set of terms over a signature in a neat and compact way, the main emphasis has been put on jungle preservation. We have specified a class of graph rewrite rules which yield jungles whenever they are applied to jungles. Moreover, jungle evaluation has been related to algebraic specifications. We have demonstrated how jungle rewriting can simulate term rewriting. There is some evidence that the use of jungles rather than terms may speed up the evaluation process drastically.

This paper presents a first step in the systematic investigation of jungle evaluation. More work will have to be done to realize the potential for this new graph grammar approach to the evaluation of functional expressions. We would like to point out some topics for future investigation.

[9] I.e., there is exactly one path from v_0 to $root_T$ and this path corresponds, when viewing $t \to u$ as a subtree replacement, to the path from the root of t to the node where $\sigma(l)$ is replaced by $\sigma(r)$.

(1) The prospect of efficiency: Although the sizes of terms may be multiplied in each term rewrite step, the sizes of jungles never grow beyond a constant bound in a single rewrite step. Furthermore, a jungle rewrite step can correspond to several term rewrite steps. For which examples and under which conditions do these facts pay off? We strongly believe that jungle evaluation is more efficient than term evaluation. But how can this be stated and proved in a precise way?

(2) The prospect of parallelism: The theory of graph grammars provides some concepts for parallelism and concurrency which apply to jungle rewriting. But how can this knowledge be exploited in a meaningful and advantageous way? Does this kind of parallelism help to speed up the evaluation process once more?

(3) The prospect of a new specification and programming paradigm: So far, jungle evaluation is discussed as a method for optimizing algebraic specifications in certain respects. But why should jungle rewrite rules not be interesting in their own right? There are excellent arguments for algebraic and equational specification and programming based on terms and equations. Are there good arguments for a new specification and programming paradigm based on jungles and jungle rewrite rules as well?

7 Appendix: Hypergraphs and Hypergraph Replacements

This appendix summarizes all notions concerning hypergraphs, generalizing the corresponding notions for graphs, and hypergraph replacements which are used in this paper.

7.1 Definition (Hypergraph)
1. Let $C = (C_V, C_E)$ be a pair of sets, called a pair of *label alphabets* for nodes and hyperedges respectively, which will be fixed in the following.

2. A *hypergraph* (over C) is a system $H = (V_H, E_H, s_H, t_H, l_H, m_H)$, where V_H is a finite set of *nodes*, E_H is a finite set of *hyperedges* (or *edges* for short), $s_H : E_H \to V_H^*$ and $t_H : E_H \to V_H^*$ [10] are two mappings assigning a sequence of *sources* $s_H(e)$ and a sequence of *targets* $t_H(e)$ to each $e \in E_H$, and $l_H : V_H \to C_V$ and $m_H : E_H \to C_E$ are two mappings assigning *labels* to nodes and hyperedges.

3. The set of all hypergraphs (over C) is denoted by $\mathcal{H}_C$.

4. Let $H \in \mathcal{H}_C, e \in E_H, s_H(e) = x_1 \dots x_m$ and $t_H(e) = x_{m+1} \dots x_{m+n}$ with $x_i \in V_H$ for $i = 1, \dots, m+n$. Then $NODES_H(e) = \{x_i \in V_H \mid i = 1, \dots, m+n\}$ denotes the set of nodes related by the hyperedge e.

Remarks
1. In drawings of hypergraphs, a circle represents a node and the label is inscribed in the circle; a graphical structure of the form

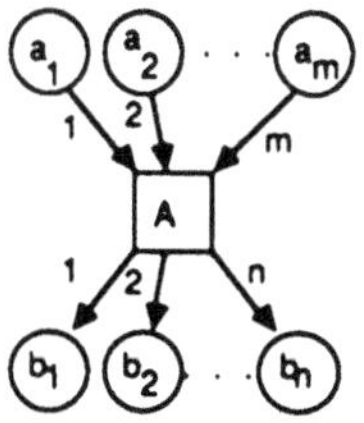

depicts a hyperedge with sources and targets where the label of the hyperedge is inscribed in the box, the i-th arrow incoming into the box starts at the i-th source (i=1,...,m) and the j-th arrow outgoing from the box reaches the j-th target (j=1,...,n). In other words, our graphical representation makes use of the one-to-one correspondence between hypergraphs and bipartite graphs.

2. There is a one-to-one correspondence between hypergraphs and bipartite graphs: On one hand, for each hypergraph H there is an underlying graph $U(H)$, whose nodes are the nodes as well as the hyperedges of H and whose edges are the "tentacles" of the hyperedges of H. On the other hand, each (directed) bipartite graph G may be seen as a hypergraph choosing the one set of nodes as the set of nodes and the other set

[10] Let A be a set. Then A^* denotes the set of finite sequences over A, including the empty sequence λ.

as the set of hyperedges. This close relationship between hypergraphs and bipartite graphs is interesting in several respects: (1) Graph-theoretic notions can be adapted to hypergraphs. (2) Various known results on graph grammars can be applied to hypergraph grammars (see, i.e., [EK 76], [Eh 79], [Kr 87]).

7.2 Definition (Subhypergraph and Hypergraph Morphism)
1. Let $G, H \in \mathcal{H}_C$. Then G is called a *subhypergraph* of H, denoted by $G \subseteq H$, if $V_G \subseteq V_H, E_G \subseteq E_H$ and s_G, t_G, l_G, and m_G are restrictions of the corresponding mappings in H.

2. Let $G, H \in \mathcal{H}_C$ and $V \subseteq V_H$. Then G is said to be the *subhypergraph of H induced by V* if $G \subseteq H$, $V_G = V$, and $E_G = \{e \in E_H \mid NODES_H(e) \subseteq V\}$.

3. Let $G, H \in \mathcal{H}_C$. A *hypergraph morphism* $h : G \to H$ consists of two mappings $h_V : V_G \to V_H$ and $h_E : E_G \to E_H$ such that $s_H(h_E(e)) = h_V^{*}(s_G(e))$, $t_H(h_E(e)) = h_V^{*}(t_G(e))$,[11] $l_H(h_V(v)) = l_G(v)$, and $m_H(h_E(e)) = m_G(e)$ for all $e \in E_G$, $v \in V_G$. h is called *injective* (*surjective, bijective*) if both h_V and h_E are injective (surjective, bijective).

4. A bijective hypergraph morphism $h : G \to H$ is called an *isomorphism*. In this case, G and H are said to be *isomorphic*, denoted by $G \cong H$.

Remark
Each hypergraph morphism $h : G \to H$ determines a subhypergraph of H, denoted by $h(G)$.

7.3 Definition (Hypergraph Rule)
A (*gluing*) *rule* $r = (L \supseteq K \subseteq R)$ consists of three hypergraphs L, R and K with $K \subseteq L$ and $K \subseteq R$. L is called the *left-hand side*, R the *right-hand side*, and K the *gluing hypergraph* of r.

7.4 Definition (Hypergraph Derivation)
1. Let $G, H \in \mathcal{H}_C$ and $r = (L \supseteq K \subseteq R)$ be a rule. Then G *directly derives H through r*, if H is isomorphic to the hypergraph $GLUE$ constructed in the following four steps:

1. *CHOOSE* a hypergraph morphism $g : L \to G$, called the (*left-*)*occurrence map*.

2. *CHECK* the following *gluing condition* (consisting of the *contact condition* and the *identification condition*):

   - For all $v \in V_L$, if $g_V(v) \in NODES_G(e)$ for some $e \in E_G - E_{g(L)}$, then $v \in V_K$.
   - For all $x, y \in L$,[12] if $x \neq y$ but $g(x) = g(y)$, then $x, y \in K$.

3. *REMOVE* the occurrence $g(L)$ of L in G up to $g(K)$ from G yielding the *remainder* $REM = G - (g(L) - g(K))$.[13]

4. *ADD* the right-hand side R up to K to REM yielding the *gluing* $GLUE = REM + (R - K)$ [14] the components of which are defined as follows:

   - $V_{GLUE} = V_{REM} + (V_R - V_K)$ and $E_{GLUE} = E_{REM} + (E_R - E_K)$,
   - each node and each hyperedge keeps its label,
   - each hyperedge of E_{REM} keeps its sources and targets,
   - each hyperedge of $E_R - E_K$ keeps its sources and targets provided that they are in $V_R - V_K$; otherwise sources and targets are handed over to V_{REM}: $s_{GLUE}(e) = h_V^{*}(s_R(e))$ and $t_{GLUE}(e) = h_V^{*}(t_R(e))$ for $e \in E_R - E_K$ where $h_V : V_R \to V_{GLUE}$ is given by $h_V(v) = v$ for $v \in V_R - V_K$ and $h_V(v) = g_V(v)$ for $v \in V_K$.

[11] Let $f : A \to B$ be a mapping. Then $f^{*} : A^{*} \to B^{*}$ denotes the free symbolwise extension of f given by $f^{*}(a_1 \ldots a_k) = f(a_1) \ldots f(a_k)$ for all $k \in \mathcal{N}$ and $a_i \in A (i = 1, \ldots, k)$.

[12] "$x \in L$" is a short denotation for "$x \in V_L$ or $x \in E_L$" and is used whenever nodes and hyperedges do not have to be destinguished. Similarly, "$g(x)$" is short for "$g_V(x)$ or $g_E(x)$".

[13] " $-$ " denotes the difference of sets for nodes and hyperedges separately.

[14] " $+$ " denotes the disjoint union of sets for nodes and hyperedges separately.

Such a *direct derivation* is denoted by $G \Rightarrow H$ *through* r (*based on* g) or $G \underset{r}{\Rightarrow} H$.

2. A sequence of direct derivations of the form $H_0 \underset{r_1}{\Rightarrow} H_1 \underset{r_2}{\Rightarrow} \ldots \underset{r_k}{\Rightarrow} H_k$ constitutes a *derivation from* H_0 *to* H_k *through* $r_1, \ldots, r_k$. Such a derivation may be denoted by $H_0 \overset{*}{\underset{RULES}{\Longrightarrow}} H_k$ if $r_1, \ldots, r_k \in RULES$.

Remarks

1. The occurrence map $g : L \to G$ locates the *occurrence* $g(L)$ *of* L *in* G.
2. The gluing condition ensures that REM is a subhypergraph of G.
3. Let $REM = G - (g(L) - g(K))$. Then, for $x \in K$, $d(x) = g(x)$ defines a hypergraph morphism $d : K \to REM$ locating $g(K)$ in REM.
4. Let H be isomorphic to $GLUE$ and $i : GLUE \to H$ be the corresponding isomorphism. Then $h(x) =$ **if** $x \in R - K$ **then** $i(x)$ **else** $i(d(x))$ defines a hypergraph morphism $h : R \to H$, called the *right-occurrence map*. Respectively, $h(R)$ is called the *occurrence of* R *in* H. Further the restriction of $i : GLUE \to H$ to $REM \subseteq GLUE$ defines a hypergraph morphism.
5. All hypergraph morphisms involved in a direct derivation can be grouped into two squares

$$\begin{array}{ccccc} L & \leftarrow & K & \rightarrow & R \\ {\scriptstyle g}\downarrow & & {\scriptstyle d}\downarrow & & {\scriptstyle h}\downarrow \\ G & \leftarrow & REM & \rightarrow & H \end{array}$$

which are actually gluing diagrams in the sense of [Eh 79], 2.6. The explicit construction of the derived hypergraph given above corresponds to the gluing analysis and the gluing construction in [Eh 79], 3.7 and 3.8.

The definition of a direct derivation is symmetric in the following sense.

7.5 Fact

Let $G \Rightarrow H$ be a direct derivation through $r = (L \supseteq K \subseteq R)$ based on the (left-)occurrence map $g : L \to G$. Let $h : R \to H$ be the corresponding right-occurrence map. Then there is a direct derivation $H \Rightarrow G$ through the *inverse rule* $r^{-1} = (R \supseteq K \subseteq L)$ based on the occurrence map $h : R \to H$.

Acknowledgment

Wolfgang Ditt, Inger Kuhlmann, Anne Wilharm, and the three authors of this paper took part in a weekend seminar on graph grammars held at the second author's private home in Summer 1985. With a lot of fun, the six of us developed the idea of jungle evaluation and outlined the basic notions and expected results. As the authors of this paper, we gratefully acknowledge Anne's, Inger's, and Wolfgang's contribution to the initial seminar.

Moreover, we would like to thank Don Sannella, Michael Löwe, and the anonymous referees for many helpful comments on the draft of this paper.

References

[BEGKPS 87] H.P. Barendregt, M.C.J.D. van Eekelen, J.R.W. Glauert, J.R. Kennaway, M.J. Plasmeijer, M.R. Sleep: *Term Graph Reduction.* University of East-Anglia and University of Nijmegen, Proc. PARLE Conference on Parallel Architectures and Languages, Eindhoven (1987).

[Eh 79] H. Ehrig: *Introduction to the Algebraic Theory of Graph Grammars.* Proc. 1st Graph Grammar Workshop, Lect. Not. Comp. Sci. 73, 1-69 (1979).

[EK 76] H. Ehrig, H.-J. Kreowski: *Parallelism of Manipulations in Multidimensional Information Structures.* Proc. MFCS'76, Lect. Not. Comp. Sci. 45, 284-293 (1976).

[EM 86] H. Ehrig, B. Mahr: *Fundamentals of Algebraic Specifications. Part I: Initial Semantics.* Springer, Monographs in Computer Science, New York-Berlin-Heidelberg (1986).

[ER 76] H. Ehrig, B.K. Rosen: *Commutativity of Independent Transformations on Complex Objects.* Research Report RC 6251. IBM T.J. Watson Research Center, Yorktown Heights (1976).

[HO 80] G. Huet, D.C. Oppen: *Equations and Rewrite Rules, A Survey.* In R.V. Book (ed.): *Formal Language Theory: Perspectives and Open Problems.* Academic Press, 349-405 (1980).

[Kl 87] J.W. Klop: *Term Rewriting Systems. A Tutorial.* EATCS Bulletin 32, 142-182 (1987).

[Kr 87] H.-J. Kreowski: *Is Parallelism Already Concurrency? - Part 1: Derivations in Graph Grammars.* Proc. 3rd Graph Grammar Workshop, Lect. Not. Comp. Sci. 291, 343-360 (1987).

[Pa 82] P. Padawitz: *Graph Grammars and Operational Semantics.* Theor. Comp. Sci. 19, 117-141 (1982).

[Pl 86] D. Plump: *Im Dschungel: Ein neuer Graph-Grammatik-Ansatz zur effizienten Auswertung rekursiv definierter Funktionen.* Diplomarbeit, Studiengang Informatik, Universität Bremen (1986).

[St 80] J. Staples: *Computation on Graph-like Expressions.* Theor. Comp. Sci. 10, 171-185 (1980).

The ACT-System
- Experiences and Future Enhancements -

Horst Hansen

Institute for Software and Theoretical Computer Science
Department of Computer Science
Technical University of Berlin
Franklinstraße 28/29
D-1000 Berlin 10

Abstract

The ACT-system, which comprises an implementation of the algebraic specification language ACT ONE, an Interpreter, a Persistency Checker and a Pretty-Printer, is a specification environment, which is used for the development of specifications for software systems. Here we focus on the environment of the Interpreter, which includes implementations for the concept of object-variables with assignment and the concept of input and output conversion. The former concept is analogous to variables and assignment as known from programming languages while the latter is equivalent to the concept of input- and output-formats of high-level programming languages. It will be shown that this environment greatly enhances the usability of the Interpreter in the ACT-system. Furthermore a new interpretation technique is proposed, which works with arbitrary algebraic specifications. These concepts together allow testing of all algebraic specifications with initial or free functor semantics as well as using them as prototypes of software systems in a convenient way.

1. Introduction

In 1983 the algebraic specification language ACT ONE was introduced in [EFH 83]. Very soon the need arose to have some automated tool (i.e. program) to check the syntax of large specifications. Theoretical work of P. Padawitz [Pad 83] in addition showed that there was even the possibility to check some crucial semantical conditions of specifications (e.g. 'persistency' [TWW 78], [Pad 83], [EM 85]) using algorithms, which check some sufficient syntactical criteria.
The current version of the *ACT-system* (developed 1984/85) comprises the *Language Implementation*, which is a program that computes the *flat specification* from a specification text (see [EFH 83], [EM 85]), an *Interpreter*, a *Persistency Checker* (see [Lan 85a], [Lan 85b]) and a *Pretty-Printer*.

1.1 Example Applications developed using the ACT-system

The ACT-system has been used with great success in our practical course 'algebraic specification of software systems', which is being taught during the winter semester 1987/88 for the 4th time.
Within these courses larger algebraic specifications have been developed, e.g. a specification of the

- the specification language ACT ONE,
- an Interpreter for flat algebraic specifications,

- a relational database,
- the UNIX[1]-Filesystem, and different specifications of
- line- and screen-oriented editors.

Apart from teaching courses ACT ONE has for example been used to specify the transport service of the OSI communication protocol hierarchy (see [HM 85]), a reasonable part of the data types underlying the hardware description language EDIF ([EDIF 87], [BH 87]), and syntax-directed editors for different purposes ([Rie 85], [Sch 86]).
Since 1985 an improved descendent of the language ACT ONE has been integrated into the language LOTOS, a specification language for distributed systems. The latter language has been developed in the ESPRIT project SEDOS. ACT ONE is used for the specification of data types within this language. During the last two years a large number of LOTOS specifications have been designed, which include a lot of specifications of abstract data types from the field of OSI communication protocols (see e.g. [DVB 87]).

1.2 Related Systems

During the the last 7 years a lot of different specification languages came into existence. Some of them have been supplemented with a computer implementation of the language as well as with additional tools. The specific aims of most of these systems are quite different.
Among others there are the AFFIRM-System [Mus 80], the Wide Spectrum Language CIP-L and the CIP-System [CIP 85], the applicative language HOPE [BMS 80], the Structural Recursive Defintion Language SRDL [Kla 82], the REVE Term Rewriting System [Les 83], the LARCH Family of Specification Languages [GH 83], [Win 87], the PLUSS specification language for Structured Specifications [Gau 84] and the ASSPEGIQUE Specification Environment [BCV 85], the RAP-System for rapid prototyping of algebraic specifications [GH 85], [Hus 85], several versions of the specification language OBJ (e.g. OBJ2 [FGJM 85]), ML and its extensions [HMM 86], [San 86], [ST 85], the Specification Language of OBSCURE [LL 87], and the specification environment at Dortmund [Gan 87]. Related work has also been carried out within the ESPRIT projects SEDOS [DVB 87], METEOR, PROSPECTRA and PEACOCK.

1.3 Interpretation in the software development process

In this paper we will discuss the Interpreter and its environment in more detail. Interpreters for algebraic specifications are mainly useful for two purposes :

1. for <u>testing</u> of specifications
2. for <u>prototyping</u> of software systems .

Both aims are closely related : it is different people who are interested in the first resp. second aim. A system analyst, who is capable of writing down the requirements for a software system (or parts of it) in a formal specification language, is interested in developing from this ***requirements specification*** an ***executable specification***, which satisfies the requirements. Executability allows him to test the specification, i.e. compare the effect of specified operations against mental expectations of what the operations should do.[2]
When talking of prototyping of software systems, another group of people is involved: the customer of a

---

[1] UNIX is a trademark of AT&T Technologies, Inc.

[2] In our algebraic approach we would prefer to have explicated such expectations in the definition of a many-sorted algebra, or a class of such algebras. This would open the chance for a *correctness proof* of the specification against the algebra (or class of algebras), and this of course would render testing superfluous.

software house or (preferably) future users of the system. The customer resp. users have some expectations of what certain high level operations of the system should do. Using a prototype, which is already given by the executable specification of the system, they can compare their expectations against the functional results presented by the prototype. This of course enables the customer resp. users to clarify their requirements at an early development stage.

There are several problems related with the procedure outlined above. We will dig into two of them only :

1. There are many design specifications that cannot be executed by usual Interpreters.
2. It is inconvenient for a system analyst (and much more so for a customer or user of a software system) to test complex operations on large argument terms by inputting these terms and viewing the result as another large term.[3]

In 4.2 we will outline a solution to the first problem listed, and in section 3 we will tackle the second problem.

1.4 The Interpretation Environment

We think, the user interface of the Interpreter must be enhanced in some way to

- reduce the size of input terms, which are to be tested,
- allow more convenient representations as input than terms alone,
- allow a representation of output (results) of the interpretation procedure in easily readable and comprehensible formats, which are adequate to the needs of system analysts, customers or users respectively.

To solve this problem we propose two concepts :

- *object-variables* and assignment allow to give names to terms. These names may later be used as arguments in input terms.
- integration of *input* and *output conversion* procedures enable the system analyst to design application oriented input and output formats. This is a generalization of built-in representations for standard data types as found in other specification languages.

1.5 Acknowledgment

I would like to thank especially my colleagues Michael Löwe, Harmut Ehrig and Werner Fey, who took the patience to discuss some of the topics of this paper in great detail. Without my colleague Paul Boehm, who managed the implementation, there would not exist an ACT-system!

[3] Consider e.g. the addition of the natural numbers 100 and 50 in a specification using a unary representation: then the result would be a term with 150 operation symbols SUCC in it. Whoever would notice, if the result had only 149 such operation symbols?

2. The ACT-System

Since 1985 there exists an implementation of the algebraic specification language ACT ONE ([EFH 83], [EM 85]) at our institute in the department of computer science of the Technical University Berlin. The language implementation comprises a *Parser* and a program called *Flattener*. The specification environment, the *ACT-system*, furthermore consists of the following tools: an *Interpreter*, a *Persistency Checker*, and a *Pretty-Printer*.[4]

2.1 Structure of the ACT-System

Figure 1 shows the overall structure of the current implementation of the ACT-system. The main components, which are specific to the system are encircled boldly. Rounded boxes represent programs and rectangular boxes represent texts which either reside in files or are part of input/output in the interactive environment of the system.

The *Language Implementation* consists of two parts: a *Parser* for the underlying context free language, and a program, called *Flattener*, that checks the context conditions (static semantics) of the language and computes from an ACT TEXT all resulting flat specifications.[5]
The Parser reads a file which contains an ACT TEXT, i.e. a sequence of type definitions. These types may depend on other types which are defined in a library, which is another ACT TEXT. Types defined therein again may depend on other types in other libraries. Circular dependencies are not allowed. The Parser checks whether or not the input conforms to the context free syntax of the specification language ACT ONE and produces an internal representation of all read ACT TEXTs, as well as error marks and error messages if necessary.
The Flattener[6] uses the internal representation as established by the Parser, checks the context-conditions of the language ACT ONE (see [EM 85]) and computes the flat specification for each type definition in the ACT TEXTs. If necessary, error marks and messages are produced.
The Report generator writes a listing of all specifications including the error messages of both the Parser and the Flattener.
The Pretty-Printer and the Prolog generator work only on error free ACT TEXTs. The Pretty-Printer produces from the internal representation an ACT TEXT with standardized indentation. The Prolog generator extracts from the internal representation the flat specification of the topmost type definition and encodes this specification in form of Prolog facts, which then can be used as input to the Interpreter as well as the Persistency Checker.
The *Persistency Checker* reads a flat specification encoded as Prolog facts and then decides (possibly guided by some user input), whether the parameterized specification is persistent[7] or not (for more details see [Pad 83], [Pad 85], [EM 85], [Lan 85a], [Lan 85b]).

---

[4] The Parser, the Flattener, and the Pretty-Printer are implemented in Pascal, while the Interpreter and the Persistency Checker are written in PROLOG. The current version of the ACT-system, which runs on an IBM-mainframe computer in our department, was implemented during 1984-86 by P. Boehm, J. Buntrock, K.-P. Hasler, A. Langen, F. Nürnberg, and the author.

[5] A *flat* specification is a specification, which only contains a *parameter specification*, made up of lists of PARAMETER SORTS, PARAMETER OPNS, PARAMETER EQNS, and a *body specification*, made up of lists of SORTS, OPNS, and EQNS.

[6] In ASSPEGIQUE the corresponding program is called *specification compiler* [BCV 85].

[7] Informally speaking, a parameterized specification is called persistent, if its semantical functor transforms any parameter algebra into an algebra, in which the parameter algebra is retained without changes.

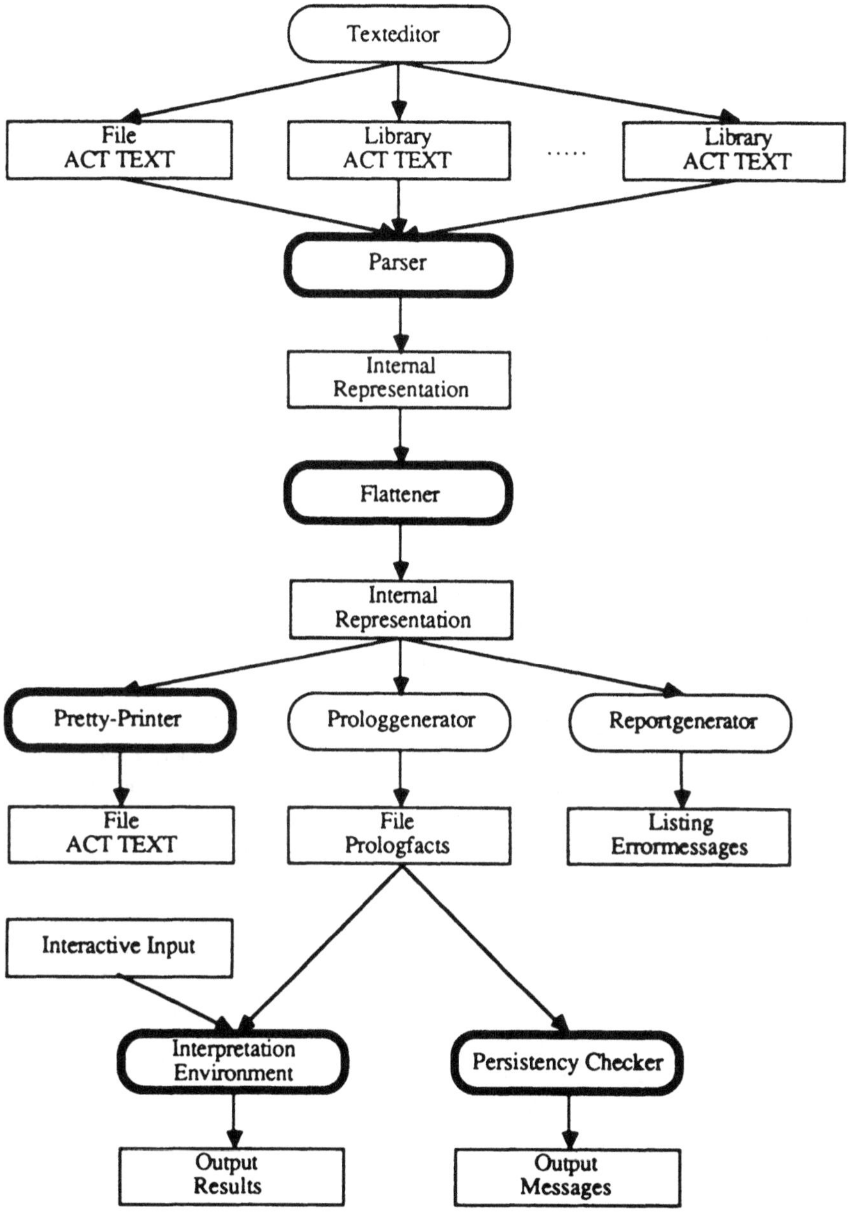

Figure 1: Structure of the ACT-system

The Persistency Checker as well as the *Interpretation Environment* including the *Interpreter* of the ACT-System are written in Waterloo-Prolog ([Wat 86], which proved to be suitable for quick implementation of prototypes of algorithms in the context of algebraic specifications. The interactive Interpretation Environment supports testing and prototyping of specifications (see [BH 86b]). It first reads as input the Prolog facts as produced from the Prolog generator and then responds to any user request. User requests may either be the interpretation of a term of the currently loaded specification (called *current specification* later on) or commands to the Interpretation Environment, e.g. definition of an interpretation strategy, definition of an object-variable (see 3.1), or usage of some input/output conversion procedures (see 3.2).

2.2 Deficiencies of ACT ONE and the ACT-System

During the last three years there have been noticed some deficiencies of ACT ONE and the ACT-System by its users. Those that were noticed most frequently are listed below:

1. The 'disjointness condition' for the actualization of parameterized specifications is very inconvenient w.r.t. basic data types as e.g. bool, natural numbers or integers.[8]
2. The language requires that each application of a construction operation (i.e. extension, actualization, union, renaming) yields a new type, which must be named.
3. The prefix notation of operation symbols renders the readability of specifications sometimes more difficult.
4. While in the specification language ACT ONE overloading of operation symbols is allowed, the current Interpreter of the system cannot cope with overloading.
5. There isn't any tool which checks whether the system of rewrite rules taken from the set of equations of a specification is terminating or not.
6. There is no Knuth-Bendix algorithm included in the system.
7. The Persistency Checker works well only on relatively small specifications.
8. The Interpreter is relatively slow and consumes much memory space.

These deficiencies can be grouped according to the reasons which induce them. They are the following:

- ACT ONE was primarily intended as an algebraic specification language for theoretical computer scientists. The main aim was the sound semantical foundation of the language. Therefore it was designed as a 'kernel language', which is in one to one correspondence with the underlying semantical concepts of extension, actualization, union and renaming of parameterized specifications as studied e.g. in [EM 85]. Deficiencies 1 through 3 are consequences of these limited design goals of the language ACT ONE.
- The current version of the ACT-system still is a kind of prototype. Using this prototype we have been learning which features are needed in a specification system (or specification environment). Its characteristic as a prototype is immediately visible in the fact that the Interpreter as well as the persistency checker are implemented in Prolog, which makes them unnecessarily slow and space consuming. The result of this are deficiencies 4, 7 and 8. Deficiencies 5 and 6 will be removed in future versions by adding these useful features.

3. The Interpretation Environment

To ease the use of the Interpreter for testing of specifications as well as for prototyping of software systems we implemented an environment around the term rewriting procedure, which manages user-created *object-variables* as well as user-defined *input* and *output procedures*.

[8] see [EM 85]

3.1 Object-variables

An *object-variable* is composed from three items: its *name*, called object name, its *sort* – which must be a sort of the currently loaded specification (current specification) – and its *value*, which is a term (more precisely a representative: see 5.1) of its sort.
Object-variables can be created and deleted dynamically in the interpretation environment. The last object-variable created is called *current object-variable*. Another (previously defined) object-variable can be made the current one by an explicit operation. So the interpretation environment at any moment consists of a *set of object-variables* – which may be empty – and one distinguished current object-variable (if the set of object-variables is not empty).

Input terms may either be terms according to the signature of the current specification or they may contain currently defined names of object-variables. In the latter case these object names first are substituted by the values of their object-variables, and afterwards the interpretation (calculation of an equivalent representative) starts.

Using object names in input terms has some consequences: The interpretation may have a side effect on the interpretation environment. This occurs, if

1. the name of the current object-variable is used in the input term , and
2. the sort of the input term is identical to the sort of the current object-variable.

In this case the value of the current object-variable is updated with the representative determined from the input term. The output also shows that this side effect has taken place: the object name of the current object-variable , its sort, and its new – updated – value are displayed.

3.1.1 Example

As a small example we first present a specification of **natural numbers** and then show, how the specification can be used in this environment as a prototype of a desk calculator.

```
ACT TEXT
   TYPE  natural  numbers   IS
   ( SORTS  nat
     OPNS   0 :                              →  nat
            SUCC, PRED  :  nat               →  nat
            ADD , MULT, EXP  :  nat nat      →  nat
     EQNS  OF  SORT   nat
            FOR ALL   n, m   IN   nat   :
     {nn1}  PRED(0) = 0
     {nn2}  PRED(SUCC(n)) = n
     {nn3}  ADD(n,0) = n
     {nn4}  ADD(n,SUCC(m)) = SUCC(ADD(n,m))
     {nn5}  MULT(n,0) = 0
     {nn6}  MULT(n,SUCC(m)) = ADD(n,MULT(n,m))
     {nn7}  EXP(n,0) = SUCC(0)
     {nn8}  EXP(n,SUCC(m)) = MULT(n,EXP(n,m))
   )
   ENDTYPE [9]
END OF TEXT
```

[9] In the remainder of this paper we will abbreviate the operation symbols introduced in this specification: S for SUCC, P for PRED, A for ADD, M for MULT, and E for EXP.

We will show a way to compute the expression $(3+2^2) * 2$ making intensive use of object-variables. In the sequel input to the interpretation environment is prefixed by '>' while output is marked by '<'. We start with an empty environment of object-variables. First we create an object-variable `N1`, to which we assign the value `2` :

```
> CREATE(N1, nat, S(S(0)))
< N1, nat :  S(S(0))
```

The result of the interpretation procedure applied to `S(S(0))` using the equations as rewriting rules from left to right, which is the unchanged term `S(S(0))`, becomes the value of `N1`. The resulting term is prefixed by the object name of the current object-variable and its sort. Creating this object-variable makes sense because we need its value several times in the sequel. We now create a second object-variable `N2`, which is used to successively compute the value we are interested in. First we assign the result of 2^2 to it :

```
> CREATE(N2, nat, E(N1,N1))
< N2, nat :  S(S(S(S(0))))
```

The value of `N2` is computed by the Interpreter after substituting the current value of the object-variable `N1` into the term `E(N1,N1)`, which gives `E(S(S(0)),S(S(0)))`. We go on:

```
> COMPUTE(A(S(N1),N2)) [10]
< N2, nat :  S(S(S(S(S(S(0))))))
```

Because `N2` is the current object-variable, which was referenced by its name in the input term, and the sort of this term is identical to the sort of the current object-variable, as a side effect the value of the object-variable `N2` is updated. In a last step we tell the Interpreter to multiply the result of the previous operations with the value `2`.

```
> COMPUTE(M(N2,N1))
< N2, nat :  S(S(S(S(S(S(S(S(S(S(S(S(0))))))))))))
```

This example shows a way to break down large input terms to smaller ones using object-variables.

Another way of getting the desired result would have been to type in the term directly without making use of object-variables :

```
> COMPUTE(M(A(S(S(S(0))), E(S(S(0)),S(S(0)))),S(S(0))))
< nat : S(S(S(S(S(S(S(S(S(S(S(S(0))))))))))))
```

But any error in the input of this term would require retyping of the whole thing, perhaps with another error in it. As we did not use any object name in the input term, there occurs no implicit updating of the current object-variable. So the resulting term is only prefixed with its sort.

3.1.2 General note on object-variables and assignment

This environment in a way introduces the idea of assignment to the Interpreter of the ACT-system. Here assignment comes in a uniform way for all kinds of specifications. This eliminates the necessity to introduce assignment as an explicit operation in specifications.

If we compare the way assignment is handled in this environment with assignment as known from programming languages, we can point out the following:

---

[10] `COMPUTE` starts the interpretation of its argument term.

- Assignment in usual *imperative high level languages* (Algol 68, Pascal, Modula 2, etc.) behaves wildly : at any point in a program all visible variables from surrounding blocks can be updated. This feature makes the mathematical (denotational) semantics of these languages additionally complex.
- *Single assignment languages* have to cope with the problems of iteration and recursion : either the idea of single assignment is given up for iterations and in recursive procedures or the name-space of such programs may become infinite. Single assignment languages have the advantage that their mathematical semantics is less complex than that of imperative languages (see e.g. [MN 84]).
- Assignment as introduced in our environment of the Interpreter lies in between the extremes of the previously mentioned concepts : we introduce a wellbehaved multiple assignment, which seems rather natural. There is one variable, i.e. the current object-variable which is updated exactly when we work with this variable.[11] Any side-computations can be done if necessary, but they do not change the current environment.

3.2 Input and output conversion

Input and output conversion allows the user of the Interpreter to define specific procedures that convert a term, which is the result of the rewriting procedure, into a more readable form, e.g. to convert a term of sort `nat`, which usually is of the form `S(...S(0)...)` into a number representation (like `1, 2,` ...). Input conversion allows this change of representation in the opposite direction : a number representation can be used as input. Before the Interpreter gets hold of the term to start the rewriting procedure, the number is converted into a term of sort `nat`.
Input and output conversion is a generalization of having predefined representations for input and output of standard data types as found in high level programming languages and many other specification languages. The feature presented here allows to have user-defined conversion routines for arbitrary data types. It is even possible to write conversion routines for standard data types replacing the ones provided by the interpretation environment of the ACT-system.

The ACT-system provides a library of basic data type definitions, which is available to every user of the system. The library includes e.g. the types **boolean , natural numbers , integers , string(data) , string(string(data)) , stack(data) , queue(data)** . Along with all of these we provide predefined output conversion procedures. For example terms of sort `string` like `ladd(n,ladd(a,ladd(t,empty)))` are converted to standard string representation and are displayed as `'nat'`. Another example are terms of sort `file`, which is the sort associated with the data type **string(string(data))** . These terms are displayed as a sequence of strings, where each string starts at the beginning of a new line.
Input conversion works as follows: For every sort `xyz` in the predefined data types there is a conversion function named `xyz` as well. If one wants to input e.g. the term `PRED(PRED(0))` , one can instead write `integer(-2)` . Then the number `-2` will be converted to the corresponding term. A more complex term could look like `ADD(integer(-2),integer(10))` . In this expression the subterms `integer(-2)` and `integer(10)` get converted to special terms (representatives: see 4.2) of sort `integer` and these are then substituted into the context term. The naming of the input conversion

[11] The way this assignment works is very similar to the way editors work on texts : there is exactly one position, the position of the cursor, where all activities take place. All updating is carried out at this position. If we want to interrupt our work on the current text we must explicitly change our current environment to another document.

procedures is similar to the naming convention for coercion functions as used e.g. in Pascal ([JW 85]). For the predefined data type specifications as well as for any user-defined specification input and output conversion procedures can be defined.[12]

With these additional features the example from 3.3.1 looks like :

```
>  COMPUTE(M(A(nat(3), E(nat(2), nat(2))), nat(2)))
<  nat : 14 .
```

The acceptance of the ACT-system has grown rapidly since these conversion-features have been added.

4. Future Enhancements of the ACT-System

Currently a reimplementation of the ACT-system is under way. The new version will be implemented under UNIX on SUN workstations. This version will include additional features which will overcome most of the deficiencies encountered with the current system (see 2.2).

4.1 Language improvements

The new abstract syntax of the language ACT ONE will allow the combination of all primitive ACT ONE operations as AND (for union of types), ACTUALIZED BY (for actualization), and RENAMED BY (for renaming) in a single type definition. The precedence of these operations is given by additional brackets to resolve multiple parses. The revised abstract syntax of ACT ONE can be found in the appendix.

Furthermore we will implement a somewhat different set of (syntactical) context conditions. These will cope with deficiency 1. The concept of *defining occurrence* of an identifier, especially of an identifier denoting a type, will help to resolve this problem partially: We automatically identify those parts of the two specifications, which have been defined at the same place as a common subtype. So for example the following specification would be correct in the future version of ACT ONE while it is erroneous in the current version:

```
ACT TEXT
   TYPE  string(data)   IS
   ( natural  numbers 13
     FORMAL  SORTS  data
     SORTS   string(data)
     OPNS    EMPTY:                          →    string(data)
             LADD:   data  string(data)      →    string(data)
             LENGTH: string(data)            →    nat
     EQNS OF SORT    nat
             FOR ALL d IN data ;  s IN string(data)  :
             LENGTH(EMPTY)  = 0
             LENGTH(LADD(d,s))  = S(LENGTH(s))
   )
   ENDTYPE
```

[12] In the current version of the ACT-system these procedures can be defined as PROLOG predicates.

[13] The type **natural numbers** is used here as given in 3.1.1 .

```
  TYPE  string(nat)  IS
  ( string(data)
     ACTUALIZED BY natural  numbers
     USING SORTNAMES    nat     FOR  data
  )
  ENDTYPE

  FROM LIBRARY   natural  numbers
END OF TEXT
```

In the new version it will be recognized that the sort nat in both specifications has been imported from the type **natural numbers** . Therefore there will be only one sort nat in the resulting value specification. Semantically the subtype **natural numbers** is handled as if it had been included in the parameter part of the type **string(data)** together with an initial constraint on it.[14, 15]
The syntax of operation symbols will be less restricted. We will allow the definition of operation symbols using 'underline' as a placeholder as e.g. in OBJ, PLUSS or LOTOS (see [FGJM 85], [Gau 84] resp. [DVB 87]).
As an additional improvement we will allow positive conditional equations instead of equations in the new version, as in PLUSS [Gau 84], or the RAP-System [GH 85].

The new Interpreter can be derived easily from an existing one which was developed as part of the SEDOS-project. This Interpreter, implemented in C, will be integrated into the system much more rigorously than the existing prototype, thereby overcoming deficiency 4. Sample measurements (in the LOTOS environment) have shown that this Interpreter yields a factor of approximately 10 in execution time performance[16] and reduces space requirements even more. (compare deficiency 8). These improvements make it possible to use much larger specifications as prototypes than before.

Another major topic of study is execution of arbitrary algebraic specifications. A possible solution to this problem will be discussed in the sequel.

4.2 Another Interpreter for algebraic specifications

As mentioned in the introduction, there are many examples of algebraic specifications, which can not be interpreted, not even if there is a Knuth-Bendix-completion-procedure available in a specification environment ([HO 80]). The problem gets even harder, if one considers specifications with conditional equations ([Gan 87]).
If there is no confluent and terminating term rewriting system for a given algebraic specification and nevertheless it is absolutely necessary to have a prototype for the specified software system, then the algebraic specification has to be changed in such a way that

1. the semantics of the original specification is not changed, (i.e. the corresponding quotient term algebras must be isomorphic after forgetting about some hidden functions) and
2. the term rewriting system generated from the changed specification is confluent and terminating.

---

[14] It must be noted that the syntactical condition used here is neither neccessary nor sufficient to guarantee that the semantics of the syntactically identical subpart is also identical (resp. isomorphic).

[15] In the module specification language ACT TWO (see [Fey 86], [Fey 88]) this situation will be handled analogously.

[16] This comparison is based on CPU time used on an IBM 4381-2 mainframe computer compared to CPU time used on a SUN 3/160 workstation.

These are conflicting goals which are not easy to achieve. The first one of course involves considerable proof efforts, while the second one may be only met by adopting some 'trial and error' approach, i.e. by running an appropriate completion procedure on the specification and changing the specification until the completion procedure terminates successfully.

4.2.1 Definitions

In this section we propose a new technique for the interpretation of algebraic specifications, which works with any equational specification. First we will fix the terminology we use in this chapter, which mainly follows [EM 85].

An *algebraic specification* (Σ, E) consists of a *signature* $\Sigma = (S,OP)$ which defines a *set of sorts* S, a *set of operation symbols* OP, and a *set of equations* E. The signature gives rise to a Σ–algebra T_Σ, called *Σ–term algebra*, and the equations allow to define a (Σ, E)–algebra $Q_{\Sigma,E}$, called *quotient term algebra* of the specification.
A *representation system* $R_{\Sigma,E}$ (called *canonical terms system* in [EM 85], p. 140) for a quotient term algebra $Q_{\Sigma,E}$ is a set of terms $R_{\Sigma,E} \subseteq T_\Sigma$ s.t. for all $t \in T_\Sigma$ there is some $r \in R_{\Sigma,E}$ with $t \equiv_E r$, i.e. such that there is at least one term in the representation system $R_{\Sigma,E}$ for any quotient class in the base sets of the quotient term algebra $Q_{\Sigma,E}$. We talk of an *unique representation system*, if in addition for any two $r, r' \in R_{\Sigma,E}$ with $r \equiv_E r'$ we have $r = r'$, i.e. if there is exactly one representative for each class of terms in the quotient term algebra. In the following we sometimes talk of a representation system for a specification rather than a representation system for the quotient term algebra of the specification. Representation systems give rise to *representation algebras* in a straightforward way (see e.g. [EM 85], [Han 87]).

4.2.2 Representation systems

In the literature there are different proposals of how to define a set of representatives. The most common approach is to define an unique representation system as the set of all terms, on which the rewriting procedure stops when using a confluent and terminating rewriting system (see e.g. [HO 80]). We cannot use this approach for our purposes, because we want to deal with arbitrary specifications, for which there do not exist such rewriting systems.
Some authors use a subsignature Σ' of the signature Σ, called set of *constructors* or *generators*, to describe a unique representation system (see e.g. [Kla 82], [GH 85], [BGM 87]). But this works only with specifications, where there are no equations between these constructors. If this assumption is not valid, then clearly it is impossible to define a unique representation system this way. Furthermore a signature only allows to specify a context free set of terms, while there are many examples of representation systems for which the terms cannot be generated context free. Consider e.g. the specification of **natural numbers** as given in 3.3.1. Then the set

$$\{ A(x,x) \mid x = S^n(0) , n \geq 0 \} \cup \{ S(A(x,x)) \mid x = S^n(0) , n \geq 0 \}$$

of course is a unique representation system for this specification. But the condition that the operation symbol A takes two identical arguments cannot be formulated context free.

At the Tapsoft Conference in Pisa in spring '87 M. Wirsing proposed to give a representation system for an algebraic specification by some algebraical means, i.e. staying in the framework of algebraic specifications, but on a meta level by using some boolean-valued functions, which separate the set of representatives from other terms. This idea, of course, has the advantage that an interpreter for algebraic specifications can also be used for deciding the question 't ∈ $R_{\Sigma,E}$ '?. But this method does not seem to work for example 3 in the next paragraph.

4.2.3 Definition of representation systems by production systems

Here we describe representation systems in a different way. We define a *R-specification* (Σ,E,P), which consists of an algebraic specification (Σ, E) and a *production system* P for a representation system $R_{\Sigma,E}$ of the corresponding quotient term algebra. So this definition includes a crucial semantic condition : P must not generate an arbitrary set of terms of the signature Σ, but a set of representatives.
A *production system* P = { r_1, ..., r_n } consists of a finite set of *rules* r_1, ..., r_n . The formal definition of a production system and the set of terms, which is generated by the system, can be found in [Han 87]. Here we will only exhibit three examples of production systems, which generate unique representation systems for the specification of **natural numbers** .

Example 1

```
REPS
  (1)               →  0 E nat
  (2)     z E nat   →  S(z)  E nat
```

The set of terms generated by this production system is { $S^n(0)$ | n ≥ 0 }.
The production procedure works as follows: In the first step the *syntactical entity* 0 E nat with the intuitive meaning '0 is E(lement) of nat' is produced by rule 1, which has no premise. In the second and all consecutive steps we can generate from the set { 0 E nat } by unifying the entity 0 E nat with the premise of the second rule the new entity S(0) E nat by substituting 0 for z in the conclusion of the rule. Thus we now have the set { 0 E nat, S(0) E nat}. By repeated application of rule 2 to this set we end up with the set of entities { $S^n(0)$ E nat | n ≥ 0 }. From the entities in this set we only use the terms, which we find before the 'E nat' - part of the entities. To this set we refer as *the set of terms generated by the production system.*

Example 2
Now let's consider another production system:

REPS
(1) → 0 E nat_0
(2) z E nat_0 → S(z) E nat_0
(3) z E nat_0 → A(z,z) E nat
(4) z E nat_0 → S(A(z,z)) E nat

Using this production system we start with { 0 E nat_0 }. Note the index 0 of nat ! Rules 2, 3 and 4 generate new entities from this set, which results in the set { 0 E nat_0 , S(0) E nat_0 , A(0,0) E nat, S(A(0,0)) E nat_0 }. Repeated application of these three rules yields the set
{ $S^n(0)$ E nat_0 | n ≥ 0 } ∪ { A($S^n(0)$,$S^n(0)$) E nat | n ≥ 0 } ∪
{ S(A($S^n(0)$,$S^n(0)$)) E nat | n ≥ 0 } .
From this set we only take all terms, which have as postfix 'E nat', but not 'E nat_i' with some index 'i'. This results in the set of terms
{ A($S^n(0)$,$S^n(0)$) | n ≥ 0 } ∪ { S(A($S^n(0)$,$S^n(0)$)) | n ≥ 0 },

which clearly is another unique representation system of the specification **natural numbers** .

Example 3

As a last example consider:

```
REPS
    (1)                 → A(0,0)  E nat
    (2)                 → S(A(0,0))  E nat0
    (3)   z E nat0      → A(z,z)  E nat0
    (4)   z E nat0      → S(A(z,z))  E nat0
    (5)   z E nat0      → z E nat
```

This production set generates by rule 1 the term `A(0,0)` as a representative. Furthermore it produces by rule 2 the intermediate term `S(A(0,0))`. By rule 5 this term becomes a representative as well. Using `S(A(0,0))` in rule 3 resp. 4 we can generate `A(S(A(0,0)),S(A(0,0)))` resp. `S(A(S(A(0,0)),S(A(0,0))))` . These terms can again be entered as premises of rule 3 and 4 respectively. By rule 5 any of these terms become representatives. So we end up with the following recursively defined set of terms

$R^+ = \{ S(A(0,0)) \} \cup \{ A(t,t) \mid t \in R^+ \} \cup \{ S(A(t,t)) \mid t \in R^+ \}$

and the set of representatives is $R^+ \cup \{ A(0,0) \}$.

This is a set of totally balanced 'binary trees', another unique representation system of the specification. Using the meta-level approach sketched above it is quite easy to give equations for a boolean-valued meta-operation `IS_REPRESENTATIVE` , which yields `TRUE` for all representatives. However it is an open question how to define the negative case using equations only.

In [Han 87] the subclass of acyclic production systems has been examined more closely. Acyclic production systems give rise to a decision procedure for the question '$t \in R_{\Sigma,E}$?' for any $t \in T_\Sigma$. This decision procedure will be used as a termination criterion for the interpretation procedure described in the next section. Furthermore there is another efficient decision procedure, which determines whether or not a production system is acyclic.

4.2.4 The interpretation algorithm

Now we will present the alternative interpretation technique. After giving an informal introduction we will outline the main algorithm of the Interpreter in a Pascal like language.

The Interpreter starts with any valid term of the *current specification* (cf. section 2) and generates from this in a first step equivalent terms by applying all equations of the current specification to the term at all possible positions. Remember, we are using equations, i.e. we match the left hand sides of an equation as well as the right hand sides! Then we use the decision procedure sketched above to examine all previously generated terms. If in this set we find a term, which is a representative, then this term is the result of our interpretation procedure. Of course, the result of this interpretation procedure is uniquely defined if and only if the representation system used is a unique one. Otherwise the result is defined only up to equivalence: any term from the set of representatives, which are in the same equivalence (more precisely congruence) class, may be the result of the interpretation procedure.

For the algorithm we assume a surrounding program block, which contains a variable `SetofEquations : equations` , and the declaration of a boolean-valued function `Representative(Term : term )` , which implements the decision procedure to check whether or not a term is a representative. The meaning of all other functions or procedures should be clear from the context and their names. The variable above should hold as value the set of equations of the *current specification*, which must have been extended to a *R-specification*, before the function `Interpret` is called. Furthermore there should be some means to input a term, which is to be interpreted, as well as some means to output the term which results from the interpretation procedure.

```
FUNCTION  Interpret(SetofTerms : terms) : terms ;
   BEGIN
   VAR  NewSetofTerms :  terms ;
   NewSetofTerms :=  Ø ;
   FOR ALL  T   IN   SetofTerms  DO
      BEGIN
      FOR ALL  E  IN  SetofEquations  DO
         BEGIN
         FOR ALL  Matches of LeftHandSide of  E  in  T  DO
            BEGIN
            VAR  Result : term ;
            Result := Apply  E  To  T ;
            INSERT  Result  INTO  NewSetofTerms ;
            END ; { FOR ALL Matches }
         FOR ALL  Matches of RightHandSide of  E  in  T  DO
            BEGIN
            VAR  Result : term ;
            Result := Apply  E  To  T ;
            INSERT  Result  INTO  NewSetofTerms ;
            END ; { FOR ALL Matches }
         END ; { FOR ALL E }
      END ; { FOR ALL T }
   FOR ALL T  IN  NewSetofTerms do
      IF Representative(T)  THEN  Interpret :=  T ;
   Interpret :=  Interpret(NewSetofTerms) ;
END ;
```

Figure 2 : Interpreter

For sake of clarity we have chosen do define the interpretation procedure recursively. Of course this function could easily be rewritten in an iterative version.

The algorithm developed above is an extremely inefficient one. But there are a lot of possible improvements. I will only mention the most ambitious one, which we are just developing in more detail: Consider an algebraic specification, which is extended in some way by adding new sorts and/or operation symbols as well as equations. Then it is very useful to have the property, that the semantics of the first specification (i.e. its quotient term algebra) is isomorphic to the quotient term algebra of the new specification after forgetting about any additional sorts and operations of the latter quotient term algebra. (For a detailed discussion of this semantical property, which describes that the semantics of the first specification is retained in the semantics of the new one, see e.g. [TWW 78], [EM 85].)
A proof of this property can either be done by applying some known sufficient criteria to the pair of specifications (cf. [Pad 83]) – and these can be checked by some proof tool in a specification environment – or manually by doing some explicit proof using structural induction on terms. From proofs of this type one can deduce information, which then is used to direct the interpretation procedure exhibited above. This information is sufficient to eliminate all nondeterminism, which is present in the presented

algorithm, and end up with an efficient deterministic interpretation procedure. We plan to develop a computer based system for proofs by structural induction, which helps the user to carry out such proofs explicitly. Furthermore there will a program which automatically transforms the information inherent in such proofs into strategy information for our interpreter. These ideas will be the topic of a forthcoming paper of M. Löwe and the author.

5. Conclusions

The redesign of the algebraic specification language ACT ONE and the reimplementation of the ACT-System will overcome many drawbacks encountered with the current version of the ACT-System, which in a sense still is a prototype of a specification environment.
The new version of the ACT-System will not include all language extensions and tools which could be put into such a system using existing theoretical concepts. In parallel to the current reimplementation we consider a new generation specification language, which will allow positive universal horn clauses as axioms. The theoretical foundation for such a language are currently examined in the second volume of 'Fundamentals of Algebraic Specifications' ([EM 88]).
The language of such a future system possibly will be based on the module specificaton language ACT TWO (see [Fey 86], [Fey 88]), which is under development right now.
Another important topic of future research will be the interpretation of structured algebraic specifications instead of flat specifications. In [Han 87] it has been shown, that the structuring operations for specifications as defined in ACT ONE can be extended to operations on R-specifications under certain additional assumptions. This lights a way towards using the interpretation technique proposed in 4.2 for structured specifications as well.

6. References

[ADJ 76] Goguen, J.A., Thatcher, J.W., Wagner, E.G. : An Initial Algebra Approach to the Specification, Correctness and Implementation of Abstract Data Types, IBM Research Report RC 6487, 1976
Also : Current Trends in Programming Methodology IV : Data Structuring (R. Yeh, ed.), Prentice Hall, 1978, pp. 80-144

[BCV 85] Bidoit, M., Choppy, C., Voisin, F. : The ASSPEGIQUE specification environment
In. Kreowski, H.-J. (ed.) : Informatik Fachberichte Nr. 116, Springer Verlag, 1985

[BGM 87] Bidoit, M., Gaudel, M.C., Mauboussin, A. : How to make Algebraic Specifications more understandable? Research Report Nr. 343, Laboratory of Computer Science, Universite de Paris-Sud, Orsay 1987

[BH 86a] Boehm, P., Hansen, H. : ACT-System User's Guide, Department of Computer Science, TU Berlin, 1986 (German)

[BH 86b] Boehm, P., Hansen, H. : ACT-System: Interpreter User's Guide, Department of Computer Science, TU Berlin, 1986 (German)

[BH 87] Brauer, J., Hansen, H. : Spezifikation von VLSI-Entwurfsobjeckten als abstrakte Datentypen, E.I.S. Workshop, Bonn, 13-14. October 1987

[BMS 80] Burstall, R. M., MacQueen, D. B., Sannella, D. T. : HOPE: An Experimental Applicative Language, Internal Report No. CSR-62-80, Department of Computer Science, University of Edinburgh, May 1980

[CIP 85] The CIP Language Group: The Munich Project CIP - Vol. I : The Wide Spectrum Language CIP-L, Lecture Notes in Computer Science, No. 183, Springer-Verlag, 1985

[DVB 87] Diaz, M., Vissers, C., Budkowski, S. : ESTELLE and LOTOS Software Environments for the Design of Open Distributed Systems, In : Commission of the European Communities (ed.) : ESPRIT '87 - Achievements and Impact, Proccedings of the 4th Annual ESPRIT Conference, Brussels, September 28-29, 1987; North-Holland, 1987

[EDIF 87] EDIF - Electronic Design Interchange Format (Version 2 0 0), EDIF Steering Committee, Electronic Industries

Association, Washington, D.C.

[EFH 83] Ehrig, H., Fey, W., Hansen, H. : ACT ONE : An Algebraic Specification Language with two Levels of Semantics, Research Report Nr. 83-03, Department of Computer Science, TU Berlin, 1983

[EM 85] Ehrig, H., Mahr, B. : Fundamentals of Algebraic Specification 1, Springer Verlag, Berlin, 1985

[EM 88] Ehrig, H., Mahr, B. : Fundamentals of Algebraic Specification 2, to appear, 1988

[Fey 86] Fey, W. : Introduction to Algebraic Specification in ACT TWO, Research Report No. 86-13, Department of Computer Science, TU Berlin, 1986

[Fey 88] Fey, W. : The Module Specification and Interconnection Language ACT TWO, to appear 1988

[FGJM 85] Futatsugi, K., Goguen, J. A., Jouannaud, J.-P., Meseguer, J. : Principles of OBJ2, Proceedings of the 12th ACM Symposium on Principles of Programming Languages, New-Orleans, Lousiana, January 1985, pp. 52-66

[Gau 84] Gaudel, M.-C. : A first Introduction to PLUSS, Internal draft report, LRI, UNiversité de Paris-Sud, December 1984

[Gan 87] Ganzinger, H. : A Completion Procedure for Conditional Equational Specifications, Internal Report of talk, held at the 5th Workshop on Specification of Abstract Data Types, Gullane, 1-4 September 1987

[GH 83] Guttag, J. V., Horning, J. J. : An Introduction to the LARCH Shared Language; In: Mason, R. E. A. (ed.) : Information Processing 83, Elsevier Science Publishers B.V., North-Holland, 1983

[GH 85] Geser, A., Hussmann, H. : Rapid Prototyping for Algebraic Specifications: Examples for the Use of the RAP System, Research Report Nr. MIP - 8517, University of Passau, December 1985

[Han 84] Hansen, H. : An ACT ONE Specification for User Operations of a Line-Oriented Editor, Research Report Nr. 84-20, Department of Computer Science, TU Berlin, 1984

[Han 87] Hansen, H. : Von algebraischen Spezifikationen zu algebraischen Programmen, Dissertation thesis, TU Berlin, 1986; also in: Research Report Nr. 87-02, Department of Computer Science, TU Berlin, 1987

[HLR 81] Hasler, K.-P., Löwe, M., Reisin, M. : Modell, Spezifikation und Korrektheit eines universellen Interpreters für algebraische Spezifikationen, Master thesis, TU Berlin, 1981

[HM 85] Hasler, K.-P., Meer, J. de : OSI-Transport-Service Considered as an Abstract Data Type; In: Kreowski, H.-J.: Recent Trends in Data Type Specifications, Informatik Fachberichte Nr. 116, Springer Verlag, 1985

[HMM 86] Harper, R., MacQueen, D., Milner, R. : Standard ML, LFCS Report Series No. ECS-LFCS-86-2, Department of Computer Science, University of Edinburgh, March 1986

[HO 80] Huet, G., Oppen, D.C. : Equations and Rewrite Rules : A Survey; In: Book, R. V., ed., Formal Language Theory : Perspectives and Open Problems, Academic Press, 1980

[Hus 85] Hussmann, H. : Rapid Prototyping for Algebraic Specifications - RAP Sytems User's Manual, Research Report Nr. MIP - 8504, University of Passau, March 1985

[JW 85] Jensen, K., Wirth, N. : Pascal User Manual and Report ; Third Edition, Springer-Verlag, New York 1985

[Kla 82] Klaeren, H.A. : A Constructive Method for Abstract Algebraic Software Specification, RWTH Aachen, Schriften zur Informatik und Ang. Math., Nr. 78, 1982; also in: Theoretical Computer Science, 1984

[Kla 87] Klaeren, H.A. : Efficient Implementation of an Algebraic Specification Language, Invited talk at the ESPRIT METEOR Workshop on Algebraic Methods: Theory, Tools and Application, Passau, 1987, to appear in LNCS, Springer, 1987

[Lan 85a] Langen, A. : Algorithmen zur Überprüfung der semantischen Kontextbedingungen der Spezifikationssprache ACT ONE, Research Report Nr. 85-12, Department of Computer Science, TU Berlin 1985

[Lan 85b] Langen, A. : PERSIST: ein Programm zur Überprüfung syntaktischer hinreichender Bedingungen für Persistenz parametrisierter algebraischer Spezifikationen, Research Report Nr. 85-11, Department of Computer Science, TU Berlin 1985

[Les 83] Lescanne, P. : Computer Experiments with the REVE Term Rewriting System Generator; In: Proceedings of the Symposium on Principles of Programming Languages, ACM, 1983

[LL 87] Lehmann, T., Loeckx, J. : The Specification Language of OBSCURE, Research Report No. A 87/07, Department of Applied Mathematics and Computer Science, Universität des Saarlandes, Saarbrücken, 1987

[MN 84] Mahr, B., Nürnberg, F. : DONALD - A Single Assignment Language for Non-Sequential Algorithms Over Arbitrary Data Types, Research Report Nr. 84-07, Department of Computer Science, TU Berlin, May 1984

[Mus 80] Musser, D. R. : Abstract Dta Type Specification in the AFFIRM System, IEEE Transactions on Software Engineering, Vol. SE-6, No. 1, January 1980, pp. 24-32

[Pad 83] Padawitz, P. : Correctness, Completeness, and Consistency of Equational Data Type Specifications, Dissertation thesis, TU Berlin 1983; also in: Research Report Nr. 83-15, Department of Computer Science, TU Berlin, 1983

[Pad 85] Padawitz, P. : Parameter Preserving Data Type Specifications, Proc. TAPSOFT Vol. 1, 1985, LNCS 185, pp. 323-341, Springer Verlag, 1985

[Rie 85] Rieckhoff, C. : Induzierte Korrektheit parametrisierter algebraischer Spezifikationen unter Anwendung kategorieller Methoden, Research Report Nr. 85-13, Department of Computer Science, TU Berlin, 1985

[San 86] Sannella, D. : Formal Specification of ML Programs, LFCS Report Series No. ECS-LFCS-86-15, Department of Computer Science, University of Edinburgh, November 1986

[Sch 87] Schulte, W. : A'gebraische Spezifikation und Programmentwicklung eines syntaxgesteuerten Editors, Master thesis, Department of Computer Science, TU Berlin, March 1987

[ST 85] Sannella, D., Tarlecki, A. : Extended ML: an intitution-independent framework for formal program development; In: Proceedings of the Workshop on Category and Computer Programming, Guildford, 1985

[TWW 78] Thatcher, J.W., Wagner, E.G., Wright, J.B. : Data Type Specification: Parameterization and the Power of Specification Techniques; 10th Symp. Theory of Computing, 1978, pp. 119-132; Trans. Prog. Languages and Systems 4, 1982, pp. 711-732

[Wat 86] Waterloo Prolog User's Manual (Version 1.7), Intralogic Inc., Waterloo, Canada, 1986

[Win 87] Wing, J.: Writing LARCH Interface Language Specifications, ACM Transactions on Programming Languages Vol. 9, No. 2, April 1987, pp. 1-25

7. Appendix : Revised Abstract Syntax of ACT ONE[17]

```
(0)  <spectext>   ::=  ACT TEXT {<type>}+
                         [ FROM LIBRARY <namelist> ]
                       END OF TEXT
(1)  <type>       ::=  TYPE <name> IS
                         <pexpr>
                       ENDTYPE
(2)  <pexpr>      ::=  ( <pexpr> ACTUALIZED BY <pexpr>
                         [ USING <repl> ] )
(3)  <pexpr>      ::=  ( <namelist> )
(4)  <pexpr>      ::=  ( [ <namelist> ] <pspec> )
(5)  <pexpr>      ::=  ( <pexpr> RENAMED BY <repl> )
(6)  <pspec>      ::=  [ PARAMETER SORTS <namelist>      ]
                       [ PARAMETER OPNS {<operation>}+   ]
                       [ PARAMETER EQNS {<equation>}+    ]
                       [ SORTS <namelist>                ]
                       [ OPNS {<operation>}+             ]
                       [ EQNS {<equation>}+              ]
(7)  <namelist>   ::=  { <name> , }* <name>
(8)  <repl>       ::=  [ SORTNAMES <repllist> ]
                       [ OPNAMES   <repllist> ]
(9)  <repllist>   ::=  { <name> FOR <name> }+
(10) <operation>  ::=  <namelist> : {<name>}* -> <name>
(11) <equation>   ::=  OF SORT <name>
                       [ FOR ALL <vardecl> : ]
                       {[ <eqnlist> -> ] <eqn>}+
(12) <vardecl>    ::=  { <namelist> IN <name> ; }*
(13) <eqnlist>    ::=  { <eqn> , }* <eqn>
(14) <eqn>        ::=  <term> = <term>
(15) <term>       ::=  <name> [ ( {<term> ,}* <term> ) ]
```

17 As a shorthand notation we use [...] for optional parts, { ... }+ for nonempty sequences, and { ... }* for sequences, that may be empty. Terminal symbols are written in boldface.

The specification language of *OBSCURE*[1]

Thomas Lehmann and Jacques Loeckx
Universität des Saarlandes
Fachbereich Informatik
D-6600 Saarbrücken

1 Introduction

The idea that abstract types may support the development of correct programs is now well-accepted. Meanwhile several *specification methods* have been proposed in the literature: operational specifications ([Ho 72], [Sh 81], [Li 81], [NY 83], [LG 86]), algebraic specifications ([GTW 78], [GHM 78], [TWW 82], [BW 82], [Eh 82], [EM 85]) and constructive specifications ([Ca 80], [Kl 84], [Lo 87], [Bu 87], [Sp 88]). These three specification methods essentially differ by the way operations are defined. In the operational specification method operations are defined as function procedures in an imperative programming language. In the algebraic specification method operations are defined implicitly by first-order formulas, usually equalities or Horn clauses. Finally, in the constructive specification method operations are defined as functions in a functional programming language.

The design of non-trivial specifications is practicable only if it is performed modularly. To this end specifications are embedded into a *specification language*. Essentially, such a language allows the construction of specifications out of more elementary ones. In the case of operational specifications the specification language is foreordained to be the imperative programming language in which the function procedures are written. For algebraic specifications several specification languages have recently been proposed: CLEAR ([Sa 84], [BG 80]), ACT-ONE and ACT-TWO ([EM 85], [Fe 87]), OBJ2 ([FGJM 85]), PLUSS ([Gd 84], [BGM 87]), ASL ([Wi 86]), ASF ([BHK 87]), Z ([Sp 88]).

Even with the use of a specification language the design of non-trivial specifications with pencil and paper is tedious and error-prone. As a solution the specification language is embedded into an adequate *specification environment*. Such an environment supports the interactive design of specifications as well as the (interactive or automatic) verification of their properties. Some more or less elaborate environments have been described or announced in the literature: OBJ2 ([FGJM 85]), an environment for a subset of the specification language PLUSS called ASSPEGIQUE ([BCV 85]), the environment RAP ([Hu 87]), an environment for the specification language ACT-ONE called the ACT-System.

The specification tool discussed in this paper is called *OBSCURE*. It consists of a specification language *together with* an environment for it. The specification language is a simple language similar to Bergstra's term language ([BHK 86]). The environment consists of a design unit and a verification unit. The design unit allows the interactive design of specifications. More precisely, with the help of a *design language* the user induces the design unit to incrementally generate syntactically correct specifications. The verification unit allows to prove properties of these specifications and, in particular, to prove their semantical correctness. The main features by which *OBSCURE* differs from the specification languages and environments described in the literature are now briefly discussed.

First, the specification language of *OBSCURE* has been designed as a language to be used in an environment, not as a language to be used with pencil and paper. As a result the specification language has a very simple syntax and semantics at the expense of more elaborate context conditions. These context conditions put no burden on the user as they are checked automatically and on-line by the design unit. Second, the specification language is independent from the specification method used, i.e. *OBSCURE* may be used in connection with algebraic, constructive or operational specification methods. *OBSCURE* even allows the use of different specification methods within a single specification. This feature results from the explicit distinction between the constructs inherent to the specification method — such as "data constraints" in CLEAR — and those inherent to the specification language — such

[1]Supported in part by the Deutsche Forschungsgemeinschaft

as the constructs putting specifications together. Third, *OBSCURE* explicitly distinguishes between the specification language and the design language: the specification language is a language to describe specifications while the design language is a language to generate specifications (with the help of the design unit). As a result parameterized specifications and user-friendly macros are part of the design language, *not* of the specification language. According to this philosophy parameterized specifications are *not* specifications but rather constitute a tool to generate specifications. Next, apart from the operations classically provided by a specification language *OBSCURE* allows to explicitly construct subalgebras and quotient algebras. Finally, *OBSCURE* directly ties the design of a specification to its verification. In particular, the design unit automatically generates formulas expressing, for instance, certain closure and congruence conditions and transmits them for verification to the verification unit.

The main goal of the present paper is to give a formal definition of the specification language of *OBSCURE*. A description of the design unit and its design language is in preparation. An informal introduction to *OBSCURE* and an illustration of its use may be found in [LL 87].

Section 2 briefly recalls some basic notions. Section 3 contains a description of the specification language; it constitutes the bulk of the paper. The case of loose specifications and the problem of overloading is treated in Section 4. Finally, Section 5 briefly discusses the design language and its parameterization mechanism. It moreover contains an overview of the environment of *OBSCURE*.

2 Basic notions

2.1 Algebras

The notions following are classical (cf. [EM 85]) except for minor differences.

2.1.1 Syntax

A *sort* is an identifier. An *operation* is a $(k+2)$-tuple, $k \geq 0$,

$$n : s_1 \ldots s_k \rightarrow s_{k+1}$$

where n is an identifier, called *operation name*, and $(s_1, \ldots, s_{k+1})$ is a $(k+1)$-tuple of sorts, called the *arity*. It is called *S-sorted*, if S is a set of sorts with $s_1, \ldots, s_{k+1}$ among its elements. By definition two operations

$$n : s_1 \ldots s_k \rightarrow s_{k+1}$$

$$m : t_1 \ldots t_l \rightarrow t_{l+1}$$

are equal, if $n = m, k = l$ and $s_i = t_i$ for all i, $1 \leq i \leq k+1$.

A *signature* is a pair (S, O) where S is a set of sorts and O a set of operations. It is called an *algebra signature* if each operation of O is S-sorted.

A *list of sorts and operations* is a $(k+l)$-tuple

$$(s_1, \ldots, s_k; o_1, \ldots, o_l) \quad (k \geq 0,\ l \geq 0)$$

where $s_1, \ldots, s_k$ are sorts and $o_1, \ldots, o_l$ operations. It is occasionally identified with the signature $(\{s_1, \ldots, s_k\}, \{o_1, \ldots, o_l\})$.

Let $\Sigma = (S, O)$ and $\Sigma' = (S', O')$ be signatures. Expressions such as $\Sigma - \Sigma'$ or $\Sigma \subseteq \Sigma'$ are used to denote $(S - S', O - O')$ or $S \subseteq S'$ and $O \subseteq O'$ respectively. Similarly, if no ambiguity arises one writes Σ instead of $S \cup O$; for instance, $c \in \Sigma$ stands for $c \in S \cup O$.

Lemma 1: If Σ and Σ' are algebra signatures, then so are $\Sigma \cup \Sigma'$ and $\Sigma \cap \Sigma'$.

2.1.2 Semantics

In order to avoid the use of classes we start from a set $\mathcal{U}$ called *universe*.

Let $\Sigma = (S, O)$ be an algebra signature. A $(\Sigma\text{-})$*algebra* is a (total) function, say A, which maps

(i) each sort s of S into a set $A(s) \subseteq \mathcal{U}$, called the *carrier set* of sort s;

(ii) each operation $n : s_1 \dots s_k \to s_{k+1}$ ($k \geq 0$) of O into a (possibly partial) function

$$A(n : s_1 \dots s_k \to s_{k+1}) : A(s_1) \times \dots \times A(s_k) \rightsquigarrow A(s_{k+1}).$$

The set of all Σ-algebras is denoted Alg_Σ.

Let $\Sigma = (S, O)$ and Σ' be algebra signatures with $\Sigma \subseteq \Sigma'$ and let A be a Σ'-algebra. By definition $A \mid \Sigma$ denotes the Σ-algebra obtained by the restriction of the function A to the domain $S \cup O$.

2.2 Algebra modules

Intuitively, algebra modules are to represent the meaning of specifications of abstract data types (cf. [BHK 86], [BEPP 87], [EM 88]). Syntactically an algebra module is characterized by an "imported" signature and an "exported" one. Semantically it is characterized by a function mapping algebras of the imported signature into algebras of the exported one - - at least in the case of non-loose specifications. The basic idea is that an exported algebra is an extension of the imported one. Actually, it is possible to "forget" sorts and operations. Hence the sorts and operations of an imported algebra are not necessarily all "inherited" by the exported one. The requirement that the exported algebra is an extension of the imported one is therefore replaced by the requirement that the inherited sorts and operations are "persistent", i.e. that their meaning in the exported algebra is the same as in the imported algebra. These notions are now made more precise. The treatment of loose specifications is delayed until Section 4.2.

A *module signature* is a pair (Σ_i, Σ_e) of algebra signatures. Σ_i is called the *imported* signature, Σ_e the *exported* one. The sorts and operations from $\Sigma_i \cap \Sigma_e$ are called the *inherited* ones.

An *(algebra) module* for the module signature (Σ_i, Σ_e) is a (possibly partial) function

$$M : Alg_{\Sigma_i} \rightsquigarrow Alg_{\Sigma_e}$$

satisfying the following *persistency condition* :

$$\text{for each algebra } A \in Alg_{\Sigma_i} \text{ from the domain of } M\text{:}$$
$$\text{for each inherited sort or operation } c \in \Sigma_i \cap \Sigma_e\text{:}$$
$$M(A)(c) = A(c)$$

Informally, the persistency condition expresses that the meaning of any sort or operation c occurring in both the imported and exported signature remains unchanged. Note that the condition has only to hold for algebras A from the domain of M, i.e. for algebras for which $M(A)$ exists.

2.3 Logic

Let $\Sigma = (S, O)$ be an algebra signature. A *(Σ-)variable (of sort s)* is a pair $(v : s)$ or, briefly, v where v is an identifier. *Formulas* are built up from operations and variables. The precise definition of the set WFF(Σ) of all formulas for the algebra signature Σ is left pending in order to keep *OBSCURE* independent from the logic.

An *assignment* for the Σ-algebra A is a function mapping each variable of sort s into an element of the carrier set $A(s)$. The *meaning* of the logic is an extension of the function A, namely

$$A : \text{WFF}(\Sigma) \to (\text{ASS} \to \{true, false\})$$

where ASS denotes the set of all assignments for the algebra A and (ASS $\to$ $\{true, false\}$) the set of all functions on ASS with values in $\{true, false\}$ (cf. [LS 87]). Again, the precise definition of this extension is left pending. Note that the meaning has to cope with undefined values in the case of partial operations. In fact, $A(w)(\sigma)$ evaluates to *true* or *false* for any formula w and assignment σ, even if w contains terms with undefined values. Examples of logics dealing with partial operations are *LCF*([Mi 72]) and the logic described in [Lo 87].

A formula w is *valid* in a Σ-algebra A if $A(w)(\sigma) = true$ for all assignments σ. One then writes $A \models w$.

These general notions suffice for a definition of the specification language of *OBSCURE*. Actually, one gets a more explicit definition by assuming the validity of the Coincidence Theorem. To this effect the logic is supposed to provide a — not further specified — notion of a *free occurrence* of a variable in a formula. The Coincidence Theorem states that the value $A(w)(\sigma)$ of a formula w for the assignment σ depends on the value $\sigma(v)$ of only those variables v which occur free in w. As a notational abbreviation one writes $A(w)$ instead of $A(w)(\sigma)$ whenever w contains no free occurrences of variables.

2.4 Renamings

A renaming is an operation on signatures performing the simultaneous substitution of "old" names by "new" ones. In a specification renamings are defined by pairs of lists of sorts and operations. These notions are now made precise. The reader may skip the formal details in a first reading.

2.4.1 Renamings

Let $\Sigma = (S, O)$ be a signature. A *renaming (on* Σ*)* (or *signature morphism*) is a pair $\rho = (\rho_S, \rho_O)$ of functions ρ_S on S and ρ_O on O such that for each operation $o = (n : s_1 \dots s_k \to s_{k+1})$ from O

$$\rho_O(o) = (n' : s'_1 \dots s'_k \to s'_{k+1})$$

with $s'_i = \rho_S(s_i)$ for $1 \leq i \leq k+1$.

The following Lemmata are immediate consequences of the definitions:

Lemma 2: Let ρ be a renaming. If $\Sigma' \subseteq \Sigma$ is an algebra signature, then so is $\rho(\Sigma')$. □

Lemma 3: Let ρ be a renaming on Σ and let $\Sigma' \subseteq \Sigma$ be an algebra signature.

(i) If A is a $\rho(\Sigma')$-algebra, then $A \circ (\rho \mid \Sigma')$ is a Σ'-algebra.

(ii) If ρ is injective on Σ' and if B is a Σ'-algebra, then $B \circ (\rho \mid \Sigma')^{-1}$ is a $\rho(\Sigma')$-algebra. □

2.4.2 Renaming pairs

A *renaming pair (on a signature* Σ*)* is a pair of lists of sorts and operations from Σ, say

$$((s_1, \dots, s_k; o_1, \dots, o_l), (s'_1, \dots, s'_k; o'_1, \dots, o'_l)) \qquad (k, l \geq 0)$$

satisfying the following conditions:

a) the sorts $s_1, \dots, s_k$ are pairwise different;

b) the operations $o_1, \dots, o_l$ are pairwise different;

c) for each $i, 1 \leq i \leq l$: if $o_i = (n : t_1 \dots t_m \to t_{m+1})$ and $o'_i = (n' : t'_1 \dots t'_{m'} \to t'_{m'+1})$, $m, m' \geq 0$, then

- $m = m'$;
- for each $1 \leq j \leq m+1$:

$$t'_j = \begin{cases} s'_p & \text{if } t_j = s_p \text{ for some } p,\ 1 \leq p \leq k \\ t_j & \text{otherwise .} \end{cases}$$

Informally, condition c) expresses that in the arities of the new operations the sorts have already been substituted.

A renaming pair $((s_1, \dots, s_k; o_1, \dots, o_l), (s'_1, \dots, s'_k; o'_1, \dots, o'_l))$ on a signature Σ induces a renaming ρ on Σ in the following straightforward way:

- for each sort s from Σ:

$$\rho(s) = \begin{cases} s'_j & \text{if } s = s_j \text{ for some } j,\ 1 \leq j \leq k \\ s & \text{otherwise} \end{cases}$$

- for each operation $o = (n : t_1 \dots t_m \to t_{m+1})$, $m \geq 0$, from Σ:

$$\rho(o) = \begin{cases} o'_j & \text{if } o = o_j \text{ for some } j, 1 \leq j \leq l \\ (n : \rho(t_1) \dots \rho(t_m) \to \rho(t_{m+1})) & \text{otherwise} \end{cases}$$

2.5 Subalgebras, quotient algebras

Two constructions are recalled yielding subalgebras and quotient algebras respectively (see e.g. [EM 85]).

Let A be a Σ-algebra, $\Sigma = (S, O)$, and w a formula from WFF(Σ) containing free occurrences of a single variable, say $(v : s_o)$. This formula defines a subset, say C, of the carrier set $A(s_o)$ of sort s_o, namely the set of all carriers from $A(s_o)$ that satisfy w. Formally

$$C = \{a \in A(s_o) \mid A(w)(\sigma[v/a]) = \mathit{true} \text{ for all } \sigma \in \text{ASS}\}^2$$

This subset in its turn defines a subalgebra of the algebra A, namely the Σ-algebra B defined by

$$B(s) = \begin{cases} A(s) & \text{if } s \in S - \{s_o\} \\ C & \text{if } s = s_o \end{cases}$$

for each $s \in S$;

$$B(o) = A(o) \mid \ (B(s_1) \times \ldots \times B(s_k))$$
$$\text{for each } o = (n : s_1 \ldots s_k \to s) \in O,\ k \geq 0.$$

It is well-known that B is effectively an algebra only if the algebra A satisfies the following *closure condition*:

$$\text{for each } o = (n : s_1 \ldots s_k \to s) \text{ from } O, k \geq 0 :$$
$$A(o)(B(s_1) \times \ldots \times B(s_k)) \subseteq B(s_{k+1})$$

Informally the condition expresses that elements from the subset are mapped into elements from the subset. The algebra B is called the *subalgebra generated by A and w*.

Let A again be a Σ-algebra and w a formula in WFF(Σ) in which exactly two variables of the same sort, say $(u : s_o)$ and $(v : s_o)$, occur free. This formula defines an equivalence relation, say $\sim_{s_o}$, in the carrier set $A(s_o)$, namely the least equivalence relation satisfying

$$\text{for all } a, b \in A(s_o) :$$

$$a \sim_{s_o} b \text{ whenever } A(w)(\sigma[u/a][v/b]) = \mathit{true} \text{ for all } \sigma \in \text{ASS}$$

In order to simplify the wording of the following definitions it is useful to provide the other carrier sets with an equivalence relation as well:

$$\text{for all sorts } s \in S - \{s_o\} :$$

$$a \sim_s b \text{ iff } a = b$$

This family of equivalence relations defines a quotient algebra of the algebra A, namely the Σ-algebra B defined by:

$$B(s) = \{[c] \mid c \in A(s)\}^3$$
$$\text{for each } s \in S;$$

$$B(o)([c_1], \ldots, [c_k]) = \begin{cases} [A(o)(c_1, \ldots, c_k)] \text{ if } A(o)(c_1, \ldots, c_k) \text{ is defined} \\ \text{undefined otherwise} \end{cases}$$

$$\text{for each } c_i \in A(s_i), 1 \leq i \leq k,$$

$$\text{for each } o = (n : s_1 \ldots s_k \to s) \in O, k \geq 0.$$

It is well-known that B is effectively an algebra only if the algebra A satisfies the *congruence condition*:

[2] $\sigma[v/a]$ denotes the assignment identical with σ except that its value for the argument v is a. Note, by the way, that the value of $A(w)(\sigma[v/a])$ does not depend on σ by the Coincidence Theorem

[3] $[c]$ denotes the equivalence class of c generated by $\sim_s$.

for each $o = (n : s_1 \ldots s_k \rightarrow s) \in O, \quad k \geq 0$:
for all $a_i, b_i \in A(s_i)$ with $a_i \sim_{s_i} b_i, \quad 1 \leq i \leq k$:
either $A(o)(a_1, \ldots, a_k)$ and $A(o)(b_1, \ldots, b_k)$ are both undefined
or $A(o)(a_1, \ldots, a_k)$ and $A(o)(b_1, \ldots b_k)$ are both defined and
$A(o)(a_1, \ldots, a_k) \sim_s A(o)(b_1, \ldots, b_k)$

Informally, the condition expresses that equivalent arguments lead to equivalent values. The algebra B is called the *quotient algebra generated by A and w*.

For a more detailed treatment the reader may consult [EM 85] or [Lo 87]. The latter of these papers also indicates methods for proving the closure and congruence conditions.

3 The specification language

The specification language of *OBSCURE* constitutes a mathematical notation for algebra modules. While its structure is very simple, specifications written in it look clumsy. For this reason *OBSCURE* also provides a language which allows to draw up specifications; this language constitutes the design language of the *OBSCURE* environment. The present Section is devoted to the description of the specification language. The design language will be briefly discussed in Section 5.

Section 3.1 contains an informal introduction to the syntax and semantics motivating the formal definitions in Section 3.2 and 3.3. The treatment of overloading and the case of loose specifications lead to less transparent formal definitions and are therefore delayed until Section 4.

3.1 An informal overview of the language

Syntactically the specification language is a formal language, the elements of which are called *specifications*. Each specification has the form of a term. In these terms *atomic specifications* play the role of constants; constructs such as "+", "o" or "□" play the role of operators. More precisely, a specification is either an atomic specification or it has one of the following nine forms:

$$(m_1 + m_2),\ (m_1 \circ m_2),\ (lso \Box m_1),\ ([lso1/lso2]m_1),\ (m_1[lso1/lso2]),$$

$$(\{w\}m_1),\ (m_1\{w\}),\ (w \mid m_1),\ (w \bowtie m_1)$$

where m_1, m_2 are specifications, *lso*, *lso*1, *lso*2 are lists of sorts and operations and w is a formula. Note that the language bears strong similarities with the term language of [BHK 86].

Following a now classical pattern ([EM 85], [Sa 84]) the semantics of the specification language are defined in two steps:

(i) a function $\mathcal{S}$, called *signature function*, maps specifications into module signatures;

(ii) a function $\mathcal{M}$, called *meaning function*, maps specifications into algebra modules; for any specification m the module signature of the algebra module $\mathcal{M}(m)$ is $\mathcal{S}(m)$.

The semantics of atomic specifications and of the different constructs of the language are now discussed successively.

An atomic specification is a specification drawn up according to one of the numerous specification methods known from the literature. In the description of the specification language the syntax and semantics of these specifications is left pending. It is merely assumed that each atomic specification defines an algebra module. In practice an atomic specification usually consists of a "heading" and a "specification body". The heading fixes the imported and exported signatures of the module signature and the specification body defines the algebra module. In the case of the initial algebra specification method, for instance, the specification body consists of a set of equalities and the algebra module maps any imported algebra into its free extension. A concrete example of an atomic specification drawn up according to the initial algebra specification method is the following: the imported signature contains the sorts *boolean* and *integer* and the pertaining operations; the exported signature moreover contains the sort *set-of-integers* and operations such as *Emptyset*, *Insert* and *Delete*: the specification body contains equations such as

$$Insert(Insert(s,i),i) = Insert(s,i)$$

and

$$Delete(Emptyset, i) = Emptyset.$$

By the way, the predicate "atomic" refers to the semantics, not to the syntax: atomic specifications usually constitute the bulk of (the text of) a specification!

Next, the nine constructs of the specification language are discussed successively. Most of them are illustrated graphically in Figure 1.

The construct "+" puts two specifications together. More precisely, when applied to the specifications m_1 and m_2 the construct yields the specification $(m_1 + m_2)$. The module signature $\mathcal{S}((m_1 + m_2))$ of this specification is defined as the union of the module signatures $\mathcal{S}(m_1)$ and $\mathcal{S}(m_2)$ (see Figure 1(a)). The module $\mathcal{M}((m_1 + m_2))$ is defined similarly: its value is obtained by uniting the values of the modules $\mathcal{M}(m_1)$ and $\mathcal{M}(m_2)$. Hence the construct "+" of *OBSCURE* is similar to (but not identical with!) the construct "+" of *CLEAR* or "and" of *ACT-ONE*. Actually, a precise definition of the semantics of this construct has to cope with the following technical problem: the algebras accepted as arguments by the modules $\mathcal{M}((m_1 + m_2))$, $\mathcal{M}(m_1)$ and $\mathcal{M}(m_2)$ have in general different signatures. Hence the module $\mathcal{M}((m_1 + m_2))$ is defined by its value for an arbitrary algebra A of the imported signature of the module signature $\mathcal{S}((m_1 + m_2))$:

$$\mathcal{M}((m_1 + m_2))(A) = \mathcal{M}(m_1)(A \mid \mathcal{S}_i(m_1)) \cup \mathcal{M}(m_2)(A \mid \mathcal{S}_i(m_2))$$

where $\mathcal{S}_i(m_1)$ and $\mathcal{S}_i(m_2)$ are the imported signatures of the module signatures $\mathcal{S}(m_1)$ and $\mathcal{S}(m_2)$ respectively. Note that the restrictions $A \mid \mathcal{S}_i(m_1)$ and $A \mid \mathcal{S}_i(m_2)$ of the algebra A to the signatures $\mathcal{S}_i(m_1)$ and $\mathcal{S}_i(m_2)$ yield algebras of the required signatures. The right-hand side of the equality denotes the algebra obtained by the union of the graphs of the algebras $\mathcal{M}(m_1)(A \mid \mathcal{S}_i(m_1))$ and $\mathcal{M}(m_2)(A \mid \mathcal{S}_i(m_2))$. (Remember that an algebra is a function!). Actually, the union of the graphs of two functions yields (the graph of) a relation which is not necessarily a function. That the right-hand side of the equality nevertheless denotes an algebra follows from "context conditions" on the specifications m_1 and m_2. Essentially, these conditions make sure that there are no "name clashes". A precise formulation of these context conditions and the pertaining proof that the definition of the module $\mathcal{M}((m_1 + m_2))$ is consistent is to be found in Sections 3.2 and 3.3.

The construct "o" composes two specifications as illustrated by Figure 1(b). In the terminology of top-down design the specification $(m_1 \circ m_2)$ constitutes a "refinement" of the specification m_1 by the specification m_2. Hence the construct can be viewed as a generalization of the `enrich`-construct of *CLEAR*. Note that according to Figure 1(b) the construct may be applied to specifications m_1 and m_2 only if the exported signature of m_2 coincides with the imported signature of m_1. Note that a relaxation of this stringent condition is obtained in the design language through the use of "macros" (see Section 5).

The next construct allows to forget sorts and operations. More precisely, if m_1 is a specification and lso is a list of sorts and operations the specification $(lso \Box m_1)$ denotes the module obtained from m_1 by deleting from its exported signature the sorts and operations of lso (see Figure 1(c)). Note that the imported signature remains unchanged. The construct allows, in particular, to get rid of auxiliary (i.e. "hidden") sorts and operations. More importantly, it allows to remove those sorts and operations that fail to comply with the closure or congruence conditions of subsequent `subset` or `quotient` constructs.

If m_1 is a specification and $(lso1, lso2)$ is a renaming pair then the specification $([lso1/lso2]m_1)$ denotes the module obtained from m_1 by renaming its exported signature according to $(lso1, lso2)$ (see Figure 1(d)). Again, the imported signature remains unchanged. In particular, if an inherited sort or operation is renamed, only its occurrences in the exported signature are modified. The construct may, for instance, be used to avoid name clashes that might arise in a subsequent "+"-construct.

Let m_1 and $(lso1, lso2)$ be as above. The specification $(m_1[lso1/lso2])$ performs a renaming of the imported signature (see Figure 1(e)). Contrasting with the previous construct the renaming of an inherited sort or operation modifies its occurrences in both the imported and exported signature. The construct allows in particular to simulate the parameter passing mechanism used in the design language: the formal parameters $lso1$ are renamed into actual parameters $lso2$ — as will be explained in Section 5.

Let m be a specification and w a formula. The effect of the specification $(\{w\}m)$ is to make sure that the formula w is valid in the algebra $\mathcal{M}(m)(A)$. The signatures remain unchanged. The construct

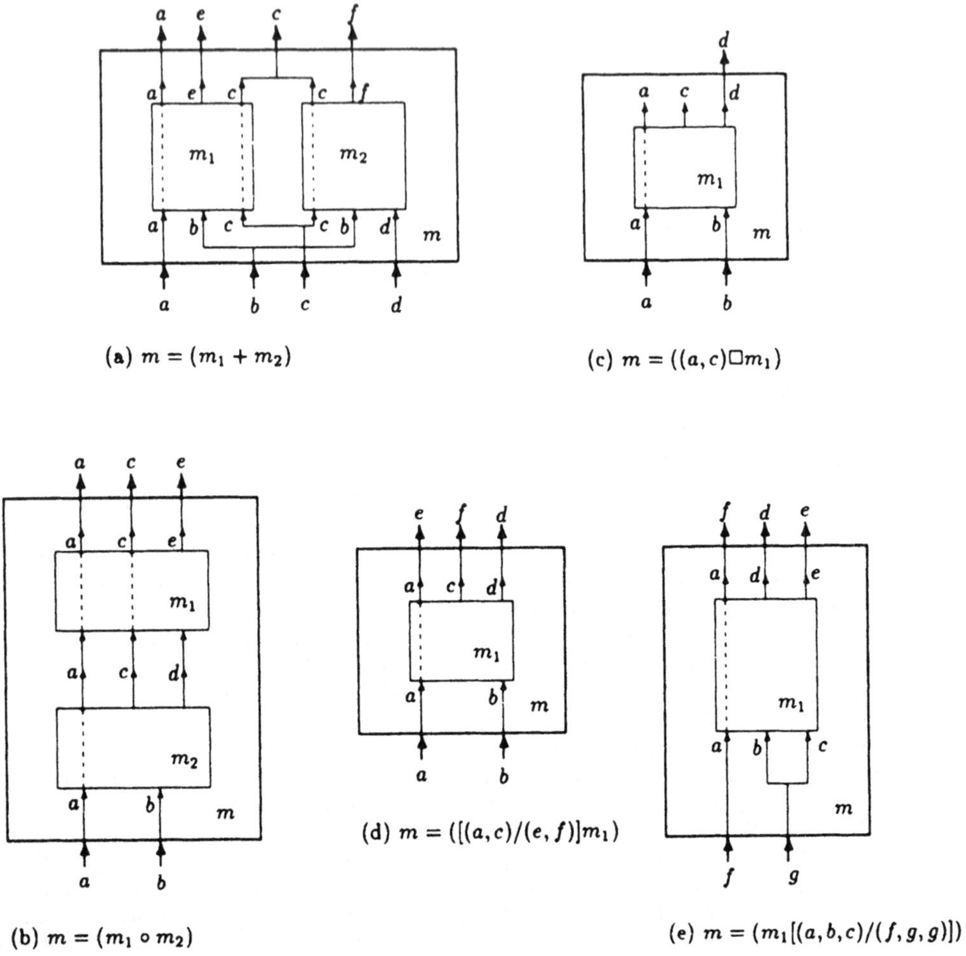

(a) $m = (m_1 + m_2)$

(c) $m = ((a,c)\Box m_1)$

(b) $m = (m_1 \circ m_2)$

(d) $m = ([(a,c)/(e,f)]m_1)$

(e) $m = (m_1[(a,b,c)/(f,g,g)])$

FIGURE 1 Graphical illustration of a few constructs of the specification language. In this illustration a specification is represented by a box. The arrows entering a box represent its imported sorts and operations, those leaving a box represent its exported sorts and operations. A dotted line represents an inherited sort or operation. Each of the symbols $a, b, \ldots, f, g$ stands for a sort or an operation.

may be used to express that the data type specified by m satisfies the property denoted by w. Formally, the effect of the construct $(\{w\}m)$ is to restrict the domain of the module $\mathcal{M}(m)$ to those algebras A for which the formula w is valid in the algebra $\mathcal{M}(m)(A)$, i.e. for which

$$\mathcal{M}(m)(A) \models w \tag{1}$$

In practice the user has to prove that (1) holds for all "intended" algebras A. To perform this proof he may make use of the verification unit of the *OBSCURE* environment.

The specification $(m\{w\})$ is similar to the previous one but now the formula w expresses a property of the imported algebra. The construct may be used to explicitly restrict the domain of the module. It will be used in Section 5 to express semantic constraints on the formal parameters of a procedure.

Let m be a specification and w a formula with free occurrences of a single variable. The specification $(w \mid m)$ performs a subalgebra construct. More precisely, $\mathcal{M}((w \mid m))(A)$ is the subalgebra generated by the algebra $\mathcal{M}(m)(A)$ and the formula w (see Section 2.5). The proof that the closure condition is satisfied is left to the user. Again, he may perform this proof by making use of the verification unit of the *OBSCURE* environment. Note that the module signature remains unchanged but that the meaning of the sort of the variable occurring free in w is "overwritten". The subalgebra construct may, for instance, be used to transform a specification of multisets into a specification of sets by eliminating the multisets containing duplicates. Subalgebra constructs are essential in the algorithmic specification method ([Lo 87]). Algebraic specifications may do without subalgebra constructs but their use may make specifications more transparent and modular.

Finally, the specification $(w \bowtie m)$ performs a quotient algebra construct along the same lines as the subalgebra construct. Again, the user has to prove that the congruence condition of Section 2.5 is satisfied. A quotient algebra may, for instance, be used to transform a specification of lists into a specification of multisets by identifying lists which differ by the order of occurrence of their elements only. The remarks on the necessity of the subalgebra construct carry over.

After this informal overview we now proceed with a formal definition of the syntax and the semantical functions $\mathcal{S}$ and $\mathcal{M}$ of the specification language. The syntax, $\mathcal{S}$ and $\mathcal{M}$ are defined inductively. The syntax and the semantical function $\mathcal{S}$ are defined by simultaneous induction and are treated first.

3.2 The syntax and the semantical function $\mathcal{S}$

The goal of this Section is to define

- a formal language **SPEC** of specifications;
- a function $\mathcal{S}$ mapping any specification of **SPEC** into a module signature.

To this end we start from a signature Σ and a set **AtSPEC**, the elements of which are called *atomic specifications*[4]. It is assumed that a module signature $\mathcal{S}_o(am) \subseteq \Sigma^2$ is associated with each specification am from **AtSPEC**.

The set **SPEC** and the function $\mathcal{S}$ are now defined by simultaneous induction. In this definition $\mathcal{S}$ is defined as a function mapping each specification from **SPEC** into a pair of signatures. That these pairs of signatures are module signatures, i.e. pairs of algebra signatures, is proved in Theorem 4.

Each step in the now following definition is accompanied by conditions denoted $(i), (ii), \ldots$. These conditions are called *context conditions*. The name stems from the fact that these conditions define a subset of the context-free language implicitly introduced by the informal definition of the syntax in Section 3.1. The aim of these context conditions is to guarantee the consistency of the definitions of the semantical functions $\mathcal{S}$ and $\mathcal{M}$, i.e. to make the proofs of Theorem 4 and Theorem 5 feasible.

Most of the formal definitions now following may be clear from the informal description of Section 3.1. Some of the "difficult" context conditions will be briefly discussed after the formal definition. The reader should remember the notations introduced in Section 2.1.1. Moreover, for each specification m $\mathcal{S}_i(m)$ and $\mathcal{S}_e(m)$ denote the imported and exported signature of the module m. Hence

$$\mathcal{S}(m) = (\mathcal{S}_i(m), \mathcal{S}_e(m)) \ .$$

Definition (The formal language **SPEC** and the semantical function $\mathcal{S}$)
(Induction basis) If $am \in$ **AtSPEC** then:

[4] Note that Σ plays the role of a "universal signature": all signatures occurring in this Section are subsets of Σ.

- $am \in$ **SPEC**
- $\mathcal{S}(am) = \mathcal{S}_o(am)$

(Induction step) If $lso, lso1, lso2$ are lists of sorts and operations from Σ, if $w \in \mathrm{WFF}(\Sigma)$ and if $m, m_1, m_2 \in$ **SPEC** then:

(1) if

(i) $\mathcal{S}_e(m_1) \cap \mathcal{S}_e(m_2) \subseteq \mathcal{S}_i(m_1) \cap \mathcal{S}_i(m_2)$
(ii) $\mathcal{S}_e(m_1) \cap \mathcal{S}_i(m_2) \subseteq \mathcal{S}_i(m_1)$
(iii) $\mathcal{S}_e(m_2) \cap \mathcal{S}_i(m_1) \subseteq \mathcal{S}_i(m_2)$

then

- $(m_1 + m_2) \in$ **SPEC**
- $\mathcal{S}((m_1 + m_2)) = \mathcal{S}(m_1) \cup \mathcal{S}(m_2)$

(2) if

(i) $\mathcal{S}_e(m_2) = \mathcal{S}_i(m_1)$
(ii) $\mathcal{S}_i(m_2) \cap \mathcal{S}_e(m_1) \subseteq \mathcal{S}_i(m_1)$

then

- $(m_1 \circ m_2) \in$ **SPEC**
- $\mathcal{S}((m_1 \circ m_2)) = (\mathcal{S}_i(m_2), \mathcal{S}_e(m_1))$

(3) if

(i) $\mathcal{S}_e(m) \setminus lso$ is an algebra signature

then

- $(lso \Box m) \in$ **SPEC**
- $\mathcal{S}((lso \Box m)) = (\mathcal{S}_i(m), \mathcal{S}_e(m) \setminus lso)$

(4) if

(i) $(lso1, lso2)$ is a renaming pair; call ρ the induced renaming
(ii) the renaming ρ is injective on $\mathcal{S}_e(m)$
(iii) none of the sorts and operations of $lso2$ are from $\mathcal{S}_i(m)$

then

- $([lso1/lso2]m) \in$ **SPEC**
- $\mathcal{S}(([lso1/lso2]m)) = (\mathcal{S}_i(m), \rho(\mathcal{S}_e(m)))$

(5) if

(i) $(lso1, lso2)$ is a renaming pair; call ρ the induced renaming
(ii) the renaming ρ is injective on the operations of $\mathcal{S}_e(m) \setminus \mathcal{S}_i(m)$
(iii) the sorts and operations of $lso1$ are all from $\mathcal{S}_i(m)$
(iv) $\rho(so) \notin \rho(\mathcal{S}_e(m) \setminus \mathcal{S}_i(m))$ for each sort or operation so of $\mathcal{S}_i(m)$

then

- $(m[lso1/lso2]) \in$ **SPEC**
- $\mathcal{S}((m[lso1/lso2])) = \rho(\mathcal{S}(m))$

(6) if

(*i*) $w \in \mathbf{WFF}(\mathcal{S}_e(m))$

then

- $(\{w\}m) \in \mathbf{SPEC}$
- $\mathcal{S}((\{w\}m)) = \mathcal{S}(m)$

(7) if

(*i*) $w \in \mathbf{WFF}(\mathcal{S}_i(m))$

then

- $(m\{w\}) \in \mathbf{SPEC}$
- $\mathcal{S}((m\{w\})) = \mathcal{S}(m)$

(8) if

(*i*) $w \in \mathbf{WFF}(\mathcal{S}_e(m))$

(*ii*) w contains free occurrences of a single variable; call s the sort of this variable

(*iii*) s is not a sort from $\mathcal{S}_i(m)$

then

- $(w \mid m) \in \mathbf{SPEC}$
- $\mathcal{S}((w \mid m)) = \mathcal{S}(m)$

(9) if

(*i*) $w \in \mathbf{WFF}(\mathcal{S}_e(m))$

(*ii*) w contains free occurrences of exactly two variables; these variables have the same sort; call s this sort

(*iii*) s is not a sort from $\mathcal{S}_i(m)$

then

- $(w \bowtie m) \in \mathbf{SPEC}$
- $\mathcal{S}((w \bowtie m)) = \mathcal{S}(m)$ □

Before proceeding we briefly comment on the intuitive meaning of the most "difficult" context conditions. The full significance of these context conditions will become clear in the proofs of Theorem 4 and 5. The context condition (1)(*i*) expresses that a sort or operation exported by both m_1 and m_2 is an inherited one of m_1 and m_2. The condition (1)(*ii*) expresses that a sort or operation exported by m_1 and imported by m_2 is inherited by m_1. The condition (1)(*iii*) is similar. The condition (2)(*ii*) expresses that a sort or operation exported by m_1 and imported by m_2 is an inherited one. The condition (4)(*ii*) avoids name clashes within the exported signature. Similarly, (4)(*iii*) avoids clashes between the new exported names and the imported ones. The condition (5)(*iii*) allows to rename only imported sorts and operations. Note that contrasting with the preceding construct the renaming has not to be injective on $\mathcal{S}_i(m)$, i.e. different names may be given the same new name; the utility of this possibility will become clear in the discussion of the parameter passing mechanism: it must be possible that different formal parameters get the same actual value. The condition (5)(*iv*) avoids clashes between the new imported names and the (new) non-inherited exported ones. Finally, the condition (5)(*ii*) expresses that the renaming does not lead to name clashes between the non-inherited exported operations. (Remember that the renaming of an imported sort may modify the arity of a non-inherited exported operation). The conditions (8)(*ii*) and (9)(*ii*) refer to the construction of subalgebras and quotient algebras in Section 2.5.

We now prove that $\mathcal{S}$ is the desired semantical function, i.e. that the values of $\mathcal{S}$ are module signatures.

Theorem 4. $\mathcal{S}(m)$ is a module signature for each specification $m \in \mathbf{SPEC}$.

Proof

$\mathcal{S}(m)$ has been defined as a pair of signatures. According to the definition of a module signature in Section 2.2 it is sufficient to prove that both signatures are algebra signatures. The proof is by induction on the structure of m and refers to the above Definition.

(Induction basis)

$\mathcal{S}(am) = \mathcal{S}_o(am)$ is a module signature by assumption.

(Induction step)

(1) $\mathcal{S}(m_1) \cup \mathcal{S}(m_2) = (\mathcal{S}_i(m_1) \cup \mathcal{S}_i(m_2), \mathcal{S}_e(m_1) \cup \mathcal{S}_e(m_2))$ is a module signature by induction hypothesis and Lemma 1.

(2) By induction hypothesis.

(3) By the context condition (3)(i) and the induction hypothesis.

(4) and (5) By induction hypothesis, Lemma 2 and context conditions (4)(i) and (5)(i) respectively.

(6) to (9) By induction hypothesis. □

3.3 The semantical function $\mathcal{M}$

Let the signature Σ, the set of atomic specifications **AtSPEC** and the semantical function $\mathcal{S}_o$ on **AtSPEC** be given as above. Let moreover **SPEC** and $\mathcal{S}$ be defined as indicated in Section 3.2. The goal of the present Section is to define a function $\mathcal{M}$ mapping any specification of **SPEC**, say m, into an algebra module with module signature $\mathcal{S}(m)$. To this end it is assumed that an algebra module $\mathcal{M}_o(am)$ with module signature $\mathcal{S}_o(am)$ is associated with each atomic specification am from **AtSPEC**.

The function $\mathcal{M}$ is now defined by its value $\mathcal{M}(m)(A)$ for an arbitrary specification $m \in \mathbf{SPEC}$ and an arbitrary algebra A of the imported signature $\mathcal{S}_i(m)$ of m. That $\mathcal{M}(m)$ is effectively an algebra module will be proved in Theorem 5. The basis of this proof is constituted by the context conditions of the definition of **SPEC**. Hence the comments on these context conditions at the end of Section 3.2 — together with the informal description of the language in Section 3.1 — may help the reader to understand the formal definitions now following.

An algebra module is a partial function. Hence a value $\mathcal{M}(m)(A)$ of $\mathcal{M}(m)$ is not necessarily defined. In fact the last four constructs of the language **SPEC** may introduce partiality, even if the "atomic specifications" $\mathcal{M}_o(am)$ are all total — as will become clear below.

The formal definition of the semantical function $\mathcal{M}$ is by structural induction on its argument m. Hence it closely follows the structure of the inductive definition of **SPEC** in Section 3.1.

Definition (The semantical function $\mathcal{M}$) Writing

"$\mathcal{M}(x)(A) = E$ iff C"

as a shorthand for

"for all algebras $A \in Alg_{\mathcal{S}_i(x)}$:
$\mathcal{M}(x)(A)$ is defined iff C holds; in that case its value is E"

one defines:

(Induction basis)

$$\mathcal{M}(am)(A) = \mathcal{M}_o(am)(A)$$
iff $\mathcal{M}_o(am)(A)$ is defined

(Induction step)

(1)

$$\mathcal{M}((m_1 + m_2))(A) = \mathcal{M}(m_1)(A \mid \mathcal{S}_i(m_1)) \cup \mathcal{M}(m_2)(A \mid \mathcal{S}_i(m_2))$$
iff $\mathcal{M}(m_1)(A \mid \mathcal{S}_i(m_1))$ and $\mathcal{M}(m_2)(A \mid \mathcal{S}_i(m_2))$ are both defined

(2)

$$\mathcal{M}((m_1 \circ m_2))(A) = \mathcal{M}(m_1)(\mathcal{M}(m_2)(A))$$

iff $\mathcal{M}(m_2)(A)$ and $\mathcal{M}(m_1)(\mathcal{M}(m_2)(A))$ are both defined

(3)

$$\mathcal{M}((lso\Box m))(A) = \mathcal{M}(m)(A) \mid (\mathcal{S}_e(m) \setminus lso)$$

iff $\mathcal{M}(m)(A)$ is defined

(4)

$$\mathcal{M}(([lso1/lso2]m))(A) = (\mathcal{M}(m)(A)) \circ (\rho \mid \mathcal{S}_e(m))^{-1}$$

iff $\mathcal{M}(m)(A)$ is defined

where ρ is the renaming induced by $(lso1,\ lso2)$

(5)

$$\mathcal{M}((m[lso1/lso2]))(A) = \{(\rho(so'), \mathcal{M}(m)(A \circ (\rho \mid \mathcal{S}_i(m)))(so')) \mid so' \in \mathcal{S}_e(m)\}$$

iff $\mathcal{M}(m)(A \circ (\rho \mid \mathcal{S}_i(m)))$ is defined

where ρ is the renaming induced by $(lso1,\ lso2)$

(6)

$$\mathcal{M}((\{w\}m))(A) = \mathcal{M}(m)(A)$$

iff $\mathcal{M}(m)(A)$ is defined and $\mathcal{M}(m)(A) \models w$

(7)

$$\mathcal{M}((m\{w\}))(A) = \mathcal{M}(m)(A)$$

iff $\mathcal{M}(m)(A)$ is defined and $A \models w$

(8)

$\mathcal{M}((w \mid m))(A) =$ the subalgebra generated by $\mathcal{M}(m)(A)$ and w

iff $\mathcal{M}(m)(A)$ is defined and $\mathcal{M}(m)(A)$ satisfies the closure condition

(9)

$\mathcal{M}((w \bowtie m))(A) =$ the quotient algebra generated by $\mathcal{M}(m)(A)$ and w

iff $\mathcal{M}(m)(A)$ is defined

and $\mathcal{M}(m)(A)$ satisfies the congruence condition

□

Theorem 5. The definition of the semantical function $\mathcal{M}$ is consistent, i.e. for each specification $m \in$ **SPEC** it is the case that $\mathcal{M}(m)$ is an algebra module with module signature $\mathcal{S}(m)$.
The proof is in the Appendix. □

4 Two Generalizations

4.1 Overloading

An operation has been defined as consisting of its name together with its arity. Actually, in terms or formulas it is usual to denote an operation by its name only. This postulates that it is possible to distinguish between operations with the same operation name. This disambiguation is classically performed by type inferencing. Type inferencing is particularly easy to perform when any two operations with the same operation name differ by the number or the sort of their arguments. These notions are now made more precise.

A signature is called *unambiguous* if for any two different operations

$$n : s_1 \ldots s_k \rightarrow s_{k+1}$$
$$n : t_1 \ldots t_k \rightarrow t_{k+1} \qquad (k \geq 0)$$

with the same operation name n and the same number k of arguments there exists i, $1 \leq i \leq k$, such that $s_i \neq t_i$.

It is easy to adapt the definition of the specification language of Section 3 to algebras with unambiguous signatures. While the definitions of the semantical functions $\mathcal{S}$ and $\mathcal{M}$ remain unchanged the formal language **SPEC** is slightly restricted by additional context conditions. More precisely, each of the constructs

$$(m_1 + m_2)$$
$$(m_1 \circ m_2)$$
$$([lso1/lso2]m)$$
$$(m[lso1/lso2])$$

is provided with additional context conditions expressing that the resulting module signature consists of a pair of unambiguous signatures. For instance, the additional context conditions for the construct $(m_1 + m_2)$ are:

(*iv*) $\mathcal{S}_i(m_1) \cup \mathcal{S}_i(m_2)$ is unambiguous

(*v*) $\mathcal{S}_e(m_1) \cup \mathcal{S}_e(m_2)$ is unambiguous

Clearly, these restrictions do not affect the validity of the Theorems 4 and 5.

4.2 Loose specifications

In Section 3 atomic specifications were assumed to be drawn up according to a non-loose specification method — such as the initial algebra specification method or a constructive specification method. We now briefly discuss the case in which loose specification methods are used, i.e. specification methods allowing several rather than a unique model. To this end it is necessary to generalize the notion of an algebra module. Next the semantics of the specification language will be modified accordingly.

A *loose (algebra) module* for the module signature (Σ_i, Σ_e) is a total function

$$M : Alg_{\Sigma_i} \rightarrow \mathcal{P}(Alg_{\Sigma_e})$$

(where $\mathcal{P}(Alg_{\Sigma_e})$ denotes the power set of Alg_{Σ_e}) satisfying the following *persistency condition*:

for each algebra $A \in Alg_{\Sigma_i}$:
for each algebra $B \in M(A)$:
for each inherited sort or operation $c \in \Sigma_i \cap \Sigma_e$:
$B(c) = A(c)$.

Informally, a loose module maps any imported algebra into a set of exported ones. Note that loose modules are total functions while — according to Section 2.2 — non-loose ones are partial: in loose modules the undefined value is "simulated" by the empty set.

The generalization of the specification language of Section 3 for loose specifications is straightforward. The definitions of the formal language **SPEC** and the semantical function $\mathcal{S}$ remain unchanged. On the other hand $\mathcal{M}_0$ now assigns a loose module $\mathcal{M}_0(am)$ to each atomic specification $am \in$ **At-SPEC**. The definition of the semantical function $\mathcal{M}$ is generalized by componentwise application. More precisely, the definition of Section 3.3 is replaced by:

(Induction basis)

$$\mathcal{M}(am)(A) = \mathcal{M}_0(am)(A)$$

(Induction step)

(1) $\mathcal{M}((m_1 + m_2))(A) =$
$\{B \cup C \mid B \in \mathcal{M}(m_1)(A \mid \mathcal{S}_i(m_1)),\ C \in \mathcal{M}(m_2)(A \mid \mathcal{S}_i(m_2))\}$

(2) $\mathcal{M}((m_1 \circ m_2))(A) = \bigcup\{\mathcal{M}(m_1)(B) \mid B \in \mathcal{M}(m_2)(A)\}$

(3) $\mathcal{M}((lso\Box m))(A) = \{B \mid (\mathcal{S}_e(m) \setminus lso) \mid B \in \mathcal{M}(m)(A)\}$

(4) $\mathcal{M}(([lso1/lso2]m))(A) = \{B \circ (\varrho \mid \mathcal{S}_e(m))^{-1} \mid B \in \mathcal{M}(m)(A)\}$
— where ϱ is the renaming induced by $(lso1, lso2)$

(5) $\mathcal{M}((m[lso1/lso2]))(A) =$
$\{\{(\varrho(so'), B(so')) \mid so' \in \mathcal{S}_e(m)\} \mid B \in \mathcal{M}(m)(A \circ (\varrho \mid \mathcal{S}_i(m)))\}$
— where ϱ is the renaming induced by $(lso1, lso2)$

(6) $\mathcal{M}((\{w\}m))(A) = \{B \in \mathcal{M}(m)(A) \mid B \models w\}$

(7) $\mathcal{M}((m\{w\}))(A) = \begin{cases} \mathcal{M}(m)(A) & \text{if } A \models w \\ \emptyset & \text{otherwise} \end{cases}$

(8) $\mathcal{M}((w \mid m))(A) =$

$$\{\text{the subalgebra generated by } B \text{ and } w \mid B \in \mathcal{M}(m)(A)\}$$

(9) $\mathcal{M}((w \bowtie m))(A) =$

$$\{\text{the quotient algebra generated by } B \text{ and } w \mid B \in \mathcal{M}(m)(A)\}.$$

The proof of Theorem 5 carries over without any difficulty (see [Kn 87]). A user of *OBSCURE* has not to explicitly indicate which of the two definitions of $\mathcal{M}$ he uses. If some of his atomic specifications make use of a loose specification method the relevant definition of $\mathcal{M}$ is of course the present one. Otherwise both the present definition and the definition of Section 3.3 apply.

5 An overview of the *OBSCURE* environment

While the specification language described in Section 3 and 4 has a transparent mathematical structure it is difficult to write specifications in it using pencil and paper. This difficulty stems from the clumsy notation, the elaborate context conditions and the primitivity of the constructs. Moreover, it is necessary to prove that the semantic constraints resulting from a subalgebra construct $(w \mid m)$, a quotient construct $(w \bowtie m)$ and a construct $(\{w\}m)$ or $(m\{w\})$ are satisfied. To this end *OBSCURE* provides an environment consisting of a design unit and a verification unit. The design unit supports the user in the development of (syntactically correct) specifications. The verification unit supports the user in the proof that the semantical constraints are satisfied. The different aspects of the *OBSCURE* environment are now briefly discussed.

5.1 The design language

To control the design unit the specifier makes use of a language called *design language*. This language may be viewed as yet another specification language. As such it differs from the specification language described above by a user-friendly notation, by additional powerful language constructs ("macros") and by the possibility to draw up parameterized specifications. Alternatively, the design language may be viewed as a programming language. The execution of a program written in this language yields a specification of the specification language, i.e. a specification of **SPEC**. We here adopt the former viewpoint.

The goal of the present Subsection is to roughly describe the main features by which the design language differs from the specification language. To this end we successively discuss the notation, the macros and the parameterization mechanism.

All constructs of the specification language are part of the design language but some "operators" are expressed in a more user-friendly notation. One writes, for instance

$$(m \textbf{ forget } lso)$$

and

$$(m \textbf{ input-rename } lso1 \textbf{ as } lso2)$$

instead of $(lso \square m)$ and $(m[lso1/lso2])$ respectively. Moreover, in the case of left associativity the brackets may be omitted. For instance, one writes $m_1 \circ m_2 + m_3$ instead of $((m_1 \circ m_2) + m_3)$.

A macro has the same form as a construct of the specification language. It may be considered as a shorthand notation for a specification. An example of a macro is

$$(m_1 \textbf{ compose } m_2)$$

the meaning of which is illustrated in Figure 2. It may be considered as a shorthand for the specification $(m_1 + 1_g) \circ (1_{a,b} + m_2)$ where — loosely speaking — 1_g and $1_{a,b}$ stand for atomic specifications with $\mathcal{S}_i(1_g) = \mathcal{S}_e(1_g) = \{g\}$ and $\mathcal{S}_i(1_{a,b}) = \mathcal{S}_e(1_{a,b}) = \{a,b\}$. By the way, this macro constitutes a generalization of the construct $(m_1 \circ m_2)$ circumventing the stringent context condition (2)(i) of Section 3.2.

Parameterization is realized with the help of two constructs called *declaration* and *instantiation* respectively. The semantical description of these constructs makes use of an *environment* consisting of the current list of all declarations.

A declaration has the form

$$\textbf{module } n(lso) \textbf{ is } m \textbf{ end}$$

where n is a name called *module name*, lso a list of sorts and operations called *formal parameters* and m a specification called *module body*. As a context condition the sorts and operations of lso have to be from the imported signature of m, i.e. $lso \subseteq \mathcal{S}_i(m)$. The effect of a declaration is the addition of the triple (n, lso, m) to the environment. A simple example of a declaration is

$$\textbf{module } \text{SET } (element) \textbf{ is } m \textbf{ end}$$

where m is a specification for the sort *set* (of elements). Hence, *element* is a sort from $\mathcal{S}_i(m)$ and *set* a sort from $\mathcal{S}_e(m)$.

An instantiation has the form

$$n(lso')$$

where n is a module name from the environment and lso' is a list of sorts and operations called *actual parameters*. An instantiation stands for a specification, namely the specification

$$(m[lso/lso'])$$

-- being understood that (n, lso, m) is the triple of the environment with module name n. Resuming the preceding example the instantiation

$$\text{SET } (integer)$$

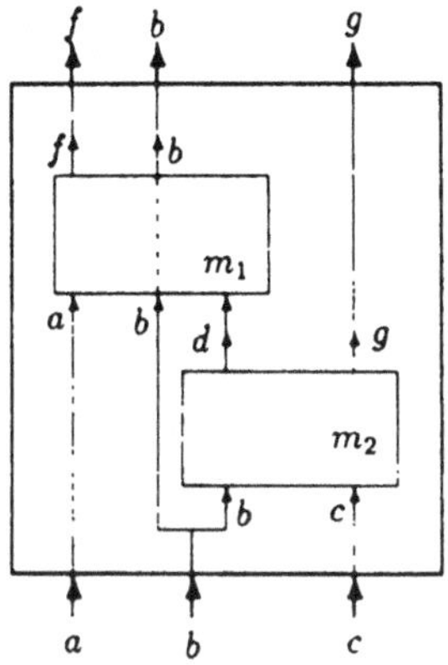

FIGURE 2 Graphical illustration of (m_1 **compose** m_2). The conventions are those of Figure 1.

stands for the specification

$$(m[element/integer])$$

This specification has *integer* instead of *element* among its imported sorts. Moreover the carrier set of the exported sort *set* consists of sets of integers rather than sets of elements.

Note that the construct $(m\{w\})$ may be used to express semantic constraints on the parameters. In the declaration

$$\textbf{module } n(lso) \textbf{ is } (m\{w\}) \textbf{ end}$$

the formal parameters *lso* — or, more precisely, the imported algebra — are bound to satisfy the formula w. This constraint on the formal parameters is automatically transformed into a constraint on the actual parameters by the renaming

$$((m\{w\})[lso/lso'])$$

induced by the instantiation

$$n(lso').$$

5.2 The design unit

The design unit supports the incremental design of specifications written in the design language. It checks the context conditions of Section 3.2 automatically and on-line. It displays the current imported and exported signatures. For the constructs yielding a subalgebra or a quotient algebra it automatically generates formulas expressing the closure or the congruence condition respectively.

The editor of the design unit may be run in two modes : pure editing or syntax-directed editing. It accepts incomplete information and asks for additional details when necessary. The user may, for instance, omit the arity of an operation, the sort of a variable or the imported signature of an atomic specification.

A prototype of the design unit has been implemented on a Siemens $MX-2$ computer [FH 88]. A final version is under design.

5.3 The verification unit

The verification of a formula in the exported signature of a specification m is performed in two steps. First the formula is transformed into an "equivalent" formula in the exported signature of an atomic specification contained by m. Next this formula is proved on the basis of the properties of this atomic specification. The first part of such a verification depends on the (properties of the) specification language of *OBSCURE* only. A calculus performing this transformation is to be presented in a forthcoming paper. The second part of a verification essentially depends on the specification method used. In the case of the algorithmic specification method one may use the proof methods described in [Lo 87]. In the case of the initial algebra specification method one may use, for instance, term rewriting.

A prototype of the verification unit is under development. The specification methods considered are the algorithmic specification method and the initial algebra specification method.

References

[BCV 85] Bidoit, M., Choppy, C., Voisin, F., "The ASSPEGIQUE specification environment — Motivations and design", *Int. Rep., Univ. Paris-Sud* (Oct. 1985)

[BEPP 87] Blum, E.K., Ehrig, H., Parisi–Presicce, F., "Algebraic Specification of Modules and Their Basic Interconnections", *JCSS* **34** (1987), pp. 293 - 339

[BG 80] Burstall, R.M., Goguen, J.A., "The semantics of Clear, a specification language", *Proc. 1979 Copenhagen Winter School, LNCS* **86** (1980), pp. 292 - 332

[BGM 87] Bidoit, M., Gaudel, M.C., Mauboussin, A., "How to make algebraic specifications more understandable? — An experiment with the PLUSS specification language", *Int. Rep. 343, Univ. Paris-Sud* (Apr. 1987)

[BHK 86] Bergstra, J.A., Heering, J., Klint, P., "Module Algebra", *Report CS-RXXX, Centre for Math. and Comp. Sc., Amsterdam* (1986), submitted for publication

[BHK 87] Bergstra, J.A., Heering, J., Klint, P., "ASF — An algebraic specification formalism", *Report CS-R 8705, Centre for Math. and Comp. Sc., Amsterdam* (1987)

[Bu 87] Burstall, R.M., "Inductively Defined Functions in Functional Programming Languages", *Int. Rep. ECS-LFCS-87-25, Univ. Edinburgh* (April 1987)

[BW 82] Broy, M., Wirsing, M., "Partial abstract types", *Acta Inform.* **18** (1982), pp. 47 - 64

[Ca 80] Cartwright, R., "A constructive alternative to abstract data type definitions", *Proc. 1980 LISP Conf., Stanford Univ.* (1980), pp. 46 - 55

[Eh 82] Ehrich, H.D., "On the theory of specifications, implementation and parameterization of abstract data types", *Journal ACM* **29** (1982), pp. 206 - 227

[En 72] Enderton, H.B., "A Mathematical Introduction to Logic", *Academic Press* (1972)

[EM 85] Ehrig, H., Mahr, B., "Fundamentals of Algebraic Specification (Part 1)", *Springer-Verlag* (1985)

[EM 88] Ehrig, H., Mahr, B., "Fundamentals of Algebraic Specification (Part 2)", *Springer-Verlag* (to appear)

[Fe 87] Fey, W., "Concepts, syntax and semantics of ACT-TWO", presented at the *5th Workshop on Specification of Abstract Data Types, Edinburgh* (Sept. 1987)

[FGJM 85] Futatsugi, K., Goguen, J., Jouannaud, J.P., Meseguer, J., "Principles of OBJ2", *Proc. POPL 85* (1985), pp. 52 - 66

[FH 88] Fuchs, J., Hoffmann, A., Loeckx, J., Meiss, L., Philippi, J., Zeyer, J., "Benutzerhandbuch des *OBSCURE*-Systems — Teil 1: Der Editor", *Int. Rep. WP 88/05, Univ. Saarbrücken* (1988)

[Gd 84] Gaudel, M.C., "A first introduction to PLUSS", *Int. Rep.*, *Univ. Paris-Sud* (Dec. 1984)

[GHM 78] Guttag, J.V., Horowitz, E., Musser, D.R., "Abstract data types and software validation", *Comm. ACM* **21** (1978), pp. 1048 - 1069

[GTW 78] Goguen, J.A., Thatcher, J.W., Wagner, E.G., "An initial algebra approach to the specification, correctness and implementation of abstract data types", *Current Trends in Programming Methodology IV* (Yeh, R., ed.), *Prentice-Hall* (1978), pp. 80 - 149

[Ho 72] Hoare, C.A.R., "Proof of correctness of data representations", *Acta Inf.* **1**, 4 (1972), pp. 271 - 281

[Hu 87] Hussmann, H., "Rapid Prototyping for Algebraic Specifications — RAP System User's Manual" (Revised edition), *Int. Rep. MIP-8504*, *Univ. Passau* (1987)

[Kl 84] Klaeren, H.A., "A constructive method for abstract algebraic software specification", *Theor. Comp. Sc.* **30**, 2 (1984), pp. 139 - 204

[Kn 87] Klein, B., "Zwei Erweiterungen von *OBSCURE*", *Diplomarbeit*, *FB* 10, *Univ. Saarbrücken* (1987)

[LG 86] Liskov, B., Guttag, J., "Abstraction and specification in program development", *The MIT Electrical Engin. and Comp. Sc. Series*, *McGraw-Hill* (1986)

[Li 81] Liskov, B., et al., "CLU Reference Manual", *LNCS* **114** (1981)

[LL 87] Lehmann, T., Loeckx, J., "*OBSCURE*: A specification environment for abstract data types", *Int. Rep. A06/87*, *Univ. Saarbrücken* (1987)

[Lo 87] Loeckx, J., "Algorithmic Specifications: A Constructive Specification Method for Abstract Data Types", *TOPLAS* **9**, 4 (1987), pp. 646 - 685

[LS 87] Loeckx, J., Sieber, K., "The Foundations of Program Verification" (Second edition), *Wiley/Teubner* (1987)

[Mi 72] Milner, R., "Logic for computable functions: description of a machine implementation", *SIGPLAN NOTICES* **7** (1972), pp. 1 - 6

[NY 83] Nakajima, R., Yuasa, T., "The IOTA Programming System", *LNCS* **160** (1983)

[Sa 84] Sannella, D., "A set-theoretic semantics for Clear", *Acta Informatica* **21**, 5 (1984), pp. 443 - 472

[Sh 81] Shaw, M., "ALPHARD, Form and Content", *Springer-Verlag* (1981)

[Sp 88] Spivey, J.M., "Understanding Z", *Cambridge University Press* (1988)

[TWW 82] Thatcher, J.W., Wagner, E.G., Wright, J.B., "Data type specification: Parameterization and the power of specification techniques", *TOPLAS* **4** (1982), pp. 711 - 732

[Wi 86] Wirsing, M., "Structured algebraic specifications: A kernel language", *Theor. Comp. Sc.* **42**, 2 (1986), pp. 124 - 249

Appendix

Proof of Theorem 5

The proof is by induction on the structure of m. To this end it is sufficient to successively consider the defining equalities of the form

$$\mathcal{M}(x)(A) = E \text{ iff } C$$

and to prove:

(I) whenever C holds the expression E yields an algebra of signature $\mathcal{S}_e(x)$ as its value;

(II) $\mathcal{M}(x)$ satisfies the persistency condition, i.e. for each inherited sort or operation so from $\mathcal{S}_i(x) \cap \mathcal{S}_e(x)$:

$$\mathcal{M}(x)(A)(so) = A(so)$$

The proposition (I) may be replaced by the following three propositions:

(Ia) whenever C holds the value of the expression E is defined;

(Ib) whenever C holds the value of the expression E is a function;

(Ic) this function is an algebra (over $\mathcal{S}_e(x)$).

In the proof now following the application of the induction hypothesis is not always explicitly mentioned.

(Induction basis)

The theorem follows from the assumption that $\mathcal{M}_o(am)$ is an algebra module.

(Induction step)

(1) $\mathcal{M}((m_1 + m_2))(A)$

As A is an algebra of signature $\mathcal{S}_i(m_1) \cup \mathcal{S}_i(m_2)$, $A \mid \mathcal{S}_i(m_1)$ is an algebra of signature $\mathcal{S}_i(m_1)$. Hence the value $\mathcal{M}(m_1)(A \mid \mathcal{S}_i(m_1))$ is well-defined. A similar remark holds for $\mathcal{M}(m_2)(A \mid \mathcal{S}_i(m_2))$. This proves (Ia).

To prove (Ib) it is sufficient to prove that any sort or operation $so \in \mathcal{S}_e(m_1) \cap \mathcal{S}_e(m_2)$ has the same meaning in the algebras $\mathcal{M}(m_1)(A \mid \mathcal{S}_i(m_1))$ and $\mathcal{M}(m_2)(A \mid \mathcal{S}_i(m_2))$, i.e.

$$\mathcal{M}(m_1)(A \mid \mathcal{S}_i(m_1))(so) = \mathcal{M}(m_2)(A \mid \mathcal{S}_i(m_2))(so)$$

By context condition (i) one obtains $so \in \mathcal{S}_i(m_1) \cap \mathcal{S}_i(m_2)$. Hence so is an inherited sort of both m_1 and m_2. By induction hypothesis one obtains

$$\begin{aligned}\mathcal{M}(m_1)(A \mid \mathcal{S}_i(m_1))(so) &= (A \mid \mathcal{S}_i(m_1))(so)\\ &= A(so)\end{aligned}$$

and a similar equality for m_2. This concludes the proof of (Ib).

(Ic) is a direct consequence of the fact that $\mathcal{M}(m)(A \mid \mathcal{S}_i(m_1))$ and $\mathcal{M}(m)(A \mid \mathcal{S}_i(m_2))$ are algebras.

To prove (II) let so be an inherited sort or operation of $(m_1 + m_2)$, i.e.

$$so \in (\mathcal{S}_i(m_1) \cup \mathcal{S}_i(m_2)) \cap (\mathcal{S}_e(m_1) \cup \mathcal{S}_e(m_2))$$

It has to be proved that so has the same meaning in A and $\mathcal{M}((m_1 + m_2))(A)$. This follows directly from the induction hypothesis using the inclusion

$$(\mathcal{S}_i(m_1) \cup \mathcal{S}_i(m_2)) \cap (\mathcal{S}_e(m_1) \cup \mathcal{S}_e(m_2)) \subseteq (\mathcal{S}_i(m_1) \cap \mathcal{S}_e(m_1)) \cup (\mathcal{S}_i(m_2) \cap \mathcal{S}_e(m_2))$$

which can be deduced from context conditions (ii) and (iii).

(2) $\mathcal{M}((m_1 \circ m_2))(A)$

(Ia) directly follows from context condition (i).

The proofs of (Ib) and (Ic) are immediate with context condition (i).

Let so be an inherited sort or operation of $(m_1 \circ m_2)$. Hence $so \in \mathcal{S}_i(m_2) \cap \mathcal{S}_e(m_1)$. By context condition ($ii$) one obtains $so \in \mathcal{S}_i(m_1) \cap \mathcal{S}_i(m_2)$. Hence (II) holds.

(3) $\mathcal{M}((lso\Box m))(A)$

The proofs of (Ia), (Ib) and (Ic) are immediate.

An inherited sort or operation of $(lso\Box m)$ is an inherited one in m. This proves (II).

(4) $\mathcal{M}(([lso1/lso2]m))(A)$

The renaming ρ is well-defined by context condition (i). The inverse function $(\rho \mid \mathcal{S}_e(m))^{-1}$: $\rho(\mathcal{S}_e(m)) \to \mathcal{S}_e(m)$ is well-defined by context condition (ii). Hence (Ia), (Ib) and (Ic) follow from Lemma 3(ii). In particular, the signature of the algebra

$$(\mathcal{M}(m)(A)) \circ (\rho \mid \mathcal{S}_e(m))^{-1}$$

is clearly $\rho(\mathcal{S}_e(m))$.

In order to prove (II) it suffices to show

$$\mathcal{S}_i(m) \cap \rho(\mathcal{S}_e(m)) \subseteq \mathcal{S}_e(m) \qquad (a)$$

and

$$\rho(so) = so \quad \text{for} \quad so \in \mathcal{S}_i(m) \cap \rho(\mathcal{S}_e(m)) \qquad (b)$$

In fact we can deduce the validity of (II) from (a) and (b) as follows:

For $so \in \mathcal{S}_i(m) \cap \rho(\mathcal{S}_e(m))$ we have by (a) :

$$so \in \mathcal{S}_i(m) \cap \mathcal{S}_e(m)$$

and therefore, with (b) and the induction hypothesis:

$$(\mathcal{M}(m)(A) \circ (\rho \mid \mathcal{S}_e(m))^{-1})(so) = (\mathcal{M}(m)(A) \circ (\rho \mid \mathcal{S}_e(m))^{-1})(\rho(so))$$

$$= \mathcal{M}(m)(A)(so) = A(so)$$

yielding (II).

It remains to prove (a) and (b).

Let so be a sort or operation from $\mathcal{S}_i(m) \cap \rho(\mathcal{S}_e(m))$. By context condition ($iii$) $so \notin lso2$. Let $so' \in \mathcal{S}_e(m)$ be the sort for which $\rho(so') = so$. Then so' cannot be an element of $lso1$. (because $\rho(so') \notin lso2$). If so and so' are sorts, it directly follows

$$so' = \rho(so') = so$$

proving (a) and (b) for sorts.

If so and so' are operations one has

$$\begin{aligned} so =& \quad (n : s_1 \ldots s_k \to s_{k+1}) \\ so' =& \quad (n : s'_1 \ldots s'_k \to s'_{k+1}) \qquad (k \geq 0) \end{aligned}$$

with $\rho(s'_i) = s_i$ $(1 \leq i \leq k+1)$ by the very definition of renaming. Since $\mathcal{S}_e(m)$ and, by Lemma 1, $\mathcal{S}_i(m) \cap \rho(\mathcal{S}_e(m))$ are algebra signatures we have

$$\begin{aligned} & s'_i \in \mathcal{S}_e(m) \\ \text{and} \quad & s_i \in \mathcal{S}_i(m) \cap \rho(\mathcal{S}_e(m)) \quad (1 \leq i \leq k+1). \end{aligned}$$

By context condition (*iii*) $s_i \notin lso2 \cup \mathcal{S}_i(m) = \emptyset$, hence

$$s'_i \notin lso1 \qquad (1 \leq i \leq k+1).$$

Hence

$$s'_i = \rho(s'_i) = s_i \qquad (1 \leq i \leq k+1).$$

This yields $so = so'$ proving (*a*) and (*b*) for operations.

(5) $\mathcal{M}((m[lso1/lso2])(A)$

Let us first prove (Ia). Clearly, $\rho \mid \mathcal{S}_i(m)$ is a function mapping $\mathcal{S}_i(m)$ into $\rho(\mathcal{S}_i(m))$. By assumption A is an algebra with signature $\rho(\mathcal{S}_i(m))$. Hence

$$A \circ (\rho \mid \mathcal{S}_i(m))$$

is an algebra with signature $\mathcal{S}_i(m)$ (see Lemma 3(*i*)). As $\mathcal{M}(m)$ is a module with signature $(\mathcal{S}_i(m), \mathcal{S}_e(m))$, it accepts $A \circ (\rho \mid \mathcal{S}_i(m))$ as an argument and yields an algebra $\mathcal{M}(m)(A \circ (\rho \mid \mathcal{S}(m)))$ with signature $\mathcal{S}_e(m)$. This algebra accepts so' as an argument. Hence the relation denoted by the righthand side of the equality is well-defined.

To prove (Ib) we prove that this relation is a function. In order to shorten the notation we put $B = \mathcal{M}(m)(A \circ (\rho \mid \mathcal{S}_i(m)))$. Let $so', so'' \in \mathcal{S}_e(m), so' \neq so''$, be sorts or operations such that

$$\rho(so') = \rho(so'') \qquad (c)$$

It is sufficient to prove that

$$B(so') = B(so'')$$

We distinguish three cases:

- so' and so'' are both inherited in m. In that case

$$\begin{aligned} B(so') &= (A \circ (\rho \mid \mathcal{S}_i(m)))(so') \quad \text{by persistency} \\ &= A(\rho(so')) \end{aligned}$$

  and similarly for so''. Hence the property results from (*c*).

- so' is inherited in m but so'' is not. Hence $so' \in \mathcal{S}_i(m)$ and $so'' \in \mathcal{S}_e(m) \setminus \mathcal{S}_i(m)$. By context condition (*iv*), $\rho(so') \notin \rho(\mathcal{S}_e(m) \setminus \mathcal{S}_i(m))$. Hence $\rho(so') \neq \rho(so'')$ which contradicts (*c*).

- neither so' nor so'' are inherited in m, i.e. so' and so'' are both from $\mathcal{S}_e(m) \setminus \mathcal{S}_i(m)$. If so', so'' are sorts, then $\rho(so') = so'$ and $\rho(so'') = so''$ by context condition (*iii*). Hence $\rho(so') \neq \rho(so'')$ which contradicts (*c*). If so', so'' are operations then context condition (*ii*) implies $\rho(so') \neq \rho(so'')$ contradicting (*c*).

  To prove (Ic) put $C = \mathcal{M}((m[lso1/lso2]))(A)$. We have to show that for any operation $o = (n : s_1 \ldots s_k \rightarrow s_{k+1}) \in \rho(\mathcal{S}_e(m))$, $(k \geq 0)$, it is the case that:

  α) The domain of $C(o)$ is contained in $C(s_1) \times \ldots \times C(s_k)$

  β) $C(o)(C(s_1) \times \ldots \times C(s_k)) \subseteq C(s_{k+1})$.

  By definition of C (and B) we have:

$$C(so) = B(so')$$

  for all $so \in \rho(\mathcal{S}_e(m))$ and $so' \in \mathcal{S}_e(m)$ with $so = \rho(so')$. Let $o' = (n' : s'_1 \ldots s'_k \rightarrow s'_{k+1}) \in \mathcal{S}_e(m)$ be such that $\rho(o') = o$. Note that

$$\rho(s'_i) = s_i \quad (1 \leq i \leq k+1) \qquad (d)$$

  The domains of $C(o)$ and $B(o')$ coincide by definition. They are contained in $B(s'_1) \times \ldots \times B(s'_k)$ because B is a $\mathcal{S}_e(m)$-algebra. By (*d*) and the definition of C we obtain

$$C(s_i) = B(s'_i) \quad (1 \leq i \leq k+1)$$

  proving α). A similar argument shows the validity of β).

Finally, we prove (II). Let

$$so \in \rho(\mathcal{S}_i(m)) \cap \rho(\mathcal{S}_e(m))$$

be a sort or operation. We have to prove that

$$A(so) = (\mathcal{M}(m)(A \circ (\rho \mid \mathcal{S}_i(m))))(so') \qquad (e)$$

for a sort or operation $so' \in \mathcal{S}_e(m)$ satisfying $so = \rho(so')$. Now we have the obvious inclusion

$$\rho(\mathcal{S}_i(m)) \cap \rho(\mathcal{S}_e(m)) \subseteq \rho(\mathcal{S}_e(m)) = \rho(\mathcal{S}_e(m) \cap \mathcal{S}_i(m)) \cup \rho(\mathcal{S}_e(m) \setminus \mathcal{S}_i(m)).$$

By context condition (iv)

$$\rho(\mathcal{S}_i(m)) \cap \rho(\mathcal{S}_e(m) \setminus \mathcal{S}_i(m)) = \emptyset$$

yielding

$$\rho(\mathcal{S}_i(m)) \cap \rho(\mathcal{S}_e(m)) \subseteq \rho(\mathcal{S}_e(m) \cap \mathcal{S}_i(m)).$$

Hence it is possible to choose so' from $\mathcal{S}_e(m) \cap \mathcal{S}_i(m)$ and

$$\mathcal{M}(m)(A \circ (\rho \mid \mathcal{S}_i(m)))(so') = (A \circ (\rho \mid \mathcal{S}_i(m)))(so')$$

$$= A(\rho(so')) = A(so)$$

by persistency of $\mathcal{M}(m)$ yielding (e).

(6) $\mathcal{M}((\{w\}m))(A)$

$\mathcal{M}(m)(A) \models w$ is well-defined by context condition (i). This proves (Ia).

The proofs of (Ib), (Ic) and (II) are immediate.

(7) $\mathcal{M}((m\{w\}))(A)$

As for (6).

(8) $\mathcal{M}((w \mid m))(A)$

The subalgebra generated by $\mathcal{M}(m)(A)$ and w is well-defined by the context conditions (i) and (ii) (and by the fact that the closure condition is satisfied). This proves (Ia), (Ib) and (Ic).

Let so be an inherited sort or operation of $(w \mid m)$. If it is a sort it cannot be s by context condition (iii). If it is an operation the sort s cannot occur in its arity — again by context condition (iii) and because $\mathcal{S}_i(m)$ is an algebra signature. Hence the meaning of so is not modified by the subalgebra construction. This proves (II).

(9) $\mathcal{M}((w \bowtie m))(A)$

As for (8). □

Algebraic Specifications of Reachable Higher-Order Algebras*

Bernhard Möller
Institut für Informatik
Technische Universität München
Postfach 20 24 20
D-8000 München 2

Andrzej Tarlecki
Institute of Computer Science
Polish Academy of Sciences
PKiN, P.O. Box 22
PL-00901 Warsaw

Martin Wirsing
Fakultät für Informatik
Universität Passau
Postfach 2540
D-8390 Passau

Abstract

We propose a way of integrating predefined data type constructions, in particular higher-order function spaces, into the framework of algebraic specifications such that some standard results such as existence of initial and terminal algebras for hierarchical specifications are preserved. The central idea is to employ the generation principle for the built-in construction of function spaces; not all functions are considered but only those that can be denoted by terms. This leads to a particularly simple theory in which the extended specifications can be related to the usual first-order ones.

1 Introduction

The design of suitable data structures is one of the crucial points in the construction of large software systems. There are two complementary approaches for describing data structures: either by using other predefined built-in data structures, such as records, arrays, sets or even function spaces (in higher-order languages), or by abstractly defining the new data structures with the help of e.g. algebraic methods.

The latter approach, known under the catchwords "abstract data types" or "algebraic specifications", permits to describe software independently from unnecessary details such as implementation decisions or overspecification caused by the programming model as it is often the case with the former approach. With few exceptions, algebraic specifications have been restricted to encompass first-order operations only. However, higher-order operations are, not only theoretically, but even more from the methodological point of view quite valuable, for example for describing schematic algorithms, such as generic tree traversals, or for structuring by extraction of common patterns in routines through suitable parameterization (for examples see [Möller 87]).

In this paper we propose a way of integrating the standard constructions of (higher-order) function spaces in the framework of algebraic specifications. Our technique preserves results such as existence of initial and terminal algebras.

*This research has been partially sponsored by the ESPRIT-project 436, METEOR (MW) and by grants from the Polish Academy of Sciences and from the Science and Engineering Research Council (AT).

Among the approaches allowing higher-order operations in algebraic specifications known from the literature, viz. [Maibaum, Lucena 80], [Parsaye-Ghomi 81], [Dybjer 83], [Poigné 84], [Poigné 86], [Möller 86], [Möller 87], [Broy 86], the last two concentrate, like in the first-order case, on algebras that follow the generation principle; this means that only term-denotable subsets of function spaces are considered as carriers of higher-order types. We follow this line since we deem it adequate for computer science; denotability is a prerequisite for effectiveness. It turns out that the generation principle leads to a particularly simple theory which allows to keep many of the structural properties of the first-order case. In the present paper we give an explanation for this phenomenon by relating higher-order specifications to first-order ones.

To avoid the technical problems associated with binding mechanisms, we do not allow λ-abstractions as terms. This is no loss in power, since $\lambda x.t$ can always be replaced by a new constant symbol f together with the axiom $fx = t$.

We consider a hierarchical approach to algebraic specifications: a hierarchical abstract type contains a designated primitive subtype that can be understood, analyzed, and implemented on its own, that is, without using any information about the overall type. On the other hand, the enclosing type can be viewed as a "black box" the behaviour of which is given by the effects w.r.t. the primitive type. This reflects a basic method in computer science: nonprimitive objects are semantically explained by the effects they have within arbitrary primitive contexts ("visible" or "observable" behaviour, "input-output" behaviour). Under suitable conditions (sufficient completeness and hierarchy-consistency), such hierarchical specifications have initial and terminal models; the isomorphism classes of their models form a complete lattice and the terminal models are fully abstract, i.e. the non-primitive objects of terminal models are characterized by their observable behaviour.

The paper is organized as follows:

In section 2 the basic definitions and some important properties of algebraic specifications are briefly presented. Algebraic specifications with higher-order operations are introduced in section 3. In general, higher-order types may be interpreted as arbitrary sets. It is only in extensional algebras that these carriers are actually isomorphic to sets of functions. This behaviour is axiomatically enforced by extensional specifications. We relate higher-order specifications to first-order ones and give a lattice theorem for non-hierarchical extensional higher-order specifications as a corollary to the corresponding theorem for first-order specifications.

In section 4 the lattice properties of hierarchical higher-order specificatons are investigated. It is shown that under the usual conditions of sufficient completeness and hierarchy-consistency (generalized to the higher-order case) every hierarchical higher-order specification admits an initial model. However, terminal models do not always exist. Full abstraction may be inconsistent with the requirement of extensionality; there are simple examples where no extensional terminal model exists. Therefore we introduce an additional semantical condition, called "distinguishability condition", which allows us to prove that the isomorphism classes of reachable higher-order (extensional) models of a hierarchical specification form a complete lattice; the smallest element of this lattice is formed by the terminal models which are fully abstract and extensional.

An early version of this paper contained also an attempt to generalise this work on higher-order specifications to other standard data type constructions such as power sets or Cartesian products. Unfortunately, only after this generalisation appeared as [Möller et al. 88] we have realised that some of its details are inaccurate (see section 5 for few more remarks on this).

2 Preliminaries on algebraic specifications

Throughout the paper we deal with many-sorted sets, functions, relations etc. (For any set S, an S-sorted set is just a family $X = (X_s)_{s\in S}$ of sets indexed by S, and similarly for functions, relations etc.) We feel free to use any standard set-theoretic notation without explicit use of indices: for example, we write $x \in X$ rather than $x \in X_s$ for some $s \in S$, and $h : X \to Y$ rather than $h = \{h_s : X_s \to Y_s\}_{s\in S}$.

We adopt the usual definitions of (many-sorted) **signature** and, for any signature $\Sigma = (S, F)$, of (discrete, total) **Σ-algebra**, **Σ-homomorphism**, **Σ-term**, **Σ-equation** and **Σ-congruence**.

For any Σ-algebra A, we denote by A_s the carrier of sort s in A.

We write A_w for the cartesian product $A_{s_1} \times \ldots \times A_{s_n}$ where $w = \langle s_1, \ldots, s_n\rangle$ and $\langle s_1, \ldots, s_n\rangle \in S$. (If n = 0, A_w is a one-element set.) By $T(\Sigma)$ we denote the **algebra of ground Σ-terms** and by $T(\Sigma, X)$ the **algebra of Σ-terms with free variables** in X (where X is an S-sorted set of free variables). Then $T(S, X)_w$ denotes the set of all w-tuples of Σ-terms. If x is a free variable of sort s, then $T(S, x{:}s)_{s_1}$ denotes the set of all **Σ-contexts** of x of sort s_1.

A **positive conditional Σ-equation** is a Σ-formula Φ of the form

$$\forall x_1{:}s_1 \ldots x_n{:}s_n.\ (\wedge_{i\in I}\ u_i = v_i) \Rightarrow u = v$$

where $n \geq 0$; $s_1, \ldots, s_n \in S$; $u_i, v_i, u, v \in T(\Sigma, \{x_1, \ldots, x_n\})$ for $i \in I$; I is a finite or infinite set of indices, hence Φ may be an infinitary formula. For any Σ-algebra A, we write $A \models \Phi$ if A satisfies Φ. We also use the notation $K \models E$, where K is a class of Σ-algebras and E is a set of Σ-formulae, with the obvious meaning.

Given a Σ-algebra A there exists a unique Σ-homomorphism ρ from $T(\Sigma)$ into A. The value of the **interpretation** $t^A = \rho(t)$ of any Σ-term $t \in T(\Sigma)$ in A is uniquely defined by this homomorphism. The image of ρ is the **least Σ-subalgebra** $\langle A\rangle_\Sigma$ of A. If $A = \langle A\rangle_\Sigma$ then A is called **reachable** (or **term-generated**) (w.r.t. Σ). In this case every carrier set A_s, $s \in S$, of A is generated by the ground terms of sort s, i.e. $A_s = \{t^A \mid t \in T(\Sigma)_s\}$.

For any Σ-algebra A and set of sorts $S' \subseteq S$, we denote by $\sim^A|_{S'}$ the **S'-restriction of the congruence** $\sim^A$ on ground terms **associated with** A, i.e. the sets $(\sim^A|_{S'})_s = \{\langle t, t'\rangle \mid A \models t = t'$, $t, t' \in T(\Sigma)_s\}$, $s \in S'$ of all (pairs of terms forming) ground Σ-equations with a sort in S' that hold in A. If $S' = S$ we simply write $\sim^A$. If A and B are reachable Σ-algebras, then there exists a Σ-homomorphism from A to B if and only if $\sim^A \subseteq \sim^B$, hence A and B are isomorphic if and only if $\sim^A = \sim^B$. Therefore in the sequel we identify isomorphism classes of reachable algebras with the associated congruences.

Given a class K of Σ-algebras, a Σ-algebra $A \in K$ is **initial** (resp. terminal) in K iff for any $B \in K$ there exists exactly one Σ-homomorphism from A to B (resp. from B to A). If K is a class of reachable Σ-algebras, then the **initial congruence** (resp. **terminal congruence**) of the set of congruences associated to K is the smallest (resp. coarsest) congruence in this set w.r.t. set-theoretic inclusion.

An algebraic specification $SP = \langle\Sigma, E\rangle$ consists of a signature Σ and a (possibly infinite) set E of positive conditional Σ-equations. When writing down the axioms of a specification we usually omit the universal quantifiers. The set of all Σ-congruences satisfying E is denoted by $RMod(\Sigma, E)$ or equivalently by $RMod(SP)$.

Theorem 2.1 The congruences of *RMod*(*SP*) form a complete lattice.

Proof The proof is standard: since all axioms in *SP* are positive conditional equations, *RMod*(*SP*) is closed under intersection and so forms a complete lower semilattice. Then, since the total relation on ground terms is a trivial, coarsest congruence which satisfies *SP*, it is the greatest element of this lattice. Thus *RMod*(*SP*) is a complete lattice. □

It is worth pointing out that infinitary conditional equations form the most general logical system for which the above theorem holds (see [Mahr, Makowsky 84, Tarlecki 85, Tarlecki 86] for an exact formulation of this result).

A **hierarchical algebraic specification** is a triple $HSP = \langle SP, P, S'_P\rangle$. Here, $SP = \langle S, E\rangle$ is a specification with $\Sigma = (S, F)$. The **primitive part** $P = \langle \Sigma_P, \sim^P\rangle$ of *HSP* consists of **a primitive signature** $\Sigma_P = (S_P, F_P)$ with $\Sigma_P \subseteq \Sigma$ and of a Σ_P-congruence $\sim^P$ on the term-algebra $T(\Sigma_P)$. Strictly speaking, P should be replaced by a specification having $\sim^P$ as, say, the initial model. Finally, $S'_P \subseteq S_P$ is a distinguished subset of **protected** primitive sorts. A term t is called **protected** if $t \in T(\Sigma_P, X)_s$ with $s \in S'_P$, it is called of **protected sort** if $t \in T(\Sigma, X)_s$ with $s \in S'_P$. For the convenience of presentation we assume that E contains all equations which hold in P, i.e. that $\sim^P \subseteq \sim$ for any $\sim \in$ *RMod*(*SP*).

As for example [Broy et al. 84], we consider only isomorphism classes for the (protected) primitive part instead of arbitrary classes of algebras (this is mainly for a simpler formulation of the theorems). We should point out, however, that our definition is slightly more general than the one in the paper cited above. In [Broy et al. 84], it is always the case that all the primitive sorts are viewed as protected; i.e., $S'_P = S_P$ is assumed. Nevertheless it is straightforward to check that all the results of that paper easily extend to the slightly more general framework we consider here.

By *HMod*(*SP*,*P*) we denote the class of all reachable hierarchical models (as usual, identified with their associated congruences) of $\langle SP, P, S'_P\rangle$; these are all Σ-congruences $\sim \in$ *RMod*(*SP*) that "protect" S'_P, i.e., such that for each protected primitive sort $s \in S'_P$

- for every term $t \in T(\Sigma)_s$, there exists a protected term $t_P \in T(\Sigma_P)_s$ such that $t \sim t_P$, and
- for any two protected ground terms $t, t' \in T(\Sigma_P)_s$, if $t \sim t'$ then $t \sim^P t'$.

In other words, the first requirement means that for any reachable Σ-algebra A associated with $\sim$, all protected primitive carrier sets A_s with $s \in S'_P$ are reachable w.r.t. the primitive signature Σ_P, i.e., $A_s = \{t^A \mid t \in T(\Sigma_P)_s\}$. Since we have assumed that *SP* contains all the equations of P, the second requirement implies that on protected ground terms $\sim$ is exactly the same as $\sim^P$.

A (hierarchical or non-hierarchical) specification *SP* is called **monomorphic**, if it admits exactly one isomorphism class of reachable (hierarchical) algebras as model, i.e., if its set of congruences contains exactly one element.

A hierarchical specification $\langle SP, P, S'_P\rangle$ is called **hierarchy-consistent** if for all ground Σ_P-equations $t = t'$ between protected terms $E \models t = t'$ implies $t \sim^P t'$. It is called **hierarchy-complete** (or **sufficiently complete**) if for every ground term $t \in T(\Sigma)_s$ of a protected primitive sort there exists a protected term t_P such that $RMod(SP) \models t = t_P$.

Notice that in the above definition we used the **semantical** notion of consequence. As is well known, it may be replaced by a corresponding proof-theoretic notion; it is possible to define a sound and complete proof system for the many-sorted equational calculus with infinitary formulae (see e.g. [Keisler 71] where such a proof system was developed for the full infinitary logic).

Theorem 2.2 Let $\langle SP, P, S'_P \rangle$ be a hierarchy-complete and hierarchy-consistent hierarchical specification.

(1) The isomorphism classes of *HMod*(*SP*, *P*) form a non-empty complete lower semilattice. In particular, *HMod*(*SP*, *P*) has an initial model I the equality of which is characterized as follows: for all ground terms $t, t' \in T(\Sigma)$, $I \models t = t'$ iff *RMod*(*SP*)$\models t = t'$.

(2) If the premises of the axioms E are of protected primitive sort then the isomorphism classes of *HMod*(*SP*,*P*) form a complete lattice. In particular, *HMod*(*SP*,*P*) has a terminal model Z the equality relation of which is characterized as follows: for all ground terms $t, t' \in T(\Sigma)$, $Z \models t = t'$ iff for all contexts $c \in T(\Sigma, x)$ of protected primitive sort, *RMod*(*SP*) $\models c[t] = c[t']$.

The **proof** can be directly taken from the proofs of theorem 1 and theorem 2 in [Broy et al. 84]. □

As an immediate corollary one gets that the terminal model Z of theorem 2.2 (2) is fully abstract, i.e., for all $t, t' \in T(\Sigma)$, $Z \models t = t'$ iff for all contexts $c \in T(\Sigma, x)$ of protected primitive sort, $Z \models c[t] = c[t']$. If the protected sorts are just the sorts of type level 0, this coincides with the notion in [Plotkin 77, Milner 77].

3 Higher-order specifications

In usual algebraic specifications functions are of first order: functions cannot occur as parameters nor as results of other functions. In contrast, in higher-order specifications functions are "first-class objects". They can occur as parameters and results of other functions. In an extensional higher-order specification certain sorts are interpreted as (subsets of) function spaces; in any higher-order model of such a specification the objects of these sorts are functions.

For a given set B of basic sorts we define the set $B^{\rightarrow}$ of higher-order sorts. A higher-order signature consists of a set B and of a $B^{\rightarrow}$-sorted family of function symbols which we interpret as constants (of higher-order sorts) and to which we add function application for each higher-order sort.

Definition 3.1 Let B be a set of basic sorts.

(1) The set $B^{\rightarrow}$ of **higher-order sorts** (generated from B) is the least set such that $B \subseteq B^{\rightarrow}$ and for any $w \in (B^{\rightarrow})^n$, $n > 0$, and $s \in B^{\rightarrow}$, $(w \rightarrow s) \in B^{\rightarrow}$.

(2) A **higher-order signature** Σ is a pair $\Sigma = (B, (F_s)_{s \in B^{\rightarrow}})$ where for each $s \in B^{\rightarrow}$, F_s is a (possibly empty) set of constant symbols of sort s. Any higher-order signature Σ determines a first-order signature $\Sigma^{\rightarrow} =_{def} (B^{\rightarrow}, (F_s)_{s \in B^{\rightarrow}} \cup \text{FFUNC}(B))$ where $\text{FFUNC}(B) = \{apply_{w \rightarrow s} : (w \rightarrow s), w \rightarrow s \mid w, s \in B^{\rightarrow}\}$.

(3) A **higher-order Σ-algebra** is a $\Sigma^{\rightarrow}$-algebra.

The only non-constant function symbols in $\Sigma^{\rightarrow}$ are the application-function symbols, each of which takes an argument of a higher-order sort and a tuple of arguments appropriate for this sort and returns a result of the sort indicated in the higher-order sort of its first argument. Other "function" symbols are represented here as constants of higher-order sorts which may be interpreted as functions via the application functions.

Since higher-order Σ-algebras are just ordinary $\Sigma^{\rightarrow}$-algebras, the notions of homomorphism, reachability, subalgebra, term, term algebra $T(\Sigma^{\rightarrow})$, congruence for many-sorted algebras carry directly over to the higher-order case. In the same way, the notions of conditional equation and satisfaction carry over.

Notation: We write $t(t_1, \ldots, t_n)$ for $apply_{w \rightarrow s}(t, t_1, \ldots, t_n)$, where $w \in (B^{\rightarrow})^n$, $s \in B^{\rightarrow}$, $t \in T(\Sigma^{\rightarrow}, X)_{w \rightarrow s}$ and $\langle t_1, \ldots, t_n \rangle \in T(\Sigma^{\rightarrow}, X)_w$, and we write $f(a_1, \ldots, a_n)^A$ for $apply^A(f, a_1, \ldots, a_n)$, where A is a higher order Σ-algebra, $f \in A_{w \rightarrow s}$, and $\langle a_1, \ldots, a_n \rangle \in A_w$.

The following property ensures that elements of higher order sorts behave like functions:

Definition 3.2 A higher order Σ-algebra is **extensional**, if for all sorts $w \rightarrow s \in B^{\rightarrow}$ and for all $f, g \in A_{w \rightarrow s}$ the following holds:

if $f(a_1, \ldots, a_n)^A = g(a_1, \ldots, a_n)^A$ for all $\langle a_1, \ldots, a_n \rangle \in A_w$, then $f = g$.

Extensional algebras are isomorphic to algebras where the elements of higher-order carrier sets are functions; every carrier set $A_{w \rightarrow s}$ of an extensional algebra A is isomorphic to a subset of the function space $[A_w \rightarrow A_s]$. This subset is countable if Σ is countable and A is reachable. Obviously, extensionality is preserved under isomorphism. It should be pointed out, though, that in general neither subalgebras nor quotients of an extensional algebra need to be extensional.

Example 3.3 Consider a signature Σ with a sort s and operations

$a,\ b : s$
$f,\ g : s \rightarrow s$

and an extensional Σ-algebra A given by

$A_s =_{def} \{a, b\},\ a^A =_{def} a,\ b^A =_{def} b$
$A_{s \rightarrow s} =_{def} \{f, g\},\ f^A(x) =_{def} a,\ g^A(x) =_{def} x$ for all $x \in \{a, b\}$.

Clearly, the reduct of A to the subsignature which contains only the operations a, f and g is extensional as well. However, its reachable subalgebra B is given by

$B_s = \{a\},\ a^B = a$
$f^B(a) = g^B(a) = a$ (but $f^B \neq g^B$)

and thus is not extensional. Moreover, the quotient of A obtained by setting $a^A = b^A$ (which looks much like B) is not extensional either. □

Extensionality of **reachable** higher-order algebras can be axiomatized by the following set of ground infinitary conditional equations:

$(\mathbf{ext})_\Sigma$: $(\bigwedge_{\langle t_1, \ldots, t_n \rangle \in T(\Sigma^{\rightarrow})_w} t(t_1, \ldots, t_n) = t'(t_1, \ldots, t_n)) \Rightarrow t = t'$,
for all $t, t' \in T(\Sigma^{\rightarrow})_{w \rightarrow s}$, $w \in (B^{\rightarrow})^n$, $s \in B^{\rightarrow}$.

Fact 3.4 A reachable higher order Σ-algebra is extensional iff it satisfies the axioms $(\mathbf{ext})_\Sigma$.

Proof Clear, since for any reachable algebra A we have $A = \{t^A \mid t \in T(\Sigma^{\rightarrow})\}$. □

For non-reachable higher-order algebras neither of the above implications needs to hold.

Example 3.5 Consider a signature Σ_1 with a sort s and operations

$$a : s$$
$$f : s \rightarrow s$$

and a non-reachable Σ_1-algebra A given by

$$A_s =_{def} \{a\},\ a^A =_{def} a$$
$$A_{s\rightarrow s} =_{def} \{f, g\},\ f^A(a) =_{def} g^A(a) =_{def} a$$

Since $(\mathbf{ext})_{\Sigma_1} = \{(\bigwedge_{n\geq 0} f(f^n(a)) = f(f^n(a))) \Rightarrow f = f\}$, A satisfies $(\mathbf{ext})_{\Sigma_1}$ without being extensional.

Conversely, consider a signature Σ_2 with a sort s and operations

$$a : s$$
$$f,\ g : s \rightarrow s$$

and a non-reachable Σ_2-algebra B given by

$$B_s = \{a, b\},\ a^B =_{def} a$$
$$f^A(x) = a,\ g^A(x) = x.$$

Because of $a = f^A(a) = g^A(a)$, B satisfies $t = a$ for all $t \in T(\Sigma_2^{\rightarrow})_s$. Hence, B satisfies the premise of the axiom

$$(\bigwedge_{t\in T(\Sigma_2^{\rightarrow})_s} f(t) = g(t)) \Rightarrow f = g$$

in $(\mathbf{ext})_{\Sigma_2}$, but not its conclusion. Hence B is extensional without satisfying $(\mathbf{ext})_{\Sigma_2}$. □

Fact 3.6 Any extensional higher-order congruence is uniquely determined by its reduction to the basic sorts, that is, given any higher-order signature $\Sigma = (B, F)$ and two extensional higher-order Σ-congruences $\sim_1$ and $\sim_2$ on $T(\Sigma)$, if their reductions to the basic sorts are the same (i.e., $\sim_1|_B = \sim_2|_B$) then they are the same ($\sim_1 = \sim_2$).

Proof We prove that $\sim_1$ and $\sim_2$ are the same on terms of each sort $s \in B^{\rightarrow}$, by induction on s. For any basic sort this is just our assumption. So, consider a higher-order sort $(w \rightarrow s) \in B^{\rightarrow}$, where we can assume that $\sim_1$ and $\sim_2$ are the same on the terms of the sorts in w, s. Let $t, t' \in T(\Sigma^{\rightarrow})_{w\rightarrow s}$. Suppose that $t \sim_1 t'$. Then since $\sim_1$ is a higher-order congruence, for all $\langle t_1, \ldots, t_n\rangle \in T(\Sigma^{\rightarrow})_w$ we have $t(t_1, \ldots, t_n) \sim_1 t'(t_1, \ldots, t_n)$, and so by the inductive assumption, also $t(t_1, \ldots, t_n) \sim_2 t'(t_1, \ldots, t_n)$. Thus, by the extensionality of $\sim_2$, $t \sim_2 t'$, which by symmetry completes the proof. □

Higher-order specifications are higher-order signatures together with higher-order conditional equations. As models only reachable, extensional algebras are considered:

Definition 3.7

(1) A higher-order specification SP is a pair $\langle \Sigma, E\rangle$ consisting of a higher-order signature Σ and a set E of higher-order conditional Σ-equations.

(2) The first-order specification $SP^{\rightarrow}$ associated with SP is defined to be $\langle \Sigma^{\rightarrow}, E \cup (\mathbf{ext})_\Sigma\rangle$.

(3) $RMod_{ext}(SP)$ is the set of all extensional $\Sigma^{\rightarrow}$-congruences which satisfy E; i.e., the subset of $RMod(\langle\Sigma^{\rightarrow}, E\rangle)$ which is extensional. (We write simply $RMod_{ext}(\Sigma)$ with the obvious meaning if E is empty.)

As an immediate consequence of fact 3.4 we get

Fact 3.8 $RMod_{ext}(SP) = RMod(SP^{\rightarrow})$.

Corollary 3.9 The congruences of $RMod_{ext}(SP)$ form a complete lattice w.r.t. $\subseteq$. In particular, any higher-order specification has an extensional reachable initial model; the terminal model is trivially extensional.

The **proof** follows directly from theorem 2.1 since all axioms of $SP^{\rightarrow}$, including the extensionality axioms $(\mathbf{ext})_{\Sigma}$, are positive conditional equations. □

4 Hierarchical higher-order specifications

A hierarchical specification *SP* is a specification where a subcongruence P of *SP* is designated as primitive. In the higher-order case, *SP* as well as P are higher-order.

Definition 4.1 **A hierarchical higher-order specification** (h.h.o. specification, for short) is a pair $\langle SP, P\rangle$ where

- *SP* is a higher-order specification $\langle\Sigma, E\rangle$ with $\Sigma = \langle B, F\rangle$ and
- P is (a higher-order specification of) a higher-order extensional Σ_P-congruence $\sim^P$, where $\Sigma_P = \langle B_P, F_P\rangle \subseteq \Sigma$ is a distinguished higher-order subsignature of S.

As for first-order hierarchical specifications, we assume that E contains all equations which hold in the primitive sorts $B_P^{\rightarrow}$, i.e., for all $\sim \in RMod_{ext}(SP)$, for all primitive sorts $s \in B_P^{\rightarrow}$ and ground primitive terms $t, t' \in T(\Sigma_P)_s$, if $t \sim^P t'$ then $t \sim t'$.

By fact 3.6, $\sim^P$ is determined unambiguously by its reduction to the basic primitive sorts and the requirement of extensionality. Then the assumption that *SP* contains all equations which hold in P may be restricted to the equations between terms of basic primitive sorts plus the axioms of extensionality for $\sim^P$ again. We write $RMod_{ext}(P)$ to denote all reachable higher-order Σ_P-algebras corresponding to $\sim^P$.

There exist (at least) two semantic notions of hierarchy: either the full higher-order specification P is encapsulated ("strongly h.h.o. specification") or only the basic part of the primitive specification is encapsulated ("h.h.o. specification").

In the former case neither new primitive basic objects nor new functions with domain and range in primitive sorts (i.e., objects of sorts in $B_P^{\rightarrow}$) can be introduced. As a consequence, all proofs of properties of the primitive specifications remain valid in the hierarchical specification; in particular, also the proofs using structural induction or/and the extensionality axioms $(\mathbf{ext})_{\Sigma_P}$ remain valid.

In the latter case only the basic primitive sorts are protected; by the hierarchical specification new objects of primitive basic sort cannot be introduced but new functions with arity in $B_P^{\rightarrow}$ can be defined. As a consequence, only those proofs for P are ensured to be valid in the hierarchical specification which do not use $(\mathbf{ext})_{\Sigma_P}$ nor structural induction for higher-order sorts.

Definition 4.2 Let *Spec* = $\langle SP, P\rangle$ be a h.h.o. specification as in definition 4.1.

(1) A higher-order Σ-algebra A is called a **strongly hierarchical higher-order model** ("strongly h.h.o. model") of *Spec* if

- $A \in RMod_{ext}(SP)$ and
- $A|_{\Sigma_{\vec{P}}} \in RMod_{ext}(P)$.

(2) A higher-order Σ-algebra A is called a **hierarchical higher-order model** ("h.h.o. model") if

- $A \in RMod_{ext}(SP)$ and
- A protects the basic primitive sorts B_P, that is, A is reachable on B_P w.r.t. Σ_P (i.e., for all $s \in B_P$, $A_s = \{t^A \mid t \in T(\Sigma_P{}^{\rightarrow})_s\}$) and A does not confuse primitive terms of basic primitive sorts (i.e., for all $s \in B_P$ and $t, t' \in T(\Sigma_P{}^{\rightarrow})_s$, if $t^A = t'^A$ then $t \sim^P t'$).

(3) The class of all strongly h.h.o. models of *Spec* is denoted by $SHMod_{ext}(Spec)$ and the class of all h.h.o. models of *Spec* is denoted by $HMod_{ext}(Spec)$.

Example 4.3
Let *Spec* = $\langle \text{ENAT}, \sim_{\text{NAT}}\rangle$ where

high-spec NAT =
  sort *nat*
  opns 0 : *nat*,
    succ: *nat* → *nat*
endspec

high-spec ENAT =
  based on NAT
  opns $.+.: nat, nat \rightarrow nat$
  axioms $0 + y = y$
    $succ(x) + y = succ(x + y)$
endspec

and $\sim_{\text{NAT}}$ is the initial reachable congruence for NAT.

Since the carrier of type $nat, nat \rightarrow nat$ is empty in $\sim_{\text{NAT}}$ but not in $\sim_{\text{ENAT}}$, $\sim_{\text{ENAT}}$ is not a strongly hierarchical h.o. model of ENAT. Since, however, the sort *nat* is interpreted equally in $\sim_{\text{NAT}}$ and $\sim_{\text{ENAT}}$, $\sim_{\text{ENAT}}$ is still a hierarchical model. □

Thus, the usual notion of enrichment is not captured by the notion of strongly h.h.o. models but rather by the weaker concept of h.h.o. models.

We aim at reducing hierarchical higher-order specifications to standard (hierarchical, first-order) specifications, just as we did in the previous section in the non-hierarchical case. Let *Spec* = $\langle SP, P\rangle$ be a hierarchical higher-order specification as in Definition 4.1. Define:

- $Spec^{\rightarrow} =_{def} \langle SP^{\rightarrow}, P, B_{\vec{P}}\rangle$
- $Spec^{b\rightarrow} =_{def} \langle SP^{\rightarrow}, P, B_P\rangle$

In the above we have identified the higher-order Σ_P-congruence P (or rather $\sim^P$) with the (first-order) $\Sigma_{\vec{P}}$-congruence it in fact is. Notice that, as should be expected, the essential difference between the two hierarchical first-order specifications, Spec$^{\rightarrow}$ and $Spec^{b\rightarrow}$ (^{b} for "basic sorts") is in which of the primitive sorts are protected. In the former specification all primitive sorts are protected; in the latter only the basic ones.

Fact 4.4 Under the notational assumptions as above,

(a) $SHMod_{ext}(Spec) = HMod(Spec^{\rightarrow})$, and

(b) $HMod_{ext}(Spec) = HMod(Spec^{b\rightarrow})$.

Proof Directly from the definitions. □

As a direct consequence of this fact one may notice that the restriction of $SHMod_{ext}(Spec)$ to Σ_P is monomorphic, whereas the restriction of $HMod_{ext}(Spec)$ to Σ_P may have non-isomorphic models.

Definition 4.5 Let *Spec* be a hierarchical h.o. specification as in definition 4.1.

(1) *Spec* is called **strongly hierarchy-complete** if $Spec^{\rightarrow}$ is hierarchy-complete, i.e., for all ground terms $t \in T(\Sigma^{\rightarrow})_s$ of primitive sort (i.e., $s \in B_{\vec{P}}$) there exists a ground primitive term $p \in T(\Sigma_{\vec{P}})_s$ such that $RMod_{ext}(SP^{\rightarrow}) \models t = p$.

(2) *Spec* is called **basic-complete** if $Spec^{b\rightarrow}$ is hierarchy-complete, i.e., for all ground terms $t \in T(\Sigma^{\rightarrow})_s$ of basic primitive sort (i.e., $s \in B_P$) there exists a ground primitive term $p \in T(\Sigma_{\vec{P}})_s$ such that $RMod_{ext}(SP^{\rightarrow}) \models t = p$.

(3) *Spec* is called hierarchy-consistent if $Spec^{\rightarrow}$ is hierarchy-consistent.

One may feel tempted to generalise the definition of hierarchy-consistency and give it in two versions, "strong" and "basic", as for sufficient completeness. However, this extra generality would be illusory:

Fact 4.6 For any h.h.o. specification $Spec = \langle SP, P \rangle$, $Spec^{\rightarrow}$ is hierarchy-consistent iff $Spec^{b\rightarrow}$ is so.

Proof The implication "⇒" is clear. For the opposite, define $\sim$ on $T(\Sigma_{\vec{P}})$ by $t_1 \sim t_2$ iff $Spec^{\rightarrow} \models t_1 \sim t_2$. By the assumption that $Spec^{b\rightarrow}$ is hierarchy-consistent, we have $\sim|_{B_P} = \sim^P|_{B_P}$. Now, by fact 3.6, we get $\sim|_{B_{\vec{P}}} = \sim^P|_{B_{\vec{P}}}$. □

Fact 4.7 Let *Spec* be a h.h.o. specification which is hierarchy-consistent.

(1) If *Spec* is strongly hierarchy-complete then the congruences of the strongly h.h.o. models of *Spec* form a complete lower semilattice w.r.t. $\subseteq$. In particular, *Spec* has an initial strongly h.h.o. model.

(2) If *Spec* is basic-complete then the congruences of the h.h.o. models form a complete lower semilattice w.r.t. $\subseteq$. In particular, *Spec* has an initial h.h.o. model.

Proof Follows directly from fact 4.4 and theorem 2.2 (1). □

In both cases the semilattices do not have to be lattices; the extensionality axiom is positive conditional, but it has premises of non-primitive sorts. In such cases, terminal models do not exist in general as the following example shows.

Example 4.8 Consider the following higher-order specification T.

high-spec $\mathbf{T} \equiv$
  based on BOOL
  sort t
  opns $a \quad : \to t$
  $f, g \quad : t \to t$
  $h \quad : (t \to t) \to bool$
  axioms $h(f) = true$
  $h(g) = false$
endspec

The following reachable hierarchical models A and B with two-element carriers of sort t are extensional but incomparable; every upper bound of A and B would identify a and b and hence also f and g by extensionality, but in any model of T, f and g have to be different because of h; i.e., any model of T has at least two elements of sort t. Therefore T does not have a terminal reachable hierarchical model.

A: $A_t =_{def} \{a, b\}$ $\quad a^A =_{def} a$
$f^A(x) =_{def} a \quad g^A(x) =_{def} b \quad$ for $x \in \{a, b\}$
$h^A(f) =_{def} true \quad h^A(g) =_{def} false;$

B: $B_t =_{def} \{a, b\}$ $\quad a^B =_{def} a$
$f^B(x) =_{def} b \quad g^B(x) =_{def} a \quad$ for $x \in \{a, b\}$
$h^B(f) =_{def} true \quad h^B(g) =_{def} false.$

□

As the above example illustrates, the reason for the non-existence of reachable terminal algebras is that contexts may distinguish higher-order objects which are not distinguishable by extensionality. The following theorem shows that a specification in which this problem does not occur and which satisfies the standard requirements of sufficient completeness and hierarchy-consistency has a terminal hierarchical model and therefore the isomorphism classes of its hierarchical models form a complete lattice.

First we define formally what it means that two terms are distinguishable.

Definition 4.9 Let SP be a higher-order specification and let $S' \subseteq sorts(\Sigma^{\to})$ be a set of sorts. Two terms $t_1, t_2 \in T(\Sigma^{\to})_u$, $u \in sorts(\Sigma^{\to})$, are called **distinguishable w.r.t.** S' in SP if there exists a context $c \in T(\Sigma^{\to}, x{:}u)_s$, $s \in S'$, such that $RMod(SP^{\to}) \not\models c[t_1] = c[t_2]$. In this case, the context c **distinguishes** t_1 and t_2.

Lemma 4.10 Let SP be a h.h.o. specification. If two terms are distinguishable w.r.t. primitive (higher-order) sorts then they are distinguishable w.r.t. basic primitive sorts.

Proof By induction on the structure of sorts.

Let $t_1, t_2 \in T(\Sigma^{\rightarrow})$ be distinguishable by a context $c \in T(\Sigma^{\rightarrow}, x)_s$, $s \in B_P^{\rightarrow}$, i.e., $RMod(SP^{\rightarrow}) \not\models c[t_1] = c[t_2]$. We distinguish two cases:

(1) $s \in B_P$, i.e. s is a basic primitive sort. Then the lemma holds obviously.

(2) $s = (w \rightarrow s_1)$, i.e. s is a higher-order primitive sort. Since $RMod(SP^{\rightarrow}) \not\models c[t_1] = c[t_2]$, there exists a reachable model A of $SP^{\rightarrow}$ such that $A \models c[t_1] \neq c[t_2]$.

Since $SP^{\rightarrow}$ contains the extensionality axioms $(\mathbf{ext})_\Sigma$, there exists a tuple of terms $t \in T(\Sigma^{\rightarrow})_w$ such that $A \models c[t_1](t) \neq c[t_2](t)$. Thus the context $c' =_{def} c[x](t) \in T(\Sigma^{\rightarrow}, x)_{s_1}$ is a context of a smaller sort than s which distinguishes t_1 and t_2. By the induction hypothesis one concludes that there exists a context of basic primitive sort which distinguishes t_1 and t_2. □

Theorem 4.11 Let *Spec* be a basic-complete and hierarchy-consistent h.h.o. specification such that

(1) the premises of the axioms are of **primitive** (possibly higher-order) sorts and

(2) the following distinguishability condition (∗) holds:
For all higher-order terms $t_1, t_2 \in T(\Sigma^{\rightarrow})_{w \rightarrow s}$ which are distinguishable w.r.t. primitive sorts there exists an "actual parameter" $t \in T(\Sigma^{\rightarrow})_w$ such that $t_1(t)$ and $t_2(t)$ are distinguishable w.r.t. primitive sorts.

Then the congruence classes of $HMod_{ext}(Spec)$ form a complete lattice w.r.t $\subseteq$. The terminal congruence $\sim^Z$ of $HMod_{ext}(Spec)$ is fully abstract w.r.t. B_P; for all $t, t' \in T(\Sigma^{\rightarrow})_s$ it is defined by

$t \sim^Z t'$ iff for all $c \in T(\Sigma, x{:}s)$ of basic primitive sort, $RMod(SP^{\rightarrow}) \models c[t] = c[t']$.

Proof By facts 4.7 (2) and 4.4 (b), it is sufficient to show that $Spec^{b\rightarrow}$ has a fully abstract terminal hierarchical model. Let $\sim^Z$ be a higher-order Σ-congruence defined as above (clearly, this indeed is a $\Sigma^{\rightarrow}$-congruence which is fully abstract). Then, let Z be the (unique to within isomorphism) higher-order reachable Σ-algebra corresponding to $\sim^Z$. We show that Z is a terminal hierarchical model of $Spec^{b\rightarrow}$.

(a) For any two terms $t, t' \in T(\Sigma^{\rightarrow})$ of a common primitive sort, $t \sim^Z t'$ iff $RMod(SP^{\rightarrow}) \models t = t'$.

Proof: The "if" part is clear directly from the definition of $\sim^Z$. To prove the "only if" part we proceed by induction on the structure of the common sort of t and t'. If it is a basic primitive sort, then the thesis follows directly from the definition of $\sim^Z$. Otherwise, let $t, t' \in T(\Sigma^{\rightarrow})_{w \rightarrow s}$ for some primitive sorts w, s. Assume $t \sim^Z t'$. Since $\sim^Z$ is a (higher-order) congruence, for all $\langle t_1, \ldots, t_n \rangle \in T(\Sigma^{\rightarrow})_w$, $t(t_1, \ldots, t_n) \sim^Z t'(t_1, \ldots, t_n)$, which by the inductive hypothesis implies $RMod(SP^{\rightarrow}) \models t(t_1, \ldots, t_n) = t'(t_1, \ldots, t_n)$. Now, since all models in $RMod(SP^{\rightarrow})$ are extensional and reachable, it follows that $RMod(SP^{\rightarrow}) \models t = t'$.

Notice that this proves that under the above assumptions the restriction of $HMod_{ext}(Spec)$ to Σ_P is monomorphic.

(b) $\sim^Z \in RMod(SP^{\rightarrow})$

Proof: Since the reachability is assumed, it is sufficient to prove that Z satisfies all ground instances of the axioms in $SP^{\rightarrow}$. This is quite obvious for the axioms in SP, which are assumed to have premises of the primitive sorts only. Namely, let

$$(\wedge_{i \in I}\ u_i = v_i) \Rightarrow u = v$$

be a ground instance of such an axiom. If $Z \models u_i = v_i$ for $i \in I$, then by fact (a) above, $RMod(SP^{\rightarrow}) \models u_i = v_i$ for $i \in I$, and so $RMod(SP^{\rightarrow}) \models u = v$, which implies $Z \models u = v$ by the definition of $\sim^Z$.

Other axioms of $SP^{\rightarrow}$ are the extensionality axioms of the form

$$(\wedge_{\langle t_1,\ldots,t_n\rangle \in T(\Sigma^{\rightarrow})_w} t(t_1,\ldots,t_n) = t'(t_1,\ldots,t_n)) \Rightarrow t = t'$$

for some terms $t, t' \in T(\Sigma^{\rightarrow})_{w \rightarrow s}$ and $w, s \in B^{\rightarrow}$. Suppose that $Z \not\models t = t'$. By the definition of Z, this means that the terms t and t' are distinguishable w.r.t. basic primitive sorts. This, however, implies by the condition $(*)$ that for some $\langle t_1,\ldots,t_n\rangle \in T(\Sigma^{\rightarrow})_w$, $t(t_1,\ldots,t_n)$ and $t'(t_1,\ldots,t_n)$ are distinguishable, which in turn means that Z does not satisfy all the premises of the above implication.

(c) Z is reachable w.r.t. Σ_P on the basic primitive sorts.

Proof: obvious by the basic-completeness of *Spec* and by fact (a) above.

(d) Z does not confuse primitive terms.

Proof: obvious by the hierarchy-consistency of *Spec* and by fact (a) above.

The three last facts prove that indeed $\sim^Z \in HMod_{ext}(Spec)$. What remains is to show that $\sim^Z$ includes any congruence $\sim \in HMod_{ext}(Spec)$.

(e) For any $\sim \in HMod_{ext}(Spec)$, $\sim \subseteq \sim^Z$.

Proof: Suppose $t \sim t'$ for some sort $s \in B^{\rightarrow}$ and $t, t' \in T(\Sigma^{\rightarrow})_s$. Then, consider any context $c \in T(\Sigma^{\rightarrow}, x{:}s)$ of a basic primitive sort. Clearly, $c[t] \sim c[t']$. Now, because *Spec* is basic-complete, there are primitive terms p and p' such that $RMod(SP^{\rightarrow}) \models c[t] = p$ and $RMod(SP^{\rightarrow}) \models c[t'] = p'$. Consequently, $p \sim p'$, and since *Spec* is hierarchy-consistent, $p \sim^P p'$, which implies that $RMod(SP^{\rightarrow}) \models p = p'$. Hence, $RMod(SP^{\rightarrow}) \models c[t] = c[t']$. Finally, since c was arbitrary, we have $t \sim^Z t'$, which completes the proof. □

Theorem 4.12 Let *Spec* be a strongly sufficiently complete and hierarchy-consistent h.h.o. specification such that

(1) the premises of the axioms are of primitive sorts, and

(2) the distinguishability condition $(*)$ of assumption (2), theorem 4.11 holds.

Then the congruences of $SHMod_{ext}(Spec)$ form a complete lattice w.r.t. $\subseteq$. The terminal congruence $\sim^Z$ of $SHMod_{ext}(Spec)$ is fully abstract (w.r.t. B_P); for all $t, t' \in T(\Sigma)_s$, $\sim^Z$ is defined by

$t \sim^Z t'$ iff for all $c \in T(\Sigma, x{:}s)$ of basic primitive sort, $RMod(SP^{\rightarrow}) \models c[t] = c[t']$.

Proof follows from theorem 4.11; the additional assumption that *Spec* is **strongly** sufficiently complete directly implies that $\sim^Z$ protects all primitive sorts, and so $\sim^Z \in SHMod_{ext}(Spec)$. □

5 Concluding Remarks

In the previous section we have shown that under reasonable assumptions reachable higher-order algebras behave as well as first-order ones. Thus, the "standard concept" of higher-order functions can be added in a convenient way to the framework of algebraic specifications. However, function spaces are not the only standard construction in programming. Perhaps the simplest and best known other examples are power sets with the membership relation as standard operation, and the Cartesian product with the pairing constructor and projections. As already mentioned in section 1, in [Möller et al. 88] we have tried to extend the definitions and theorems for higher-order specifications to a more general framework which includes other standard constructions, the two mentioned above in particular, and for which the results and examples presented here would just be particular instances. The idea was to use reachable subalgebras of algebras in which certain carriers are obtained by standard constructions (e.g. by taking function spaces or power sets) from the basic carriers. Unfortunately, higher-order algebras do not quite fall into this generalization, since subalgebras of extensional algebras do not need to be extensional themselves as has been shown in section 3 (example 3.3). A possible way to rectify this inaccuracy is to consider an iterative construction, where in each step we built one more level of standard types and use a subalgebra of the resulting standard algebra. This will be discussed in more detail in a forthcoming complete version of this paper.

It will be interesting to see whether such a generalized framework applies to algebras with some built-in concept of "processes" introducing operators for describing parallel and distributed processes.

The approach to algebraic specifications in this paper is based on total algebras. But for the specification of data structures partial algebras [Broy et al. 84] and continuous algebras [Möller 87] are equally important. Therefore we have tried to extend our approach to continuous algebraic specifications based on an infinitary least upper bound operation as in [Tarlecki, Wirsing 86]. It turns out that essentially all results carry over to this case and that conditions such as sufficient completeness and hierarchy-consistency have only to be considered for finitary terms. These results are an indication that everything should be expressible in the unifying framework of institutions (cf. [Goguen, Burstall 84], [Tarlecki 85, Tarlecki 86]).

Acknowledgement

Thanks go to Axel Poigné for many useful comments to a draft version of the paper and to Rosemarie Eggerl, Elisabeth Loibl, Sabine Mroch, Thomas Ramke and Bernhard Reus for carefully typing the manuscript; in particular without the help of Sabine it would not have been possible to finish the paper in due time.

References

[Bauer, Woessner 82] F.L. Bauer, H. Wössner: *Algorithmic Language and Program Development.* Berlin: Springer, 1982.

[Broy et al. 84] M. Broy, C. Pair, M. Wirsing: *A systematic study of models of abstract data Types.* Theoretical Computer Science 33, 1984, 139-174.

[Broy 86] M. Broy: *Partial interpretations of higher order algebraic types.* Lecture Notes of the International Summer School on Logic of Programming and Calculi of Discrete Design, Marktoberdorf, 1986.

[Burstall, Goguen 80] R.M. Burstall, J.A. Goguen: *The semantics of CLEAR, a specification language.* Proc. Advanced Course on Abstract Software Specifications, Copenhagen. Lecture Notes in Computer Science 86, Berlin: Springer, 1980, 292-332.

[Dybjer 83] P. Dybjer: *Category-theoretic logics and algebras of programs.* Chalmers University of Technology at Göteborg, Dept. of Computer Science, Ph. D. Thesis, 1983.

[Ehrig, Mahr 85] H. Ehrig, B. Mahr: *Fundamentals of Algebraic Specification 1.* EATCS Monographs on Theoretical Computer Science 6, Berlin: Springer, 1985.

[Goguen, Burstall 84] J.A. Goguen, R.M. Burstall: *Introducing institutions.* Proc. Logics of Programming Workshop, Carnegie-Mellon, Lecture Notes in Ccomputer Science 164, Springer 1984, 221-256.

[Keisler 71] H.J. Keisler: *Model Theory for Infinitary Logic.* Studies in Logic and Foundations of Mathematics, Vol. 62, 1971.

[Mahr, Makowsky 84] B. Mahr, J.A. Makowsky: *Characterising specification languages which admit initial semantics*, Theoretical Computer Science 31, 1984, 49-59.

[Maibaum, Lucena 80] T.S.E. Maibaum, C.J. Lucena: *Higher order data types.* Journal of Computer and Information Sciences 9, 1980, 31-53.

[Milner 77] R. Milner: *Fully abstract semantics of typed λ-calculi.* Theoretical Computer Science 4, 1977, 1-22.

[Möller 86] B. Möller: *Algebraic specifications with higher-order operators.* In: L. Meertens (ed.): Proc. IFIP TC2 Working Conference on Program Specification and Transformation, Bad Tölz, April 1986. Amsterdam: North-Holland, 1987, 367-392.

[Möller 87] B. Möller: *Higher-order algebraic specifications.* Fakultät für Mathematik und Informatik der TU München, Habilitationsschrift, 1987.

[Möller et al. 88] B. Möller, A. Tarlecki, M. Wirsing: *Algebraic specification with built-in domain constructions.* In: M. Dauchet, M. Nivat (eds.): Proc. 13th Colloquium on Trees in Algebra and Programming, Nancy, March 1988. Lecture Notes in Computer Science 299. Berlin: Springer 1988, 132 - 148.

[Parsaye-Ghomi 81] K. Parsaye-Ghomi: *Higher-order abstract data types.* Dept. of Computer Science, University of California at Los Angeles, Ph. D. Thesis, 1981.

[Plotkin 77] G.D. Plotkin: *LCF considered as a programming language.* Theoretical Computer Science 4, 1977, 223-255.

[Poigné 84] A. Poigné: *Higher-order data structures - Cartesian closure versus λ-calculus.* Proc. Symposium on Theoretical Aspects of Computer Science 1984. Lecture Notes in Computer Science 166. Berlin: Springer, 1984, 174-185.

[Poigné 86] A. Poigné: *On specifications, theories, and models with higher types.* Information and Control 68, 1986, 1-46.

[Tarlecki 85] A. Tarlecki: *On the existence of free models in abstract algebraic institutions,* Theoretical Computer Science 37, 1985, 269-304.

[Tarlecki 86] A. Tarlecki: *Quasi-varieties in abstract algebraic institutions,* Journal of Computer and System Sciences 33, 1986, 333-360.

[Tarlecki, Wirsing 86] A. Tarlecki, M. Wirsing: *Continuous abstract data types.* Fundamenta Informaticae 9, 1986, 95-125.

Observing Nondeterministic Data Types

Tobias Nipkow*
Laboratory for Computer Science
Massachusetts Institute of Technology
545 Technology Square
Cambridge MA 02139

1 Introduction

In [18] a theory of behavioural implementations of nondeterministic data types was developed. The main motivation for this development is the fact that the behaviour of nondeterministic data types can be observed properly only with the help of programming language constructs. This is in contrast to ordinary deterministic data types, whose behaviour in a programming context is determined completely by the behaviour of its term algebra, i.e. all finite compositions of its operations. Hence the implementation relationship between nondeterministic data types is not given *a priori* but is a function of the observing programming language and its implementation definition.

In this paper we consider the impact of both the observer and the relationship between observations on the induced relationship between nondeterministic data types. We study two observation languages of different expressive power and three important implementation concepts based on different orderings on powerdomains. We derive sound model theoretic characterizations of the induced implementation relationships which are complete for certain subclasses of data types. Our notion of nondeterministic data types is purely semantic and hence independent of any syntactic formalism for specifying them. This greater generality prohibits any proof theoretic considerations.

The literature contains many independent approaches to the problem of *representation independence*.

On the data type side there is Hoare's original contribution in [10] and a long list of publications dealing with the implementation problem for (algebraically defined) abstract data types. Of particular interest in the current context are those approaches dealing with *behavioural* or *observational* implementations (e.g. [7], [2], [21], [23], [8], [14], [22]), a discussion of which can be found in [24] and [20]. With the exception of [10], [22] and [24] none of these papers acknowledge the need to take the environment in which a data type operates into account when discussing correctness of implementations. The correctness arguments [10] are informal whereas the theory developed in [22] is rather abstract and it is not clear to me whether it can be used to develop or justify the concrete implementation relations studied in this paper. In [24], however, an implementation relation between partial algebras called *correspondence* is defined which is a specialization of (and served as a starting point for) the notion of a *simulation* used in this paper. Simulations can be seen as a generalization of correspondences to nondeterministic structures. The current work started as an attempt to generalize the approach in [10]. At the same time Hoare et al. followed a very similar route which is documented for example in [9]. In [11] Hoare has recast the whole problem in categorical terms, thus simplifying previous treatments. However, this approach is still in its infancy.

*This research was carried out at the University of Manchester

In the area of concurrency our work is close to [6]. The main difference is that de Nicola and Hennessy observe CCS processes with the help of other CCS processes, whereas we want to observe nondeterministic data types with the help of programs. Since CCS is a syntactic calculus, they can formulate proof rules for showing that certain relationships hold between given CCS terms. A similar programme is carried out in [3] where the observations about CCS processes are characterized by modal logic formulae.

The third important approach is based on representation independence in the λ-calculus, as for example in [17]. This approach is complementary to ours in that it deals with higher order functions and abstract data type definition facilities *within* the language but avoids nondeterminacy. The main tools in that study are so called *logical relations* which are strongly related to Schoett's correspondences and to what I call simulations.

Most proofs have been omitted from the current paper and can be found in [20].

2 Preliminaries

Let a *signature* $\Sigma = (S, V, O)$ be a triple of *sort names* $S \subseteq Id$, *visible sorts* $V \subseteq S$ and *operation names* $O \subseteq Id$, where Id is some infinite set of *identifiers*[1]. Every operation $r \in O$ comes with a rank which is depicted as $r : w \to s$ for $w \in S^*$ and $s \in S$. In the sequel we assume $\Sigma = (S, V, O)$.

Nondeterministic data types are modeled as so called Σ-structures. A *Σ-structure* $\underline{A}$ consists of a set A_s for every $s \in S$, a relation $r^{\underline{A}} \subseteq A_w \times A_s$ for every $r : w \to s$ in O and a set $T_{\underline{A}}[r] \subseteq A_w$ for every $r : w \to s$ in O, where $A_{s_1 \ldots s_k} = A_{s_1} \times \ldots \times A_{s_k}$. The A_s are the carriers, $r^{\underline{A}}$ is the input/output relation of operation r and $T_{\underline{A}}[r]$ the set of inputs for which termination is guaranteed. Hence $T_{\underline{A}}[r] \subseteq dom(r^{\underline{A}})$ must always hold. Elements $(a, a') \in r^{\underline{A}}$ are often written as $a \to a'$ where a is omitted if it is the empty tuple; $r^{\underline{A}}(a)$ denotes $\{a' \mid (a, a') \in r^{\underline{A}}\}$. The class of all structures with signature Σ is denoted by $Struct(\Sigma)$.

In the sequel we make the additional assumption that for every $s \in Id$ there is a "universe" U_s such that $s \neq t$ implies that U_s and U_t are disjoint. Given a Σ-structure $\underline{A}$, we further assume that $A_s \subseteq U_s$ for all $s \in S$. This restriction is necessary because the observation language we are going to define is completely untyped. Hence it allows observing programs that would fail to type check in any sensibly typed language with data abstraction facilities. Only the disjointness condition prevents elements of one type masquerading as values of a different type. It can be seen as run time type checking by tagging every element of a given sort with its sort name. If the observation language is typed, disjointness can be dropped. Finally we assume there is a visible sort $Bool$ in every signature and $U_{Bool} = \{\text{tt}, \text{ff}\}$. Booleans are required by the conditional in the observing programs.

In [18] a general framework for observing nondeterministic data types via programs is created. It requires a syntactic domain of programs $Prog$, a semantic domain Sem with a transitive and reflexive implementation ordering on it, and a mapping D which takes a program and a Σ-structure and returns a denotation in Sem. In this paper we fix both $Prog$ and Sem but vary D and the implementation relationship.

The semantic domains of our choice are so called *streams*. The following treatment of streams is based on the definitions in [4].

Let $U = \bigcup_{s \in Id} U_s$ and let $\perp$ be an element not in U. Then $Stream$ denotes the set of all those finite and infinite sequences over $U \cup \{\perp\}$ where $\perp$ appears only at the end.

On sequences we have the following operations: the empty sequence ε and the infix concatenation operation $x.y$, where x and y may either be sequences or single elements. Notice that if x is infinite $x.y$ equals x.

Sequences with a $\perp$ at the end are called *partial*, those without *total*.

[1]The fact that the set of sort and operation names are identical is of no significance.

Stream comes equipped with a partial order $\sqsubseteq$ between its elements, the approximation ordering, which is defined as follows:

$$s \preceq t \Leftrightarrow \exists s_1, t_2.(s = t) \vee (s = s_1.\bot \wedge t = s_1.t_2)$$

This partial order can be extended to a quasi-order on $\mathcal{P}(Stream)$ in many different ways, two of which give rise to important correctness concepts:

$$M \preceq_S N \Leftrightarrow \forall n \in N \exists m \in M : m \preceq n$$
$$M \preceq_H N \Leftrightarrow \forall m \in M \exists n \in N : m \preceq n$$

$\preceq_S$ and $\preceq_H$ are the orderings of the so called *Smyth* (see [25]) and *Hoare* (see [13]) powerdomains respectively. They provide the basis for two of the implementation concepts we are going to look at in detail.

In this paper the semantics of programs are elements in

$$NDF_k = Stream^k \rightarrow \mathcal{P}(Stream),$$

the set of (total) nondeterministic functions. All orderings on $\mathcal{P}(Stream)$ extend automatically to *NDF* in the canonical pointwise way. The subclass of functions on finite total streams is denoted by

$$FNDF_k = U^{*k} \rightarrow \mathcal{P}(U^*).$$

In [18] only finite total sequences are used as semantic domains. In analogy to the definition of operations in data types, the semantics of programs are given as pairs (R, T), where $R \subseteq U^* \times U^*$ is the input/output relation and $T \subseteq U^*$ the set of all inputs for which termination is guaranteed. In order to translate notions on streams to these simpler semantic domains we define a mapping $pd : \mathcal{P}(U^* \times U^*) \times \mathcal{P}(U^*) \rightarrow NDF_1$:

$$pd(R, T) = \lambda s.\{t \mid (s, t) \in R\} \cup \{\bot \mid s \notin T\} \tag{1}$$

3 Observation Languages

The syntax of our observation languages is almost identical to the one use in [18] which is a subset of Broy's AMPL (see [4]). It is a first-order applicative language over streams.

$$
\begin{array}{lll}
Expr & ::= & <> \mid <U>\&Expr \mid Expr\&Expr \mid \{\underline{\text{first}} \mid \underline{\text{rest}} \mid \underline{\text{ismt}}\} Expr \mid \\
 & & \underline{\text{if}}\ Expr\ \underline{\text{then}}\ Expr\ \underline{\text{else}}\ Expr \mid Choice \mid Appl \mid Id \mid \bot \mid U^\infty \\
Choice & ::= & Expr \,\Box\, Expr \mid Expr \nabla Expr \\
Appl & ::= & Id(Expr^*) \mid (Abstr)(Expr^*) \\
Abstr & ::= & \lambda Id^*.Expr \\
U^\infty & ::= & <U>\&U^\infty \\
Fundef & ::= & Id = Abstr \\
Prog & ::= & Fundef^*; Abstr
\end{array}
$$

Notice that the term "syntax" is used very liberally since the set *Expr* also contains values from U and in particular the infinite objects in U^∞. Their only purpose is to model the operational behaviour of a program *during* execution. U^∞ deals with infinite input. Values from U are not supposed to be part of user programs because that would be a breach of representation independence. Therefore the following restrictions apply to all user programs.

Given a signature Σ, $Prog(\Sigma)$ denotes the subset of programs $f_1 = A_1; \ldots; f_n = A_n; A$ in *Prog* which meet the following context conditions:

- No operation is defined twice: $i \neq j \Rightarrow f_i \neq f_j$
- No operation in O is redefined: $\forall 1 \leq i \leq n. f_i \notin O$
- Every application $f(E_1, \ldots, E_m)$ is well formed: either $f \in O$ and $m = 1$ or $f = f_i$ for some i and A_i is of the form $\lambda x_1, \ldots, x_m.E$.
- No expression $<u>$ with $u \in U$ occurs in the program.

In [18] the above language is given a simple denotational semantics based on flat domains. In the sequel we shall call this language L1. The semantics of L1 is given by two families of functions $R_\Sigma : Prog(\Sigma) \times Struct(\Sigma) \to FNDF$ and $T_\Sigma : Prog(\Sigma) \times Struct(\Sigma) \to \mathcal{P}(U^*)$ which compute the input/output function and the set of inputs for which the program is guaranteed to terminate. In the sequel we will just write R and T.

However, it turns out that L1 is not expressive enough in the following sense: there are data types which need to be distinguished but which no L1-observation can tell apart. Hence we associate a more expressive semantics with the above syntax and call the resulting language L2.

Below we give an operational semantics for L2. In contrast to denotational semantics based on powerdomains, which lead to undesirable identifications (see e.g. [1]), this ensures maximum expressiveness.

The operational semantics is defined with the help of the two relations $\to$ and $\xrightarrow{s}$. $E \to F$ should be read as "E rewrites to F in one step" and $E \xrightarrow{s} F$ as "E rewrites to F prefixed by the output string s". Both relations are defined w.r.t. a Σ-structure $\underset{\sim}{A}$ and a list of function definitions FD of the form $f_1 = A_1; \ldots; f_n = A_n$.

Given two expressions E and F and an identifier x, $E[F/x]$ denotes the result of substituting all *free* (w.r.t. the conventions of the λ-calculus) occurrences of x in E by F. This can be extended to $E[F_i/x_i \mid i \in I]$, which denotes $E[F_1/x_1] \ldots [F_n/x_n]$ for $I = \{1, \ldots, n\}$. Therefore it is necessary that $i \neq j$ implies $x_i \neq x_j$ and x_i is not free in F_j.

$\to$ and $\xrightarrow{s}$ steps can be combined to yield longer $\xrightarrow{s'}$ steps:

$$\begin{array}{rcl} & & E \xrightarrow{\epsilon} E \\ E \to F \wedge F \xrightarrow{s} G & \Rightarrow & E \xrightarrow{s} G \\ E \xrightarrow{\epsilon} <e>\&F \wedge F \xrightarrow{s} G & \Rightarrow & E \xrightarrow{e.s} G \end{array}$$

The conditions of if-then-else-expressions are evaluated lazily. Only the first item in the stream determines which branch is selected.

$$\begin{array}{rrcl} & \underline{\text{if}}\ <\text{tt}>\&E\ \underline{\text{then}}\ F\ \underline{\text{else}}\ G & \to & F \\ & \underline{\text{if}}\ <\text{ff}>\&E\ \underline{\text{then}}\ F\ \underline{\text{else}}\ G & \to & G \\ & \underline{\text{if}}\ <>\ \underline{\text{then}}\ F\ \underline{\text{else}}\ G & \to & \bot \\ e \notin \{\text{tt}, \text{ff}\} \Rightarrow & \underline{\text{if}}\ <e>\&E\ \underline{\text{then}}\ F\ \underline{\text{else}}\ G & \to & \bot \\ C \to D \Rightarrow & \underline{\text{if}}\ C\ \underline{\text{then}}\ F\ \underline{\text{else}}\ G & \to & \underline{\text{if}}\ D\ \underline{\text{then}}\ F\ \underline{\text{else}}\ G \end{array}$$

Free identifiers $x \in Id$ and $\bot$ give rise to infinite rewrites without output, i.e. they diverge. This rule is important for function evaluation. It must be possible to rewrite the body of a function even if some of the formal parameters cannot be instantiated because the respective actual parameters diverge.

$$\begin{array}{c} x \to x \\ \bot \to \bot \end{array}$$

The erratic choice operator $\square$ picks an arbitrary subexpression:

$$\begin{array}{c} E \,\square\, F \to E \\ E \,\square\, F \to F \end{array}$$

The angelic choice operator ∇ diverges only if both subexpressions diverge. Otherwise a non-diverging subexpression is selected:

$$\begin{array}{rcl} E \to E' \wedge F \to F' & \Rightarrow & E\nabla F \;\to\; E'\nabla F' \\ E \xrightarrow{\epsilon} <> & \Rightarrow & E\nabla F \;\to\; <> \quad \wedge \;\; F\nabla E \to <> \\ E \xrightarrow{\epsilon} <e>\&E' & \Rightarrow & E\nabla F \;\to\; <e>\&E' \;\wedge\; F\nabla E \to <e>\&E' \end{array}$$

Operations in O are treated as if they have only one argument that is passed by value:

$$\begin{array}{rcl} E \to F & \Rightarrow & r(<e_1>\&\ldots<e_m>\&E) \to r(<e_1>\&\ldots<e_m>\&F) \\ (e_1\ldots e_m, e) \in r^{\Delta} & \Rightarrow & r(<e_1>\&\ldots<e_m>\&<>) \to <e>\&<> \\ (e_1\ldots e_m) \notin T_{\Delta}[r] & \Rightarrow & r(<e_1>\&\ldots<e_m>\&<>) \to \bot \end{array}$$

Calls to functions defined in FD are treated by unfolding:

$$f_i(E_1,\ldots E_k) \to (A_i)(E_1,\ldots E_k)$$

Function application: Let $E = (\lambda x_1,\ldots,x_n.B)(E_1,\ldots,E_n)$, and let I, J and K be three disjoint sets such that $I \cup J \cup K = \{1,\ldots,n\}$ and

- $\forall i \in I : E_i \to F_i$
- $\forall j \in J : E_j \xrightarrow{s_j} F_j \wedge s_j \neq \epsilon$
- $\forall k \in K : E_k \xrightarrow{s_k} <>$

Hence all arguments indexed by K can be evaluated completely, those indexed by J can be evaluated partially and yield some result, and those indexed by I may not yield any result at all. Let $B' = B[s_j\&x_j/x_j \mid j \in J][s_k/x_k \mid k \in K]$ be the result of substituting the partially and the totally evaluated parameters into the function body. Finally let $\{i_1,\ldots,i_m\} = I \cup J$.

$$\begin{array}{lcl} B' = <> & \Rightarrow & E \to <> \\ B' = <e>\&C & \Rightarrow & E \to <e>\&(\lambda x_{i_1},\ldots,x_{i_m}.C)(F_{i_1},\ldots,F_{i_m}) \\ B' \to C & \Rightarrow & E \to (\lambda x_{i_1},\ldots,x_{i_m}.C)(F_{i_1},\ldots,F_{i_m}) \end{array}$$

The list manipulation functions are lazy and behave as expected:

$$\begin{array}{l} (E\&F)\&G \to E\&(F\&G) \\ <>\&E \to E \\ E \to E' \Rightarrow E\&F \to E'\&F \\ \underline{\text{first}}<> \to \bot \\ \underline{\text{first}}(<e>\&E) \to <e>\&<> \\ \underline{\text{rest}}\ <> \to \bot \\ \underline{\text{rest}}(<e>\&E) \to E \\ \underline{\text{ismt}}\ <> \to <tt>\&<> \\ \underline{\text{ismt}}\ (<e>\&E) \to <ff>\&<> \\ E \to F \Rightarrow \underline{\text{first}}\ E \to \underline{\text{first}}\ F \wedge \underline{\text{rest}}\ E \to \underline{\text{rest}}\ F \wedge \underline{\text{ismt}}\ E \to \underline{\text{ismt}}\ F \end{array}$$

The complexity of the above operational semantics is due to the combination of lazy evaluation and angelic choice. Lazy evaluation requires the function body and the arguments to be evaluated in parallel or in an interleaved fashion. Angelic choice may however require some arguments to be evaluated arbitrarily far. Consider the expression $E = (\lambda x.(\underline{\text{rest}}^n x)\nabla <>)(F)$, where $\underline{\text{rest}}^n$ is the n-fold composition of $\underline{\text{rest}}$. In order to give both ∇-branches in the body a chance to be selected, F must be evaluated far enough to yield a stream of length at least n. Hence we need to know how the arguments of an application behave w.r.t. $\xrightarrow{s}$ before the application itself can be rewritten by $\to$.

The above set of rewrite rules defines the relations $\rightarrow$ and $\stackrel{\bullet}{\longrightarrow}$ uniquely because all rules are Horn clauses. Hence we can associate a continuous transformation as in [26] with the set of rules and take its fixpoint as the unique semantics. Although some of the rules are actually rule *schemes* which stand for an infinite number of rules, and we are dealing with potentially infinite objects (U^∞), this does not destroy continuity of the transformation. The exact details can be found in [16].

The rewrite relations can now be used to define a function $B : Expr \rightarrow \mathcal{P}(Stream)$ from expressions to sets of streams.

$$\begin{aligned} B[E] \;=\; & \{s \mid E \stackrel{s}{\longrightarrow} <>\} \cup \\ & \{s.\bot \mid E \stackrel{s}{\longrightarrow} E_0 \rightarrow E_1 \rightarrow E_2 \rightarrow E_3 \rightarrow \ldots\} \cup \\ & \{e_1.e_2.e_3\ldots \mid E \rightarrow <e_1>\&E_1 \wedge E_1 \rightarrow <e_2>\&E_2 \wedge E_2 \rightarrow <e_3>\&E_3 \wedge \ldots\} \end{aligned}$$

Of course B depends on $\underset{\sim}{A}$ and FD just as $\rightarrow$ and $\stackrel{\bullet}{\longrightarrow}$ do.

To define the semantics of a program we need to take I/O into account. For that purpose the function $\ll . \gg$ defined below translates streams into expressions.

$$\begin{aligned} \ll \epsilon \gg \;&=\; <> \\ \ll e.s \gg \;&=\; <e>\&\ll s \gg \end{aligned}$$

In addition we need to enforce information hiding by preventing I/O of hidden values. In most programming languages this restriction is captured by a type system which only admits those programs which do not read or write hidden values. Since our observation language is untyped we enforce this restriction by explicitly filtering hidden values in the input and output. The function *filter* defined below terminates a stream with $\bot$ upon detection of hidden values. It can be seen as a run time system enforcing information hiding.

$$\begin{aligned} filter(\epsilon, H) \;&=\; \epsilon \\ filter(e.s, H) \;&=\; if\; e \in H\; then\; \bot\; else\; <e>\&filter(s, H) \end{aligned}$$

The overall semantics of a program $p = FD; P$, where $P = \lambda x_1, \ldots, x_k.E$, w.r.t. a Σ-structure $\underset{\sim}{A}$ is defined as a function $D[p](\underset{\sim}{A}) \in NDF_k$:

$$\begin{aligned} D[p](\underset{\sim}{A}) \;=\; & \lambda s_1, \ldots, s_k.filter(B[(P)(filter(\ll s_1 \gg, H), \ldots, filter(\ll s_k \gg, H))]) \\ & \text{where } H = \bigcup_{h \in S \setminus V} A_h \end{aligned}$$

Notice that the λ in this definition is a meta-level symbol and not part of an element of *Expr*.

4 Three Implementation Concepts

We can now discuss the three notions of loose, partial and robust implementations defined in [5] to capture different aspects of correctness. In the sequel remember that $\subseteq$, $\preceq_S$ and $\preceq_H$ extend from $\mathcal{P}(Stream)$ to *NDF*.

Definition 1 *Let $I, S \in NDF$ be two nondeterministic functions.*
I is a loose implementation *of S iff $I \subseteq S$ holds.*
I is a partial implementation *of S iff $I \preceq_H S$ holds.*
I is a robust implementation *of S iff $S \preceq_S I$ holds.*

Loose correctness is the strongest of the three notions. It reflects the view that an implementation may be more deterministic than the corresponding specification.

An implementation is partially correct if its behaviour is consistent with the specification. For finite total streams this notion coincides with loose correctness. However it is coarser in that it allows the implementation to diverge at any point. In concurrent systems this is often called a *safety property*. Partial correctness alone is usually not satisfactory. The advantage of proving it in isolation is that the termination proof can be tackled separately.

Robust correctness, the dual of partial correctness, asserts that for every behaviour of the implementation there is a behaviour in the specification that is consistent with it. For finite total streams this notion does again coincide with loose correctness. However it allows nontermination in the specification to be replaced by arbitrary behaviour of the implementation. This corresponds to the view that nontermination is actually underspecification permitting any implementation.

Although any loose implementation is also a partial and a robust one, the reverse does not hold: an implementation which is both partial and robust need not be loosely correct.

The above correctness notions carry over to data types as follows: $\underline{C}$ is a loose / partial / robust implementation of $\underline{A}$ w.r.t. a set of programs P with semantics $D[\![.]\!]$, if $D[\![p]\!](\underline{C})$ is a loose / partial / robust implementation of $D[\![p]\!](\underline{A})$ for all $p \in P$. What we are interested in is to characterize the induced relationships without any reference to observing programs, purely as a set-theoretic relation between data types. Our main tools for that purpose are the so called simulations.

Definition 2 *Let $\underline{C}, \underline{A}$ be two Σ-structures and let $\sqsubseteq$ be an S-sorted relation $\sqsubseteq_s \subseteq U_s \times U_s$ such that $\sqsubseteq_v = \{(u,u) \mid u \in U_v\}$ for all $v \in V$. For $w \in S^*$ let $\sqsubseteq_w$ be the componentwise extension of $\sqsubseteq_s$.*

$\sqsubseteq$ *is called a* partial simulation *iff for all operations $r : w \to s$ in Σ and all $c \sqsubseteq_w a$ we have*

$$\forall c' \in r^{\underline{C}}(c) \exists a' \in r^{\underline{A}}(a) : c' \sqsubseteq_s a'$$

$\sqsubseteq$ *is called a* (loose) simulation *iff it is a partial simulation, and for all operations $r : w \to s$ in Σ and all $c \sqsubseteq_w a$ we have*

$$a \in T_{\underline{A}}[\![r]\!] \Rightarrow c \in T_{C}[\![r]\!]$$

$\sqsubseteq$ *is called a* robust simulation *iff for all operations $r : w \to s$ in Σ and all $c \sqsubseteq_w a$ we have*

$$a \in T_{\underline{A}}[\![r]\!] \Rightarrow (c \in T_{\underline{C}}[\![r]\!] \wedge \forall c' \in r^{\underline{C}}(c) \exists a' \in r^{\underline{A}}(a) : c' \sqsubseteq a')$$

If the carriers of $\underline{C}$ and $\underline{A}$ are identical, it is verified easily (by translating operations of $\underline{C}$ and $\underline{A}$ to elements in *NDF* via *pd*) that loose, partial and robust simulations coincide with loose, partial and robust correctness respectively. This shows that simulations have a twofold task: to relate different carriers and to guarantee the desired correctness notion.

In the rest of the paper we establish the exact connection between the three simulations and implementations w.r.t. both L1 and L2. The two questions we are interested in are *soundness* and *completeness* of simulations as an implementation criterion:

- Does the existence of a loose/partial/robust simulation between $\underline{C}$ and $\underline{A}$ imply that $\underline{C}$ is a corresponding implementation of $\underline{A}$ w.r.t. programs in L1 and L2?

- If $\underline{C}$ is a loose/partial/robust implementation of $\underline{A}$ w.r.t. programs in L1 and L2, does that imply the existence of a corresponding simulation between $\underline{C}$ and $\underline{A}$?

It turns out that simulations are sound in all cases. Completeness, however, depends crucially on the expressiveness of the observing language and does sometimes hold only for subclasses of data types.

5 Loose Implementations

5.1 Soundness

For L1, the soundness result carries over from [18]: the language L used in [18] is, apart from minor syntactic details, equivalent to L1; using the translation *pd* defined in (1) above, it is easily verified that in [18] we were working with loose simulations and implementations. Hence we have immediately:

Theorem 1 *Simulations are a sound criterion for loose implementations w.r.t. programs over L1.*

More importantly, we can reuse the approach to verifying soundness used in [18]. The idea is to decompose simulations into a combination of simpler relations like homomorphisms. This in turn leads to a number of simpler requirements for soundness. It is shown that simulations decompose into homomorphisms, inclusions, reducing nondeterminism and increasing termination. Consequently it suffices to show that D is

1. insensitive to taking substructures: if $\underline{B}$ is a substructure of $\underline{A}$, i.e. $\underline{B}$ contains less "unreachable" junk than $\underline{A}$, then $D[\![p]\!](\underline{B}) = D[\![p]\!](\underline{A})$ should hold.

2. monotone w.r.t. nondeterminism: if $\underline{B}$ is obtained from $\underline{A}$ by reducing the nondeterminism of operations, $D[\![p]\!](\underline{B})$ should be a loose implementation of $D[\![p]\!](\underline{A})$

3. anti-monotone w.r.t. termination: if $\underline{B}$ is obtained from $\underline{A}$ by increasing the termination sets of operations, $D[\![p]\!](\underline{B})$ should be a loose implementation of $D[\![p]\!](\underline{A})$

4. compatible with homomorphisms.

For exact definitions see [18] or [20].

It is easily shown that the operational semantics of L2 satisfies all four requirements and hence that

Theorem 2 *Simulations are a sound criterion for loose implementations w.r.t. programs over L2.*

5.2 Completeness

In most cases we are going to consider, completeness can only be achieved for restricted classes of data types. First we show that, independent of the power of the observation language, we need to restrict to finite signatures and countable nondeterminism.

Example 1 Let $S = \{H, N\}$, $V = \{N\}$ and $O = \{c :\to H\} \cup \{e_i : H \to N \mid i \in \mathbf{N}\}$ and let $\underline{A}$ and $\underline{C}$ be the following Σ-structures:

$$\begin{array}{ll} \underline{A}: & A_H = \{a_i \mid i \in \mathbf{N}\}, \quad A_N = \{0,1\} \\ & c^{\underline{A}} = \{\to a_i \mid i \in \mathbf{N}\}, \quad e_i^{\underline{A}} = \{a_i \to 1\} \cup \{a_j \to 0 \mid j \neq i\} \\ \underline{C}: & C_H = A_H \cup \{\omega\}, \quad C_N = A_N \\ & c^{\underline{C}} = c^{\underline{A}} \cup \{\to \omega\}, \quad e_i^{\underline{C}} = e_i^{\underline{A}} \cup \{\omega \to 0\} \end{array}$$

We assume all operations are total.

The only difference between $\underline{C}$ and $\underline{A}$ is the fact that for any output a of $c^{\underline{A}}$ there is an operation e_i such that $e_i^{\underline{A}}(a) = \{1\}$. In $\underline{C}$ this is not the case because $e_i^{\underline{A}}(\omega) = \{0\}$ holds for all i. However, since we do not know which e_i will reveal the difference, we need to test the results of c with an ***unbounded*** number of operations e_i. As programs are finite, they can only contain finitely many different e_i. Hence there is no program that can distinguish $\underline{C}$ from $\underline{A}$. Therefore $\underline{C}$ is a loose implementation of $\underline{A}$.

However, there is no simulation $\underline{C} \sqsubseteq \underline{A}$: because of c, $\omega \sqsubseteq a_i$ would have to hold for some i, which implies $0 \sqsubseteq 1$ because of e_i.

A very similar example showing that uncountable nondeterminism can lead to incompleteness is contained in [20]. Hence we confine ourselves to Σ-structures with finitely many operations and countable nondeterminism. In a computer science context these are rather natural assumptions anyhow.

An operation $r : w \rightarrow s$ of a data type $\underline{A}$ is called *finitely nondeterministic* if the set $r^{\underline{A}}(a)$ is finite for all $a \in A_w$. $\underline{A}$ is called finitely nondeterministic if all its operations are.

Theorem 3 *Simulations are a complete criterion for loose implementations w.r.t. L1 for the subclass of finitely nondeterministic data types $\underline{A}$ such that*

- *every operation $r \in O$ is* termination-deterministic*: $T_{\underline{A}}[r] = dom(r^{\underline{A}})$, and*
- *every visible sort $v \in V$ has an* equality predicate *$eq_v : v \times v \rightarrow Bool$ with*

$$eq_v^{\underline{A}} = \{(a,a) \rightarrow tt \mid a \in A_v\} \cup \{(a,b) \rightarrow ff \mid a,b \in A_v \wedge a \neq b\}.$$

The corresponding result for L2 is far cleaner:

Theorem 4 *Simulations are a complete criterion for loose implementations w.r.t. L1 for the subclass of finitely nondeterministic data types.*

Although we have not been able to prove it, we conjecture that completeness holds for countably nondeterministic data types too.

The discrepancy between L1 and L2 is not surprising: after all, L2 is a more expressive language. Although theorem 3 is not very interesting in itself, in relation to theorem 4 it shows that a weakening of the observation language can easily destroy completeness of the implementation criterion. However, it seems pointless to try and find an implementation criterion that exactly matches the expressive power of an arbitrary language. As a consequence we would get implementations which are only valid in the context of that language but may become invalid in a more expressive context. Therefore we have tried to find an implementation criterion that matches the most expressive language we could conceive of, L2.

5.3 Total Correctness

Total correctness, as defined in [5], is the equality relation on *NDF*. Since we have shown that for L2 simulations are sound and complete criteria for loose implementations (modulo unbounded nondeterminism), it follows that the existence of two simulations, one in each direction, is a sound and complete criterion for total correctness.

It should be pointed out that there is the slightly stronger notion of a *bisimulation* for Σ-structures (see [19]) which also guarantees total correctness. However [19] contains an example which shows that bisimulations are not complete, i.e. the existence of two simulations does not imply the existence of a bisimulation.

6 Partial Implementations

6.1 Soundness

Following the method outlined in section 5.1, we can decompose partial simulations as in theorem 3.10 of [18] and obtain

Lemma 1 *If $\underline{C} \sqsubseteq \underline{A}$ is a partial simulation, there exist Σ-structures $\underline{B}$ and $\underline{D}$ such that there is a closed homomorphism which is the identity on V from $\underline{B}$ to $\underline{A}$ and from $\underline{D}$ to $\underline{C}$, and $\underline{D}$ is obtained from the smallest substructure of $\underline{B}$ by suitable reduction of nondeterminism.*

This is very similar to the decomposition of simulations, except that there is no increased termination. Hence requirements 1, 2 (with "partial" instead of "loose") and 4 of section 5.1 suffice to imply soundness. But since L1 and L2 meet these conditions w.r.t. loose correctness, they meet them in particular w.r.t. partial correctness. Thus we have as a corollary of theorems 1 and 2:

Corollary 1 *Partial simulations are sound implementation criteria w.r.t. both L1 and L2.*

6.2 Completeness

All completeness proofs follow the same basic pattern. The one for partial simulations w.r.t. L1 exhibits this patter in its simplest form, which is why it is sketched below.

For deterministic data types, the completeness proof is relatively straightforward: if $\underline{C}$ is a partial implementation of $\underline{A}$, there is a smallest partial simulation between them which can be constructed explicitly (see for example lemma 4.3.9 in [24], where partial simulations are called "correspondences"). For Σ-structures this does not hold any more as the following example shows.

Example 2 Let $S = \{H, Bool\}$, $V = \{Bool\}$ and $O = \{c :\rightarrow H, eq : H \times H \rightarrow Bool\}$ and let $\underline{A}$ be the following Σ-structure:

$$A_H = \{a, b\}, \quad A_{Bool} = \{\text{tt}, \text{ff}\}$$
$$c^{\underline{A}} = \{\rightarrow a, \rightarrow b\}, \quad eq^{\underline{A}} = \{(a,a) \rightarrow \text{tt}, (b,b) \rightarrow \text{tt}, (a,b) \rightarrow \text{ff}, (b,a) \rightarrow \text{ff}\}$$

There are exactly two partial simulations $\underline{A} \sqsubseteq \underline{A}$, showing that $\underline{A}$ is a partial implementation of itself:

$$\sqsubseteq_1 = \{(a,a), (b,b), (\text{tt},\text{tt}), (\text{ff},\text{ff})\} \text{ and } \sqsubseteq_2 = \{(a,b), (b,a), (\text{tt},\text{tt}), (\text{ff},\text{ff})\}$$

Unfortunately there is no largest or smallest partial simulation, because neither $\sqsubseteq_1 \subseteq \sqsubseteq_2$ nor $\sqsubseteq_2 \subseteq \sqsubseteq_1$.

Let $\underline{C}$ and $\underline{A}$ be two Σ-structures such that $\underline{C}$ is a partial implementation of $\underline{A}$ and $\underline{A}$ is finitely nondeterministic. Let F be the subset of single argument abstractions in *Abstr* which do not contain any function calls apart from those to operations in Σ and which denote functions that only return visible values. Notice that elements of F can also be considered as programs with an empty sequence of function definitions. We call an S-sorted relation $\sqsubseteq_s \subseteq U_s \times U_s$ *consistent* if $\sqsubseteq_v = \{(u,u) \mid u \in U_v\}$ for all $v \in V$ and if the following holds: given two sequences $\underline{c} \in C_w$ and $\underline{a} \in A_w$, $w \in S^*$, such that $\underline{c} \sqsubseteq_w \underline{a}$, then $R[\![p]\!](\underline{C})(\underline{c}) \subseteq R[\![p]\!](\underline{A})(\underline{a})$ holds for all $p \in F$.

Because $\underline{C}$ is a partial implementation of $\underline{A}$, the S-sorted relation which is the (total) identity on U_s for all $s \in V$ and empty for all $s \in S \backslash V$ is easily seen to be consistent. One can also show that a non-empty set of consistent relations has maximal elements (w.r.t. $\subseteq$), but not necessarily a largest element. It remains to be shown that maximal consistent relations are in fact partial simulations.

Let us assume that there is a maximal consistent relation $\sqsubseteq$ which is not a partial simulation. By definition of consistency $\sqsubseteq$ is the identity on visible sorts. Thus there must be an operation $r : w \rightarrow s$, tuples $\underline{c}_0 \in C_w$ and $\underline{a}_0 \in A_w$ with $\underline{c}_0 \sqsubseteq_w \underline{a}_0$ such that

$$\exists c' \in r^{\underline{C}}(\underline{c}_0) \forall a' \in r^{\underline{A}}(\underline{a}_0) : c' \not\sqsubseteq a'.$$

Let the offending element be called c' and let $r^{\underline{A}}(\underline{a}_0) = \{a_1, \ldots, a_n\}$. Because $\sqsubseteq$ is maximal, for any $i \in \{1, \ldots, n\}$, $c' \not\sqsubseteq a_i$ implies that $\sqsubseteq \cup \{(c', a_i)\}$ is not consistent, i.e. there is an abstraction $e_i \in F$ and there are inputs $\underline{c}_i \sqsubseteq \underline{a}_i$ such that $R[\![e_i]\!](\underline{C})(\underline{c}_i . c') \not\subseteq R[\![e_i]\!](\underline{A})(\underline{a}_i . a_i)$. Let $d_i \in R[\![e_i]\!](\underline{C})(\underline{c}_i . c')$ such that $d_i \notin R[\![e_i]\!](\underline{A})(\underline{a}_i . a_i)$. We can now construct some input $\underline{c} \sqsubseteq \underline{a}$ and a program $p \in F$ such that $R[\![p]\!](\underline{C})(\underline{c}) \not\subseteq R[\![p]\!](\underline{A})(\underline{a})$, which contradicts the consistency of $\sqsubseteq$. Let $\underline{a} = \underline{a}_0 . \underline{a}_1 \cdots \underline{a}_n$ and $\underline{c} = \underline{c}_0 . \underline{c}_1 \cdots \underline{c}_n$, and let f_i be an abstraction which extracts $\underline{c}_i$ and $\underline{a}_i$ from $\underline{c}$ and $\underline{a}$ respectively, $i \in \{0, \ldots, n\}$. It is an easy exercise in string manipulation using first and rest to construct the f_i. Finally let

$$p = \lambda x.(\lambda y.e_1(f_1(x)\&y)\& \ldots \&e_n(f_n(x)\&y))(r(f_0(x))).$$

It is easy to show that $d_1 \dots d_n \in R[\![p]\!](\underline{C})(\underline{c})$ but $d_1 \dots d_n \notin R[\![p]\!](\underline{A})(\underline{a})$.

For L2 the proof is almost identical. Overall we have:

Theorem 5 *Partial simulations are a complete criterion for partial implementations w.r.t. L1 and L2 for the subclass of finitely nondeterministic data types.*

It is interesting to note that the completeness proof makes use only of a small subset of L1 and L2, basically abstraction, application and sequence manipulation. The completeness proof for loose simulations given in [20] uses all language constructs except recursion. Only dealing with unbounded nondeterminism seems to require recursion, as an example in [18] suggests.

7 Robust Implementations

7.1 Soundness

Unfortunately, robust simulations are not sound w.r.t. to all L1/L2 programs. The reason is that robust implementations do not necessarily compose in L1/L2: even if the p_i are robust implementations of the q_i, their composition $C(p_1, \dots, p_k)$ does not yield a robust implementation of $C(q_1, \dots, q_k)$ for every syntactic construct C. The offending construct is ∇, the angelic choice. Robust implementations compose only in contexts where nonterminating components do not affect the behaviour of the overall system (e.g. because they are guarded) or lead to nontermination of the whole system. In both cases any replacement of the nonterminating components yields a robust implementation of the system. Contexts which are both nondeterministic and nonsequential (see [27]) do not have this property: although 0 is a robust implementation of 0, and 1 a robust implementation of $\perp$ (anything is), $0\nabla 1$ is *not* a robust (or any kind of) implementation of $0\nabla\perp$. This shows that, although some authors use robust implementations as their standard implementation definition (e.g. [12]), this is only valid in a (in the technical sense of [27]) sequential environment. Consequently we concentrate on the subset of L1/L2 without ∇ which we call L1'/L2'.

Decomposing robust simulations as in lemma 1, we find that the decomposition is similar to the one for loose simulations, except that we have an additional relation:

Definition 3 *Given two Σ-structures $\underline{A}$ and $\underline{B}$ with the same carriers, we write $\underline{B} \subseteq_{R/T} \underline{A}$ if for all operations $r : w \longrightarrow s$*

$$T_{\underline{B}}[\![r]\!] = T_{\underline{A}}[\![r]\!] \wedge r^{\underline{B}} = \{(a, a') \in r^{\underline{A}} \mid a \in T_{\underline{A}}[\![r]\!]\}$$

Thus for soundness of robust simulations we need to show requirements 1-4 (with "robust" instead of "loose") of section 5.1 plus the following condition:

5. insensitive to behaviour outside guaranteed termination: $\underline{B} \subseteq_{R/T} \underline{A}$ should imply that $D[\![p]\!](\underline{A})$ is a robust implementation of $D[\![p]\!](\underline{B})$.

¿From section 5.1 we know that L1 and L2 meet conditions 1-4 w.r.t. loose implementations. Therefore L1' and L2' meet 1-4 w.r.t. robust implementations. Since one can also show that L1' and L2' (but not L1 or L2!) satisfy condition 5, we conclude

Theorem 6 *Robust simulations are sound criteria for robust implementations w.r.t. L1' and L2'.*

It should be noted that $\underline{B} \subseteq_{R/T} \underline{A}$ implies $pd(r^{\underline{A}}, T_{\underline{A}}[\![r]\!]) \preceq_S pd(r^{\underline{B}}, T_{\underline{B}}[\![r]\!])$ for all operations r. Hence condition 5 is equivalent to requiring monotonicity of D in the Smyth powerdomain.

7.2 Completeness

For robust simulations, we can only obtain limited completeness results. The problem is the combination of partiality with nondeterminism as in the following example:

Example 3 Let $S = \{H, N\}$, $V = \{N\}$ and $O = \{c :\rightarrow H, f, g : H \rightarrow N\}$ and let $\underline{A}$ and $\underline{C}$ be the following Σ-structures

$$\begin{array}{ll} \underline{A}: & A_H = \{a_1, a_2\}, \quad A_N = \{0,1\} \\ & c^{\underline{A}} = \{\rightarrow a_1, \rightarrow a_2\}, \quad f^{\underline{A}} = \{a_1 \rightarrow 0\}, \quad g^{\underline{A}} = \{a_2 \rightarrow 0\} \\ \underline{C}: & C_H = \{b\}, \quad C_N = A_N \\ & c^{\underline{C}} = \{\rightarrow b\}, \quad f^{\underline{C}} = \{b \rightarrow 1\}, \quad g^{\underline{C}} = \{b \rightarrow 1\} \end{array}$$

and assume that $\mathcal{T}[\![r]\!] = dom(r)$ holds for all operations in both $\underline{A}$ and $\underline{C}$.

There no robust simulation $\underline{C} \sqsubseteq \underline{A}$: because of c, $b \sqsubseteq a_i$ would have to hold for either $i = 1$ or $i = 2$, which would force $1 \sqsubseteq 0$ via either f or g. Yet $\underline{C}$ *is* a robust implementation of $\underline{A}$ w.r.t L1' and L2'. The reason is that $\underline{A}$ is a completely useless data type from the robust point of view: because there is no way of detecting whether c has returned a_1 or a_2, it is never safe to apply f or g as they may both diverge. The only safe way of applying f or g is in parallel, because one of them must always terminate. However ∇ is not available any more. Hence *any* Σ-structure where c always terminates is a robust implementation of $\underline{A}$.

However we can identify two subclasses of data types for which robust simulations are complete.

Theorem 7 *Robust simulations are a complete criterion for robust implementations w.r.t L1' and L2' for the subclass of all data types $\underline{A}$ which are either*

- result-deterministic*: for all operations $r : w \rightarrow s$ and all $a \in A_w$: $|r^{\underline{A}}(a)| \leq 1$.*
- *or finitely nondeterministic and* total*: $dom(r^{\underline{A}}) = A_w$ holds for all operations $r : w \rightarrow s$.*

Notice that result-deterministic operations are almost, but not quite, partial functions.

8 Comparisons and Conclusions

The only other approach that is close enough to ours to permit direct comparison is that in [9]. In the context of a simpler observation language (only finite I/O and no angelic nondeterminism) they prove that two variants of simulations, *upward* and *downward* simulations, are both sound and, *together*, complete. That however means that one may have to construct a third data type $\underline{B}$ and show that there is an upward/downward simulation between it and $\underline{A}/\underline{C}$.

The formalism employed in [9] is considerably simpler than the one used in this paper. To a large extent this is reflected in the simpler semantic concepts treated in [9]. In [11], Hoare aims for an even simpler framework using category theory. The main advantage seems to be that the soundness theorems for simulations are less tightly bound to particular programming languages. Completeness issues are not treated.

The framework in this paper is not as unified as for example in [6] because we have to deal with both data types and programs. A more unified approach would result from treating operations on data types as arbitrary stream processing functions, i.e. elements in *NDF*. However that would be a further significant move away from the traditional point of view of data types as algebras.

Within this unified framework, it should be possible to develop a theory of *context-dependent* simulations along the lines of [15]. This might allow us to derive soundness and completeness results for different languages (which can now be treated as contexts) and different correctness notions in a unified manner.

Acknowledgements

I am grateful for the perceptive comments on a previous version made by Andrzej Tarlecki and an anonymous referee. They uncovered a number of mistakes and hopefully led to an improved presentation.

References

[1] S. Abramsky: On Semantic Foundations of Applicative Multiprogramming, *in* Proc. 10th ICALP. LNCS 154, pp. 1-14, 1983

[2] K. Bothe: A Comparative Study of Abstract Data Type Concepts, Elektronische Informationsverarbeitung und Kybernetik 17 (1981), 237 - 257

[3] S.D. Brookes, W.C. Rounds: Behavioural Equivalence Relations Induced by Programming Logics, *in* Proc. 10th ICALP, LNCS 154, 1983

[4] M. Broy: A Theory for Nondeterminism, Parallelism, Communication, and Concurrency, TCS 45 (1986), pp. 1-61

[5] M. Broy: Extensional Behaviour of Concurrent, Nondeterministic, Communicating Systems, *in* Control Flow and Data Flow: Concepts of Distributed Programming (M. Broy, ed.), Springer Verlag, 1985

[6] R. de Nicola, M.C.B. Hennessy: Testing Equivalences for Processes, *in* Proc. 10th ICALP, LNCS 154, pp. 548-560, 1983. Full version in TCS 34, pp.83-133, 1984

[7] V. Giarratana, F. Gimona, U. Montanari: Observability Concepts in Abstract Data Type Specifications, in: 5th MFCS, LNCS 45, 1976

[8] J.A. Goguen, J. Meseguer: Universal Realization, Persistent Interconnection and Implementation of Abstract Modules, in: Proc. ICALP '82, LNCS 140, 1982

[9] J. He, C.A.R. Hoare, J.W. Sanders: Data Refinement Refined, Proc. ESOP'86, LNCS 213, 1986

[10] C.A.R. Hoare: Proof of Correctness of Data Representation, Acta Informatica 1, 1972

[11] C.A.R. Hoare: Data Refinement in a Categorical Setting, Manuscript, June 1987

[12] C.B. Jones: Systematic Software Development Using VDM, Prentice-Hall International, 1986

[13] M.C.B. Hennessy: Powerdomains and Nondeterministic Recursive Definitions, LNCS 137, pp. 178-193, 1982

[14] S. Kamin: Final Data Types and their Specification, TOPLAS 5, 1, 1983

[15] K.G. Larsen: Context-Dependent Bisimulations Between Processes, PhD Thesis, Tech. Rep. CST-37-86, Dept. of Comp. Sci., Univ. of Edinburgh, 1986

[16] J.W. Lloyd: Foundations of Logic Programming, Springer Verlag, 1984

[17] J.C. Mitchell: Representation Independence and Data Abstraction (Preliminary Version), *in* Proc. 13th POPL (1986), pp. 263-286

[18] T. Nipkow: Nondeterministic Data Types: Models and Implementations, Acta Informatica 22, pp. 629-661, 1986

[19] T. Nipkow: Are Homomorphisms Sufficient for Behavioural Implementations of Deterministic and Nondeterministic Data Types?, *in* Proc. 4th STACS, LNCS 247, pp. 260-271, 1987

[20] T. Nipkow: Behavioural Implementations Concepts for Nondeterministic Data Types, PhD Thesis, Tech. Rep. UMCS-87-5-3, Dept. of Comp. Sci., The Univ. of Manchester, 1987

[21] H. Reichel: Behavioural Equivalence: A Unifying Concept for Initial and Final Specification Methods, *in*: Proc. 3rd Hung. Comp. Sci. Conf., (M. Arato, L. Varga, eds.), Budapest, 1981, 27-39

[22] D. Sannella, A. Tarlecki: On Observational Equivalence and Algebraic Specification, Proc. CAAP'85, LNCS 185, 308-322

[23] O. Schoett: Ein Modulkonzept in der Theorie Abstrakter Datentypen, Report IfI-HH-B-81/81, Universität Hamburg, Fachbereich Informatik, 1981

[24] O. Schoett: Data Abstraction and the Correctness of Modular Programming, PhD Thesis, Tech. Rep. CST-42-87, Dept. of Comp. Sci., Univ. of Edinburgh, 1987

[25] M.B. Smyth: Power Domains, JCCS 2, pp. 23-36, 1978

[26] M.H. van Emden, R.A. Kowalski: The Semantics of Predicate Logic as a Programming Language, JACM 23, 4, pp. 733-742, 1976

[27] J. Vuillemin: Correct and Optimal Implementation of Recursion in a Simple Programming Language, JCSS 9 (1974), 332-354

Initial Behaviour Semantics for Algebraic Specifications

Mª P. Nivela
F. Orejas
Facultat d'Informàtica
Universitat Politècnica de Catalunya
Barcelona, Spain

1. Introduction

Initial algebra semantics [GTW 78] is, probably, the most popular method for giving semantics to algebraic specifications. Several reasons justify this popularity, among them the methodological appeal of the "closed world assumption" [GoMe 83], the simplicity and power of the technical constructions used and the power of the associated methods and tools [HuOp 80].

However, from the very beginning [GGM 76, GuHo 78], initial algebra semantics was criticized for not supplying the appropriate degree of abstraction in semantic definitions. Initial algebra semantics was supplying abstraction "up to isomorphism", where, it was argued, "behavioural abstraction" was needed.

The first answer to initial semantics was final semantics [GGM 76, Kam 83, Wan 79] but, although it was based on using some observability criteria in definitions, it was also a semantics up to isomorphism, not fully capturing the behavioural abstraction idea. Moreover, the kind of constructions associated to this semantics were technically more complicated than for the initial one.

Since then, a certain number of approaches [Rei 81, GoMe 82, MeGo 85, HeWi 85, Rei 81, SaWi 83, SaTa 85, Sch 82] have appeared studying behavioural abstraction and its associated semantics. Most of the work done has just dealt with studying the adequate definition of behavioural equivalence.

Being convinced of the technical advantages of initial semantics and its associated constructions and being also convinced of the methodological appeal of behavioural semantics, we have tried to obtain a synthesis of both. That is to provide initial algebra-like constructions with behavioural semantics.

Up to now, only Reichel [Rei 81, Rei 84] and, at a first level, Goguen and Meseguer [GoMe 82] have followed a similar approach. However their notion of behavioural equivalence was too limited. Reichel's notion, based on the existence of common reductions, would consider as not equivalent algebras differing on non observable junk. This is also the case for Goguen and Meseguer's notion which, moreover, needs equality on observable sorts, not admitting renaming of observable values. Later, the same authors [MeGo 85] presented a more suitable definition (in fact, in this paper, we use their notion of behavioural equivalence), but they did not redo their previous work.

In this paper we provide, what in our opinion is, the right foundations for giving behavioural semantics to algebraic specifications within the initial algebra spirit. An institution [GoBu 84] for behaviour specifications is defined in which the semantics of the usual constructions found in algebraic specification languages can be defined with the technical simplicity of initial semantics. Based on these results, in [Niv 87] the complete two-level behavioural semantics of an algebraic specification language a la Act One [EhMa 85] is provided, together with the proof of the compatibility of the two levels.

A key point for achieving these results has been the notion of homomorphism used in our category of models. In this category, isomorphism coincides with behavioural equivalence, thus obtaining the simplicity of the constructions up to isomorphism together with real behavioural abstraction. Indeed, in our opinion, some of the problems that impeded the obtaining of better results in previous work was caused by working, in this context, with loose semantics.

The other change with respect to the "standard" institution is to the definition of the satisfaction relation, which, according to the whole philosophy, has been converted into "observable" satisfaction.

The simplicity of the institution has also allowed without additional complication to define more general constructions, relaxing constraints, not fully justified from the methodological point of view, imposed in other approaches. For instance, in parameterized specifications there may be observable sorts in the body which are not in the formal parameter. Also, in parameter passing we allow changes in observability, i.e. we allow the binding of a nonobservable actual sort to an observable formal sort.

The paper is organized as follows. The first section is this introduction. In the second section the basic institution for dealing with behavioural semantics is presented. This includes the proof of existence of initial behaviours and the relations between our category of models and the usual one. Finally, in the third section, we study parameterized specifications. Their semantics is given by means of free constructions and their correctness (persistency) is characterized. Also, semantics of parameter passing is presented, characterizing its correctness in terms of persistency and proving its associativity.

In this paper a lot of easy proofs have been omitted and others are presented in a reduced form. Complete proofs can be found in [Niv 87] and in a longer version of this paper in preparation. The reader is assumed to have a good knowledge of the usual algebraic specification stuff, for instance [EhMa 85].

ACKNOWLEDGEMENTS

The authors would like to thank J. Goguen, J. Meseguer and D. Sannella for some fruitful conversations. Also, the careful reading of the referees has contributed to improving the presentation of the paper. This work has been partially supported by Comisión Asesora de Investigación (ref. 2704-83).

2. An institution for behavioural semantics

Most of the work on giving behavioural semantics for algebraic specifications has concentrated the effort on defining an appropriate notion of behavioural equivalence between models. Then, the semantics of a specification is the class of models behaviourally equivalent to certain models (in the usual sense) of the specification (for instance, the initial ones).

These approaches have, in our opinion, one main drawback: extensions to define the semantics of the usual constructions found in algebraic specification languages are, often, too complicated for the purposes of this paper. For instance, we may have problems in defining (equivalent notions of) free constructions for these approaches. The reason is that, if we take two classes of algebras, say Alg(SP1) and Alg(SP2), there may be algebras which do not satisfy the specification SP1 but which are adequate "behavioural models" of SP1. Thus a direct extension of the usual free construction from Alg(SP1) to Alg(SP2) would not usually work. Also, since the semantics of most constructions found in algebraic specification languages may be based on such constructions (for instance, parameterization), if we succeeded in obtaining such a definition, we would have to extend the notion of behavioural equivalence from algebras to functors, to achieve an uniform semantic definition. Then the whole semantics will, probably, be more complicated.

We think that the way to overcome these problems is to define a new framework, a new *institution* [GoBu 84], to deal with algebraic specifications with behavioural semantics. In this new institution only syntax remains the same (we consider the usual equational algebraic specifications), except that a distinguished subset of the set of sorts denotes which of them are observable. The category of models is a new one. Objects are the usual Sig-algebras, but morphisms change in two respects:

- Morphisms are maps defined only on the observable sorts. Since values of non-observable sort are non-observable there is no need to define morphisms on them.
- Morphisms commute with respect to **observable computations** (terms constructed from the operations with observable inputs and observable result) and not necessarily with respect to any operation in the signature.

Finally, the satisfaction relation is also different. We consider that an algebra satisfies a given equation if it satisfies (in the classical sense) all its observable consequences.

This institution has a certain number of nice properties that eliminate the problems mentioned above:

- Behavioural equivalence coincides with isomorphism.
- The class of models of a given specification, SP, contains all the models which are behaviourally equivalent to algebras in Alg(SP)
- There are initial models and free constructions. In particular, the class of initial models is the class of algebras behaviourally equivalent to the usual initial algebra T_{SP}. Also, the class of free functors is the class of functors behaviourally equivalent to the usual free construction. Obviously, this equivalence of functors should be considered in an intuitive sense, since not only the categories on which they are defined are different, but, as said above, even the models belonging to these categories are not the same. For these reasons initial behaviours and free behaviour constructions may be seen as adequate for giving semantics to, respectively, non-parameterized and parameterized specifications.

In this section, we will present the basic definitions and results concerning this new institution. In the first subsection we define the categories of behaviours and the satisfaction relation associated to a given set of equations. Additionally, we provide a syntactic characterization of the behaviour theory associated to a specification. In the second subsection we prove the existence of initial behaviours providing a meaning to non-parameterized specifications. Finally, in the last subsection we establish some connections between the categories of behaviours and the usual categories of algebras, specifically a forgetful functor and the notions of initial and final realization are defined.

2.1 Basic definitions

As in [Rei 81, GoMe 82], observability is established in a specification (or, rather, in a signature) by means of a distinguished subset, denoted Obs, of the set of sorts. The sorts in this subset are said to be observable.

Definition 2.1.1

A **behaviour signature** Sig is a triple Sig = (Obs,S,Σ) with Obs ⊆ S.The sorts in Obs are called **observable sorts**.

To every signature Sig, we may associate two categories of models: Alg(Sig), and the one we will use for defining behavioural semantics, Beh(Sig). In this category models are Sig-algebras, as in Alg(Sig), but morphisms, as said above, are different. To avoid confusion, from now on, morphisms in Alg(Sig) will be called Sig-homomorphisms, while morphisms in Beh(Sig) will be called Sig-behaviour morphisms.

Definition 2.1.2

Let A be a Sig-algebra. A **computation** (resp. an **observable computation**) over A is a term in $T_\Sigma(A_{Obs})$ (resp. $T_\Sigma(A_{Obs})_s$ with $s \in Obs$. As usual, we may provide an evaluation function, denoted ε_A, which is the unique Sig-homomorphism extending the inclusion of A_{Obs} into A.

Given two Sig-algebras A and B, a **Sig-behaviour morphism** f: A → B is a family of functions $f=\{f_s\}_{s\in Obs}$ such that for all observable computations $t \in T_\Sigma(A_{Obs})_s$, $s \in Obs$, the following equality holds

$$f_s(\varepsilon_A(t)) = \varepsilon_B(f^{\#}_s(t))$$

where $f^{\#}$: $T_\Sigma(A_{Obs}) \rightarrow T_\Sigma(B_{Obs})$ is the unique Sig-homomorphism which extends f. Sig-algebras together with Sig-behaviour morphisms, form the category **Beh(Sig)**. It can be noted that if Obs coincides with S then Beh(Sig) is exactly the same as Alg(Sig).

A Sig-behaviour morphism establishes a relationship between the observable computations and their results in A and B respectively. To every observable computation t over A corresponds the observable computation $f^{\#}(t)$ over B and to the result $\varepsilon_A(t)$ of this computation over A corresponds the result $\varepsilon_B(f^{\#}(t))$ in B. Thus an Obs-indexed family $f = \{f_s\}_{s\in S}$ is a Sig-behaviour morphism if these observable computations over A yield in B the same value as in A, up to the transformation determined by f. This means that the following diagram commutes:

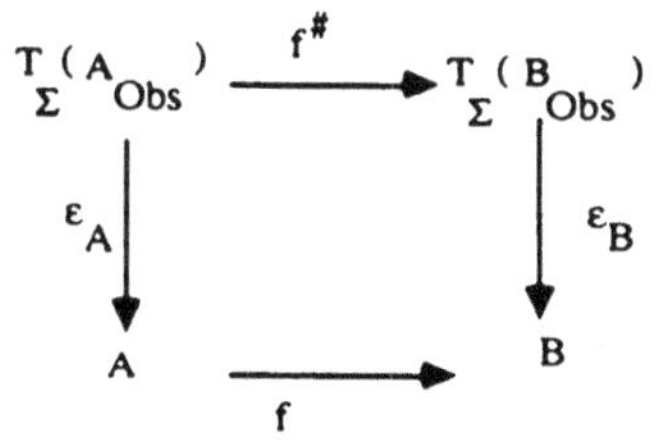

for all sorts in Obs.

If the converse holds, that is, if all the observable computations over B yield in A the same value as in B up to the transformation determined by f, and f itself is a bijection, then A and B give the same answers to the same questions, that is, they *show the same observable behaviour*. Hence, in our framework, behavioural equivalence is characterized by isomorphism in the category Beh(Sig). In particular, isomorphism in Beh(Sig) coincides with the notion of behavioural equivalence from [MeGo 85, HeWi 85, SaWi 83, SaTa 85].

Definition 2.1.3

A and B are **behaviourally equivalent**, denoted $A \equiv_{Sig} B$, if there exists a Sig-behaviour morphism f : A → B which is a Sig-behaviour isomorphism.

The second change in the institution we propose for dealing with behavioural semantics is in the notion of satisfaction. In particular, it seems reasonable that if we are interested in observable behaviour, to consider that an algebra satisfies a given equation we should only ask for satisfaction of its observable consequences.

Definition 2.1.4

Let Sig = (Obs,S, Σ) be a behaviour signature, X_{Obs} an Obs-indexed family of variables and z a variable symbol of sort s not belonging to X. A **Sig-context over the sort** s (resp. **Sig-context for** a Sig-algebra A **over the sort** s) is a term $c[z] \in T_\Sigma(X_{Obs} \cup \{z\})_{s'}$ with $s' \in Obs$ (resp. $c_A[z] \in T_\Sigma(A_{Obs} \cup \{z\})_{s'}$ with $s' \in Obs$).

Given a context c[z], (resp. $c_A[z]$) and a term t in $T_\Sigma(X_{Obs})_s$ (resp. in $T_\Sigma(A_{Obs})_s$), by c[t] (resp. $c_A[t]$) we denote the **application of the context over** t, that is, $\bar{\sigma}(c[z])$ (resp. $\bar{\sigma}(c_A[z])$), where σ is the assigment $\sigma : X_{Obs} \to T_\Sigma(X_{Obs})$ (resp. $\sigma : \{z\} \to T_\Sigma(X_{Obs})$ defined by $\sigma(z) = t$ and $\sigma(x) = x$ for every x in X_{Obs} (resp. $\sigma(z) = t$).

If we consider contexts as observations, it would seem quite natural to assert that "an algebra A behaviourally satisfies the equation e if A satisfies c[t1] = c[t2] for every Sig-context c[y] over the sort s". In this way, an equation of observable sort would be satisfied in the classical sense and an equation of nonobservable sort would be satisfied up to observable contexts. This is the notion of behavioural satisfaction defined in [Rei 84]. However, in our framework, this definition is not appropriate because the replacement of the variables in the equation by "nonobsevable inputs " (more specifically, by nonobservable junk) can cause that behavioural equivalent algebras do not behaviourally satisfy the same equations. This problem is not present in [Rei 84] because of his different notion of behavioural equivalence. Let us consider for instance the following specification for sets:

<u>spec</u> sets_of_values = Bool + Values
<u>sorts</u> <u>observable</u> bool, value
set
<u>ops</u> $\emptyset : \to$ set
push : set value $\to$ set
$\_ \cup \_$: set set $\to$ set
belongs? : set value $\to$ bool
<u>eqns</u> x, y: value; c, c1, c2: set
belongs? ($\emptyset$, x) = false
belongs? (push(c, x), y) = (x = y) <u>or</u> belongs? (c, y)
belongs?(c1 $\cup$ c2, x) = belongs?(c1, x) <u>or</u> belongs?(c2, x)
<u>end spec</u>

and let A and B be the algebras, extensions of the Bool algebra, defined by:

$A_{value} = \{0\}$	$\emptyset \cup_A \emptyset = \emptyset$	$belongs?_A(\emptyset,0) = false$
$A_{set} = \{\emptyset, \{0\}\}$	$\emptyset \cup_A \{0\} = \{0\}$	$belongs?_A(\{0\},0) = true$
$\emptyset_A = \emptyset$	$\{0\} \cup_A \emptyset = \{0\}$	
$push_A(\emptyset,0) = \{0\}$	$\{0\} \cup_A \{0\} = \{0\}$	
$push_A(\{0\},0) = \{0\}$		

$B_{value} = \{0\}$	$\emptyset \cup_B \emptyset = \emptyset$	$\{0\} \cup_B * = *$
$B_{set} = \{ \emptyset, \{0\}, * \}$	$\emptyset \cup_B \{0\} = \{0\}$	$* \cup_B \{0\} = *$
$\emptyset_B = \emptyset$	$\{0\} \cup_B \emptyset = \{0\}$	$* \cup_B * = \emptyset$
$push_B(\emptyset,0) = \{0\}$	$\{0\} \cup_B \{0\} = \{0\}$	$belongs?_B(\emptyset,0) = false$
$push_B(\{0\},0) = \{0\}$	$\emptyset \cup_B * = *$	$belongs?_B(\{0\},0) = true$
$push_B(*,0) = *$	$* \cup_B \emptyset = *$	$belongs?_B(*,0) = true$

These two algebras behave in the same way since there is a trivial behaviour isomorphism between them (remember that behaviour morphisms are only defined on observable sorts). Nevertheless, if it were allowed to substitute a variable of sort set for the "*" junk element, then A and B would satisfy different equations, for instance the equation:

belongs?(c1 $\cup$ c2, x) = belongs?(c1, x) <u>or</u> belongs?(c2, x)

would be satisfied by A but not by B (it suffices to substitute c1 and c2 by "*" and x by 0).

This problem arises when nonobservable junk is assigned to the variables in the equation. We will only allow to substitute them by values finitely generated from the observable ones. This is coherent with the intuitive idea that "we do not care about the nonobservable part".

<u>Definition 2.1.5</u>
Let A be a Sig-algebra and e: $\lambda Y.t1=t2$ a Sig-equation of sort s. A **behaviourally satisfies** e, denoted $A \models_B e$, if A satisfies $\lambda X_{Obs}.c[\ \overline{\sigma}(t1)]=c[\ \overline{\sigma}(t2)]$ for every Sig-context c[z] over the sort s and every assignment $\sigma: Y \to T_\Sigma(X_{Obs})$.

This is equivalent to saying that A behaviourally satisfies e if $\varepsilon_A(c_A[\ \overline{\alpha}(t1)]) = \varepsilon_A(c_A[\ \overline{\alpha}(t2)])$, for every Sig-context for A over the sort s, $c_A[z]$, and for every assignment $\alpha: Y \to T_\Sigma(A_{Obs})$.

From now on, in order to enhance readability, we will omit the explicit quantification of variables in equations, though technically needed [GoMe 81].

<u>Definition 2.1.6</u>
Let A be a Sig-algebra. A is **Obs-reachable**, or, also, **finitely generated from the observable part**, if the evaluation $\varepsilon_A : T_\Sigma(A_{Obs}) \to A$ is surjective.

This means that all the nonobservable values in A can be constructed from the signature operations and from the observable values in A.

<u>Definition 2.1.7</u>
A **behaviour specification** SP is a 4-tuple, SP = (Obs,S,Σ,E), where Sig = (Obs,S,Σ) is a behaviour signature and E is a set of Sig-equations. **Beh(SP)** is the full subcategory of Beh(Sig) of all Sig-algebras which behaviourally satisfy the equations in E.

<u>Definition 2.1.8</u>
Let A be a Sig-algebra. The **observable equations**, eobs(A), of A are

$$eobs(A) = \{t1 = t2 \mid t1,t2 \in T_\Sigma(A_{Obs})_s, s \in Obs, \varepsilon_A(t1) = \varepsilon_A(t2)\}$$

As said before, in Beh(SP) are all and only all the algebras which are behaviourally equivalent to an algebra in Alg(SP):

Proposition 2.1.9
A belongs to Beh(SP) if and only if there exists an algebra A' in Alg(SP) such that $A \equiv_{Sig} A'$.

Proof
Given A it suffices to choose $A' = T_\Sigma(A_{Obs}) / \equiv_{eobs(A) + E}$. Conversely, if A is behaviourally equivalent to an algebra A' in Alg(SP) then, trivially, A' behaviourally satisfies SP and therefore, since A and A' are behaviourally isomorphic, A belongs to Beh(SP). []

Algebraic theories may be defined as usual:

Definition 2.1.10
Let M be a set of Sig-algebras. The **behaviour theory of** M, **BTh(M)**, is the set of all Sig-equations which are behaviourally satisfied by every algebra in M.

$$BTh(M) = \{t1=t2 \mid \forall A \in M\ A \models_B t1=t2\}$$

Definition 2.1.11
Let SP be a behaviour specification. A Sig-equation e **is behaviourally deducible from** SP, denoted $SP \vdash_B e$, if $SP \vdash c[\ \bar{\sigma}(e)]$ (i.e. $c[\ \bar{\sigma}(e)]$ may be deduced from SP, cf. [EhMa 85]) for every assignment $\sigma : var(e) \rightarrow T_\Sigma(X_{Obs})$ and for every context c[z] over the sort of e.

The name *behavioural deduction* may be, perhaps, considered not very adequate since no deduction rules have been defined. In fact, it would be impossible to provide a sound and complete set of finitary rules for such relation. We have the following syntactic characterization of the class BTh(Beh(SP)).

Proposition 2.1.12
Let e be a Sig-equation. $SP \vdash_B e$ if and only if e belongs to BTh(Beh(SP)).

Proof
If $SP \vdash_B e$ then $SP \vdash c[\sigma(e)]$ for every assignment σ and every suitable context c[z]. So every algebra in Alg(SP) satisfies $c[\sigma(e)]$. This means that e is satisfied by every algebra in Beh(SP), because (a) in every behaviour there always exists an algebra which satisfies SP and (b) the equation $c[\sigma(e)]$ is of observable sort, since it only contains observable variables and all the algebras of the same behaviour satisfy the same equations of this kind. Conversely, if e is an equation in BTh(Beh(SP)) then every algebra in Beh(SP) satisfies $c[\sigma(e)]$ for every s and c[z]. In particular, this will also be true for all algebras in Alg(SP). Hence $SP \vdash c[\sigma(e)]$, that is, $SP \vdash_B e$.[]

2.2 Initial behaviour semantics

As has been previously said, within our institution, semantics of specifications can be defined also in terms of initiality. In fact, as the following theorem states T_{SP} is also initial in Beh(SP) (and, hence, every algebra behaviorally equivalent to T_{SP} will also be initial). This means, that we can have behavioural semantics with most of the advantages of the initial one. However, it must be mentioned that, to our knowledge, no powerful deductive methods have been designed yet.

Theorem 2.2.1

T_{SP} is initial in Beh(SP).

Proof

Let A be an algebra in Beh(SP), according to proposition 2.1.9, there is an A' in Alg(SP) such that A $\equiv_{Sig}$ A'. Since T_{SP} is initial in Alg(SP) there is a Sig-homomorphism h from T_{SP} to A'. In particular, h may be seen as a Sig-behaviour morphism. Then, as A and A' are behaviourally isomorphic, there is a Sig-behaviour morphism from T_{SP} to A. This morphism is unique because T_{SP} is finitely generated. []

2.3 Realizations of a behaviour

In this subsection we will study certain connections between categories of algebras and of behaviours. On one hand, we know that the objects of Alg(Sig) and Beh(Sig) coincide. This is not true, in general for Alg(SP) and Beh(SP) (every algebra in Alg(SP) is also in Beh(SP)). However, from SP we may define a new specification SP^* such that the models in Alg(SP^*) and Beh(SP) coincide [SaTa 85]:

Definition 2.3.1

Let SP = (Obs, S, Σ, E) be a behaviour specification. The specification **behaviourally derived from SP** is $SP^* = (S, \Sigma, E^*)$ where

$$E^* = \{ t_1 = t_2 \mid t_1, t_2 \in T_\Sigma(X_{Obs})_s, s \in Obs, E \vdash t_1 = t_2 \}$$

is the set of all equations of observable sort over observable variables which may be deduced from E.

Now, the category Beh(SP) has the same objects as Alg(SP^*), but behaviour morphisms are in a sense "weaker" than homomorphisms: every Sig-homomorphism may be seen as a behaviour morphism forgetting about the functions defined on nonobservable sorts. That is, we may define a forgetful functor:

$$U_{SP} : Alg(SP^*) \to Beh(SP)$$

such that $U_{SP}(A) = A$ for every A in Alg(SP^*) and to every Σ-homomorphism f corresponds $U_{SP}(f) = f|_{Obs}$, that is, the same f viewed as a Σ-behaviour morphism by its restriction to the observable sorts.

This forgetful functor has been called by Goguen and Meseguer [GoMe 82] the *behaviour* functor and the constructions from Beh(SP) to Alg(SP^*) that we will study below *realizations*. The reason is that we can see isomorphic classes of objects in Alg(SP^*) as concrete realizations of behaviours in Beh(SP), and, conversely, isomorphic classes of objects in Beh(SP) may be seen as the behaviour of objects in Alg(SP^*).

Goguen and Meseguer studied two realizations, the so-called initial and final realizations. The initial realization associates to every behaviour A in Beh(SP) the Obs-reachable algebra in this behaviour, I(A), with *least confusion* (two elements are equivalent if and only if they can be demonstrated as equal by the sole use of the observable relations of equality which hold in A), i.e. I(A) is initial (up to renaming of the observable values) in the subcategory of SP^*-algebras that are behaviourally equivalent to A. Conversely, the final realization associates to every behaviour A in Beh(SP) the Obs-reachable algebra in this behaviour, F(A), with *most confusion* (two elements are equivalent if and only if their equality is observably satisfied by A), i.e. F(A) is final (up to renaming of the observable values) in the subcategory of SP^*-algebras that are behaviourally equivalent to A and Obs-reachable.

In what follows we will study initial and final realization in our framework showing that initial realization is a left adjoint functor to U_{SP}. However, surprisingly, we will also show that final realization is not a functorial construction.

Definition 2.3.2

The **initial realization** of the behaviour of A is

$$I(A) = T_\Sigma(A_{Obs}) / \equiv_{eobs(A)}$$

The *initiality* of I(A) is reflected in the sense that there exists a unique Sig-homomorphism from I(A) to every other algebra belonging to the same behaviour as A. This uniqueness is given up to a Sig-behaviour isomorphism between the observable parts.

Proposition 2.3.3

Let A be a Sig-algebra. For the initial realization I(A) the following properties hold:

1. $I(A) \equiv_{Sig} A$
2. Let A' be a Sig-algebra such that $A \equiv_{Sig} A'$ and $\alpha: A \to A'$ is a Sig-behaviour isomorphism. Then, there is a unique Sig-homorphism $f : I(A) \to A'$ extending α.

The proof is not difficult and similar to the one in [MeGo 85].The construction of the initial realization can be extended to a functorial construction which associates to every algebra in Beh(SP) its initial realization in the category Alg(SP*).

Proposition 2.3.4

The construction of the initial realization extends to a functor called the **initial realization functor**

$$Ini : Beh(SP) \to Alg(SP^*)$$

which is also free with respect to the forgetful functor $U_{SP} : Alg(SP^*) \to Beh(SP)$.

The construction of the final realization [GGM 76, GoMe 82, Kam 83, Wan 79] is similar to the classic one for automata minimization, where internal states that cannot be distinguished by the application of observations are identified. This identification is carried out by the so-called Nerode congruence.

Definition 2.3.5

Let t_1, t_2 be two terms in $T_\Sigma(A_{Obs})_s$ with $s \in S$. We say that $t_1 \equiv_{N(A),s} t_2$ if for every context $c_A[z]$ over s

$$\varepsilon_A(c_A[t_1]) = \varepsilon_A(c_A[t_2])$$

The relation $\equiv_{N(A)}$ extends to a congruence called the **Nerode congruence** over A. Although it is an abuse of notation, we will also denote the Nerode congruence over A by $\equiv_{N(A)}$. The final realization is defined as follows

Definition 2.3.6

Let A be an Obs-reachable algebra. The **final realization** of the behaviour of A is

$$F(A) = T_\Sigma(A_{Obs}) / \equiv_{N(A)}$$

As for initial realization, the final realization F(A) is behaviourally equivalent to A and does not contain nonobservable junk. Moreover it is final among Obs-reachable algebras in the realized behaviour up to renaming of observable values.

Proposition 2.3.7

Let A be a Sig-algebra. The final realization F(A) satisfies the following properties:

1. $F(A) \equiv_{Sig} A$
2. If A' is an Obs-reachable algebra such that $A \equiv_{Sig} A'$ and $\alpha : A' \to A$ is a Sig-behaviour isomorphism then there is a unique Sig-homomorphism $f: A' \to F(A)$ extending α.

The final realization of a behaviour satisfies all the equations which are behaviourally satisfied by all the algebras in its class.

Proposition 2.3.8

Let A be a Sig-algebra. $F(A) \models t1=t2$ if and only if for every A' such that $A' \equiv_{Sig} A$, $A' \models_B t1=t2$.

It would seem quite reasonable that, as for initial realization, the construction of the final one determines a functorial transformation Fin from Beh(SP) to Alg(SP*) defined by:

a) to every object A in Beh(SP) corresponds the object F(A).

b) to every morphism $f : A \to B$ in Beh(SP) corresponds $Fin(f)([t]) = [f^\#(t)]$.

However, this is not possible in general, because Fin(f) is not necessarily a welldefined mapping since $[t] \equiv_{N(A)} [t']$ does not imply, in general, $[f^\#(t)] \equiv_{N(B)} [f^\#(t')]$. The reason is that if A and B are not behaviourally equivalent then $\equiv_{N(A)}$ and $\equiv_{N(B)}$ identify values in a non comparable way. The difference between the observable junk of A and B can lead to contexts which make distinction between values in B which can not be distinguished in A. For instance, let us consider the specification

```
spec SP =  sorts s, s1
           observable s
           ops  v : → s
              v1, v2 : → s1
              c : s1 s → s
end spec
```

and let A and B be two Sig-algebras with

$A_s = \{v_A\}$	$B_s = \{v_B, b\}$
$c_A(v1_A, v_A) = v_A$	$c_B(v1_B, v_B) = v_B$
$c_A(v2_A, v_A) = v_A$	$c_B(v2_B, v_B) = v_B$
	$c_B(v1_B, b) = b$
	$c_B(v2_B, b) = v_B$

and f defined over s by $f_s(v_A) = v_B$. It holds that $v1 \equiv_{N(A)} v2$ but $f^{\#}(v1) \equiv_{N(B)} f^{\#}(v2)$ does not hold since the context c(y,b) can distinguish them.

This fact has various consequences. The main one is that final realizations are not good canonical representatives for behavioural classes when dealing with algebras containing junk on observable sorts, although, due to results like prop. 2.3.8, this has often been the case: this is, for instance, the intuition behind final algebra semantics. The nonfunctoriality of final realization makes it difficult to work with such representatives.This was the case with the proof of theorem 3.2.9 below, showing the correctness of parameter passing. In this theorem, at a certain moment, there is the need to obtain a realization of the actual parameter specification satisfying the formal parameter equations. The final realization would have been the best candidate if it had been a functorial construction.

Another consequence is that initial behaviours are not "typical" in their variety, as it happens with initial algebras in the standard case. That is, if $t_1, t_2 \in T_\Sigma$ $T_{SP} \models_B t1{=}t2$ does not imply that for every A in Beh(SP) A $\models_B t1{=}t2$ (this implication is only true if t1 and t2 are of observable sort). To see this, it is enough to consider a specification SP for which the algebra A of the above example is initial.

3. Parameterized behaviour specifications

In the previous section we defined what in our opinion is the right institution to work with behavioural semantics. An adequate notion of homomorphism and of satisfaction with respect to behaviour allowed us to give to nonparameterized specifications an "initial" behaviour semantics. In what follows, we will define the semantics of a parameterized specification and of parameter passing along the same lines.

First, we will prove the existence of free constructions associated to specification morphisms in the categories of behaviours. Since, in these categories, isomorphism coincides with behavioural equivalence, any construction "behaviourally equivalent" to a free construction is free. This allows us to define the semantics of a parameterized specification as its associated free construction.

Then, we will study parameter passing. Two aspects must be stressed: on one hand, consistently with the whole approach, actual parameters have just to satisfy the formal parameter requirements with respect to observability. On the other hand, we allow to "change observability" in parameter passing; that is, we allow to bind a nonobservable sort of the actual parameter specification to an observable sort of the formal parameter specification (all formal parameter sorts are observable). This seems to be absolutely needed when working with parameterized behaviour specifications, although it is not considered in most other approaches. For instance, in a parameterized specification of "stacks of values" it seems reasonable to have sort "values" as observable and sort "stacks" as non-observable, but if we want to define "stacks of stacks of values" we have to bind sort "stacks" (non-observable actual parameter sort) to sort "values" (observable formal parameter sort). The consequence of fulfilling this requirement is, as we will see, that parameter passing "morphisms" are not really morphisms: they are not closed under composition. However, this causes no problem: as we will also see, we can prove the associativity of iterated parameter passing.

A parameterized specification is, as usual, a pair of (behaviour) specifications. As said above, all parameter sorts will be assumed to be observable. This condition is technically needed to obtain all our results. Also, it seems a reasonable assumption from a methodological point of view assumed by all other authors. Anyhow, it must be taken into account that in our context it should not be seen as a constraintt, since according to our definition of parameter passing morphism, our only limitation would be that we would be incapable of imposing that certain actual parameter sorts (i.e. those bound to a nonobservable formal sort) should be nonobservable. But, in our opinion, from a methodological standpoint, this is not a limitation.

3.1 Free constructions and semantics of a parameterized specification

To define specification morphisms for behaviour specifications we may use any reasonable definition of *standard* morphisms, but then we must make clear how observability criteria are "translated" by the morphism. In our opinion, the relation that seems most suitable from a methodological standpoint is $h(Obs1) \subseteq Obs2$, for a given morphism $h : SP1 \to SP2$. We could also have required $h(S1\text{-}Obs1) \subseteq S2\text{-}Obs2$, but this relation seems to be not so clear and, on the other hand, we would lose some generality without getting anything.

Definition 3.1.1
Let $SP1=(Obs1,S1,\Sigma1,E1)$ and $SP2=(Obs2,S2,\Sigma2,E2)$ be two specifications. A **behaviour specification morphism** $h : SP1 \to SP2$ is a specification morphism (i.e. h is a signature morphism and $h(E1) \subseteq E2$) such that $h(Obs1) \subseteq Obs2$.

The forgetful functor associated to h, $U_h : Beh(SP2) \to Beh(SP1)$, is defined as usual. There is a free functor, $Free_h$, left adjoint to the forgetful functor U_h. This result may be seen as a special case of a result in [Tar 85], stating the existence of free constructions in certain institutions.

Theorem 3.1.2
Let $SP1 = (Obs1, S1, \Sigma1, E1)$ and $SP2 = (Obs2, S2, \Sigma2, E2)$ be two specifications and $h : SP1 \to SP2$ a behaviour specification morphism. For every algebra A in Beh(SP1), the algebra defined by $Free_h(A) = T_{\Sigma2}(A_{Obs1})/\equiv_{eobs(A)+E2}$ (interpreting the values $a \in A_s$, $s \in Obs1$, as values of sort h(s)) is a free construction over A with respect to U_h which extends to a free functor $Free_h : Beh(SP1) \to Beh(SP2)$.

Proof
It suffices to take as unit of the adjunction $\eta_{A,s} : A_s \to U{\cdot}Free(A)_s$ defined by $\eta_{A,s}(a)=[a]_{\equiv\, eobs(A)+E2}$ for every s in Obs1 and a in A_s, which is welldefined because the elements we are considering belong to carriers of sort in Obs1 (note that for nonobservable sorts there may be terms t1 and t2 in $T_{\Sigma1}(A_{Obs1})$ such that $\varepsilon_A(t1)=\varepsilon_A(t2)$ but $\varepsilon_{U\cdot Free(A)}(t1) \neq \varepsilon_{U\cdot Free(A)}(t2)$). Moreover, η_A is a $\Sigma1$-behaviour morphism: if $t \in T_{\Sigma1}(A_{Obs1})_s$, $s \in Obs1$ is an observable computation over A such that $\varepsilon_A(t) = a$ then $t = a \in eobs(A)$, $\eta_A(\varepsilon_A(t)) = \eta_A(a) = [a]$ and $\varepsilon_{U\cdot Free(A)}(\eta_A{}^{\#}(t)) = [t]$, that is $\eta_A(\varepsilon_A(t)) = \varepsilon_{U\cdot Free(A)}(\eta_A{}^{\#}(t))$.

Let B be an algebra in Beh(SP2) and $f : A \to U(B)$ a $\Sigma1$-behaviour morphism then we may define $g : Free(A) \to B$ by $g([t])=\varepsilon_B(f^*(t))$ over the observable sorts of SP2, where $f^* : T_{\Sigma2}(A_{Obs1}) \to T_{\Sigma2}(U(B)_{Obs1})$ is the extension of f to a $\Sigma2$-homomorphism. It is not difficult to prove that g is a well defined $\Sigma2$-behaviour morphism and that the following diagram commutes:

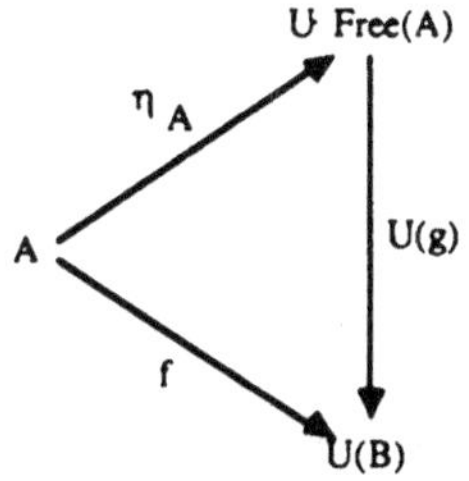

Let us notice that if Obs1 = S1 then for every SP1-algebra A, Free(A) is the usual free construction. The behavioural equivalence relation may be extended uniformly from algebras to functors. That is, in our context, behavioural equivalence of functors should coincide with natural isomorphism:

Definition 3.1.4

Let F1 and F2 be two functors from Beh(SP1) to Beh(SP2). F1 and F2 are **behaviourally equivalent,** denoted F1 ≡ F2, if they are naturally isomorphic.

Therefore, we immediately have that any functor behaviourally equivalent to a free functor is also free. This fact may be seen as a justification, in our context, for using free functors as the semantics of parameterized specifications.

Definition 3.1.5

Let SPp=(Obsp,Sp,Σp,Ep) and SPb=(Obsb,Sb,Σb,Eb) be two behaviour specifications. A **parameterized behaviour specification** SPP is a pair of behaviour specifications SPP = (SPp, SPb) such that Obsp=Sp and SPp $\subseteq$ SPb. SPp is called the **formal parameter specification** and SPb the **body specification**. The semantics of SPP = (SPp,SPb) is the (class of) free functor(s) associated to the inclusion morphism.

We will sometimes consider Obsb=Obsp+S0, Sb=Sp+S1 with S0 $\subseteq$ S1, Σb=Σp+Σ1 and Eb=Ep+E1 where + stands for disjoint union. Also, SPb(SPp) will often denote the parameterized specification SPP.

Correctness of parameterized specifications is often expressed in terms of persistency of the associated free functor. Persistency assures that parameter algebras are "protected" in the parameterization. For this reason persistency seems to be an important property from the methodological point of view. But persistency is also very important technically since it guarantees the compatibility of the two levels of semantics of parameter passing [EKTWW81, Ore87].

In [Gan 83], Ganzinger gave a syntactic characterization of persistency (for standard algebraic specifications) in terms of consistency and sufficient completeness conditions. Persistency on behaviour specifications admits the same kind of characterization as the following theorem states. Its proof will be omited since it is essentially similar to the one in [Gan 83].

Definition 3.1.6

Let SP1=(Obs1,S1,Σ1,E1) and SP2=(Obs2,S2,Σ2,E2) be two behaviour specifications, such that SP1$\subseteq$SP2, and X_{Obs1} is an Obs1-sorted set of variables.

a) SP2 is **behavioural consistent** with respect to SP1 if for every pair of terms t and t' in $T_{\Sigma 1}(X_{Obs1})_s$, s $\in$ Obs1, such that E2 |- t = t' it follows that E1 |- t =t'.

b) SP2 is **behavioural sufficiently complete** with respect to SP1 if for every term t in $T_{\Sigma 2}(X_{Obs1})_s$, s $\in$ Obs1, there exists a term t' in $T_{\Sigma 1}(X_{Obs1})_s$ such that E2 |- t = t'.

Theorem 3.1.7

Let SP1 = (Obs1,S1,Σ1,E1) and SP2 = (Obs2,S2,Σ2,E2) be two specifications such that SP1 $\subseteq$ SP2. SP2 is behavioural consistent and behavioural sufficiently complete with respect to SP1 if and only if the functor Free (associated to the inclusion) is persistent.

From now on, given two specifications SP1 and SP2 such that SP1 $\subseteq$ SP2, we will say that (SP1, SP2) is persistent if the associated free functor is. It may be thought that persistency only provides protection for observable sorts since, if (SP1,SP2), with SP1 $\subseteq$ SP2, is persistent then behavioural consistency and sufficient completeness refer only to observable sorts of SP1. However, this is not quite true since (SP1,SP2) is persistent iff there is a strongly persistent free functor F associated to the inclusion, that is U(F(A)) = A, for every A in Beh(SP1). The intuition behind this is that, in our context, persistency means observable protection of the whole algebra A, rather than full protection of the observable parts of A.

3.2 Parameter passing

To define parameter passing in a specification language (and, indeed, in any language) we must make precise three aspects:

- The binding mechanism between the actual and the formal parameter specifications.
- The construction yielding the result specification.
- The correctness conditions under which this construction works properly.

When dealing with algebraic specifications, the binding mechanism is a specification morphism. This is quite natural for the standard case since, on one hand, the connection established between signatures is adequate and, on the other hand, the connection between equations (for instance, h(E1) $\subseteq$ E2 or E2 $\vdash$ h(E1), where E1 and E2 are, respectively, the equations from the formal and the actual parameter specifications) seems to guarantee that the actual parameter "fulfils" the requirements of the formal parameter specification.

However, in our framework, specification morphisms (as we defined them in the previous section) are not adequate as binding mechanisms for parameter passing. Two aspects seem inappropriate: on one hand, it seems coherent with the whole motivation to relax the connection between equations, specifically we ask SP2 $\vdash_B$ h(E1), since it seems reasonable to ask the actual parameter to behaviourally fulfil the requirements established by the formal parameter specification. On the other hand, as mentioned above, it should be possible to "alter" observability, i.e. we should not ask h(Obs1) $\subseteq$ Obs2. Although this condition is assumed by most other authors, it is unrealistic from a practical point of view. For instance, in the parameterized specification "sets of elements", most probably, sort "elements" would be observable and sort "sets" would not. Then, we will not have any problem in defining the specification "sets of naturals" because the sort "nat" would probably be considered as observable. Nevertheless, we would get into troubles if we try to have "sets of sets of naturals" because the sort "sets" would be nonobservable in the specification "sets of naturals" and, therefore, the binding "elements" to "sets" would be forbidden.

Our binding mechanism is going to be called "parameter passing morphisms", although the name is not very accurate, since these "morphisms" are not closed under composition.

Definition 3.2.1

Let SP and SP' be two behaviour specifications. A **parameter passing morphism** h: SP $\rightarrow$ SP' is a signature morphism such that (1) h(S-Obs) $\subseteq$ S'-Obs' and (2) SP'$\vdash_B$ h(E).

Condition 1) may seem useless, since formal parameter sorts are all observable. However, for technical reasons, it is convenient to see, in parameter passing diagrams (presented below), the extension of the passing morphism, that connects the body to the result specification, also as a parameter passing morphism.

As mentioned above, parameter passing morphisms are not really morphisms because they are not closed under composition. This can be seen in the following example.

Let SP1, SP2 and SP3 be the following specifications:

```
spec SP1 =
    sorts  observable s

    ops    a : → s
           b : → s


    eqs    a = b
end spec
```

```
spec SP2 =
    sorts observable s1
          s
    ops   a : → s
          b : → s
          f : s → s1

    eqs   f (a) = f (b)
end spec
```

```
spec SP3 =
    sorts observable s1, s2
          s
    ops   a : → s
          b : → s
          f : s → s1
          g : s → s2
    eqs   f (a) = f (b)
end spec
```

The signature inclusions from SP1 to SP2 and from SP2 to SP3 are, obviously, parameter passing morphisms. Nevertheless the signature inclusion from SP1 to SP3 it not a parameter passing morphism. The reason is that the operation g introduces new contexts to "observe" the elements of sort s, in particular, from SP3 we cannot deduce g(a)=g(b), consequently a = b is not behaviourally deducible from SP3.

The problem arises because of the "closed world assumption" related to behavioural deduction: the observability criterion, which permits us to define if some property holds in a behavioural sense, is limited by the contexts that can be constructed from the given signature. This property is lost when a nonsurjective morphism is established. Specifically, the fact that in SP2 all the equations from SP1 are behaviourally satisfied does not mean that all these equations are also behaviourally satisfied in SP3. This is motivated by the additional observations that the "world" of SP3 allows with respect to the ones that SP2 allowed.

In [Gan 83], Ganzinger used a condition similar to our second one for parameter passing. Also, he presented its characterization in terms of a consistency condition:

Proposition 3.2.2

A signature morphism h : SP → SP', such that h(S-Obs) ⊆ S'-Obs', is a parameter passing morphism if and only if for every pair of terms t and t' in $T_{\Sigma'}(X_{Obs'})_{s'}$, s' ∈ Obs' E'+ h(E) |- t = t' ⇒ E' |- t = t.

In order to define the semantics of parameter passing it is necessary to describe how the models of the actual parameter specification are "seen" from the formal parameter "point of view". In the standard approach, this is done by means of the forgetful functor associated to the passing morphism. In our framework this construction is more complicated. The problem is that SP' $|\!-_B$ h(E) implies that every algebra A in Beh(SP') behaviourally satisfies E with respect to the observability criteria of SP'. But A may not satisfy E if we consider observable all sorts in Obs, although some other algebras behaviorally equivalent to A (w.r.t. SP') may do. As a consequence, we cannot be sure that for any A in Beh(SP') we have U_h(A) is in Beh(SP) (where U_h is the forgetful functor associated to h considered as a signature morphism).

Hence, we need some construction allowing any A in Beh(SP') to be viewed as a model in Beh(SP). This construction is done in two steps. The first one is a realization construction, i.e. a functor is defined from Beh(SP') to Alg(SP'*+h(E)) associating, to every A, an algebra A' behaviourally equivalent to A. This construction may be seen as a generalization of the initial realization, in the sense that it yields an algebra which is initial (up to renaming of observable values) among the algebras in its behaviour satisfying h(E).

The second step is a forgetful functor from Alg(SP'*+h(E)) to Beh(SP). This forgetful functor is the composition of two other functors, U1: Alg(SP'*+h(E)) → Alg(SP) and U2: Alg(SP) → Beh(SP).

Definition 3.2.3
Let SP be a behaviour specification and E a set of equations such that SP $\vdash_B$ E, and A in Beh(SP). The **E-realization** of A is the algebra $E\text{-}R(A) = T_\Sigma(A_{Obs}) / \equiv_{eobs(A)+E}$

This construction extends to a functor E-R: Beh(SP) $\rightarrow$ Alg(SP*+E), which is left adjoint to the forgetful functor U: Alg(SP*+E) $\rightarrow$ Beh(SP), defined as the composition of the forgetful functors U1: Alg(SP*+E) $\rightarrow$ Alg(SP) and U_{SP}: Alg(SP*)$\rightarrow$ Beh(SP)

Proposition 3.2.4
The E-realization of A is behaviourally equivalent to A.

Definition 3.2.5
Given two specifications SP and SP' and a parameter passing morphism h: SP $\rightarrow$ SP' we define the functor V_h : Beh(SP')$\rightarrow$ Beh(SP), called **view associated to** h, as the composition of the functors h(E)-R : Beh(SP') $\rightarrow$ Alg(SP'*+h(E)) and of the forgetful functor U: Alg(SP'*+h(E))$\rightarrow$ Beh(SP).

Having defined the parameter binding mechanism, we are now able to define the construction yielding the result of an instantiation of a parameterized specification. The usual construction, at the syntactic level, for defining this result specification is a pushout diagram. In our framework we will use a similar construction, although it is not, obviously, a pushout. In what follows, we will study nonparameterized parameter passing. In the following subsection we will study the parameterized case.

Definition 3.2.6
Let SPb(SPp) be a parameterized behaviour specification, with SPp = (Obsp,Sp,Σp,Ep) and SPb = SPp + (Obs1,S1,Σ1,E1). Let SPa = (Obsa,Sa,Σa,Ea) be another behaviour specification and h : SPp $\rightarrow$ SPa a parameter passing morphism. The **instantiation** of SPb(SPp) **with the actual parameter** SPa **through** h is

1. **Syntactically** : the specification SPr = (Obsr, Sr, Σr, Er) defined by

Obsr = Obsa + Obs1 Sr = Sa + S1

Σr = Σa + h'(Σ1) Er = Ea + h'(Eb)

where h' is a parameter passing morphism from SPb to SPr extending h:

a) $h'_{sorts}(s)$ = if $s \in Sp$ then h(s) else s

b) $h'_{ops}(\sigma)$ = if $\sigma : s_1...s_n \rightarrow s_{n+1} \in \Sigma p$ then $h(\sigma)$ else $\sigma : h'(s_1)....h'(s_n) \rightarrow h'(s_{n+1})$

We will also denote by $SPb(Spa)^h$ the result specification SPr. An instantiation determines a diagram called the **parameter passing diagram**

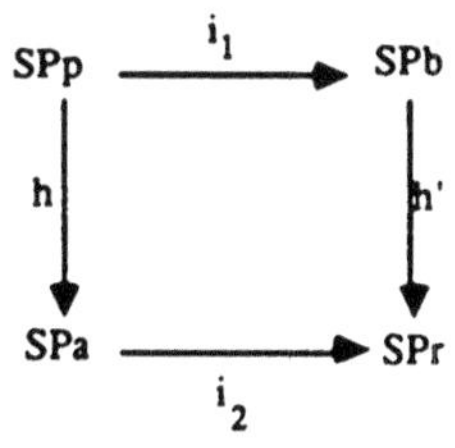

where i_1 and i_2 are inclusion morphisms.

2. **Semantically**: the pair of functors {Free : Beh(SPp) $\rightarrow$ Beh(SPb) , Free' : Beh(SPa) $\rightarrow$ Beh(SPr)}

Let us observe that the equations of SPr are Ea + h'(Eb). This means that in the result specification equations of h(Ep) are also included, even if they were not deducible from SPa. This may seem a bit strange, but it is absolutely needed from the technical point of view. On the other hand, in our opinion the technical reasons are methodologically justified.

The problem consists in assuring that Free' : Beh(SPa) → Beh(SPr) is, at least under reasonable assumptions (like persistency), a uniform extension of Free : Beh(SPp) → Beh(SPb). That is, even if the given specification is persistent we will not be able to assure the "passing compatibility" property (see below) of parameter passing. Let us see a very simple example:

```
spec SPp =                  spec SPb =                     spec SPa =
   sorts observable s          sorts observable s, s1         sorts observable s2
   ops   a : → s               ops   f : s → s1                     s
         b : → s            end spec                          ops   a : → s
   eqs   x:s                                                        b : → s
         x = a                                                      g : s → s2
end spec                                                      eqs   x:s
                                                                    g(x) = g(a)
                                                           end spec
```

In this example, (SPp,SPb) is a very simple specification: its associated free functor, given a one-valued algebra, constructs another algebra with an additional single-valued sort. This specification is trivially persistent. SPa is an admissible actual parameter (with respect to the inclusion morphism), since on sort s there is, observably, a single value. However if in the result specification the equation x=a is not included, i.e. Er={g(a) = g(X)}, then (SPa, SPr) would define a construction associating to every algebra in Obs(SPa) an algebra with an additional sort s1 and two values of this sort (one for f(a) and the other for f(b)).

From a methodological standpoint, the proposed solution, i.e. including the equations from SPp into SPr, seems reasonable. When the parameterized specification was designed, the specifier was relying on certain equations in Ep to define the effect of the parameterization. Thus, the construction associated to parameter passing should *uniformly produce the same effect* over a given actual parameter, even if it does not satisfy the equations in Ep (although it must satisfy them behaviourally). In [Gan 83] a similar solution is provided.

The last aspect that must be studied with respect to parameter passing is the kind of conditions that assure that the defined constructions work properly. We consider, as in [EKTWW 81], two correctness conditions. The first one guarantees the protection of the actual parameter in the result specification, while the second one guarantees that the free construction associated to (SPa,SPr) is an extension (in the same sense as in the last paragraph) of the semantics of the parameterized specification. As for the standard case [EKTWW 81], it is proved that these conditions are equivalent to persistency of the parameterized specification.

Definition 3.2.7

Parameter passing is **correct** if:

1. **Actual parameter protection:** $\forall A \in Beh(SPa)\ A \equiv_{\Sigma a} U_{i2} \cdot Free'(A)$.
2. **Passing compatibility:** $Free \cdot V_h \equiv V_{h''} \cdot Free'$.

Note that actual parameter protection means *observable protection* (see the comment after Th. 3.1.7).

Theorem 3.2.8

Let SPb(SPp) be a parameterized behaviour specification. Let SPa be the specification of an admissible actual parameter and $SPr=SPb(SPa)^h$ the result specification. If (SPp,SPb) is persistent then (SPa,SPr) is persistent.

Proof

Let us consider the specification SPa' defined by SPa' = SPa + (Ø, Ø, Ø, h(Ep)). The parameter passing corresponding to the diagram

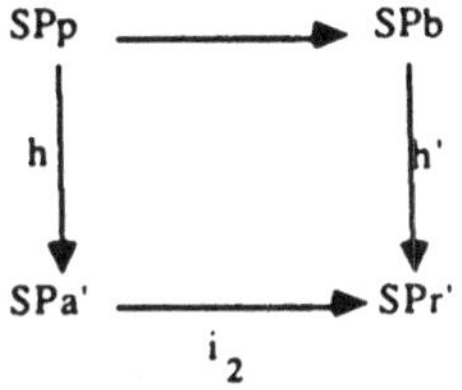

defines a specification SPr' such that (SPa', SPr') is persistent, because SPa' is an admissible parameter in the standard sense (without taking into account observability). But SPr is the same specification that we would get as result in the standard case, hence, (SPa', SPr) is persistent.

On the other hand, (SPa,SPa') is persistent. It is sufficiently complete because for every t in $T_{\Sigma a'}(X_{Obsa})_s$, $s \in$ Obsa, there is a t' in $T_{\Sigma a}(X_{Obsa})_s$ (we can take the same t), such that Ea' $\vdash t = t'$. Moreover, it is consistent since if t_1 and t_2 are in $T_{\Sigma a}(X_{Obsa})_s$, $s \in$ Obsa, and Ea + h(Ep) $\vdash t_1 = t_2$, then Ea $\vdash t_1 = t_2$ because Ea $\vdash_B$ h(Ep). So (SPa, SPr) is persistent. []

Theorem 3.2.9

Let SPP = (SPp, SPb) be a parameterized behaviour specification. Parameter passing is correct for SPP and for every parameter passing morphism h : SPp → SPa if and only if the specification SPP is persistent.

Sketch of the Proof

If parameter passing is correct for every specification morphism then, trivially, SPP is persistent. Conversely, if SPP is persistent according to the previous theorem (SPa,SPr) is persistent, and, therefore, actual parameter protection condition is satisfied. To prove passing compatibility we can show that the following diagram commutes:

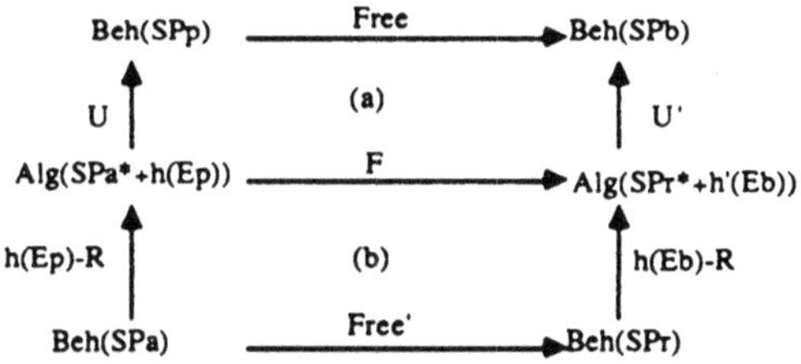

Diagram (a) is commutative because it corresponds to parameter passing in the standard case (every sort is observable in the formal and actual parameter) and SPb(SPp) is persistent. To prove that Diagram (b) is also commutative it is enough to see F(B) is the h(Eb)-realization of Free'(B) for every B such that B is its own h(Ep)-realization. Since, in that case, for every A in Beh(SPa), if B is its h(Ep)-realization (considered as a Beh(SPa)-algebra) then:

$$h(Ec)\text{-}R(Free'(A)) \cong h(Ec)\text{-}R(Free'(B)) \cong F(h(Ep)\text{-}R(A))$$

[]

3.3. Parameterized parameter passing

The fact that parameter passing morphisms are not closed under composition may lead one to think that some problems will arise when dealing with parameterized parameter passing. In what follows, we are going see that these problems do not exist. Moreover, we will see that parameterized parameter passing is associative since all compositions of parameter passing morphisms that appear in iterated parameter passing diagrams are, in this specific case, parameter passing morphisms.

As usual, parameterized parameter passing may be defined as a slight extension of (nonparameterized) parameter passing.

Definition 3.3.1

Let $SPP_1 = (SPp_1, SPb_1)$ and $SPP_2 = (SPp_2, SPb_2)$ be two behaviour specifications and $h : SPp_1 \rightarrow SPb_2$ a parameter passing morphism. The **instantiation of SPP_1 with the actual parameter SPP_2 through** h is

1. **Syntactically** : the parameterized specification $SPPr = (SPp_2, SPr)$ where SPr is defined as in 3.2.6. We will denote by $SPP_1(SPP_2)^h$ this instantiation.

An instantiation determines the following **parameterized parameter passing diagram**

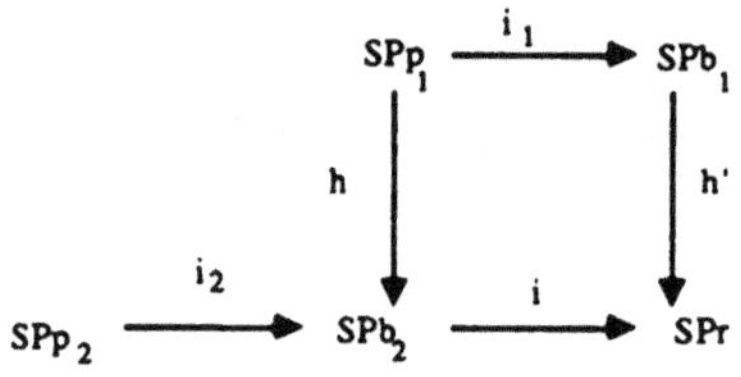

where h' is defined as in 3.2.6.

2. **Semantically** : the pair of functors $\{Free_1: Beh(SPp_1) \rightarrow Beh(SPb_1), Free_r: Beh(SPp_2) \rightarrow Beh(SPr)\}$ where $Free_r$ is the composition of functors $Free_r = Free \cdot Free_2$, with Free: $Beh(SPb_2) \rightarrow Beh(SPr)$ being the functor defining the semantics of the parameterized specification (SPb_2, SPr) and $Free_2 : Beh(SPp_2) \rightarrow Beh(SPb_2)$ the functor defining the semantics of the parameterized specification SPP_2:

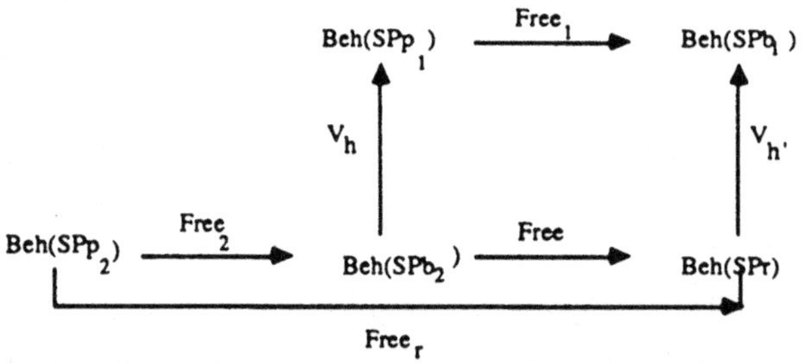

Definition 3.3.2

Parameterized parameter passing is **correct** for SPP_1, SPP_2 and h if the following properties hold:

1. **Parameterized actual parameter protection:** $\forall$ A in $Beh(SPp_2)$ $A \equiv U_{i \cdot i2} \cdot Free_r(A)$.
2. **Parameterized passing compatibility:** $V_{h'} \cdot Free_r \equiv Free_1 \cdot V_h \cdot Free_2$.

Again, persistency guarantees correctness of parameterized parameter passing:

Theorem 3.3.3 (Correctness of parameterized parameter passing)

Let $SPP_1 = (SPp_1, SPb_1)$ and $SPP_2 = (SPp_2, SPb_2)$ be two persistent parameterized behaviour specifications and $h : SPp_1 \rightarrow SPb_2$ a parameter passing morphism. It holds:

1. The specification $SPP_r = (SPp_2, SP_r)$ is persistent.
2. Parameter passing is correct for SPP_1, SPP_2 and h.

Sketch of the Proof

Persistency of SPP1 implies (according to theorem 3.2.8) persistency of (SPb2,SPr) and, therefore, persistency of (SPp_2, SP_r) which, on the other hand, is equivalent to parameterized actual parameter protection. For proving parameterized passing compatibility it is enough to see $V_{h''} \cdot Free_r \equiv V_{h''} \cdot Free \cdot Free_2 \equiv$ (cf. theorem 3.2.9) $Free_1 \cdot V_h \cdot Free_2$. []

To end, we will prove, as said above, that iterated parameter passing is associative. This is an immediate consequence of the following theorem:

Theorem 3.3.4

Let $SPP_1 = (SPp_1, SPb_1)$, $SPP_2 = (SPp_2, SPb_2)$ and $SPP_3 = (SPp_3, SPb_3)$ be three parameterized behaviour specifications and $h1 : SPp_1 \rightarrow SPb_2$, $h2 : SPp_2 \rightarrow SPb_3$ two parameter passing morphisms defining the diagrams:

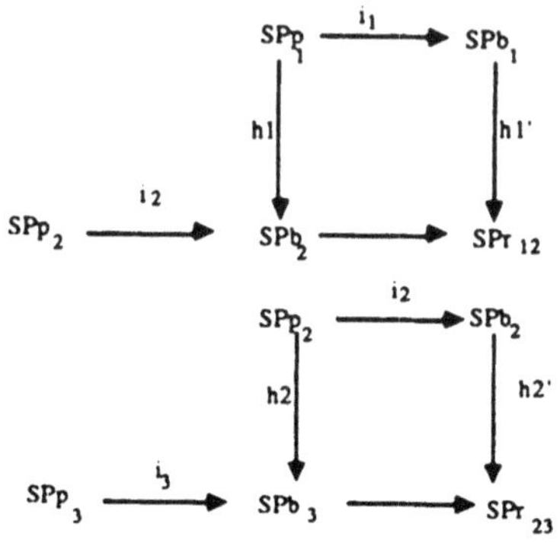

then $h2' \cdot h1$ is a parameter passing morphism from SPp1 to SPr_{23}.

Sketch of the Proof

Let $e \in Ep_1$ and let us denote by $e_1 : t_1 = t_1'$ the equation $h2' \cdot h1(e)$. It must be proved

$$Er_{23} \vdash c[\ \bar{\sigma}(t_1)] = c[\ \bar{\sigma}(t_1')]$$

for every assignment σ: var(e1) $\rightarrow T_{\Sigma r_{23}}(X_{Obsr_{23}})$ and every context $c[z] \in T_{\Sigma r_{23}}(X_{Obsr_{23}} \cup \{z\})_s$ with $s \in Obsr_{23}$ and $sort(z) = sort(e_1) \in h2'(Sb_2)$. In order to do that we may use the following two lemmas:

Lemma 3.3.5

Let z be a variable such that $sort(z) \in h2'(Sb_2)$. There exists a mapping

$$\rho : T_{\Sigma r_{23}}(X_{Obsr_{23}} \cup \{z\})_{|Obsr_{23}} \rightarrow h2'(T_{\Sigma b_2}(X_{Sb_2} \cup \{z'\})_{|Obsr_{23}}$$

and an assignment

$$\sigma_\rho : h2'(X_{Sb_2}) \cup \{z'\} \rightarrow T_{\Sigma r_{23}}(X_{Obsr_{23}} \cup \{z\})$$

such that $\bar{\sigma}_\rho(\rho(c[z])) \ll c[z]$ (where $\ll$ denotes the subterm relation).

Lemma 3.3.6

There is a mapping

$$\tau : T_{\Sigma r_{23}}(X_{Obsr_{23}})_{|h2'(Sb_2)} \rightarrow h2'(T_{\Sigma b_2}(X_{Obsb_2}))$$

and an assignment

$$\sigma_\tau : h2'(X_{Obsb_2}) \rightarrow T_{\Sigma r_{23}}(X_{Obsr_{23}})$$

such that $\bar{\sigma}_\tau(\tau(t)) = t$.

Lemma 3.3.5 states that contexts from SPr_{23} may be *subsumed* via a transformation ρ and a substiturion σ_ρ by contexts from SPb_2. Then, to prove the theorem it is enough to show:

$$Er_{23} \vdash \bar{\sigma}_1(\rho(c[t_1])) = \bar{\sigma}_1(\rho(c[t_1']))$$

where σ_1 is the union of σ_ρ and σ.

Lemma 3.3.6 states a similar thing with respect to substitutions with respect to a transformation τ and a substitution σ_τ. But, then, if we define $\sigma_2(x) = \tau(\sigma_1(x))$

Since $Eb_2 \vdash_B h1(Ep_1)$ it holds that:

$h2'(Eb_2) \vdash \bar{\sigma}_2(\rho(c[t_1])) = \bar{\sigma}_2(\rho(c[t_1'])) \Rightarrow Er_{23} \vdash \bar{\sigma}_2(\rho(c[t_1])) = \bar{\sigma}_2(\rho(c[t_1'])) \Rightarrow$

$\Rightarrow Er_{23} \vdash \bar{\sigma}_\tau \cdot \bar{\sigma}_2(\rho(c[t_1])) = \bar{\sigma}_\tau \cdot \bar{\sigma}_2(\rho(c[t_1])) \Rightarrow Er_{23} \vdash \bar{\sigma}_1(\rho(c[t_1])) = \bar{\sigma}_1(\rho(c[t_1]))$ [].

Corollary 3.3.7

Parmeterized parameter passing is associative, i.e. $(SPP_1(SPP_2)^{h1})(SPP_3)^{h2} = SPP_1(SPP_2(SPP_3)^{h2})^{h2' \cdot h1}$ or expressed with a commutative diagram:

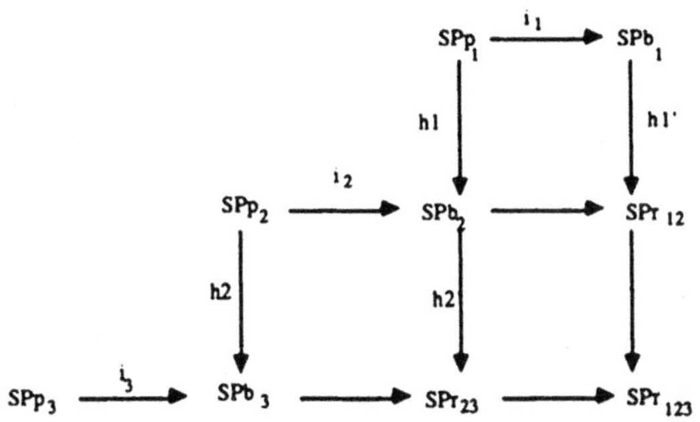

4. Conclusion

In this paper we have presented what we think is the appropiate institution for dealing with equational algebraic specifications with behavioural semantics, showing that, within this institution, we can have constructions similar to those of the standard initial algebra approach. Based on these constructions, in [Niv 87], a complete two-level behavioral semantic definition, a la Act One [EhMa 85], has been provided for a given specification language.

This work may be continued along different lines. A very important issue is loose semantics: when designing a specification, at several stages, before certain decisions have been taken, we should not expect to have a complete description of the specified object (or of part of it), not even a complete description of its behaviour. Then, in these situations, the adequate semantics to associate to specifications is the loose one. In a general framework, loose semantics and behavioural equivalence have been quite thoroughly studied in [SaTa 85a].

In [ClOr88] our view of specification design by means of loose semantics and an inheritance relation was presented. However, in that paper, the semantics of the main constructions was given in terms of data constraints, without taking into account any behavioural aspect. Therefore, to continue along this line, the definition and study of "behavioural data constraints" would be needed. This should not present many problems since we already have free constructions and most of the results obtained for the standard case seem to apply in our behaviour approach. Within his approach, Reichel has already dealt with this kind of issue.

A more difficult problem is behavioural deduction. In our paper we defined the behaviour theory associated to a specification as:

$$BTh(SP) = \{t1=t2/ \forall A \text{ in } Beh(SP_{P2})\ A \models_B t1=t2\} \quad (a)$$

It does not seem possible to obtain a sound and complete set of finitary deduction rules for this kind theory. However, if we slightly change the definition:

$$BTh(SP) = \{t1=t2/ \forall A \text{ in } Beh(SP_{P2})\ A \models t1=t2\} \quad (b)$$

then it is not difficult to obtain an associated sound and complete set of rules. [HeWi 85] deal with such theories.

Anyhow, even if we cannot have sound and complete proof rules for (a) we might be interested in having complete, under reasonable assumptions, deductive methods for such theories. Since belonging to the behavioural theory means being consistent with it, with respect to observable terms (cf. proposition 3.2.1), then techniques used in inductionless inductive theorem proving [Gog 80, HuHu 80, JoKo 85, Mu 80], also based on consistency checking, could be of value.

5. References

[ClOr 88] Clerici, S.; Orejas, F., GSBL: an algebraic specification language based on inheritance, to appear in *Proc. Europ. Conf. on Object Oriented Prog.*, Springer LNCS, 1988.

[EKTWW 82] Ehrig, H.; Kreowski, H.-J.; Thatcher, J.W.; Wagner, E.G.; Wright, J.B. Parameter passing in algebraic specification languages, *Proc. Workshop on Program Specification*, Aarhus, Denmark, Springer LNCS **164** (1983) 221-256.

[EhMa 85] Ehrig, H.; Mahr, B., *Fundamentals of algebraic specification 1*, EATCS Monographs on Theor. Comp. Sc., Springer, 1985.

[Gan 83] Ganzinger, H., Parameterized specifications: parameter passing and implementation with respect to observability, *ACM Transactions on Programming Languages and Systems* **5** (3) (1983) 318-35.

[GGM 76] Giarratana, V.; Gimona, F.; Montanari, U., Observability concepts in abstract data type specification, *Proc. 5th Intl. Symp. on Mathematical Foundations of Computer Science*, Gdansk, Springer LNCS **45** (1976) 567-587.

[GoBu 84] Goguen, J.A.; Burstall, R.M., Introducing institutions. *Proc. Logics of Programs Workshop*, Springer LNCS **164** (1984) 221-256.

[Gog 80] Goguen, J. A. "How to prove algebraic inductive hypotheses without induction, with application to the correctness of data types implementation", *Proc. 5th. Conf. on Aut. Deduction*, 1980.

[GoMe 82] Goguen, J.A.; Meseguer, J., Completeness of many-sorted equational logic, *Sigplan Notices* **17**,1 (1982) 9-17.

[GoMe 82] Goguen, J.A.; Meseguer, J., Universal realization, persistent interconnection and implementation of abstract modules, *9th Colloquium on Automata, Languages and Programming*, Aarhus, Springer LNCS **140** (1982) 265 -281.

[GoMe 83] Goguen, J.A.; Meseguer, J., Initiality Primer, Preliminary Draft (March 1983), SRI Int.

[GTW 78] Goguen, J.A.; Thatcher, J.W.; Wagner, E.G., An initial algebra approach to the specification, correctness and implementation of abstract data types, *Current Trends in Programming Methodology, Vol IV: Data Structuring*, R.T. Yeh (ed.), Prentice Hall (1978) 80-149.

[GuHo78] Guttag, J.V.; Horning, J.J., The algebraic specification of abstract data types, *Acta Informatica* **10** (1978), 27-52.

[HeWi 85] Hennicker, R.; Wirsing, M. , Observational Spécification: A Birkhoff-Theorem , *Recent Trends in Data Type Specification*, Informatik-Fachberichte, Springer **116** (1985) 119-135.

[HuHu 80] Huet, G.; Hullot, J.M. Proofs by induction in equational theories with constructors, *Proc. 21st. FOCS*, Los Angeles (1980), 96-107.

[HuOp 80] Huet, G.; Oppen, D., Equations and rewrite rules: a survey, in *Formal Language Theory: Perspectives and open problems*, R.V. Book (Ed.), Ac. Press (1980).

[JoKo 85] Jouannaud, J.P.; Kounalis, E. Proofs by induction in equational theories without constructors, C.R.I. Nancy Report 85-R-042, 1985.

[Kam 83] Kamin, S., Final data type and their specification, *ACM Transactions on Programming Languages and Systems* **5** (1983) 97 -123.

[MeGo 85] Meseguer, J.; Goguen, J.A., Initiality, induction and computability, *Algebraic Methods in*

Semantics, M. Nivat and J. Reynolds (eds.), Cambridge Univ. Press (1985) 459-540.

[Mus 80] Musser, D. On proving inductive properties of abstract data types, *Proc. 7th. POPL*(1980), 154-162.

[Niv 87] Nivela Alós, Mª P., Semántica de comportamiento en lenguajes de especificación, PhD. Thesis, Facultat d'Informàtica, Universitat Politècnica de Catalunya, Barcelona (1987).

[Ore 87] Orejas, F., A characterization of passing compatibility for parameterized specifications, *Theor. Comp. Sc.* **51** (1987), 205-214.

[Rei 81] Reichel, H., Behavioural equivalence - a unifying concept for initial and final specification methods, *Proc. 3rd Hungarian Computer Science Conf.*, Budapest (1981) 27-39.

[Rei 84] Reichel, H., Behavioral validity of equations in abstract data types, *Contributions to General Algebra 3, Proc.of the Vienna Conference*, Verlag B. G. Teubner, Stuttgart (1985) 301-324.

[SaTa 85] Sannella, D.; Tarlecki, A., On observational equivalence and algebraic specification*Journal of Computer and System Sciences* **34**(2/3)(1987)150-178.

[SaWi 83] Sannella, D.; Wirsing, M., A kernel language for algebraic specification and implementation. *Proc. Intl. Conf. on Foundations of Computation Theory* Sweden. Springer LNCS **158** (1983) 413-427.

[Sch 82] Schoett, O., A theory of program modules, their specification and implementation (extended abstract), Univ. of Edinburgh, Rep. CSR-155-83, 1982.

[Tar 85] Tarlecki, A., On the existence of free models in abstract algebraic institutions, *Theor. Comp. Sc.* **37** (1985) 269-304.

[Wan 79] Wand, M., Final algebra semantics and data type extensions. *Journal of Computer and System Sciences* **19** (1) (1979) 27-44.

PARTIAL ALGEBRAS, SUBSORTING, AND DEPENDENT TYPES

- Prerequisites of Error Handling in Algebraic Specifications -

Axel Poigné

GMD F2G2
Postfach 1240
D-5205 St.Augustin 1
ap%gs2@gmdzi.uucp

0. Introduction

Handling of errors has always been a challenge to the theory of abstract data types [Goguen 77], [ADJ 78], [Goguen 78], [Poigné 84], [Gogolla 86]. Order sorted algebras [Goguen 78], [Gogolla 83], [Poigné 84], [Smolka 86] so far provide the most suitable framework to deal with errors. Some worries, however, still remain. This paper is yet another attempt to clarify the subject.

Initial algebra semantics considers errors just as ordinary data and then spends some efforts to discriminate errors from correct data. I challenge this point of view and propose to conceive errors as exceptions or interrupts as in operating systems and to use a typing mechanism to define a precise interface. We introduce classified algebras as a formal basis for this intuition.

The paper starts with a discussion of errors in two sections outlining the problems and suggesting a solution. A brief section then explains the structure of the subsequent parts.

1. Outlining the Problem

To start with I believe that

- error handling should (essentially) be confined to the module the errors stem from
- error handling should be uniform and automatic except for exception handling facilities.

Errors conceived as just another sort of data results in messy techniques ([ADJ 78] seems to be the only "pure" initial algebra approach handling errors) which are by no means uniform (several examples to this effect are given in [ADJ 78]), and which do not allow for modularization error handling; given the usual specification of arrays with parameter sorts <u>index</u> and <u>data</u>, a get operation causes a <u>data</u> error if a cell is not initialized. If we update the parameter <u>data</u> by an actual parameter, say natural numbers, the actual parameter does not supply a denotation for "errors", or in more practical terms, the implementation of the natural numbers does not provide an implementation of error elements. As an alternative one might argue that denotations for "error terms" must be provided by the implementation of arrays. Then, however, application of operators of an actual parameter to "error" cause new errors which could not be foreseen when implementing the arrays, hence again no denotation is provided. To avoid such a phenomenon one might assume that all "errors" are part of the formal parameter (which allows to refer to errors as well in the array module as in all actual parameters) and that certain correctness criteria hold for parameter passing [EKTWW 84]. Unfortunately, as a consequence any update of the sort data must provide its own error handling (not necessarily being an inherent feature of an actual parameter such as the natural numbers). Even worse, errors propagate if we update the sorts data and index by the same sort and thus create errors on the sort index.

In general, adding a new module to the system may cause a re-specification of the error handling of all other modules in contradiction to the principle of modularity.

Several suggestions have been made to reconcile equational specification and error handling. Order-sorted algebras emerge as a more solid theoretical underpinning. Roughly, order-sorted algebras have carriers which are partially ordered by inclusion (specified by a subsort relation) and operators which are overloaded in that operators may have several types but applied to the same arguments must have the same results independent of typing. Subsorting can be used in various ways for error handling (compare [Futatsugi-Goguen-Meseguer 85]):

- to add "error" - supersorts as in

```
spec  NATE  is
sorts nat < naterr
ops   0 : → nat
      suc : nat → nat
      suc : naterr → naterr
      pred : naterr → naterr
      error : → naterr
vars  n : nat
eqns  pred(suc(n)) = n
      suc(pred(n)) = n
      pred(0) = error
      pred(error) = suc(error) = error
```

(overloading of suc is necessary as otherwise terms of the form ...suc(pred(...)) are syntactically incorrect)

- to avoid errors at all

```
spec NATD is
sorts nat+ < nat
ops   0 : → nat
      suc : nat → nat+
      pred : nat+ → nat
vars  n : nat
eqns  pred(suc(n)) = n
      suc(pred(n)) = n
```

This option appears most attractive but terms such as pred(pred(suc(suc(0)))) are no longer syntactically correct though "semantically correct". A way out is to add a "retract" [Goguen-Jouannaud-Meseguer 85] by

```
spec NATD+ is
NAT with
ops   r : nat → nat+
vars  n : nat+
eqns  r(n) = n
```

with the convention that retracts are automatically inserted if necessary to adapt sorts, e.g. pred(r(0)), pred(r(pred(suc(suc(0))))). Terms are erroneous if the retracts cannot be deleted. "Error recovery" is provided in that

pred(r(pred(suc(suc(0))))) = 0.

Automatic error recovery, however, is dubious:

```
spec STACKD is
sorts $data, nestack < stack
ops   empty : → stack
      push : stack data → nestack
      pop : nestack → stack
      top : nestack → data
vars  s : stack, d : data
eqns  pop(push(s,d)) = s
      top(push(s,d)) = d
```

allows to recover errors such as in pop(push(empty, top(empty)))), a result one does not accept in every case.

Explicit specification of errors as in NATE is not any better if parameterization is considered: The data component of stacks is guarded against propagation of errors if the junk is confined to non-parameter sorts

```
spec STACKE is
sorts $data < errdata, stack < errstack
ops   empty : → stack
      push : stack data → stack
      push : errstack errdata → errstack
      pop : errstack → errstack
      top : errstack → errdata
      derr : → errdata
      serr : → errstack
vars  s : stack, d : data, s' : errstack, d' : errdata
eqns  pop(push(s,d)) = s
      top(push(s,d)) = d
      top(empty) = top(serr) = derr
      pop(empty) = pop(serr) = serr
      push(s',derr) = push(serr,d') = serr
```

The problem is the same as with NATD; updating yields a specification such that the operators of the actual parameter cannot access the data on the stack, e.g. suc(top(push(empty,0))) is syntactically incorrect.

So are we back at our starting point and do we have to pass error data to the actual parameter?

2. Towards a Solution

The question is biased in that errors are conceived as proper data. If we interpret errors as interrupts of "execution" errors are data on a meta level only and error recovery mechanisms are control structures on the meta level which may eventually resume "execution" on the object level.

For intuition: one might animate specifications by term rewriting.

But can we distinguish between a meta and an object level of an abstract data type?
Let a specification consist of two components, a **language specification** and a **data type specification** which are linked by an (in general obvious) **interface**, e.g.

```
spec NAT is
syntax  sorts  NAT
        ops    0: → NAT
               suc : NAT → NAT
               pred : NAT → NAT
data    sorts  nat+ < nat < NAT
        ops    0: → nat
               suc : nat → nat+
               pred : nat+ → nat
        vars   n : nat, m : nat+
        eqns   pred(suc(n)) = n
               suc(pred(m)) = m
```

Terms are called **admissible** if they are well-formed with regard to the **syntax** signature (being the "compile-time" component of type checking), e.g. pred(pred(suc(0))), pred(pred(suc(suc(0)))). A term is **typed** if it is well-formed with regard to the **data** signature. Admissible terms may have no denotation in that there is no "equivalent" term which is typed. Terms are equivalent if they can be transformed into each other by application of the equations to subterms. Hence

pred(pred(suc(suc(0)))) = pred(suc(0)) = 0 has a denotation, but

pred(pred(suc(0))) = pred(0) has no denotation.

To refer to this mechanism as **run-time type checking** is justified as a (partial) computation of the result is needed in order to decide if the term denotes some proper data or prompts an error message.

The idea is more precisely captured in the framework of partial algebras:
We distinguish (compile time) sorts and (run time) types, the latter being unary predicates and stipulate that a term has a denotation (resp. is defined) if and only if it can be typed. The type predicates thus state *definedness* in a more sophisticated way than a single definedness predicate does.

```
spec NAT is
sorts   NAT
ops     0: → NAT
        suc : NAT → NAT
        pred : NAT → NAT
types   _ ε nat+ , _ ε nat : NAT
```

var n : NAT

axioms ∴ 0 ε nat

n ε nat+ ∴ n ε nat

n ε nat ∴ suc(n) : nat+

n ε nat+ ∴ pred(n) ε nat

n ε nat ∴ pred(suc(n)) = n

n ε nat+ ∴ suc(pred(n)) = n

n ε nat+ ∴ n ε nat states subsorting as a conditional axiom

Even then the standard theory of partiality does not naturally provide a framework which captures our intuition in that models do not comprise *undefined entities*, i.e. errors in our context. Scott's theory of partiality [Scott 77], [Scott-Fourman 77] distinguishes between total and partial elements. The latter are instantiations of "*undefined*" in that all partial element behave in the same way in any context. Strictness of partial operations then states propagation of errors. The point will be discussed more precisely in section 4.

The concept of partial elements is a necessary prerequisite to deal with **error messages** and **error recovery**:
Erroneous terms are the most precise error messages. But one might insist on error messages like "error_stack_underflow". Equalities such as top(empty) = error_stack_underflow state existence in the world of partial algebras (see section 4), thus generate proper data from errors in contrast to all we advocated for. Moreover error recovery is non-strict while partial operations should be strict in that data cannot be generated from the undefined, mimicking error propagation. Hence we strive for inconsistent goals; operators should behave uniformly in order to confine error handling to modules, in contrast error procedures should react differently on different errors.

If we take the idea of interrupts seriously, errors should be handled by an altogether different system of error procedures necessarily consistent with the data specification:

recovery : DATA → data

recovery (top(push(s,d)) = d where s : STACK, d ε data

or

message : STACK → ERRORMESSAGES

message(pop(empty)) = error_stack_underflow

message(push(error_stack_underflow, d)) = error_stack_underflow, etc.

Though applied to the same elements the error equations constitute a second equational system. Application of error procedures depends on an exact understanding of what erroneous data are, even more, on some insight of how errors are represented. Our notion of errors as type errors provides such an exact interface, and we shall develop a semantics which reflects these purposes.

Finally, our type mechanism is too weak to specify bounded stacks [Goguen&al 85]

$n \, \varepsilon \, \underline{nat}, s \, \varepsilon \, \underline{stack}, \text{length}(s) < n \; \therefore \; \text{push}(s,n) \, \varepsilon \, \underline{stack}$

We cater for such situations and introduce a more sophisticated type discipline with dependent types borrowed from [Cartmell 78]. Here we claim originality for the amalgamation of partiality, dependent types, subsorting and overloading.

3. Plan of the Paper

In section 4 we review of Scott's logic of partiality [Scott 77] and the corresponding model theory but cut down to its algebraic part [Fourman-Scott 77]. We will argue that the Scott's theory of partiality mimics our intuitions about error handling. Section 5 considers elementary classified algebras which are in close relation to order-sorted algebras. This chapter is an intermediate step to the more sophisticated type discipline of classified algebras discussed in chapter 6. Section 7 relates the results to other work, and section 8 resumes the theme of the first section in that we give a formal definition of what we mean by an error specification. We do not have the space to investigate the concept more thoroughly but consider an example.

4. A Review of Partial Algebras

We work out Scott's theory of partiality [Scott 77], [Scott-Fourman 77] for the restricted case that the internal logic is given by the two-point boolean algebra of truth values. Following the recommendations of a referee we take the chance to motivate some of the particular choices made in this approach.

Partial algebras are usually defined as given by a carrier set A_s for every sort s and a partial function $\sigma^A : A_{s_1} \times ... \times A_{s_n} \rightarrow A_s$ for every operator $\sigma : s_1...s_n \rightarrow s$. As inductive evaluation of terms may not be successful in a partial algebra one distinguishes different concepts of equality [Grätzer 78]:

Weak equality $x \doteq y$ states that "x and y are defined and equal"
Strong equality $x \equiv y$ states that "y is defined and equal to x if x is defined, and x is defined and equal to y if y is defined".

This has some bearing on the proof system; e.g. given a signature $0 : \rightarrow \underline{nat}$, $suc : \underline{nat} \rightarrow \underline{nat}$, $pred : \underline{nat} \rightarrow \underline{nat}$ with natural numbers as a model where the "predecessor" of 0 is undefined, the term pred(x) may be undefined if we assign 0 to x. The model satisfies $pred(suc(x)) \doteq x$ but fails to satisfy the equation $pred(suc(pred(x))) \doteq pred(x)$ obtained by (syntactical) substitution. The discrepancy creeps in because satisfaction substitutes variables only by defined data, namely the elements of the model,while (syntactic) substitution replaces a variable by a term the interpretation of which is potentially undefined.

The usual strategy resolves the problem by restriction of substitution in that variables replaced only by terms which are "defined", i.e. it is weakly equal to itself $t \doteq t$. Formally, one modifies the substitution rule $\varphi \, , t \doteq t \vdash \varphi[x/t]$.

The standard substitution rule, however, is sound with regard to a different concept of model. Assume that models comprise *undefined values* (or just one element "undefined" for every carrier) and stipulate that operations are *strict* in that they preserve *undefinedness*. Clearly, this concept of model is equivalent to the standard one (any partial function $f: X \to Y$ can be turned into a strict total function $f: X \cup \{\bot\} \to Y \cup \{\bot\}$ and vice versa). The semantics of "weak equality", however, change considerably: $pred(suc(x)) \doteq x$ implicitly states $x \doteq x$, hence existence of all values, specifically pred(0), due to strictness (the conditioned equation $x \doteq x \to pred(suc(x)) \doteq x$ retains the "old meaning" of weak equality).

One may go on step further and abandon the strictness condition on operations. Then the equality $pred(suc(x)) \doteq x$ may hold for defined and undefined arguments but one would rather insist that undefined arguments are handled uniformly, i.e. suc(pred(0) and suc(pred(pred(0))) should yield the "same" result if pred(0) and pred(pred(0)) are undefined. Formally, operations should preserve strong equality: $\sigma(a_1,...a_n) \equiv \sigma(a'_1,...,a'_n)$ if $a_i \equiv a'_i$.

One has to pay a price, though, in that the identity rule

$$\frac{\Phi \vdash \varphi[x/t] \qquad \Phi \vdash t \doteq t'}{\Phi \vdash \varphi[x/t']}$$

no longer guarantees completeness of equational deduction: assume that $suc(x) \doteq suc(x)$ and that pred(0) and pred(pred(0)) are undefined. Preservation of strong equality implies $suc(pred(0)) \doteq suc(pred(pred(0)))$ semantically but to prove this equality by the identity rule one needs $pred(0) \doteq pred(pred(0))$ which states definedness of pred(0) and pred(pred(0)). Scott therefore strengthens the identity rule to the *equivalence rule*

$$\frac{\Phi \vdash \varphi[x/t] \qquad \Phi, t \doteq t \vdash t \doteq t' \qquad \Phi, t' \doteq t' \vdash t \doteq t'}{\Phi \vdash \varphi[x/t']}$$

which allows to replace undefined terms by undefined terms. Then completeness of deduction is obtained again.

Though we restrict our attention to models with strict operations (and relations) our proofs refer to the equivalence rule in order to cater for more general situations. Such a model theory has been advocated for in [Broy 86].

For our purposes, the particular attraction of Scott's theory of partiality is that it allows several "undefined" values in a model with the proviso that all "undefined" or "partial" values behave in the same way. Formally, each carrier consists of a set of **total** and **partial** elements which are discriminated by a partial equivalence relation (i.e. a symmetric and transitive relation). Total elements are those which are reflexive with regard to the partial equivalence. Operations are functions of suitable arity which may be partial but which uniformly behave on partial elements.

A *(p-) set* A is a set | A | equipped with a relation $\_\doteq\_ \subseteq |A| \times |A|$ (*p-equality*) which is symmetric and transitive.

Extent and ***equivalence*** are defined by

$$Ea := a \doteq a \qquad a \equiv b := Ea \vee Eb \rightarrow a \doteq b.$$

The extend predicate determines the total elements.

A *(p-) **mapping*** $f : A \dot{\rightarrow} B$ (with A, B p-sets) is a mapping $f : EA \rightarrow EB$ which ***preserves** p-equality*, i.e. $f(a) \doteq f(b)$ if $a \doteq b$ where $EA = \{a \in |A| \mid Ea\}$.

An ***operation*** $\sigma : A_{s_1} \times ... \times A_{s_n} \rightarrow A_s$ is a mapping $\sigma_A : |A_{s_1}| \times ... \times |A_{s_n}| \rightarrow |A_s|$ such that $\sigma_A(a_1,...,a_n) \equiv \sigma_A(b_1,...,b_n)$ if $\bigwedge_i a_i \equiv b_i$. A ***relation*** is a subset $\rho \subseteq |A_{s_1}| \times ... \times |A_{s_n}|$ such that $\rho(b_1,...,b_n)$ if $\rho(a_1,...,a_n)$ and $\bigwedge_i a_i \equiv b_i$.(Note: $\_\doteq\_$ is in general not a congruence)

An operation resp. a relation is ***strict*** if $E\sigma_A(a_1,...,a_n)$ resp $\rho(a_1,...,a_n)$ implies $\bigwedge_i Ea_i$, and ***total*** if the converse holds.

A ***signature*** SIG comprises a set of sorts S, a set of operators of the form $\sigma : w \rightarrow s$ and a set of relation symbols of the form $\rho : w$. A many-sorted p-set A (i.e. a family A_s of p-sets indexed by some set S of sorts) with strict operations $\sigma : A_w \rightarrow A_s$ and strict relations $\rho \in A_w$ of suitable arity is called a SIG-***model*** or an SIG-***algebra*** in case that only operators are given. We ambiguously use σ and ρ as notation for operators and operations, resp. relators and relations.

(p-) ***homomorphisms*** $h : A \dot{\rightarrow} B$ (with A,B SIG-models) are families $(h_s : A_s \dot{\rightarrow} B_s \mid s \in S)$ of (p-) mappings which satisfy the condition that $h_s(\sigma_A(a_1,...,a_n)) \doteq \sigma_B(h_{s_1}(a_1),..., h_{s_n}(a_n))$ if $E\sigma_A(a_1,...,a_n))$ and $\rho_B(h_{s_1}(a_1),..., h_{s_n}(a_n))$ if $\rho_A(a_1,...,a_n)$. A (p-)homomorphism is ***strong*** iff $E\sigma_B(h_{s_1}(a_1),..., h_{s_n}(a_n))$ implies $E\sigma_A(a_1,...,a_n))$ and if $\rho_B(h_{s_1}(a_1),..., h_{s_n}(a_n))$ implies $\rho_A(a_1,...,a_n)$.

One may abandon the strictness condition but then homomorphisms must be modified accordingly (compare [Broy 86]).

Evaluation of terms and formulas (implicitly defined) in a model A is given by (compare [Fourman-Scott 77]:

terms $[\![x]\!]_A\xi := \xi(x)$

$[\![\sigma(t_1,...,t_n)]\!]_A\xi := \sigma([\![t_1]\!]_A\xi,..., [\![t_n]\!]_A\xi)$

formulas $[\![\rho(t_1,...,t_n)]\!]_A\xi := \rho([\![t_1]\!]_A\xi,...,[\![t_n]\!]_A\xi)$

$[\![t \doteq_s t']\!]_A\xi := [\![t_1]\!]_A\xi \doteq_s [\![t']\!]_A\xi$

$[\![\varphi_1,...,\varphi_n \vdash_{\chi w} \psi]\!]_A\xi := \bigwedge_i [\![\varphi_i]\!]_A\xi \rightarrow [\![\psi]\!]_A\xi$

where $\xi : \{\chi : w\} \rightarrow A$ is a variable substitution (all free variables are supposed to occur in the list $\chi = x_1,...,x_n$ of sort $w = s_1,...,s_n$). For ***satisfaction*** we quantify over all substitutions: $\varphi_1,...,\varphi_n \vdash_{\chi w} \psi$ if $\forall\xi. [\![\varphi_1,...,\varphi_n \vdash_{\chi w} \psi]\!]_A\xi$

We use the notation $\Phi \vdash^{Ax}_{\chi w} \psi$ to state that $\Phi \vDash_{\chi w} \psi$ holds for all models A which satisfy a set Ax of axioms which are of the form $x_1 \doteq x_1,...,x_n \doteq x_n,\varphi_1,...,\varphi_n \vdash_{\chi w} \psi$ (for which we will use the abbreviation $\varphi_1,...,\varphi_n \therefore_{\chi w} \psi$).

Notation • We will use $E_s t$ as a shorthand for $t \doteq_s t$.

• We omit all sub- and superscripts if the context is unambiguous.

• We often use $\_\xi$ as a shorthand for $[\![\_]\!]_A \xi$.

Remark In Scott's theory of partiality universally bound variables can only be replaced by total elements. We mimic universal quantification in that we stipulate definedness of variables in axioms. This retains the conventional interpretation of weak equality.

Technical Convention Relations $\rho : w$ can be expressed as operations $\rho : w \to 1$ where 1 is a sort with $tt : \to 1$ such that $E\,tt$ and $E_1 x \vdash x \doteq tt$. We obtain isomorphic categories of models if we replace atomic propositions $\rho(t_1,...,t_n)$ by $\rho(t_1,...,t_n) = tt$ (the reader may check that all the stipulations concerning relations fall out from those for operations. It is quite important that $E_1\,tt$ holds as otherwise predicates may depend on the existence of tt). We use this observation in that all proofs only argue about operations though retaining relations as a convenient syntactic device.

The definitions conceive weak and strong equality [Grätzer 78] as semantical concepts and thus avoid to bother about existence predicates explicitly. For my part I consider this as a virtue, conceptually and technically as indicated by following observations:

• Models define standard (total) models if we forget about partial equality. Hence, standard homomorphisms between models are well defined. Then

4.1 Proposition *Each standard homomorphism* $h : A \to B$ *defines a (strong) p-homomorphism if* h *preserves partial equality (and* ***reflects*** *existence, i.e.* Ea *if* Eh(a)).

Proof h restricts to EA and EB as it preserves p-equality. $E\sigma_A(a_1,...,a_n)$ implies $Eh(\sigma_A(a_1,...,a_n))$. $h(\sigma_A(a_1,...,a_n)) = \sigma_B(h(a_1),...,h(a_n))$ then implies $Eh(a_i)$ by strictness of σ_B. $E\sigma_B(h(a_1),...,h(a_n))$ implies $Eh(\sigma_A(a_1,...,a_n))$ as $\sigma_B(h(a_1),...,h(a_n)) = h(\sigma_A(a_1,...,a_n))$.

•• We obtain a kind of inverse if we consider canonical models: Let A be a model. The model A^c consists of the term algebra $T_\Sigma(EA)$ (generated from EA) modulo the (standard) congruence generated by "$\sigma(a_1,...,a_n) \sim \sigma_A(a_1,...,a_n)$ if $E\sigma_A(a_1,...,a_n)$" ($a_i \in EA$). P-equality is defined by $[a] \doteq_{A^c} [b]$ if $a \doteq_A b$ for all $a,b \in |A|$, similarly the other relations. We say that A is ***canonical*** if $A \cong A^c$ (standard isomorphism).

The idea is to generate the partial elements freely to have scope for inductive definitions.

Remark An algebra is canonical if the carrier is a term algebra.

Lemma $a \sim \sigma(t_1,...,t_n)$ iff exist $t_i \sim a_i$ with $a_i \in EA$, $E\sigma_A(a_1,...,a_n)$ and $\sigma_A(a_1,...,a_n) = a$.

Proof We use thar the congruence can be defined as least transitive and reflexive closure of the union of relations $t \sim_n t'$ defined inductively by $\sigma(a_1,...,a_n) \sim_0 \sigma_A(a_1,...,a_n)$ if $E\sigma_A(a_1,...,a_n)$ and $t \sim_{n+1} t'$ if $t \sim_n t'$ or if $t = \sigma(t_1,...,t_n)$, $t' = \sigma(t'_1,...,t'_n)$ and $t_i \sim_n t'_i$. Induction on the "length of proofs" then proves the claim.

4.2 Proposition • $A \stackrel{\bullet}{\cong} A^c$ (as SIG-models)

•*Each p-homomorphism* h : $A \stackrel{\bullet}{\to} B$ *uniquely extends to a (standard) homomorphism* $h^c : A^c \to B$ such that $h^c{}_{/EA} = h$. h^c *preserves partial equality (and reflects existence if h is strong).*

Proof • The operations are well defined and strict by the lemma. The isomorphism is given by $a \leftrightarrow [a]$. This clearly defines p-mappings. $E\sigma_A(a_1,...,a_n)$ implies $[\sigma_A(a_1,...,a_n)] = [\sigma(a_1,...,a_n)] = \sigma_B([a_1],...,[a_n])$. Vice versa, $E\sigma([a_1],...,[a_n]) = E[\sigma(a_1,...,a_n)]$ implies $E\sigma_A(a_1,...,a_n)$ by the lemma.
• $h : EA \to EB$ uniquely extends to $h : T_\Sigma(EA) \to B$. $h(\sigma(a_1,...,a_n)) = (h(a_1),...,h(a_n)) = h(\sigma_A(a_1,...,a_n))$ as $E\sigma_A(a_1,...,a_n)$, hence $h^c : A^c \to B$ is uniquely defined. P-equality is preserved as h preserves p-equality. For reflection of existence we observe that for $Eh^c(x)$ either $x = [a]$ with $a \in EA$ or $x = \sigma(x_1,...,x_n)$. Then $h^c(x) = \sigma_B(x_1,...,x_n)$ and $Eh^c(x_i)$ by strictness of σ_B and Ex_i by inductive assumption.

Remark Strong homomorphisms preserve partiality in that h^c maps partial elements to partial elements.

The propositions give a systematic account of well known practice in the theory of partial algebras and map out a strategy how to explore the world of partial algebras, namely to use the standard constructions but ensure that all homomorphisms involved preserve p-equality. As an example we prove some results about partial algebras relevant for the next sections.

The **logic of partial equality** of [Scott 77] is given by the rules

(sym) $x \doteq y \vdash_{x,y:s} y \doteq x$ **(trans)** $x \doteq y, y \doteq z \vdash_{x,y,z:s} x \doteq z$

The deduction system (in sequent form) moreover comprises rules for *substitution*

$$\text{(sub)}\quad \frac{\Phi \vdash_{y:w} \Psi}{\Phi \vdash_{x:s,y:w} \Psi} \qquad \frac{\Phi \vdash_{x:s,y:w} \Psi}{\Phi[x/t] \vdash_{y:w} \Psi[x/t]}$$

where t is of sort s the only variables occurring are in the list y

a rule for *equivalence*

$$\text{(eq)}\quad \frac{\Phi \vdash_{y:w} \Psi[x/t] \qquad \Phi, Et \vdash_{y:w} t \doteq t' \qquad \Phi, Et' \vdash_{y:w} t \doteq t'}{\Phi \vdash_{y:w} \Psi[x/t']}$$

(where x and y occur in y.w), and the standard axioms for *sequents*

$$\text{(id)}\quad \varphi \vdash_{y:w} \varphi \qquad\qquad \text{(mon)}\quad \frac{\Phi \vdash_{y:w} \Psi}{\Phi, \varphi \vdash_{y:w} \Psi}$$

$$\text{(mp)}\quad \frac{\Phi \vdash_{y:w} \varphi \qquad \Phi, \varphi \vdash_{y:w} \Psi}{\Phi \vdash_{y:w} \Psi}$$

We enrich the deduction system by *strictness* axioms for operations and relations

(strict) $E\sigma(x_1,\dots,x_n) \vdash_{x_1:s_1,\dots,x_n:s_n} Ex_i$ $\rho(x_1,\dots,x_n) \vdash_{x_1:s_1,\dots,x_n:s_n} Ex_i$

$\Phi \vdash^{Ax}_{y:w} \psi$ states that $\Phi \vdash_{y:w} \psi$ is derivable in the proof system from a set of axioms Ax.

4.3 Proposition *We can replace the equivalence rule by the standard rule of identity*

$$\text{(eq')} \qquad \frac{\Phi \vdash_{y:w} \psi[x/t] \qquad \Phi \vdash_{y:w} t \doteq t'}{\Phi \vdash_{y:w} \psi[x/t']}$$

Proof ψ is of the form $\rho(t_1,\dots,t_n)$ or $t \doteq t'$. Strictness implies $\Phi \vdash t \doteq t'$ if x occurs in ψ (by induction over the structure of terms). Then the identity rule implies the equivalence rule as we can eliminate the existence conditions. If x does not occur the conclusion is trivial anyway.

Remark • Though the proof system with the identity rule is simpler our proofs use the equivalence rule because than most of the proofs transfer to models with non-strict operations and relations. Such models are closely related to generalizations of partial models as considered in [Broy 86] which will be discussed elsewhere.

4.4 Proposition *Deduction is sound.* I.e. $\Phi \vdash^{Ax}_{y:w} \psi$ implies $\Phi \models^{Ax}_{y:w} \psi$

Proof Induction on terms, formulas and sequents proves some standard facts concerning assignment, namely that $[\![\varphi[x/t]]\!]\,\zeta \leftrightarrow [\![\varphi]\!]\,\zeta+[x \to [\![t]\!]\,\zeta]$, $[\![\varphi]\!]\,\zeta \leftrightarrow [\![\varphi]\!]\,\zeta+[x \to v]$ and $[\![\varphi]\!]\,\zeta \leftrightarrow [\![\varphi]\!]\zeta[x \to v]$ provided that $v \doteq \zeta(y)$ where $\zeta[x \to v]$ is ζ except that $\zeta(x) = v$ and $\zeta+[x \to v]$ adds a new argument x to ζ with $\zeta(x) = v$. Then soundness follows by a straightforward computation, e.g.

$$[\![\Phi]\!]\,\zeta[x \to [\![t]\!]\,\zeta] \to [\![\psi]\!]\,\zeta[x \to [\![t]\!]\,\zeta] \quad \text{implies} \quad [\![\Phi[x/t]]\!]\,\zeta \to [\![\psi[x/t]]\!]\,\zeta.$$

The equivalence rule is slightly more sophisticated; semantically, the assumption can be rephrased to $[\![\Phi]\!]\,\zeta \to [\![\psi[x/t]]\!]\,\zeta \wedge ([\![Et]\!]\zeta \vee [\![Et']\!]\zeta \to [\![t]\!]\zeta) \doteq [\![t']\!]\zeta)$ resp. to $[\![\Phi]\!]\,\zeta \to [\![\psi[x/t']]\!]\,\zeta \wedge [\![t]\!]\zeta \equiv [\![t']\!]\zeta$. One then uses $[\![\varphi[x/t']]\!]\,\zeta \leftrightarrow [\![\varphi]\!]\,\zeta[x \to [\![t']\!]\,\zeta]$ and $[\![\varphi]\!]\,\zeta \leftrightarrow [\![\varphi]\!]\zeta[x \to v]$ if $v \equiv [\![t]\!]\zeta$. (Note that the form of the equivalence rule is due to the restriction to conjunction in formulas)

A ***specification*** SPEC consists of a signature SIG and a set of axioms of the form $\varphi_1,\dots,\varphi_n \therefore \varphi_{n+1}$. SPEC-***models*** are SIG-models which satisfy all the axioms of SPEC. SPEC-models and SIG-homomorphisms form a category we denote by $\mathbf{SPEC^b}$.

$\Phi \vdash^{SPEC}_{x:w} \psi$ states that $\Phi \vdash_{x:w} \psi$ is derivable in the deduction system augmented by the axioms of SPEC.

4.5 Proposition *The term algebra* T_{SIG} *with p-equality* $[\![\, t = t']\!]$ iff $\vdash^{SPEC} t \doteq t'$ *is an initial* SPEC-*model we denote by* T_{SPEC}.

Remark We use p-homomorphisms.

Proof T_{SPEC} satisfies the axioms and operators are strict by definition. Operators preserve equivalence:
We observe that $t \equiv t' \Leftrightarrow [\![Ex \vdash x \doteq y]\!]\zeta[x \to t, y \to t'] \wedge [\![Ey \vdash x \doteq y]\!]\zeta[x \to t, y \to t'] \Leftrightarrow (Et \vdash t \doteq t') \wedge (Et' \vdash t \doteq t')$. Hence preservation of equivalence follows if $E\sigma(t_1,\ldots,t_n) \vdash \sigma(t_1,\ldots,t_n) \doteq \sigma(t'_1,\ldots,t'_n)$ and $E\sigma(t'_1,\ldots,t'_n) \vdash \sigma(t_1,\ldots,t_n) \doteq \sigma(t'_1,\ldots,t'_n)$ can be deduced from the assumption $Et_i \vdash t_i \doteq t'_i$ and $Et'_i \vdash t_i \doteq t'_i$:
We expand the premise of the assumptions by $z = \sigma(t_1,\ldots,t_n)$ and iterate the equivalence rule to obtain $z = \sigma(t_1,\ldots,t_n) \vdash z = \sigma(t'_1,\ldots,t'_n)$. Then substitution yields $\sigma(t_1,\ldots,t_n) = \sigma(t_1,\ldots,t_n) \vdash \sigma(t_1,\ldots,t_n) = \sigma(t'_1,\ldots,t'_n)$.

For initiality T_{SIG} we only need to check if the initial standard homomorphism to another SPEC model preserves partial equality (as T_{SIG} is canonical due to the results above) which holds as any SPEC model satisfies the axioms.

The construction of free algebras over some generators proceeds along the standard lines (by adding the generators as constant operators) as does the proof of

4.6 Proposition *Deduction is complete.* I.e. $\Phi \models^{Ax}_{y.w} \psi$ implies $\Phi \vdash^{Ax}_{y.w} \psi$.

using relatively free functional models, i.e. one uses free models over the set of variables and proves that only those axioms over the variables hold in the free algebra which are deducible.

Our development of partial algebras is easily linked to more standard approaches (e.g. [Burmeister 86]): Let A be a model, and let $[a] := \{ b \mid a \equiv b \}$. Operations and relations are well defined on these equivalence classes. Denote the resulting model by A^f where $[a] \doteq [b]$ iff $a \doteq b$ defines p-equality. This process is a trivial instance of sheafification [Fourman-Scott 77]. Clearly, the

4.7 Proposition $A^f \equiv A$. (in $\mathbf{SIG^b}$)

holds. If all operations and relations of A are total A^f is just an ordinary total algebra and sheafification is factorization by a congruence relation, otherwise all partial elements are identified. Omitting the only partial element gives us a standard partial algebra with partial operations. Hence we have equivalent categories of partial algebras.

In general the underlying sorted sets of A^f and A are not isomorphic. We could say that an algebra A presents A^f by sorted sets with partial equivalences which is exactly the way an algebra is presented in computer programming. In practical terms, A might be considered as an implementation of A^f, e.g. lists with the suitable equality represent sets. The bonus of partiality is the possible multiple representation of "undefined". Partial or undefined values will be interpreted as errors. This is a necessary prerequisite for error handling as discussed below. Let us consider an example:

> **spec** NAT **is**
> **sorts** <u>nat</u>
> **ops** $0 : \to$ <u>nat</u>
>   suc : <u>nat</u> $\to$ <u>nat</u>
>   pred : <u>nat</u> $\to$ <u>nat</u>
> **axioms** $\therefore$ E 0
>   E x $\therefore$ E suc(x)

$E\,x \therefore \text{pred}(\text{suc}(x)) \doteq x$

$E\,\text{pred}(x) \therefore \text{suc}(\text{pred}(x)) \doteq x$

One possible initial algebra comprises terms of the form $\text{suc}^n(0)$ and terms of the form ...(pred(0)) with partial equivalence $\text{suc}^n(0) \doteq \text{suc}^n(0)$ with operations defined in the obvious way. All terms of the form ...(pred(0)) are instantiations of "undefined" or errors. Sheafification identifies all such terms.

5. Elementary Classified* Models

We have argued in section 2 that a "type predicates" are a natural tool to express the partiality inherent in order-sorted specifications. This chapter formalizes the intuition. We provide a suitable deduction system and check existence of initial algebras. A result of practical importance we prove in 5.9 that a term is defined if and only if it is equal to a term which is *strongly typed* in the sense that it is "typed with regard to the data signature". The typing mechanism is given by a deduction system.

5.1 Definition (Typing as Deduction)

- Formulas are of the form $t\,\varepsilon\,\tau$ where t is a term and τ a *type*.
- a ***declaration*** is of the form $x_1\,\varepsilon\,\tau_1,\ldots,x_n\,\varepsilon\,\tau_n \therefore t\,\varepsilon\,\tau$

  where the x_i's are not necessarily distinct. T abbreviates $x_1\,\varepsilon\,\tau_1,\ldots,x_n\,\varepsilon\,\tau_n$.

  Operator declarations are of the form $x_1\,\varepsilon\,\tau_1,\ldots,x_n\,\varepsilon\,\tau_n \therefore \sigma(x_1,\ldots,x_n)\,\varepsilon\,\tau$ where the x_i's are pairwise distinct.

  Γ abbreviates $x_1\,\varepsilon\,\tau_1,\ldots,x_n\,\varepsilon\,\tau_n$ where the x_i's are pairwise distinct.
- We introduce a deductive system $\Phi \vdash_t^D \varphi$ where D is a sequence of declarations.

  The deduction system comprises the rules

  •• **(mon)**, **(sub)**, **(id)**, **(mp)** with superscript D

  •• **(monD)**
  $$\frac{\Phi \vdash_t^D \varphi}{\Phi \vdash_t^{D,d} \varphi}$$

  (decl1) $\Gamma \vdash_t^{D,d} \sigma(x_1,\ldots,x_n)\,\varepsilon\,\tau$ where $d = \Gamma \therefore \sigma(x_1,\ldots,x_n)\,\varepsilon\,\tau$

  •• **(decl2)**
  $$\frac{T \vdash_t^D t\,\varepsilon\,\tau}{T \vdash_t^{D,d} t\,\varepsilon\,\tau'}$$
  where $d = T \therefore t\,\varepsilon\,\tau'$.

  Here and henceforth D ranges over a sequence of declarations, d over declarations. We omit the sort information $x_1 : s_1,\ldots,x_n : s_n$ for readability.
- A term t is called ***strongly typed*** wrt. D if $\vdash_t^D t\,\varepsilon\,\tau$ for some type τ.

---

* Tom Maibaum has pointed out the connection of what earlier was called "order-sorted partial algebra" to the classified algebras of [Wadge 82]. I have adopted the terminology though the concept proposed here is different but similar in spirit.

5.2 Definition An ***elementary classified specification*** SPEC comprises

- a set S of sorts,
- a set **types** T
- a set Σ of operators and relators of the form $\sigma : w \to s$ resp. $\rho : w$ with $w \in S^*$, $s \in S$ such that the set of relators include a unary ***type predicate*** $\_\varepsilon\, \tau : s$ for every type $\tau \in$ T, and
- a sequence D of ***declarations*** such that $T \vdash_t^D t\, \varepsilon\, \tau$ for every declaration $T \therefore t\, \varepsilon\, \tau$ in D, and
- a set of axioms of the form

$T \therefore t \doteq t'$ where $T \vdash_t^D t\, \varepsilon\, \tau$ and $T \vdash_t^D t'\, \varepsilon\, \tau$

$T \therefore \rho(t_1,\ldots,t_n)$ where $T \vdash_t^D t_i \varepsilon\, \tau_i$ and where ρ is not a type predicate.

Remarks • Subsorting is expressed by $x\, \varepsilon\, \tau \therefore x\, \varepsilon\, \tau'$.
• Elementary classified specification extend order-sorted specification in that one may for instance define "intersection types" by $x\, \varepsilon\, \tau, x\, \varepsilon\, \tau' \therefore x\, \varepsilon\, \tau \cap \tau'$, $x\, \varepsilon\, \tau \cap \tau' \therefore x\, \varepsilon\, \tau$ and $x\, \varepsilon\, \tau \cap \tau' \therefore x\, \varepsilon\, \tau'$. This is a mild generalization already to be found in [Goguen 78] and [Wadge 82].
• We incorporate the "construction of strongly typed terms" into the proof system as suggested by E.Moggi.
• In practical terms the system $\Phi \vdash_t^D \varphi$ determines the type checking algorithm.
• One might restrict declarations to operator declarations and "subsorting declarations" of the form $x\, \varepsilon\, \tau_1,\ldots,x\, \varepsilon\, \tau_n \therefore x\, \varepsilon\, \tau$ as declarations of the form $T \therefore t\, \varepsilon\, \tau$ may be simulated by introduction of a new operator σ of suitable arity for which the equality $\sigma(x_1,\ldots,x_n) \doteq t$ holds. Eventually one has to introduce "intersection types" if a variable occurs more than once in T.

Notation For technical convenience we use ρ to refer to relators which are not type predicates, while we use $\_\,\varepsilon\, \tau$ to refer to type predicates.

Notation We use the standard format for specifications, e.g.

spec NAT **is**
sorts NAT
ops $0 : \to$ NAT
suc : NAT $\to$ NAT
pred : NAT $\to$ NAT
types nat+ , nat : NAT
var n : NAT
axioms
$\therefore 0\, \varepsilon$ nat
$n\, \varepsilon$ nat+ $\therefore n\, \varepsilon$ nat
$n\, \varepsilon$ nat $\therefore$ suc(n) : nat+
$n\, \varepsilon$ nat+ $\therefore$ pred(n) ε nat
$n\, \varepsilon$ nat $\therefore$ pred(suc(n)) $\doteq$ n
$n\, \varepsilon$ nat+ $\therefore$ suc(pred(n)) $\doteq$ n

Under the keyword **types** we not only introduce types but relate them to sorts.

Classified specifications are designed to confine definedness statements to "operator declarations", hence:

5.3 Definition A model A of SPEC is called ***elementary classified*** if the following properties hold for all elements a, a', $a_1,...,a_n$ of A:

(i) Ea iff $a \varepsilon \tau$ for some type τ.

(ii) $E\sigma(a_1,...,a_n)$ iff $a_i \varepsilon \tau_i$ for some operator declaration

$$x_1 \varepsilon \tau_1,...,x_n \varepsilon \tau_n \therefore \sigma(x_1,...,x_n) \varepsilon \tau .$$

The full subcategory of elementary classified SPEC-algebras will be denoted by $\mathbf{SPEC^{ecl}}$.

Remarks • In case that the only axioms for relations state subsorting ($x \varepsilon \tau \therefore x \varepsilon \tau'$) the conditions guarantee equivalence of elementary classified models to order-sorted algebras in the sense of [Gogolla 83], [Poigné 84], [Smolka 86].

• Both condition are relevant for practical and theoretical (see section 7) purposes. The first condition ensures that definedness statements reduce to type checking while the second condition states that type checking is "compositional", i.e. a type must be determined by matching the operator to the arguments. The list of types thus obtained need not be exhaustive due to the other declarations. In case that we have only order-sorted declarations (apart from operator declarations) we only have to add all "supersorts".

5.4 Definition (Elementary classified deduction)

The deduction system of the previous section is extended by the axiom

(ex) $\quad x \varepsilon \tau \vdash Ex$

in order to match the semantic requirements of elementary classified algebras.

The superscript SPEC in $\Phi \vdash^{SPEC} \varphi$ indicates that the declarations and axioms of SPEC are added, but will be omitted if clear from the context.

Remark $\Phi \vdash_t^{D} \varphi$ implies $\Phi \vdash^{SPEC} \varphi$ where D are the declarations of SPEC (note that $x_i \varepsilon \tau_i \vdash Ex_i$)

The development suggests that T_{SPEC} (defined as in the previous section but with regard to the extended deductive system) is an initial algebra which would be the case if T_{SPEC} is elementary classified. We need two lemmas to prove this conjecture.

5.5 Definition φ is Ψ***-typeable*** ("$\Psi \Vdash_t \varphi$") if for all subterms t of φ it holds that

- $\Psi \vdash t \varepsilon \tau$ if φ is of the form $t \varepsilon \tau$ and that
- if $t = x$ then $\Psi \vdash x \varepsilon \tau$ for some type τ, and
- if $t = \sigma(t_1,...,t_n)$ then $\Psi \vdash t_i \varepsilon \tau_i$ for some declaration $x_1 \varepsilon \tau_1,...,x_n \varepsilon \tau_n \therefore \sigma(x_1,...,x_n) \varepsilon \tau$.

The definition canonically extends to sets of formulas.

5.6 Lemma $\Phi \vdash_t^D \varphi$ *and* $\Psi \Vdash_t \Phi\xi$ *implies* $\Psi \overset{d}{\cup} \Phi\xi \Vdash_t \varphi\xi$ *for all substitutions* ξ

where $\Psi \overset{d}{\cup} \Phi\xi := \Psi \cup \{\psi \in \Phi\xi \mid \Psi \nvdash \psi\}$ and where γ_ξ is the formula obtained from γ by substituting all variables x in γ by $\xi(x)$.

Proof By induction on the structure of proofs $\Phi \vdash_t \varphi$:

(decl1): Let $\Psi \Vdash_t \xi(x_i) \varepsilon \tau_i$. Thus $\Psi \vdash \xi(x_i) \varepsilon \tau_i$. Modus ponens yields $\Psi \vdash \sigma(\xi(x_1),...,\xi(x_n)) \varepsilon \tau$. All proper subterms satisfy the conditions by assumption and $\sigma(\xi(x_1),...,\xi(x_n))$ by the structure of declarations. Hence

$\Psi \Vdash_t \sigma(\xi(x_1),...,\xi(x_n))\ \varepsilon\ \tau$.

(decl2): The inductive hypothesis yields all the properties except that $\Psi \vdash t\ \varepsilon\ \tau'$ which follows by **(mp)**.
The argument for **(sym)**, **(trans)**, **(id)** is trivial as well as the argument for **(mon)**, **(monD)** and **(sub1)**.
(sub2): Let $\Psi \Vdash_t \Phi[x/t]\xi$. Then $\Psi \Vdash_t \Phi\xi[x\to t]$. By inductive assumption $\Psi \overset{d}{\cup} \Phi\xi[x\to t] \Vdash_t \varphi\,\xi[x\to t]$) and $\Psi \overset{d}{\cup} \Phi[x/t]\xi \Vdash_t \varphi[x/t]$ ξ).
(mp): $\Psi \Vdash_t \Phi\xi$ implies $\Psi \overset{d}{\cup} \Phi\xi \Vdash_t \varphi\xi$ by inductive assumption, thus $\Psi' \Vdash_t \Phi\xi \cup \{\varphi\xi\}$ Again by inductive assumption and as $\Psi \overset{d}{\cup} \Phi\xi \vdash \varphi\xi$ we have $\Psi \overset{d}{\cup} \Phi\xi \Vdash_t \psi\xi$.

5.7 Lemma $\Phi \vdash \varphi$ *and* $\Psi \Vdash_t \Phi\xi$ *implies* $\Psi \overset{d}{\cup} \Phi\xi \Vdash_t \varphi\xi$ *for all substitutions* ξ.

Proof The proof proceeds in analogy to 5.6 except that additional cases must be considered.
"Non-operator declarations and axioms": Let $T\ \therefore\ \rho(t_1,...,t_n)$ be an axiom and let $\Psi \Vdash_t \xi(x_i)\ \varepsilon\ \tau_i$. We have $T \Vdash_t t_i\ \varepsilon\ \tau_i$ as by the proviso $T \vdash_t^D t_i\ \varepsilon\ \tau_i$ (by 5.6). We now prove by induction on the structure of the terms t_i that $\Psi \Vdash_t t_i\xi\ \varepsilon\ \tau_i$. Inductive statement is that $T \vdash_t^D t'\ \varepsilon\ \tau'$ implies $\Psi \Vdash_t t'\xi\ \varepsilon\ \tau'$ for subterms t' of t_i of length at most n:
If t_i is a variable x then the subterm $\xi(x)$ satisfies the necessary properties as $\Psi \Vdash_t \xi(x_i)\ \varepsilon\ \tau_i$. If t_i is of the form $\sigma(t_1,...,t_n)$ we know (as $T \vdash_t^D \sigma(t_1,...,t_n)\ \varepsilon\ \tau$ implies $T \vdash_t^D \sigma(t_1,...,t_n)\ \varepsilon\ \tau$) that $T \vdash_t^D t_i\ \varepsilon\ \tau_i$ for some declaration $x_1\ \varepsilon\ \tau_1,...,x_n\ \varepsilon\ \tau_n\ \therefore\ \sigma(x_1,...,x_n)\ \varepsilon\ \tau$. By inductive assumption $\Psi \Vdash_t t_i\xi\ \varepsilon\ \tau_i$. This and modus ponens yields $\Psi \vdash \sigma(t_1,...,t_n)\xi\ \varepsilon\ \tau$, thus $\Psi \vdash_t \sigma(t_1,...,t_n)\xi\ \varepsilon\ \tau$.
(ex) : Immediately by form of the premise.
(strict): As $\Psi \Vdash_t E\sigma(t_1,...,t_n)$ all subterms of Et_i are subterms of $E\sigma(t_1,...,t_n)$, hence they satisfy the necessary conditions for $\Psi \Vdash_t Et_i$.
(eq): Let $\Psi \Vdash_t \Phi\xi$. Then $\Psi \overset{d}{\cup} \Phi\xi \Vdash_t \varphi[x/t]$ by inductive assumption. By **(mon)** we can extend the typing environment $\Psi \overset{d}{\cup} \Phi\xi \cup \Phi\xi \Vdash_t \varphi[x/t]$. Application of substitution and monotonicity rule yields $\Psi \overset{d}{\cup} \Phi\xi \cup \Phi\xi,\ t\xi \doteq t\xi \vdash t\xi \doteq t'\xi$ and $\Psi \overset{d}{\cup} \Phi\xi \cup \Phi\xi,\ t'\xi \doteq t'\xi \vdash t\xi \doteq t'\xi$. We can now apply the equivalence rule to all instances of typeability separately, e.g. if φ is $z\ \varepsilon\ \tau$ and $t'\xi = z$ then $\Psi \overset{d}{\cup} \Phi\xi \cup \Phi\xi \vdash z\ \varepsilon\ \tau$ induces $\Psi \overset{d}{\cup} \Phi\xi \cup \Phi_\xi \vdash t'\xi\ \varepsilon\ \tau$. Finally we eliminate $\Phi\xi$ by modus ponens as $\Psi \overset{d}{\cup} \Phi\xi$ $\vdash \Phi\xi$.

Remark The use of "double closure" against substitution and additional assumptions appears to be an important proof technique in the context of natural deduction systems of the kind we consider.

5.8 Proposition T_{SPEC} *is elementary classified.*

Proof We only need to check the "only if" part of the conditions for elementary classified models.
Let $\vdash Et$. Application of 5.7 yields $\emptyset \Vdash_t Et$, thus $\vdash t\ \varepsilon\ \tau$ for some type τ.
Similarly, $\vdash E\sigma(t_1,...,t_n)$ implies $\emptyset \Vdash_t E\sigma(t_1,...,t_n)$ and $\vdash \sigma(t_1,...,t_n)\ \varepsilon\ \tau$ for some τ. But $\emptyset \Vdash_t \sigma(t_1,...,t_n)\ \varepsilon\ \tau$ by 5.7, thus $\vdash t_i\ \varepsilon\ \tau_i$ for some declaration $x_1\ \varepsilon\ \tau_1,...,x_n\ \varepsilon\ \tau_n\ \therefore\ \sigma(x_1,...,x_n)$.

5.9 Proposition *If* $\Phi \vdash t\ \varepsilon\ \tau$ *then* $\Phi_\varepsilon \vdash_t^D t'\ \varepsilon\ \tau$ *and* Φ, $Et \vdash t \doteq t'$ *and* Φ, $Et' \vdash t \doteq t'$ *for some term* t' *where* $\Phi_\varepsilon := \{\ t\ \varepsilon\ \tau \mid t\ \varepsilon\ \tau$ occurs in $\Phi\}$.

Proof By induction over the length of proofs:
Base case: Only **(Id)** and declarations are of suitable form. The statement holds by the form of the axioms and as Φ, $Et \vdash t \doteq t$ holds for all terms.
Inductive case:
(mp): We have $\Phi \vdash \varphi$ and $\Phi,\ \varphi \vdash t\ \varepsilon\ \tau$.

If φ is not of the form $t' \in \tau'$ then $\Phi_\varepsilon \vdash_t^D t'' \varepsilon \tau$ and Φ, φ, $Et' \vdash t' \stackrel{\bullet}{=} t''$ and $\Phi, \varphi, Et'' \vdash t' \stackrel{\bullet}{=} t''$ for some term t'' by inductive hypothesis. Modus ponens yields Φ, $Et' \vdash t' \stackrel{\bullet}{=} t''$ and Φ, $Et'' \vdash t' \stackrel{\bullet}{=} t''$.
If φ is of the form $t_1 \in \tau_1$ we can apply the inductive assumption twice and obtain: $\Phi_\varepsilon \vdash_t^D t_3 \varepsilon \tau_1$ and Φ, $Et_1 \vdash t_1 \stackrel{\bullet}{=} t_3$ and Φ, $Et_3 \vdash t_1 \stackrel{\bullet}{=} t_3$ for some term t_3 and $\Phi, t_1 \in \tau_1 \vdash_t^D t_2 \varepsilon \tau$ and Φ, $Et \vdash t \stackrel{\bullet}{=} t_2$ and Φ, $Et_2 \vdash t \stackrel{\bullet}{=} t_2$ for some term t_2. By lemma 5.10 there exists a t_4 such that $\Phi_\varepsilon \vdash_t^D t_4 \varepsilon \tau$ and $\Phi, Et_2 \vdash t_2 \stackrel{\bullet}{=} t_4$ and $\Phi, Et_4 \vdash t_2 \stackrel{\bullet}{=} t_4$. We now use that $t \stackrel{\bullet}{=} t_2$ implies Et_2 resp. that $t_4 \stackrel{\bullet}{=} t_2$ implies Et_2 and transitivity to show Φ, $Et \vdash t \stackrel{\bullet}{=} t_4$ and Φ, $Et_4 \vdash t \stackrel{\bullet}{=} t_4$.
(sub): The inductive hypothesis can be applied to $\Phi \vdash t \varepsilon \tau$, and substitution can be applied to the components of conclusion.
(mon) Monotonicity can be applied componentwise.
(eq): The inductive hypothesis can be applied to $\Phi \vdash t[x/t_1] \varepsilon \tau$ (where Φ, $Et_1 \vdash t_1 \stackrel{\bullet}{=} t_2$ and Φ, $Et_2 \vdash t_1 \stackrel{\bullet}{=} t_2$) to obtain $\Phi_\varepsilon \vdash_t^D t' \varepsilon \tau$, Φ, $Et[x/t_1] \vdash t[x/t_1] \stackrel{\bullet}{=} t'$ and Φ, $Et' \vdash t[x/t_1] \stackrel{\bullet}{=} t'$. Application of the equivalence rule yields Φ, $Et[x/t_2] \vdash Et[x/t_1]$ which allows to deduce $\Phi, Et[x/t_2] \vdash t[x/t_1] \stackrel{\bullet}{=} t'$. Again by equivalence we obtain $\Phi, Et[x/t_2] \vdash t[x/t_2] \stackrel{\bullet}{=} t'$ and Φ, Et' $\vdash t[x/t_2] \stackrel{\bullet}{=} t$

5.10 Lemma *Let* $\Phi_\varepsilon, t_2 \varepsilon \tau \vdash_t^D t_3 \varepsilon \tau'$. *Then for all* $\Phi_\varepsilon \vdash_t^D t_1 \varepsilon \tau$ *and* Φ, $Et_1 \vdash t_1 \stackrel{\bullet}{=} t_2$ *and* Φ, $Et_2 \vdash t_1 \stackrel{\bullet}{=} t_2$ *there exists a* t_4 *such that* $\Phi_\varepsilon \vdash_t^D t_4 \varepsilon \tau'$ *and* Φ, $Et_3 \vdash t_3 \stackrel{\bullet}{=} t_4$ *and* Φ, $Et_4 \vdash t_3 \stackrel{\bullet}{=} t_4$.

Proof By induction over the length of proofs of $\Phi_\varepsilon, t_2 \varepsilon \tau \vdash_t^D t_3 \varepsilon \tau'$:
The only proofs of length 1 which are of interest are
(id) the statement is trivially satisfied, and
("declarations") then t_2 is a variable x. We substitute $\Phi_\varepsilon, t_1 \varepsilon \tau \vdash_t^D t_3[x/t_1] \varepsilon \tau'$. We apply the equivalence rule to obtain Φ, $Et_3 \vdash t_3 \stackrel{\bullet}{=} t_3[x/t_1]$ and Φ, $Et_3[x/t_1] \vdash t_3 \stackrel{\bullet}{=} t_3[x/t_1]$ (just as in 5.7 case **(eq)**).
(sub), **(mon)** Substitutivity and monotonicity can be used for all components.
(mp) Assume that $\Phi_\varepsilon, t_2 \varepsilon \tau \vdash_t^D t'' \varepsilon \tau''$ and $\Phi_\varepsilon, t_2 \varepsilon \tau, t'' \varepsilon \tau'' \vdash_t^D t_3 \varepsilon \tau'$. By monotonicity rule $\Phi_\varepsilon, t'' \varepsilon \tau'' \vdash_t^D t_1 \varepsilon \tau$ and Φ, $Et_1, t'' \varepsilon \tau'' \vdash t_1 \stackrel{\bullet}{=} t_2$ and Φ, $Et_2, t'' \varepsilon \tau'' \vdash t_1 \stackrel{\bullet}{=} t_2$. Application of the inductive assumption yields a t_4 such that $\Phi_\varepsilon, t'' \varepsilon \tau'' \vdash_t^D t_4 \varepsilon \tau'$ and Φ, $Et_3, t'' \varepsilon \tau'' \vdash t_3 \stackrel{\bullet}{=} t_4$ and Φ, $Et_4, t'' \varepsilon \tau'' \vdash t_3 \stackrel{\bullet}{=} t_4$. We eliminate $t'' \varepsilon \tau''$ by modus ponens.

5.11 Proposition Let t be a term and $\Phi \vdash t_1 \stackrel{\bullet}{=} t_2$. Then Φ, $Et[x/t_1] \vdash t[x/t_1] \stackrel{\bullet}{=} t[x/t_2]$.

Proof We start with Φ, $t[x/z] \stackrel{\bullet}{=} t[x/t_1] \vdash t[x/z] \stackrel{\bullet}{=} t[x/t_1]$ and apply the equivalence rule by expanding the assumption to obtain Φ, $t[x/z] \stackrel{\bullet}{=} t[x/t_1] \vdash t[x/z] \stackrel{\bullet}{=} t[x/t_2]$. Then substitution yields the statement.

Proposition 5.9 and 5.11 formalize the intuition expressed in section 2; there we have argued that admissible terms have a denotation if and only if we can apply equations within a potentially undefined term in order to compute an equal term which can be (strongly) typed with regard to the "data signature". Clearly, the deduction system defining $\_ \vdash_t^D \_$ mimics the concept of a "data signature". The result is important for practical applications in that it allows to separate equational reasoning and definedness proofs which reduce to type checking. In terms of animation by rewriting application of a rewrite rule is restricted to typed subterms. After each rewrite step the type checker is applied to type a greater section of the term to be computed. The independence of type checking and rewriting should allow to apply standard rewrite and completion techniques to order-sorted specifications with the only additional component being the type checker.

Remark The results reflect our particular view of subsorting where the result of an application of operations or relations to total elements is independent of the typing information. The same view of subsorting is expressed in [Gogolla 83], [Poigné 84], [Smolka 86](the latter being closely related to this work. The main difference is that Smolka does not consider types as unary predicates) which contrast that of [Goguen&al 85] (the relations between [Gogolla 83], [Poigné 84], [Smolka 86], [Goguen&al 85] are worked out in the complementary [Poigné 87]).

If we are not yet satisfied with the expressive power of classified specifications there is no difficulty to add conditional axioms, only the conclusions must be restricted in the obvious way, e.g.

$$\Phi, \varphi_1 \;, \ldots, \varphi_n \therefore t \doteq t' \quad \text{where} \quad T \vdash_t^D t \in \tau \text{ and } T \vdash_t^D t' \in \tau$$

where the φ_i's are atomic. The proof of initiality is easily extended.

6. A Discipline of Dependent Types

More sophisticated types are obtained by parameterization, e.g.

$$\text{empty} \therefore \underline{\text{stack}}(0)$$
$$n \in \underline{\text{nat}}, s \in \underline{\text{stack}}(n), d \in \underline{\text{data}} \therefore \text{push}(s,d) \in \underline{\text{stack}}(\text{suc}(n))$$
$$n \in \underline{\text{nat}}, s \in \underline{\text{stack}}(\text{suc}(n)) \therefore \text{pop}(s) \in \underline{\text{stack}}(n)$$

where $s \in \underline{\text{stack}}(n)$ stands for a binary predicate "s is a stack of length n". The "type" $\underline{\text{stack}}(n)$ depends on the variable n of type $\underline{\text{nat}}$.

In general, we will consider n+1-ary predicates $x_{n+1} \in \underline{\sigma}(x_1,\ldots,x_n)$ were $\underline{\sigma}(x_1,\ldots,x_n)$ is a **dependent type**. The n+1-th position is used to express typing just as the unary type predicates have been used in the previous section. $\underline{\sigma}$ may be seen as a *type constructor*. We use the underlining to distinguish these operators from standard operators.

However, care has to be applied to avoid unwanted (i.e. *untyped*) generation of existence as in

$$n \in \underline{\text{nat}}, s \in \underline{\text{stack}}(n) \therefore \text{pop}(s) \in \underline{\text{stack}}(\text{pred}(n))$$

where existence of pred(0) is implicitly stated (whatever the intention might have been).

Type dependencies must as well be used cautiously in premises. For instance,

$$x \in \underline{\sigma}(y) \therefore \sigma(x) \in \tau$$

does not ensure definedness of σ as no y may exist. Similarly, but more sophisticated, the axiom

$$x \in \tau, z \in \underline{\text{eq}}(\sigma(x),\sigma(x)) \therefore \sigma(x) \in \tau$$

may not guarantee definedness of $\sigma(x)$ where

$$x \in \tau \therefore r(x) \in \underline{\text{eq}}(x,x)$$
$$x,y \in \tau, z \in \underline{\text{eq}}(x,y) \therefore x \doteq y$$
$$x,y \in \tau, z,z' \in \underline{\text{eq}}(x,y) \therefore z \doteq z'$$

The example is recoded from [Benecke-Reichel 83]. One notes that $x,y \in \tau \vdash x \doteq y$ implies $x,y \in \tau \vdash r(x) \in \underline{\text{eq}}(x,y)$.

We avoid these difficulties if we impose an existence condition on the subterms t_i occurring in a predicate

$t \,\varepsilon\, \underline{\sigma}(t_1,...,t_n)$. As in [Cartmell 78] (and other references of this kind, e.g. [Coquand 85]) we introduce environments to ensure proper type dependencies in the premises.

The examples expose the rationale of dependent types; operator declarations may be guarded by types which encode proposition which do not refer to the operator to be declared. From a practical point of view this implies that we may need "computations" to "satisfy" the type conditions on arguments but that the computations are never reflexive, i.e. in order to establish applicability of an operator declaration the operator declaration itself has to be used (similar to the hierarchy conditions in [Benecke-Reichel 83]). In terms of animation by rewriting it should be possible to construct termination and confluence proofs along the inductive definition of the typing system (the other declarations may however confuse the picture).

6.1 Definition (Typing as Deduction)

- ***Types*** are of the form $\underline{\sigma}(t_1,...,t_n)$ where $\underline{\sigma}(\_,...,\_)$ are *type constructors* and the t_i's are terms.

  We use τ to range over types.
- ***Environments*** are of the form $x_1 \,\varepsilon\, \tau_1,\ x_2 \,\varepsilon\, \tau_2(x_1),...,\ x_n \,\varepsilon\, \tau_n(x_1,...,x_{n-1})$

  where the xi's pairwise distinct and the notation $\tau(x_1,...,x_j)$ states that the variables $x_1,...,x_j$ may occur in the term expression T. We use Γ to range over environments.
- ***Operator declaration*** are of the form $\Gamma \therefore_{x_1:s_1,...,x_n:s_n} \sigma(x_{i_1},...,x_{i_m}) \,\varepsilon\, \underline{\sigma}(t_1,...,t_n)$

  where $i_j \in \{1,...,m\}$ for $i = 1,...,m$.

  Remark The use of the x_{i_j}'s in $\sigma(x_{i_1},...,x_{i_m})$ allow to forget about preconditions.
- (Other) ***Declarations*** are of the form

  $$x_1 \,\varepsilon\, \tau_1,...,\ x_n \,\varepsilon\, \tau_n \therefore\ t \,\varepsilon\, \underline{\tau}$$

  the x_i's not necessarily distinct.
- The deduction system $\Phi \vdash_t^D \varphi$ comprises deduction rules

•• **(sub)**, **(mp)** with superscript D

•• **(monD)**

$$\frac{\Phi \vdash_t^D \varphi}{\Phi \vdash_t^{D,d} \varphi}$$

•• **(env)**

$$\frac{\Gamma \vdash_t^D t_i \,\varepsilon\, \tau_i}{\Gamma, x_{n+1} \,\varepsilon\, \tau_{n+1} \vdash_t^D x_i \,\varepsilon\, \tau_i}$$

where $\tau_{n+1} = \underline{\sigma}(t_1,...,t_n)$

(env) replaces **(mon)** and **(id)**

•• **(decl1)**

$$\frac{\Gamma \vdash_t^D t_i \,\varepsilon\, \tau_i}{\Gamma \vdash_t^{D,d} \sigma(x_1',...,x_m') \,\varepsilon\, \underline{\sigma}(t_1,...,t_n)}$$

where $d = \Gamma \therefore \sigma(x_{i_1},...,x_{i_m}) \,\varepsilon\, \underline{\sigma}(t_1,...,t_n)$

•• (decl2)

$$\frac{T \vdash_t^{D} t \in \tau}{T \vdash_t^{D,d} t \in \tau'} \qquad \text{where } d = T \therefore t \in \tau'.$$

6.2 Definition • A ***classified specification*** SPEC comprises

- a set S of sorts,
- a S-sorted set **type constructors** (of the form $\underline{\sigma}(\_,...,\_) : s_1...s_n$)
- a set Σ of operators and relators of the form $\sigma : w \to s$ resp. $\rho : w$ with $w \in S^*$, $s \in S$ such that the set of relators include a unary ***type predicate*** $\_\varepsilon\ \underline{\sigma}(\_,...,\_) : s\ s_1...s_n$, and
- a sequence D of declarations such that $T \vdash_t^D t \in \tau$ for each declaration $T \therefore t \in \tau$.
- a set of ***axioms*** of the form

$$T \therefore t \doteq t' \qquad \text{where} \quad T \vdash_t^D t \in \tau \text{ and } T \vdash_t^D t' \in \tau$$

$$T \therefore \rho(t_1,...,t_n) \qquad \text{where} \quad T \vdash_t^D t_i \in \tau_i$$

where all the free variables occurring are bound in T (ρ is not a type predicate).

Remark Compared to [Cartmell 78] we separate the typing system and the equational system in order to obtain a analogous result to 5.9.

6.3 Definition A ***classified model*** is a model A which satisfies the following properties for all elements a,a',a_i :

(i) Ea iff $a \in \underline{\sigma}(a_1,...,a_n)$ for some elements $a_1,...,a_n$ in A.

(ii) $E\sigma(a_{i_1},...,a_{i_m})$ iff $a_{i+1} \in \tau_i(a_1,...,a_i)$

for some operator declaration $\Gamma \therefore \sigma(x_{i_1},...,x_{i_m}) \in \underline{\sigma}(t_1,...,t_n)$

The notation $\tau_i(a_1,...,a_i)$ states that the variables x_i in $\tau_i(x_1,...,x_i)$ are replaced by a_i.

A SPEC-***model*** satisfies all the axioms of SPEC.

The full subcategory of classified SPEC-models is denoted by $\mathbf{SPEC}^{cl}$.

6.4 Definition (Classified Deduction)

We note that the type τ in the additional axiom for classified deduction

$$x \in \tau \vdash Ex$$

is of the form $\underline{\sigma}(t_1,...,t_n)$ by notational convention.

The notation has been designed in order to transpose the proofs in the previous section.

6.5 Definition φ is Ψ-***typeable*** ("$\Psi \Vdash_t \varphi$") if for all subterms t of φ it holds that

- $\Psi \vdash t \in \tau$ for $\varphi = t \in \tau$ and that
- if $t = x$ then $\Psi \vdash x \in \tau$ for some type τ, and
- if $t = \sigma(t_{i_1},...,t_{i_m})$ then $\Psi \vdash t_{i+1} \in \tau_{i+1}(t_1,...,t_i)$ for t_i and some declaration

$$x_1 \in \tau_1,...,x_n \in \tau_n(x_1,...,x_{n-1}) \therefore \sigma(x_{i_1},...,x_{i_m}) \in \underline{\sigma}(t_1,...,t_n).$$

The definition canonically extends to sets of formulas.

6.6 Lemma $\Phi \vdash_t^D \varphi$ *and* $\Psi \Vdash_t \Phi_\xi$ *implies* $\Psi \overset{d}{\cup} \Phi_\xi \Vdash_t \varphi_\xi$ *for all substitutions* ξ.

Proof The proof proceeds along the lines of 5.6 with substitution applied to types ("τ_ξ"). The only changes are
(env)
(decl1): Let $\Psi \Vdash_t \xi(x_{i+1})\ \varepsilon\ \tau_i(\xi(x_1),...,\xi(x_i))$. Thus $\Psi \vdash \xi(x_{i+1})\ \varepsilon\ \tau_i(\xi(x_1),...,\xi(x_i))$. Modus ponens yields $\Psi \vdash \sigma(\xi(x_1)),...,\xi(x_m))\ \varepsilon\ \tau(t_1\xi,...,t_n\xi)$. All proper subterms satisfy the conditions by assumption and $\sigma(\xi(x_1),...,\xi(x_m)$ by the structure of declarations. Hence $\Psi \Vdash_t \sigma(\xi(x_1,...,\xi(x_m)\ \varepsilon\ \tau(t_1\xi,...,t_n\xi)$.

6.7 Lemma $\Phi \vdash \varphi$ *and* $\Psi \Vdash_t \Phi_\xi$ *implies* $\Psi \overset{d}{\cup} \Phi_\xi \Vdash_t \varphi_\xi$ *for all substitutions* ξ.

Proof Along the lines of 5.7.

6.8 Proposition • T_{SPEC} *is classified.*

Proof We only need to check the "only if" part of the conditions for elementary classified models.
Let $\vdash$ Et. Application of 6.7 yields $\emptyset \Vdash_t$ Et , thus $\vdash t\ \varepsilon\ \underline{\sigma}(t_1,...,t_n)$ for some type $\underline{\sigma}$ and some t_i.
Similarly, $\vdash E\sigma(t_1,...,t_n)$ implies $\emptyset \Vdash_t E\sigma(t_1,...,t_n)$ and $\vdash \sigma(t_1,...,t_n)\ \varepsilon\ \tau$ for some τ. But $\emptyset \Vdash_t \sigma(t_1,...,t_n)\ \varepsilon$) by 6.7, thus $\vdash t_i\ \varepsilon\ \tau_i$ for some declaration $x_1\ \varepsilon\ \tau_1,...,x_n\ \varepsilon\ \tau_n\ \therefore\ \sigma(x_1,...,x_n)$.

Remark As for elementary classified algebras free models exist, and classified deduction is sound.

6.9 Proposition *If* $\Phi \vdash t_{n+1}\ \varepsilon\ \underline{\sigma}(t_1,...,t_n)$ *then* $\Phi_t \vdash_t^D t'_{n+1}\ \varepsilon\ \underline{\sigma}(t'_1,...,t'_n)$ *and* Φ, $Et_i \vdash t_i \doteq t'_i$ *and* Φ, $Et'_i \vdash t_i \doteq t'_i$ *for some terms* t'_i, $i = 1,...,n+1$.

Proof The proof proceeds along the lines of 5.9. As in the proofs of 6.6-6.8 one carefully replaces $t\ \varepsilon\ \tau$'s by $t_{n+1}\ \varepsilon\ \underline{\sigma}(t_1,...,t_n)$ and checks the statements for all t_i's instead of t only.

As for the elementary case we can separate type checking and equality. Clearly, type checking is considerably more sophisticated than in the elementary case and so far we do not have ideas about an efficient algorithm.

Some notational conventions The example of encoding equality suggest that every relation may be turned into a type. This may be achieved in that we introduce

$$\{ x : s \mid \rho(x_1,...,x_n)\} \qquad \{ x : s \mid x_1 \doteq x_2)\}$$

as a standard format for type constructors where x may occur in the list $x_1,...,x_n$ of variables. x is bound in that terms can only replace the variables not equal to x.
$\{ x : s \mid \varphi\}$ may be replaced by φ if s is 1 (and if the type φ and the proposition φ cannot be confused).

Example With this conventions we can specify categories (which are an archetypal example for dependent types) in a rather natural style

> **spec** CATEGORY **is**
> **sorts** $\underline{OB}$, $\underline{MOR}$
> **ops** id : $\underline{OB} \rightarrow \underline{MOR}$
> $\_ ; \_ : \underline{MOR}\ \underline{MOR} \rightarrow \underline{MOR}$
> d, c : $\underline{MOR} \rightarrow \underline{OB}$
> **rels** $\underline{ob} : \underline{OB}$
> $\underline{mor} : \underline{MOR}$
> **axioms** $A \,\varepsilon\, \underline{ob} \;\therefore\; id(A) \,\varepsilon\, \underline{mor}$
> $f \,\varepsilon\, \underline{mor} \;\therefore\; d(f) \,\varepsilon\, \underline{ob}$
> $f \,\varepsilon\, \underline{mor} \;\therefore\; c(f) \,\varepsilon\, \underline{ob}$
> $f, g \,\varepsilon\, \underline{mor},\ c(f) = d(f) \,\varepsilon\, \underline{ob} \;\therefore\; f ; g \,\varepsilon\, \underline{mor}$
> $f,g,h \,\varepsilon\, \underline{mor},\ c(f) = d(g) \,\varepsilon\, \underline{ob},\ c(g) = d(h) \,\varepsilon\, \underline{ob} \;\therefore\; f ; (g ; h) = (f ; g) ; h \,\varepsilon\, \underline{mor}$
> $A \,\varepsilon\, \underline{ob},\ f \,\varepsilon\, \underline{mor},\ d(f) = A \,\varepsilon\, \underline{ob} \;\therefore\; id(A) ; f = f \,\varepsilon\, \underline{mor}$
> $B \,\varepsilon\, \underline{ob},\ f \,\varepsilon\, \underline{mor},\ c(f) = B \,\varepsilon\, \underline{ob} \;\therefore\; f ; id(B) = f \,\varepsilon\, \underline{mor}$

7. Relation to other Work

I reiterate that I only claim originality for the amalgamation of the various concepts.

Compared to [Benecke-Reichel 83] we have a syntactic discipline how to generate correct hep-specifications [Reichel 84] (which have the only generic type "existence" for each sort). Moreover we allow for a type discipline without coding the types by equations.

In general our theory is not well behaved a theory of partial algebras in that the categories of algebras are not varietal [Burmeister 82]. This is due to the fact that injective and surjective homomorphisms are not necessarily strong (let $a \,\varepsilon\, \tau$ and not $a \,\varepsilon\, \tau$ in a model A but $h(a) \,\varepsilon\, \tau$ and $h(a) \,\varepsilon\, \tau'$ where an operator $x \,\varepsilon\, \tau' \therefore \sigma(x) \,\varepsilon\, \tau'$ is declared. Then $\sigma(a)$ is defined in B but not in A).

7.1 Proposition *Let* SPEC *be a classified specification such that all operator declarations are of the form* $\Gamma \therefore \sigma(x_1,...,x_n) \,\varepsilon\, \underline{\sigma}(x_1,...,x_n)$, *i.e. all variables occur in* $\sigma(x_1,...,x_n)$.
A homomorphism between classified models is strong if it ***reflects types***, *i.e.* $h(a) \,\varepsilon\, \underline{\sigma}(h(a_1),...,h(a_n))$ *implies* $a \,\varepsilon\, \underline{\sigma}(a_1,...,a_n)$.

Proof If $E\sigma_B(h(a_1),...,h(a_n))$ then $h(a_{i+1}) \,\varepsilon\, \underline{\sigma}_{i+1}(a_1,...,a_i)$ for some declaration $\Gamma \therefore \sigma(x_1,...,x_n) \,\varepsilon\, \underline{\sigma}(x_1,...,x_n)$. By assumption $a_i \,\varepsilon\, \tau_i$ and $E\sigma_A(a_1,...,a_n)$ due to the declaration.

Remark The proof paraphrases that of [Benecke-Reichel 83]. The proof does not work if we relax the conditions for classified models in that we omit the axiom about existence by declarations.

Reflection of types is given only if there is a unique existence predicate or if there is a disjointness axiom in that $A_\tau \cap A_{\tau'} = \emptyset$ if $\tau \neq \tau'$ where $A_\tau := \{a \in A \mid a \varepsilon \tau\}$. Clearly then all declarations must be operator declarations as otherwise we have inconsistencies. In case of elementary classified specifications this implies that models are those of a standard heterogeneous signature (given by the types and operator declarations), while in the case of classified specifications we obtain models as for generalized algebraic theories [Cartmell 78].

These remarks may suffice to indicate that we have the deductive power of theories which come under the names of essentially algebraic theories [Freyd 72], ∃!-theories [Coste 76], finitely presented theories[Gabriel-Ulmer 71] and under several other names. In fact, the deductive power of these theories and the one proposed here should be equal as in all these theories subsorting is available in form of injective (coercion) operators while we insist that subsorting should be interpreted as inclusion, the hope being that we gain "more efficient" representation of such theories (a hope which still has to be substantiated).

8. Errors Formally

Errors are instantiations of undefinedness. The isomorphic copies of an algebra have quite a different understanding of undefinedness; the canonical algebra A^c makes the finest (reasonable) distinctions in that every term constitutes an error message if it is not typed. The coarsest error handling is given by the algebra A^f obtained by sheafification; there is only one error message. If no more restrictions are imposed it is at the discretion of an implementer to choose his favourite error handling, the only restriction being that he correctly implements correct=typed data.

For some reason errors may be bundled to error messages and/or error recovery may be appropriate. We remember that ordinary total algebra are underneath our partial algebras, hence allow for a standard equational specification. So we can add new data and impose equations such as

pop(empty) = error_stack_underflow

recovery(top(push(s,d)) = d

provided that correct data are not identified.

The following idea is quite tempting: We have a forgetful functor $\_^c$: $SPEC^{cl} \rightarrow SIG^b$ which maps a (partial) classified algebra to its canonical instantiation seen as a total algebra (SIG being the underlying signature). One adds error handling by a combination ERROR = SIG + ($\emptyset$, Σ_{ERROR}, E_{ERROR}) which is "persistent". Obviously, the idea does not work as homomorphisms do not "preserve" errors in that they are not necessarily strong (compare the example of natural numbers in the introduction). So one has to look for less semantic interpretation of error handling.

Data type specification, at least under the optics of initial algebra semantics, is interested only in algebras which are term generated in a broad sense, e.g. initial algebras for flat specifications, freely generated algebras for parameterized specifications, or reducts of such algebras. Hence we restrict error handling to parameterized specifications with "free semantics".

Let PSPEC $\subseteq$ SPEC be a parameterized specification. An ***error specification*** (wrt SPEC) is a combination ERROR = SIG + ($\emptyset$, Σ_{ERROR}, E_{ERROR}). An error specification is ***correct*** wrt. SPEC if for all PSPEC-algebras A it holds that

- for all elements t $\in$ $T_{SIGERROR}(A)$ there exists an element t' $\in$ $T_{SIG}(A)$ such that $x =_{ERROR} y$,
- for all elements t,t' $\in$ $T_{SIG}(A)$ $x \equiv y$ in $T_{SPEC}(A)$ if $x =_{ERROR} y$

where $T_{SIGERROR}(A)$, $T_{SIG}(A)$ are the term algebras generated by A., and $T_{SPEC}(A)$ is the free SPEC-algebra over A, and where $x =_{ERROR} y$ is the (standard) congruence on $T_{SIGERROR}(A)$ generated from the error equations.

A ***module*** consists of a parameterized specification and an error specification which is correct wrt. SPEC.

Remark The definition states that additional terms in ERROR can be reduced to a term in the original specification in such a way that no new identification of the original data are caused. In other words, error handling does not interfere with the original structure.

It is beyond the scope of this paper to discuss modularization techniques for this concept of modules but an informal example may help. Assume we have the specification STACKD of section 1 in classified form. We can add an error specification with the only error message error_stack_underflow and the obvious equations

top(empty) = error_stack_underflow
pop(empty) = error_stack_underflow
push(error_stack_underflow, d) = error_stack_underflow, etc.

This makes sense whatever the parameter data are. Moreover let the actual parameter be NAT with error messages

pred(0) = error_negative, etc.

Updating yields a specification which combines the error handling of the components though a wealth of new errors is created, e.g. suc(error_stack_underflow).

This may look clumsy but is the best we can expect from an error handling which is uniform and confined to modules; in a module one can only speak about what you know within the module. The strict interface by typing may, however, allow for global strategies, for instance to single out a class of "error messages" with regard to which operators are strict, e.g. push(error_stack_underflow, error_negative) = error_stack_underflow and error_negative. The mechanics of such global strategies need to be explored as do modularization techniques. The paper only provides what maybe a semantical basis.

9. Some Alternatives

The conditions imposed on classified algebras might be considered as too severe. For instance, a morphism h : SPEC $\rightarrow$ SPEC' between classified specifications (defined in the standard way) induces a forgetful functor

$\_{h} : \mathbf{SPEC'^{cl}} \rightarrow \mathbf{SPEC^{cl}}$

where

$A_{h,s} := A_{h(s)}$ with partial equivalence

$a \doteq_s b$ in A_h iff $a \doteq_{h(s)} b$ in A, and
$a \,\varepsilon\, h(\tau)$ for some type τ in SPEC, and
$a_{i+1} \,\varepsilon\, h(\underline{\sigma}_i)(a_1,...,a_i)$ for some a_i's
and for some declaration $\Gamma \therefore \sigma(x_{i_1},...,x_{i_m}) \,\varepsilon\, \underline{\sigma}(t_1,...,t_n)$ in SPEC.

Remark Without proof we state that a left adjoint exists which is obtained by the free construction where we add the generators as constants and construct the initial algebra modulo evaluation of SPEC-operators applied to generators, i.e. modulo $\sigma_A(a_1,...,a_n) \doteq \sigma(a_1,...,a_n)$.

In general the forgetful functor does not coincide with the forgetful functor for partial algebras as it may "forget existence". Forgetful functors are used as semantics for *reducts* in abstract data type theory. Reducts allow to specify with hidden operations which is a useful and sometimes necessary technique. At the moment I do not know if one needs "hidden definedness" statements in the context of classified specifications but one may introduce a (virtual) supertype $\_ \,\varepsilon\, \underline{E_s}$ for each sort s such that $x \,\varepsilon\, \tau \therefore x \,\varepsilon\, \underline{E_s}$ and stipulate that specification homomorphisms preserve this type predicate. Then the forgetful functors for classified algebras and partial algebras coincide, and reducts "preserve definedness". Such a theory needs to be investigated.

Remark • The supertypes $\_ \,\varepsilon\, \underline{E_s}$ correspond to the extent predicate $E_s\_$ semantically. The difference is that the use of supertypes is restricted in declarations. The use of an existence statement may confuse our type discipline.
• Another hint that supertypes may be necessary is implicit in [Poigné 87]. There we argued that "maximal instances" of operators must exist and be preserved by specification morphisms in order to guarantee correct parameter passing. Supertypes implicitly define maximal instances of operators in that an operator is defined on supertypes if it is defined for other types.

The representation of dependent types by atomic predicates may be another point of discussion. We have chosen this approach because of the uniformity of the semantics. There are several alternatives, the most attractive being the following:
One considers type constructors as ordinary operators in that one introduces a sort $\underline{TYPE}$. Type operators then are operators of the form $\underline{\sigma} : s_1...s_n \rightarrow \underline{TYPE}$ where the s_i's are not equal to $\underline{TYPE}$. With a constant type : $\underline{TYPE}$ such that Etype and relations $\_ \,\varepsilon\, \_ : s\,\underline{TYPE}$ one declares dependent types by

$$x_1 \,\varepsilon\, \tau_1,...,x_n \,\varepsilon\, \tau_n(x_1,...,x_{n-1}) \therefore \underline{\sigma}(x_1,...,x_n) \,\varepsilon\, \text{type}$$

and declares other operators by

$$x_1 \,\varepsilon\, \tau_1,...,x_n \,\varepsilon\, \tau_n(x_1,...,x_{n-1}) \therefore \sigma(x_1,...,x_m) \,\varepsilon\, \underline{\sigma}(t_1,...,t_n).$$

Clearly, the deduction system for typing has to be modified suitably (this is basically the mechanism in [Cartmell 78]).

Remark One may even go one step further and differentiate *types* and *judgements* via a unary predicate $\_!$: TYPE with declarations of the form

$$x_1 \varepsilon \tau_1,...,x_n \varepsilon \tau_n(x_1,...,x_{n-1}) \therefore \underline{\sigma}(t_1,...,t_n)!$$

$$x_1 \varepsilon \tau_1,...,x_n \varepsilon \tau_n(x_1,...,x_{n-1}) \therefore \underline{\sigma}(x_1,...,x_n) \varepsilon T$$

provided that $t_i \varepsilon \tau_i$ resp. T ! in the environment $x_1 \varepsilon \tau_1,...,x_n \varepsilon \tau_n(x_1,...,x_{n-1})$.
Clearly T! should imply ET, and some other axioms have to be adjoined.
This looks very much like LF [Haeper-Honsell-Plotkin 87] cut down to algebra.

The approach is attractive syntactically (not least because of the obvious generalization to use types as arguments for type constructors). However, models then have (defined) *types* (i.e. elements of sort TYPE) which are not generated from other data via type constructors unlike to the approach pursued in section 5 and 6. One might wonder about the relative advantages or disadvantages. Definitely, we loose the possibility to simulate heterogenuity via types and a disjointness axiom (as the forgetful functors do not "forget definedness"; where specification morphisms canonically preserve the sort TYPE and the element type : TYPE) which, in a sense, implies that we are, in a sense, less expressive than essentially algebraic theories [Freyd 72] (resp. all the equivalent incarnations). One might recover the expressiveness via a data constraint expressing that types are generated though the theory then is less lucid. The relative merits need some investigation from a practical point of view which will be the yardstick ultimately.

10. Outlook

The previous two section suggests a direction of future research as far as error specification is concerned, namely to establish all the properties advocated for in our introductory sections. The most exciting area, however, should be to see the impact of our formalism on rewriting techniques. I believe that there should be some advantages in the separation of equality and type checking but I am not specialist enough to pinpoint the problems. Another task is to find efficient type checking mechanism.

Another lines of thought is to enrich the sort structure with "products" and "function spaces" (e.g. [Poigné 86b]) with some reflection of this structure on the type level. The result should be closely related to Martin-Löf's type theory with quantifications being available as dependant "products" and "function spaces". Clearly, there is scope to go further.

Acknowledgement I thank all referees, especially Eugenio Moggi, for their very helpful comments which hopefully led to an improvement of an error-prone first draft.

References

[ADJ 78] J.A.Goguen, J.W.Thatcher, E.G.Wagner, J.B.Wright, A Uniform Approach to Inductive Posets and Inductive Closure, Proc. MFCS'77, LNCS 53, 1977, and TCS 7, 1978

[Benecke-Reichel 83] K.Benecke, H.Reichel, Equational Partiality, Algebra Universalis 16, 1983

[Broy-Wirsing 82] M.Broy, M.Wirsing, Partial Abstract Data Types, Acta Informatica 18, 1982

[Broy 86] M.Broy, Partial Interpretation of Higher Order Algebraic Types, Int. Summer School, Marktoberdorf, 1986

[Burmeister 82] P.Burmeister, Partial Algebras - Survey of a Unifying Approach towards a Two-Valued Model Theory for Partial Algebras, Algebra Universalis 15, 1982

[Burmeister 86] P.Burmeister, A Model Theoretic Oriented Approach to Partial Algebras, Akademie Verlag, Berlin 1986

[Cartmell 78] J.Cartmell, Generalised algebraic Theories and Contextual Categories, PhD thesis, Oxford, Short version: Annals Pure Appl. Logic 32, 1986

[Coquand 83] Th.Coquand, Une Théorie des Constructions, Thèse 3ème Cycle, Paris 1985

[Coste 76] M.Coste, Une Approche Logique des Théories Definissable par Limites Projectives Finies, Manuscript 1976

[EKTWW 84] H.Ehrig, H.-J.Kreowski, J.W.Thatcher, E.G.Wagner, J.B.Wright, Parameter Passing in Algebraic Specification Language, TCS 33, 1984

[Fourman-Scott 77] Sheaves and Logic, In: Applications of Sheaves, Proc. Durham, LNiMath 753, 1979

[Freyd 72] P.Freyd, Aspects of Topoi, Bull. Austral. Math. Soc. 7, 1972

[Futatsugi-Goguen-Jouannaud-Meseguer 85] K.Futatsugi, J.A.Goguen, J.P.Jouannaud, J.Meseguer, Principles of OBJ2, CLSI Rep. No. 85-22, Stanford University, 1985

[Gabriel-Ulmer 71] P.Gabriel, F.Ulmer, Lokal präsentierbare Kategorien, LNiMath 221, 1971

[Gogolla 83] M.Gogolla, Algebraic Specifications with Subsorts and Declarations, FB Nr. 169, Abt.Informatik, Universität Dortmund, 1983, also: Proceedings CAAP'84, Cambridge University Press, 1984

[Gogolla 86] M.Gogolla, Über partiell geordnete Sortenmengen und deren Anwendung zur Fehlerbehandlung in Abstrakten Datentypen, Dissertation, Braunschweig 1986

[Goguen 77] J.A.Goguen, Abstract Errors for Abstract Data Types, IFIP Working Conf. on Formal description of Programming Concepts, MIT, 1977

[Goguen 78] J.A.Goguen, Order Sorted Algebras, UCLA Comp. Sci. Dept., Semantics and Theory of Comp. Rep. 14, 1978

[Goguen-Jouannaud-Meseguer 85] J.A.Goguen, J.-P.Jouannaud,J.Meseguer, Operational Semantics for Order Sorted Algebras, ICALP'85,LNCS , 1985

Goguen-Meseguer 85] J.A.Goguen, J.Meseguer, Order-Sorted Algebra: Partial and Overloaded Operations, Errors and Inheritance, SRI International, Computer Science Lab, to appear

[Grätzer 78] G.Grätzer, Universal Algebra, Princeton 1978

[Harper-Honsell-Plotkin 87] R.Harper, F.Honsell, g.Plotkin, A Ramework for defining Logics, proc. LICS87

[Howard 68,80] W.A.Howard, The Formulae-as-Types Notion of Construction, In: To H.B.Curry: Essays on Combinatory Logic, Lambda-Calculus and Formalism, ed. J.P.Seldin and J.R.Hindley, Academic Press 1980

[Johnstone 77] P.T.Johnstone, Topos Theory, Cambridge University Press 1977

[Manes 74] E.G.Manes, *Algebraic Theories*, Springer 1974

[Poigné 84] A.Poigné, Another Look at Parameterization Using Algebraic Specifications with Subsorts, Proc. MFCS, LNCS 176, 1984

[Poigné 85] A.Poigné, Error Handling for Parameterized Data Types, Proc.3rd Workshop on Abstract Data Types, Bremen 1984, GI-Fachbericht 116, 1985

[Poigné 86a] A.Poigné, Algebra Categorically (Tutorial), Workshop on Category and Computer Programming, Guildford 1985, LNCS240, 1986

[Poigné 86b] A.Poigné, On Specifications, Theories, and Models with Higher Types, Inf.&Contr. Vol. 68, 1986

[Poigné 87] A.Poigné, Modularization Techniques for Specifications with Subsorts, manuscript 1984, To appear JCSS

[Reichel 84] H.Reichel, Structural Induction on Partial Algebras, Akademie Verlag, Berlin 1984

[Schmidt 87] H.W.Schmidt, Specification and Correct Implementation of Non-Sequential Systems Combining Abstract Data Types and Petri Nets, submitted as PhD thesis, 1987

[Scott 77] D.S.Scott, Identity and Existence in Intutionistic Logic, In: Applications of Sheaves, Proc. Durham, LNiMath 753, 1979

[Smolka 86] G.Smolka, Order-Sorted Horn Logic Semantics and Deduction, SEKI-Rep. SR-86-17, Universität Kaiserslautern 1986

[Wadge 82] W.W.Wadge, Classified Algebras, Theory of Comp. Rep. 46, Univ. of Warwick, 1982

OPERATIONAL SEMANTICS OF BEHAVIOURAL CANONS BASED ON NARROWING

Horst Reichel
Informatik-Zentrum, TU Dresden
Mommsenstrasse 13
Dresden, DDR-8027
German Democratic Republic

1. Introduction

The paper deals with problems which are caused by partiality on the one hand and by behavioural semantics on the other hand.

At the moment we are not able to present a comprehensive solution of the problems raised by partiality. As a first step we give a generalization of Hussmann's Conditional Narrowing Algorithm to the case of equationally partial algebras. A straightforward generalization leads to a rather inefficient operational semantics, since one has to prove at each step again by narrowing that the terms produced by a most general unifier can be evaluated (or executed). In this way there comes into narrowing a second recursion. A further reason for inefficiency is the fact that conditional equations may express both definedness requirements on partial operations and interrelations between composed applications of the fundamental operations. We suggest in this paper a way to overcome this last problem by declaring explicit domain equations for each operation and by restricting to normalized conditional equations which are incapable of expressing definedness requirements.

We have not yet compared the resulting operational semantics with those approaches where partial algebras are transformed into total algebras by the means of ok-predicates, see for instance [GM 86] and [GDLH 84].

Behavioural semantics can improve the efficiency of operational semantics based on narrowing if one agrees that it is only of interest to evaluate those terms that produce values of visible sorts, and that one only wants to search for solutions of those term equations where both lefthand side and righthand side produce visible values. In the case that a produced solution is of hidden (non-observable) sort, in the approach used in this paper, one obtains a state that incorporates a description of how it has was created and has developed since creation.

2. Basic Concepts

In the following we give a sketch of the concepts and notions used. An extended presentation of behavioural canons can be found in [Rei 86].

We start with an example which specifies the set of finite and co-finite (being the complement of a finite subset) subsets of a parametric set of elements, where the parametric set of elements is assumed to be typed and types are elements of a second parametric set. It will be allowed to put together only elements of equal types.

The behavioural specification EXAMPLE assumes as predefined the specification BOOL of truth values and truth functions where truth values are specified as observable values. In the first part, between <u>with requirement</u> and <u>with definition</u> , it is specified that there are given two sets of observable values. The parametric set represented by the sort name 'elem' represents the typed universe of elements and the sort name 'types' represents the parametric set of types. The typing of the elements is represented by the operation TYPE and additionally it is required that for both parametric sets equality predicates are given.

Following the key word <u>with definition</u> the behavioural specification of the set of finite and cofinite subsets is given. The sort name 'sets' is declared as a state sort which means that the elements of that sort are not observable. Objects of sort 'sets' can be observed only by the membership relation and by the second typing operation which associates with each finite and cofinite subset the type of its elements. It is assumed that for each type t there is an empty set O(t) and a universal set 1(t) representing the universe of all elements of type t. Since objects of sort 'sets' can be observed by the membership relation and by the typing operation, the empty sets O(t1), O(t2) behave differently if T-EQ(t1,t2)=FALSE.

Beside the third unary constructor {_}, representing the construction of singletons, we use symmetric difference $s1+s2 = (s1 \cup s2)-(s1 \cap s2)$ as the final constructor. However, the requirement that only elements of equal types can be put together makes symmetric difference a partial constructor. This partial constructor has a necessary and sufficient domain condition which is the term equation TYPE(s1) = TYPE(s2) given as an optional part of the declaration. If the declaration of an operation does not contain a domain equation, then this makes the corresponding operation a total one.

The following example is a modification of a specification in [GM 86].

EXAMPLE <u>is</u> BOOL <u>with requirement</u>

```
I/O-sorts types, elem
op         T-EQ:types,types ---> bool
           E-EQ:elem,elem ---> bool
           TYPE:elem ---> types
axioms  t,t1,t2: types; x,x1,x2: elem
     T-EQ(t,t) = TRUE;
     if T-EQ(t1,t2) = TRUE then t1 = t2;
     E-EQ(x,x) = TRUE;
     if E-EQ(x1,x2) = TRUE then x1 = x2;       __↓__  T2
with definition
state sorts  sets
op              O:types ---> sets
                1:types ---> sets
              {_}:elem ---> sets
             TYPE:sets ---> types
              _+_:(s1:sets,s2:sets) ---> sets
                   iff TYPE(s1) = TYPE(s2)
              _∈_:elem,sets ---> bool
axioms s,s1,s2,s3: sets; x,y: elem; t: types
     TYPE(O(t)) = t;
     TYPE(1(t)) = t;
     TYPE({x}) = TYPE(x);
     if s = s1+s2 then TYPE(s) = TYPE(s1);
     s + s = O(TYPE(s));
     if s = s1+s2 then s1+s2 = s2+s1;
     if s = s1+(s2+s3) then (s1+s2)+s3 = s1+(s2+s3);
     O(TYPE(s)) + s = s;
     x∈1(t) = T-EQ(TYPE(x),t);
     x∈O(t) = FALSE;
     x∈{y} = E-EQ(x,y) & T-EQ(TYPE(x),TYPE(y));
     if x∈s1 = TRUE, x∈s2 = FALSE, s = s1+s2
               then x∈s = TRUE;
     if x∈s1 = TRUE, x∈s2 = TRUE, s = s1+s2
               then x∈s = FALSE;
     if x∈s1 = FALSE, x∈s2 = FALSE, s = s1+s2
               then x∈s = FALSE;
end
```

On the formal level X,X1,...,Y,Y1,... will denote sets of variables such that each variable is of the form 'x:s' where 's' denotes a sort name. As a starting point for behavioural semantics we use two kinds of sort names. I/O-sorts represent ordinary value types. State sorts represent object types where each object has internal states and the operations on objects are used to modify the internal states or to evaluate objects in order to obtain values. In the preceding example the membership relation and the typing function are the only operations to obtain values from an object of sort 'sets'.

Mathematically we deal with partial, many-sorted algebras, SIG-algebras for short, where

SIG = (SORT,OP,I/O-SORT)

denotes a *signature* consisting of a finite set SORT of sort names together with a distinguished subset I/O-SORT, and of a finite set OP of operation names, where each element of OP is of the form
op: w ---> s, $w \in SORT^*$, $s \in SORT$.

A partial *SIG-algebra* A consists of a SORT-indexed family of sets A_s, $s \in SORT$, and of an OP-indexed family of partial operations

$$op_A : A_{s1} X \ldots X A_{sn} \text{ --o--> } A_s$$

for op: s1...sn ---> s in OP.

P-ALG(SIG) denotes the class (category) of all partial SIG-algebras, where a *SIG-homomorphism* h: A ---> B, $A,B \in$ P-ALG(SIG), is given by an SORT-indexed family of mappings $h_s : A_s \text{ ---> } B_s$ such that
$(a1,\ldots,an) \in dom(op_A)$ with op: s1...sn ---> s in OP implies

(i) $(h_{s1}(a1),\ldots,h_{sn}(an)) \in dom(op_B)$

(ii) $h_s(op_A(a1,\ldots,an)) = op_B(h_{s1}(a1),\ldots,h_{sn}(an))$.

For any set X of variables T(SIG,X) denotes the total SIG-algebra of SIG-terms with variables of X. An assignment **a**:X ---> A, for A in P-ALG(SIG), is a mapping assigning a value in A_s to x:s of X. A_X denotes the set of all assignments. For any homomorphism h: A ---> B, A,B in P-ALG(SIG), and any set X of variables we set

$$h_X : A_X \text{ ---> } B_X \text{ with } h_X(\mathbf{a})(x{:}s) = h_s(\mathbf{a}(x{:}s)).$$

Inductively we define the *partial term function*

$$t_A : A_X \text{ --o--> } A_s$$

for $A \in$ P-ALG(SIG), $t \in T(SIG,X)_s$, $s \in SORT$, where
$\mathbf{a} \in dom(op(t1,\ldots tn))$ iff $\mathbf{a} \in dom(ti_A)$ for $i=1,\ldots,n$ and
$(t1_A(\mathbf{a}),\ldots,tn_A(\mathbf{a})) \in dom(op_A)$.

If X is any set of variables and x:s in X, then X-{x:s} denotes the set of variables resulting from X by removing the indicated variable.
If $\mathbf{m} \in M_{X-\{x:s\}}$ and $m \in M_s$ then $\mathbf{m}+(x=m) \in M_X$ denotes the extended assignment.
For a finite set of variables Y, for a variable y:s1 in Y, for an element $a \in A_{s1}$ and for a term $t \in T(SIG,X)_{s2}$ we define the *partial derived polynomial function*

$$t_{A,y=a} : A_{Y-\{y:s1\}} \text{ --o--> } A_{s2}$$

by setting $\mathbf{a} \in dom(t_{A,y=a})$ iff $\mathbf{a}+(y=a) \in dom(t_A)$ and by setting
$t_{A,y=a}(\mathbf{a}) = t_A(\mathbf{a}+(y=a))$.

Based on this definition we can define *behavioural equivalence of elements* $a1, a2 \in A_{s1}$, $s1 \in SORT$, in symbols

$$a1 \equiv a2 \bmod I/O\text{-}SORT,$$

as follows:

$a1 \equiv a2 \bmod I/O\text{-}SORT$ iff for each term $t \in T(SIG,X)_{s2}$ such that X is finite, $x{:}s1 \in X$, and $s2 \in I/O\text{-}SORT$ the partial derived polynomial functions $t_{A,x=a1}$ and $t_{A,x=a2}$ are equal, i.e., if $dom(t_{A,x=a1}) = dom(t_{A,x=a2})$ and $t_{A,x=a1}(a) = t_{A,x=a2}(a)$ if both sides are defined and $a \in A_{X-\{x:s1\}}$.

In the following a term $t \in T(SIG,X)_s$ is called an *output term* if X is finite and $s \in I/O\text{-}SORT$. The distinguished subset I/O-SORT will be abbreviated by 'I' in the following.

For any set Y of variables we define an *equivalence modulo I*, denoted by

$$Y.\ l=r \bmod I,$$

with $l,r \in T(SIG,Y)_s$ for some $s \in SORT$. For any $A \in P\text{-}ALG(SIG)$ we define

$$A_{Y.l=r \bmod I} = \{ a \in A_Y \mid a \in dom(l_A) \cap dom(r_A)\ \&\ l_A(a) \equiv r_A(a) \bmod I \}.$$

A *conditional equivalence modulo I* is of the form

$$Y.\ l1=r1\&\ldots\&ln=rn \dashrightarrow l=r \bmod I$$

with $li,ri \in T(SIG,Y)_{si}$, $i=1,\ldots,n$, $l,r \in T(SIG,Y)_s$. It is called *proper* if $si \in I$ for $i=1,\ldots,n$. It is satisfied by $A \in P\text{-}ALG(SIG)$, in symbols

$$A \models Y.\ l1=r1\&\ldots\&ln=rn \dashrightarrow l=r \bmod I,$$

iff

$$A_{Y.\ l1=r1\&\ldots\&ln=rn \bmod I} = A_{Y.\ l=r \bmod I}$$

where

$$A_{Y.l1=r1,\ldots,ln=rn} = \begin{cases} \bigcap \{A_{Y.li=ri \bmod I} \mid i \in \{1,\ldots,n\}\} & \\ A_Y \ (= A_{Y.\emptyset}) & \text{if } n = 0. \end{cases}$$

(SIG,AX mod I) will be called a *behavioural theory*, if AX mod I is a finite set of conditional equivalences modulo I = SORT(SIG).

Behavioural equivalence and model classes of proper conditional equivalences have been studied in [Rei 85]. In [Wol 87] it is proved that conditional equivalences are a generalization of conditional equations, since there are model classes of finite sets of conditonal equivalences which can not be finitely axiomatized by conditional equations.

For a better understanding we summarize some results from [Rei 85]:

B1: The behavioural equivalence modulo I is an equivalence relation over each carrier set A_s, s ∈ SORT.

B2: For a1,a2 ∈ A_s where s is an I/O-sort a1 ≡ a2 mod I holds if and only if a1 = a2.

B3: The corresponding notion of *behaviourally equivalent algebras* can be defined by special homomorphisms, called *I-reductions*, r:A ---> B being surjective in each sort, injective in each I/O-sort, preserving and reflecting definedness. One defines

A ≡ B mod I

if there are I-reductions f: A ---> C, g: B ---> C, i.e., if A and B can be reduced to a common algebra by means of I-reductions.

B4: If P-ALG(SIG,AXmodI) denotes the class of all SIG-algebras which satisfy each proper conditional equivalence modulo I in AX mod I, then one can prove that P-ALG(SIG,AXmodI) has an initial algebra and that forgetful functors have left adjoint functors.

F:(SIG1,AX1modI1) ---> (SIG2,AX2modI2) is called a *theory morphism*, if F: SIG1 ---> SIG2 is a signature morphism such that

(a) $F_{SORT}(I1) \subseteq I2$ and

(b) A ∈ P-ALG(SIG2,AX2modI2), ceq ∈ AX1 mod I1 implies A |= F(ceq) mod I2.

For any theory morphism

_↓F: P-ALG(SIG2,AX2modI2) ---> P-ALG(SIG1,AX1modI1)

denotes the induced *forgetful functor* and

_↑F: P-ALG(SIG1,AX1modI1) ---> P-ALG(SG2,AX2modI2)

denotes the *left adjoint functor* of the forgetful functor (free construction). If the theory morphism represents an inclusion T1 ⊆ T2 we will also use the notions _↓T1 and _↑T2 respectively.

The last concept is that of an *initial restriction of behaviour* in a behavioural theory T being an ordered pair

(T2, F: T1 ---> T)

which consists of a theory morphism F: T1 ---> T and of a subtheory T2 ⊆ T1. For each A ∈ P-ALG(T) we set

A |= (T2, F: T1 --->T)

if

(c) ((A↓F)↓T2)↑T1 is an extension of (A↓F)↓T2, i.e., if (((A↓F)↓T2)↑T1)↓T2 = (A↓F)↑T2 and

(d) The unique extension of $id_{(A↓F)↓T2}$ to a T1-homomorphism f: ((A↓F)↓T2)↑T1 ---> A↓F yields a reduction of behaviour.

Finally, a *behavioural canon*

BC = (SIG,AXmodI,RES)

consists of a signature SIG with a distinguished subset $I \subseteq SORT$ of I/O-sorts, a finite set AX mod I of proper conditional equivalences modulo I, and a finite set RES of initial restrictions of behaviour in (SIG,AXmodI).

In the behavioural specification EXAMPLE the following two initial restric-tions of behaviour are described:

{(∅,incl: T1 --->t), (T2, id: T ---> T)}

where T1 denotes the theory which corresponds to the specification BOOL of the truth values, and T2 denotes the theory which is given by the sorts, operation symbols and axioms declared up to the key word <u>with definition</u> (also indicated by an arrow ↓). The first initial restriction of behaviour, not explicitly written, defines the value type of truth values, and the second initial restriction of behaviour defines the intended object type of typed finite and cofinite subsets of the parametric set of typed elements.

If we define an algebra A by

A_{bool} = {TRUE,FALSE}, A_{types} , A_{elem} arbitrary sets,

A_{sets} = set of all set-sorted terms built up using the elements of A_{types} and A_{elem} as variables,

$E\text{-}EQ_A$ = equality in A_{elem} , $T\text{-}EQ_A$ = equality in A_{types} ,

$TYPE_A$ = arbitrary typing function,

then A satisfies all conditional equivalences and the two initial restrictions of behaviour, and so A represents a model of the behavioural specification. Note that A would not be a model if we had used ordinary validity instead of behavioural validity, or if the sort name ´sets´ had been declared as an I/O-sort.

If B is an algebra with A↓T2 = B↓T2 that satisfies the axioms identically, i.e. with respect to ordinary validity of conditional equations, then there is a reduction r: A ---> B and so B represents another model of the behavioural specification which is certainly not isomorphic to A .

The intended algebra C is given by C↓T2 = A↓T2 and

C_{sets} = set of all typed finite and cofinite subsets of C_{elem} ,

$1_C(t) = \{x \in C_{elem} \mid TYPE_C(x) = t\}$,

$0_C(t) = (\emptyset, t)$, $\{m\}_C = \{m\}$,

$s1 +_C s2$ is defined if and only if all elements of s1 and s2 are of the same type and then $s1 +_C s2 = (s1 \cup s2) - (s1 \cap s2)$ holds.

The algebra C gives a third model of the behavioural specification which is not isomorphic to B in the case where C_{elem} is a finite set.

In the model C any two behaviourally equivalent elements are equal, so C represents a model of minimal redundancy, whereas the model A is a model of maximal redundancy within the same class of pairwise behaviourally equivalent algebras.

3. Conditional Narrowing

In [Rei 87b] the Conditional Rewriting Calculus of Hussmann [Hus 85] has been extended from total many-sorted algebras to partial many-sorted algebras and we will therefore omit this topic here.

In the following we will discuss only the generalization of the Conditional Narrowing Algorithm of Hussmann [Hus 85]. As we will see in the following section it is sufficient to deal with ordinary conditional equations and algebras which identically satisfy these conditional equations. As mentioned above, identical satisfaction is the ordinary satisfaction concept and it is defined analoguously to behavioural satisfaction except that behavioural equivalence of elements is substituted by identity. But, due to result B2, see above, behavioural satisfaction of conditional equivalences coincides with identical satisfaction of conditional equations if all sorts dealt with are I/O-sorts. Using behavioural satisfaction is suggested by the concept of *institutions* introduced in [GB 84], where the validity relation is one of the parameters of an institution.

We are aware that our notion of behavioural satisfaction is not the only one that can be thought up and that can be used in behavioural semantics. Roughly speaking, one can say that our concept of behavioural satisfaction with the corresponding concept of behaviourally equivalent algebras yields the smallest classes of behaviourally equivalent algebras.

The conditional narrowing algorithm of Hussmann starts with a goal of the form

X.G <u>with</u> id: X ---> T(SIG,X)

and tries to derive a subgoal

Y.S <u>with</u> sub: X ---> T(SIG,Y)

until a final form

Z.∅ <u>with</u> sub′: X ---> T(SIG,Z)

is reached.

The substitution sub′: X ---> T(SIG,Z) is called a *computed answer* for X.G , where X.G and Y.S represent finite sets of term equations.

In the case of total algebras there are two derivation rules, the narrowing and the unification rule, and it is sufficient to apply the unification rule only once as the final step.

In the case of partial algebras it becomes necessary to prove for every substitution that all substituted terms and all resulting terms are executable. Difficulties arise from the fact that the most general unifier of two terms may be a substitution that produces non-executable terms although there is a unifier of the given two terms which produces executable terms. The executability of a term t is expressed in our approach by a so-called *existence equation* of the form Y.t=t . To prove the executability of t one can use a third derivation rule which reduces an existence equation Y.t=t to a possibly empty set of equations by using an axiom Z.H ---> l=r if t can be unified with a subterm of l or of r.

The generalization of the conditional narrowing algorithm to partial algebras becomes an iteration of the following three derivation rules:

I. Modified Narrowing:

```
Y.S with sub: X ---> T(SIG,Y)
------------------------------------------------------------
Z.(sub'(H) ∪ sub'(S[u<-r]) ∪ {sub'(y)=sub'(y) | y ∈ Y}
            with sub sub': X ---> T(SIG,Z)
```

where (Y'.H ---> l=r) ∈ AX, u ∈ O(S) is an occurrence in S, S/u is not a variable and sub': Y ---> T(SIG,Z) is the most general unifier of S/u and l .

II. Modified Unification:

```
Y.S with sub: X ---> T(SIG,Y)
------------------------------------------------------------
Z.(sub'(S) ∪ {sub'(x)=sub'(x) | x ∈ X & sub'(x) ∉ Z}
            with sub sub': X ---> T(SIG,Z)
```

where sub': Y ---> T(SIG,Z) is the most general unifier of Y.S.

III. Reduction:

```
Y.S with sub: X ---> T(SIG,Y)
------------------------------------------------------------
Z.(sub'(S') ∪ sub'(H)) with sub sub': X ---> T(SIG,Z)
```

where (Y'.H ---> l=r) ∈ AX, (Y.t=t) ∈ S, S' = S - {Y.t=t}, sub': Y ---> T(SIG,Z) is the most general unifier of t with a subterm of l or of r .

Since each conditional equation may cause definedness requirements, each axiom has to be checked or has to be used for proving that some term t is executable. From an abstract point of view, a calculus which uses only conditional equations for defining the domains of the fundamental partial operations is the most concise one. But the narrowing algorithm based on that calculus, described above, has a rather inefficient operational semantics. The inefficiency is caused by the twofold use of conditional equations. Firstly they are used to define the domains of the fundamental operations and secondly they are used to express the interrelations between the fundamental operations. In the case of total algebras, equations and conditional equations are only used for the second aim.

In the example above we have used domain equations as part of the declaration of operation symbols. If each declaration of an operation symbol contains a possibly empty set of equations as necessary and sufficient domain equations, one can modify the conditional equations in such a way that no additional definedness requirements arise. In general it is recursively undecidable whether a given conditional equation causes additional definedness requirements with respect to a given set of conditional equations.

Let 'def(op)' denote the set of necessary and sufficient domain equations of the operation symbol op ∈ OP, which is part of its declaration. Then one can inductively define X.def(t), for each term t ∈ T(SIG,X), the set of necessary and sufficient domain conditions of the term t . For the beginning of the inductive definition we define that each variable, considered as a term, has an empty set of domain equations. For more details see [Rei 87]. Now we allow as axioms only those conditional equations for which the premise consists at least of def(l) U def(r) , where l=r is the conclusion of the conditional equation. Conditional equations of this kind will be called *'normalized'*. Restricting axioms to normalized conditional equations one can agree upon the convention that def(l) and def(r) as part of the premise will have no explicit textual representation.

Using this convention, the axioms of the defining extension in the example above can be presented as follows:

```
axioms s,s1,s2,s3:sets; x,y:elem; t:types
    TYPE(0(t)) = t;
    TYPE(1(t)) = t;
    TYPE({x}) = TYPE(x);
    TYPE(s1+s2) = TYPE(s1);
    s + s = 0(TYPE(s));
    s1 + s2 = s2 + s1;
    (s1 + s2) + s3 = s1 + (s2 + s3);
    0(t) + s = s;
    x∈1(t) = T-EQ(TYPE(x),t);
```

```
    x∈0(t) = FALSE;
    x∈{y} = E-EQ(x,y) & T-EQ(TYPE(x),TYPE(y));
    if x∈s1 = TRUE, x∈s2 = FALSE then x∈s1+s2 = FALSE;
    if x∈s1 = TRUE, x∈s2 = TRUE then x∈s1+s2 = FALSE;
    if x∈s1 = FALSE, x∈s2 = FALSE then x∈s1+s2 = FALSE;
end
```

The restriction of specifications in the described way has a positive effect on the operational semantics, since the reduction rule is no longer necessary. If one uses the following version of the modified narrowing and unification rule, no equation of the form Z.t=t will arise in the derivation process, except when such an equation is contained in an axiom or in the domain equations of one of the operation symbols.

I* Modified Narrowing:

Y.S __with__ sub: X ---> T(SIG,Y)
____

Z.(sub′(H) U sub′(S[u<-r]) U {def(sub′(y)) | y ∈ Y }
__with__ sub sub′: X ---> T(SIG,Z)

II* Modified Unification:

Y.S __with__ sub: X ---> T(SIG,Y)
____

Z.(def(sub′(S))) __with__ sub sub′: X ---> T(SIG,Z).

It is worth mentioning that the restriction to specifications with explicit domain equations as part of the declarations of operation symbols and with normalized conditional equations does not restrict the expressiveness of specifications. However, as one can see in the specification of the ′while statement′, see [Rei 87], the use of explicit domain equations may cause the introduction of additional operations, since an operation symbol cannot be used for the definition of its own domain condition.

The correctness and completeness result of Hussmann can be generalized to the case of partial algebras.

__Theorem__ (Hussmann 1985):
Let AX represent a confluent system of conditional equations and Y.S a system of equations.

(1) If sub is a computed answer for Y.S then sub is an AX-unifier of Y.S .
(2) If a normalized substitution sub is an AX-unifier of Y.S, then there is a computed answer sub′ for Y.S and a substitution sub″ such that sub = sub′ sub″.

A detailed proof of the generalized correctness and completeness theorem is given in [Wol 88]. The author wants to acknowledge U.Wolter for pointing out an error in a previous version of the generalization of the conditional narrowing algorithm.

4. Conditional Narrowing and Behavioural Semantics

In the case of initial or final semantics the meaning of an algebraic specification is an isomorphism class of SIG-algebras, so that in both cases a uniquely determined congruence relation on the term algebra represents the corresponding semantics. This unique congruence relation is described by the operational semantics. In the case of behavioural semantics the meaning is in general not an isomorphism class, see for instance the example above. Now one can make a choice among a set of possible congruence relations. In the following we suggest that by the operational semantics the model of maximal redundancy should be represented, since this model corresponds to the minimal congruence on the term algebra.

To see the advantages of this choice we give first a description of the model of maximal redundancy.

Let A Xmod I be any finite set of normalized conditional equivalences and let X.G mod I be any set of equivalences. Then we define a set $AX_I(X.G)$
of equations (notice, not a set of equivalences!) as follows:

$AX_I(X.G)$ = { X.l=r ¦ X.l=r can be derived from X.G by the use of axioms of AX and either l equals r or both l and r produce values of a sort contained in I }.

In [Rei 85] it was proved that a SIG-algebra F which is freely generated by $AX_I(X.G)$ in the class of all SIG-algebras is an algebra freely generated by the set X.G mod I of equivalences modulo I in the class P-ALG(SIG,AXmodI).

Behavioural satisfaction of conditional equivalences modulo I does not necessarily imply the identification of elements, i.e.

M ¦= X. l1=r1&...&ln=rn ---> l=r mod I

with $l,r \in T(SIG,X)_s$, $s \notin I$, does not require the identity of $l_M(m)$ with $r_M(m)$ for an assignment $m \in M_X$ which is a solution of the premise. This fact implies that in a model F which is freely generated in P-ALG(SIG,AXmodI) terms that represent internal states will not be identified. Since on the other hand behavioural equivalence of elements in carriers of I/O-sorts coincides with identity one obtains that in a model $F \in$ P-ALG(SIG,AXmodI) which is freely generated by a set X of generators and by a set X.G of defining relations, which formally means freely generated by X.G mod I, the internal states can be represented by *I-pruned* terms, where a term is called I-pruned if all subterms pro-ducing values in a carrier of a sort in I are either constants or variables.

An operational semantics that realizes calculation in the model of maximal redundancy is obtained, if one uses the following *restricted application of the narrowing step*:

An axiom $(Y'.H \dashrightarrow l=r) \in AXmodI$ with $l,r \in T(SIG,Y')_s$, $s \notin I$ can be applied only if l can be unified with a subterm inside an I-subterm of Y.S , i.e. if $u \in O(S)$ is an occurrence inside a subterm t in Y.S which produces a value of a sort in I .

The unrestricted application of the narrowing step defines an operational semantics that realizes calculation in the model which is freely generated with respect to identical satisfaction of the axioms and defining relations. Since both these models are behaviourally equivalent this operational semantics would also be correct. But the operational semantics defined by the restricted application minimizes the number of applications of the narrowing step and so makes the operational semantics more efficient.

REFERENCES:

[GDLH 84] Gogolla,M., Drosten,K., Lipeck,U., Ehrich,H.-D.: Algebraic and Operational Semantics of Specifications Allowing Exceptions and Errors. TCS 34(3),1984

[GB 84] Goguen,J.A., Burstall,R.M.:Introducing Institutions, Proc. Logics of Programming Workshop (E.Clarke, D.Kozen,eds.) Carnegie-Mellon University, Springer LNCS 164,221-256,1984

[GM 86] Goguen,J.A., Meseguer,J.: EQLOG: Equality, Types, and Generic Modules for Logic Programming. In: DeGroot,D., Lindstrom,G.(eds.), Logic Programming, Prentice-Hall, 1986

[Hus 85] Hussmann,H.: Unification in conditional-equational theories. MIP-8502, University of Passau, 1985

[Rei 85] Reichel,H.: Behavioural validity of conditional equations in abstract data types. In: Contributions to General Algebra 3, Proc. Vienna Conf., June 1984, Verlag Hoelder - Pichler - Tempsky, Wien,1985

[Rei 86] Reichel,H.: Behavioural Program Specification. In: Category Theory and Computer Programming, Pitt,D. et al (eds), LNCS 240, Springer-Verlag, Berlin Heidelberg, 1986

[Rei 87] Reichel,H.: Initial Computability, Algebraic Specifications, and Partial Algebras. Oxford Science Publication, Clarendon Press, Oxford 1987

[Rei 87b] Reichel,H.: Narrowing in Partial Algebras. In: Proc. EUROCAL'87, Leipzig, June 1987 (to appear)

[Wol 87] Wolter,U.: The Power of Behavioural Validity, Preprint MATH 1/87, June 1987, Sektion Mathematik, TU Magdeburg

[Wol 88] Wolter,U.: Ein algebraischer Zugang zur operationalen Semantik gleichungs-partieller Horn-Theorien. Dissertation TU Magdeburg, 1988

The Algebraic Specification of Semicomputable Data Types

J.L.M. Vrancken

Programming Research Group, University of Amsterdam,
Aten Laboratorium, Kruislaan 409 , 1098 SJ Amsterdam.

Abstract : A proof is given for a theorem stating that every semicomputable data type can be specified with only one hidden sort. Preceding this, definitions for the notions signature and algebra are given in the setting of category theory and the notion of a (semi-)computable algebra is discussed.

1. Introduction.

The notion of a (semi-)computable algebra was introduced by Rabin and Mal'cev in the early sixties. A (semi-)computable algebra A can be written as the surjective image of a number algebra in which the functions are recursive and the inverse image of the equality relations on the sorts of A are recursive (or recursively enumerable). In computer science many-sorted algebras are used as a means to model data types and ever since the early seventies the question has been studied how to specify algebras by means of equations. The question which algebras allow specification by equations, can be answered to a certain extent by referring to the computability properties of an algebra. It soon turns out that even very simple algebras can not be specified right away but need the use of extra (hidden) functions or even extra (hidden) sorts. For instance the algebra of the natural numbers with zero, successor and squaring can only be specified by adding extra functions, addition and multiplication being the obvious candidates (see [BT1]).

In a series of papers (for instance [BT1 - BT3]) Bergstra and Tucker studied from a theoretical point of view, the subject of algebraic specifications with emphasis on recursion theoretic aspects. In [BT1] a theorem was given for the specifiability of semicomputable algebras, but the proof was only for single-sorted algebras. (Some reading in [BT1] is highly recommended before studying the present paper). The purpose of this paper is to supply a proof for the general case. In order to do so, we considered it useful to give sharper definitions for notions like signature and algebra (in [BT1] these notions are not made sufficiently precise) and to discuss the notion of a (semi-) computable algebra.

Concerning the notions of signature and algebra, we might have adopted the usual definitions, given for instance in [MG] or, with a slight change, in [EM]. They do not however give the required notions and operations in a readily accessible form. Therefore we have decided to supply our own definitions within this paper.

It is a well-known open problem whether every semicomputable algebra can be specified with a finite number of equations and no hidden sorts (hidden functions are sometimes necessary). In section 4 we will show that in any case at most one hidden sort (for the natural numbers of course) is needed.

Acknowledgements.
We express our gratitude for useful comments to Jan Bergstra, Karst Koymans, several anonymous referees and especially to Piet Rodenburg who carefully read the previous version.

2. Signatures and Algebras.

2.1 In [BT1] a proof is given for a theorem about the specifiability of semicomputable single-sorted algebras, notational complications being mentioned as the main hurdle for a proof for many-sorted algebras. In our view however, the real problem is that the definitions they are using for the basic notions like signature and algebra are not sufficiently precise. In this section, we will supply definitions that are sharp enough to give a proof for the many-sorted case. The natural setting for this treatment is of course category theory. We will be using the terminology of [MacL].

Sections 3 and 4 are also readable with other definitions in mind. Maybe the following notions deserve some attention :

- the composition operator as used in this paper (2.2);
- opposite algebra morphisms (2.3);
- unions of signatures or algebras with overlap (2.5).

2.2 Intuitively, a signature may be seen as an object that contains a set of sort names, a set of function names and a type function which assigns to each function name its origin sorts and its image sort. The specific character of the elements of these two sets is irrelevant. This is expressed by defining a category **Sig** of signatures with morphisms as given below and the requirement that any operation on signatures must be categorical. This means that the same operation on isomorphic signatures must yield equal or isomorphical results. One may check, with the definition below, that for instance determining the number of sorts is a categorical operation whereas taking the set theoretic intersection of the sets of sort names and of function names is not.

We will be using the word *object* also in the general sense (for instance in the definition below), not only in the specific category theoretic sense.

<u>Definition</u> A **signature** Σ is a compound object that contains

a set Σ_S (the sort names)

a set Σ_F (the function and constant names)

a function $ty_\Sigma : \Sigma_F \rightarrow (\Sigma_S)^*$ (the type of a function)

$(\Sigma_S)^*$ denotes the set of finite words of elements of Σ_S. For a function name f,the last element of the word $ty_\Sigma(f)$ denotes the image sort, the other elements denote the origin sorts of f. ty_Σ never returns the empty word. Σ_S and Σ_F may be empty. If Σ_S is empty, then Σ_F should also be empty. Two signatures Σ_1 and Σ_2 are equal if the objects of Σ_1 are equal to the corresponding objects of Σ_2.

A **signature morphism** $\sigma : \Sigma_1 \rightarrow \Sigma_2$ is a compound mapping (an object that contains several mappings, to be accessed by means of indices) that contains the mappings

$$\sigma_S : \Sigma_{1S} \rightarrow \Sigma_{2S}$$

$$\sigma_F : \Sigma_{1F} \rightarrow \Sigma_{2F}$$

Moreover it obeys $ty_{\Sigma_2} \circ \sigma = \sigma \circ ty_{\Sigma_1}$ (for o see remark below).

A **signature isomorphism** is a signature morphism which is a bijective compound mapping (each component is bijective). The compound mapping in the other direction is then also a morphism.

The category of signatures and signature morphisms is denoted by **Sig**.

Remark.

- The use of compound mappings together with a powerful composition operator o happens to be very convenient. The operator o chooses the right components from a compound mapping, as required by the context. For instance, the formula $ty_{\Sigma 2} \circ \sigma = \sigma \circ ty_{\Sigma 1}$ should actually read

$$ty_{\Sigma 2} \circ \sigma_F = \sigma_S \circ ty_{\Sigma 1}$$

or even more complicated, as $ty_{\Sigma 1}$ yields a word and not a single element of Σ_{1S}. All this is taken care of by o. On the other hand, the ways in which this operator can be applied may be rather diverse and it is hard to give a general definition. Much of its convenience lies in its being *associative*. In unusual applications, one should check if it is still the case.

2.3 One may define an algebra as a set of universes (or base-sets or domains) and a set of functions and constants having these universes as origin and image sets. This precludes however the possibility to have several copies of the same universe. Moreover the type of the functions of the algebra is not readily accessible. Therefore we will put an explicit signature in our algebras.

Once the notion of an algebra is defined, the algebra morphisms are not problematic. Algebras and algebra morphisms form the category **Alg**. The isomorphism classes of this category are called *abstract data types*. Again, it goes without saying that we are only interested in categorical operations on algebras.

Definition An **algebra** A is an object that contains a signature Σ (or $\Sigma(A)$) and mappings

$S^A : \Sigma_S \rightarrow$ sets (see remark below)

$F^A : \Sigma_F \rightarrow$ functions and constants.

If $f \in \Sigma_F$ then $F^A(f)$ must have a type as given by $ty_\Sigma(f)$. The sets $S^A(s)$ for $s \in \Sigma_S$ are called the *domains* or *universes* or *base sets* of A.

A **(straight) algebra morphism** $\tau : A_1 \rightarrow A_2$ is a compound mapping that contains

- a signature morphism $\tau_{sm} : \Sigma(A_1) \rightarrow \Sigma(A_2)$ whose components, the sort names mapping and the function names mapping, will often be denoted τ_S and τ_F
- for each sort name i of $\Sigma(A_1)$ a *universe mapping*

$$\tau_i : S^{A1}(i) \rightarrow S^{A2}(\tau_S(i))$$

For each function symbol f of $\Sigma(A_1)$ the following morphism property should hold :

$$\tau \circ F^{A1}(f) = F^{A2}(\tau_F(f)) \circ \tau \qquad \text{(see the remark in section 2.2)}$$

An algebra morphism τ is called **signature preserving** if τ_{sm} is an isomorphism. The category of algebras and algebra morphisms is called **Alg**.

An **opposite algebra morphism** $\tau : A_1 \rightarrow A_2$ is a compound mapping that contains

- a signature morphism $\tau_{sm} : \Sigma(A_2) \rightarrow \Sigma(A_1)$ (reversed indices !)
- for each sort name i of $\Sigma(A_2)$ a *universe mapping*

$$\tau_i : S^{A1}(\tau_S(i)) \rightarrow S^{A2}(i)$$

For each function symbol f of $\Sigma(A_2)$ the following morphism property should hold :

$$\tau \circ F^{A1}(\tau_F(f)) = F^{A2}(f) \circ \tau$$

The category of algebras and opposite **Alg** morphisms is called **oppAlg**.

The subcategory of **Alg** consisting of algebras with a given signature Σ is called **Alg**$_\Sigma$.

Remarks.
- If we think of this whole story as being told in the context of Zermelo-Fraenkel set theory, then it is no problem to talk about sets like in

  $$S^A : \Sigma_S \rightarrow \text{sets}$$

  In this context it is also clear what functions (certain special sets) and constants (elements of sets) are.
- The definition may seem somewhat complicated, especially the morphism properties. Let us consider an easy case : algebras A_1 and A_2 have equal signature and the **Alg** morphism

  $$\tau : A_1 \rightarrow A_2$$

  contains the identity morphism as the signature morphism τ_{sm}. Let f be a function name in the signature and let g_1, g_2 be the corresponding functions ($F^{A1}(f)$, $F^{A2}(f)$) in A_1, A_2. Then the difficult equation above becomes the well-known :

  $$\tau \circ g_1 = g_2 \circ \tau$$

  The definition above is just extending this simple case with the possibility that the signatures are not equal but that a morphism is given from one signature into the other. This signature morphism may have the same direction as the whole morphism or it may have the opposite direction (in the opposite algebra morphisms). One should not confuse **oppAlg** with the dual of **Alg**. Only part of an **Alg** morphism is reversed, not the whole morphism.

2.4 We will not give an exhaustive treatment of the properties of the categories **Sig** and **Alg** but restrict ourselves to what is needed in sections 3 and 4. It will be convenient to take the category **Set** (sets and all functions between sets) along in the treatment as a steppingstone to the more complicated situations in **Sig** and **Alg**.

Subsignatures and *subalgebras* can be defined in the usual way : A is a substructure of B if there exists a monomorphism

$$m : A \rightarrow B$$

Monomorphisms (monics) in **Sig** are exactly the injective morphisms (both components injective) and *epimorphisms* (epis) the surjective morphisms.

2.5 How should we formalize the intuitive notion of a *union with overlap* of signatures (or algebras) ? Let us first consider this in **Set**. Given two objects A, B in **Set**, the usual union operation is not categorical, isomorphic images of A and B may have a completely different union. If we want to do this categorically we somehow have to specify the overlap of A and B categorically, for instance with a third set I and monomorphic embeddings i_A, i_B, as shown in figure 1. The union U should have the following properties :
- there are monic embeddings from A and B into U
- the images of I in A and B should coincide in U
- U must be the smallest set with these properties

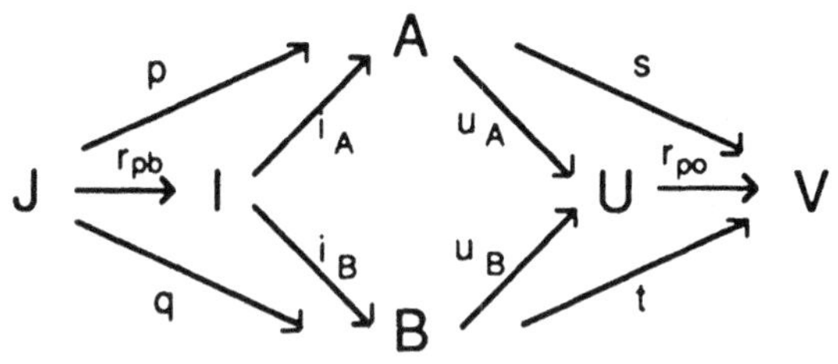

fig. 1

The pushout is an obvious candidate for fulfilling these properties. It can be constructed by taking the disjoint union of A and B and identifying in this set the elements $i_A(z)$ with $i_B(z)$ for each $z \in I$. u_A and u_B are the required monic embeddings. It is easy to show that the diagram IAUB in fig. 1 is a pushout. The mappings u_A and u_B are jointly epi. The universality of the pushout is a way to express that U is the smallest set with the first two properties : for each V with morphisms $s : A \rightarrow V$ and $t : B \rightarrow V$ and $s \circ i_A = t \circ i_B$ there exists a unique $r_{po} : U \rightarrow V$ such that $s = r_{po} \circ u_A$ and $t = r_{po} \circ u_B$.

An analogous story can be told for a categorical *intersection*. The way to specify which elements should coincide may be done by giving a third set U (fig. 1) with embeddings u_A and u_B with the intention that $x \in A$ and $y \in B$ will coincide if $u_A(x) = u_B(y)$. The intersection I should have the properties :

- there are monic embeddings from I into A and B
- the images of I in A and B coincide in U
- I is the largest set with these properties

Now the pullback is the obvious candidate. It exists whenever u_A and u_B are monic. It is easy to show that the required properties hold.

In **Sig** the same story can be told. As a signature consists of two sets (and a type function which does no harm) the constructions and properties follow easily from those in **Set** : given two signatures A and B (fig.1) and a signature I with monic embeddings i_A and i_B then a signature U (the union with overlap) with monic embeddings u_A and u_B exists such that the diagram IAUB is a pushout. The embeddings u_A and u_B are jointly epi. And given two signatures A and B and a signature U with monic embeddings u_A and u_B, then a signature I (the intersection) with monic embeddings i_A and i_B exists such that the diagram IAUB is a pullback.

In **Alg** the story is somewhat more complicated. We restrict ourselves to what is needed in section 4 and will only consider algebra morphisms with *bijective* universe mappings. Then the construction of union and intersection is essentially the same as in **Set**. Again we refer to fig. 1 : given two algebras A and B and an algebra I with monic embeddings i_A and i_B (with bijective universe mappings) then an algebra U (the union with overlap) with monic embeddings u_A and u_B (with bijective universe mappings) exists such that the diagram IAUB is a pushout. The embeddings u_A and u_B are jointly epi. And given two algebras A and B and an algebra U with monic embeddings u_A and u_B (with bijective universe mappings), then an algebra I (the intersection) with monic embeddings i_A and i_B (with bijective universe mappings) exists such that the diagram IAUB is a pullback.

In all these categories, the disjoint union is of course a special case of the general union in which the overlap is empty. In this case one should take for I the empty set, the empty signature and the empty algebra respectively.

2.6 The last construction needed in section 4 is the *restriction of an algebra* to a subsignature of its signature : given an algebra A with signature Σ and a signature Π with monic embedding $\pi : \Pi \rightarrow \Sigma$, we can form the restriction of A to (Π, π), denoted by $A|_{(\Pi,\pi)}$, by removing from the signature Σ all the sort names and function names not in $\pi(\Pi)$ and by removing from the algebra all the universes and functions that have lost their names.
The morphism π may seem superfluous but it is needed in order to make this restriction operation categorical.

3. Computable and Semicomputable Algebras.

3.1 In this section we want to extend a passage in [BT1] section 3 about the nature of the usual definition of computable and semicomputable algebras. Among other things, two skipped proofs in that paper will be written out here and a counter–example supplied. In sections 3 and 4, all signatures are assumed to be finite.

3.2 Definition A **recursive number algebra** is an algebra whose universes are recursive subsets of ω and whose functions are recursive.

A **coordinatization** of an algebra A with signature Σ is an epimorphism $\alpha : C \to A$ where C is a recursive number algebra with the same signature Σ. This coordinatization will also be denoted by (C, α)

A coordinatization is called **minimal** if its number algebra is minimal (each element reachable by a term).

A coordinatization is called **computable, semicomputable or cosemicomputable** if the sets

$$\{ (x, y) \in C_i \mid \alpha_i(x) = \alpha_i(y) \text{ in } A_i \}$$

for each sort name i of Σ, are recursive, r.e. or co-r.e. respectively.

The algebra A is called **computable, semicomputable or cosemicomputable** if it has a computable, semicomputable or cosemicomputable coordinatization respectively.

Remarks

- The notion of a recursive function in the definition above needs some comment as the universe is not necessarily ω. It differs from a partial recursive function in that its universe is recursive and that it is not considered partial. More about this slight extension of the theory of recursive functions can be found in [MG] where such a function is defined as the restriction of a recursive function $\omega \to \omega$ to a recursive subset of ω.
- If $\alpha : C \to A$ is epi and C, A have the same finite signature, then one may show that α_{sm}, the signature morphism in α, is an isomorphism. It can almost always be taken to be the identity morphism.
- Definition 3.2 indeed ensures that the notions of computability etc. for an algebra are independent of any specific coordinatization. But one might prefer the situation where each coordinatization would lead to the same conclusion. In the remainder of section 3 we will treat the question to what extent this is possible.

3.3 Definition Given two coordinatizations (Ω_α, α) and (Ω_β, β) of an algebra A with signature Σ, we say that α **recursively reduces** to β if there exists a compound mapping $f : \Omega_\alpha \to \Omega_\beta$, indexed by the sorts of Σ, with each component being recursive, such that $\alpha = \beta \circ f$.
Two coordinatizations are **equivalent** if they reduce to each other.

Lemma Given two coordinatizations (Ω_α, α) and (Ω_β, β) of an algebra A with signature Σ, such that α recursively reduces to β and β is computable (semicomputable, cosemicomputable), then α is also computable (semicomputable, cosemicomputable).

The proof is quite trivial and the result can easily be extended from the equality relation to arbitrary relations on A. (Realize that the sets mentioned in definition 3.2 are the inverse images under α of the equality relation on each universe.)

3.4 Henceforth we consider only minimal algebras. Let A be a minimal algebra with signature Σ. We denote the term algebra for signature Σ by $T(\Sigma)$. One can give a bijective Gödel numbering for each universe of $T(\Sigma)$. These Gödel numberings and their universes can be taken together into a coordinatization (G, γ_*) of $T(\Sigma)$. The functions on G, as required by the signature Σ, can easily be supplied because γ_* is bijective (each component is). This makes γ_* an isomorphism and $T(\Sigma)$ computable.

The composition $\gamma_A = \nu_A \circ \gamma_*$ of γ_* with the evaluation morphism $\nu_A : T(\Sigma) \to A$ yields a coordinatization (G, γ_A) of A which has the property that it factorizes via $T(\Sigma)$. This algebra is useful for proving the existence of minimal coordinatizations for minimal algebras. But the reduction lemma 3.8 in [BT1] that deals with this coordinatization is practically speaking a special case of the following theorem about minimal coordinatizations. The difference is just that in [BT1] the algebra G (there it has each universe equal to ω) does not need to be minimal. Inspection of the proof below shows that this is a harmless difference.

Theorem A minimal coordinatization recursively reduces to every coordinatization.

Proof

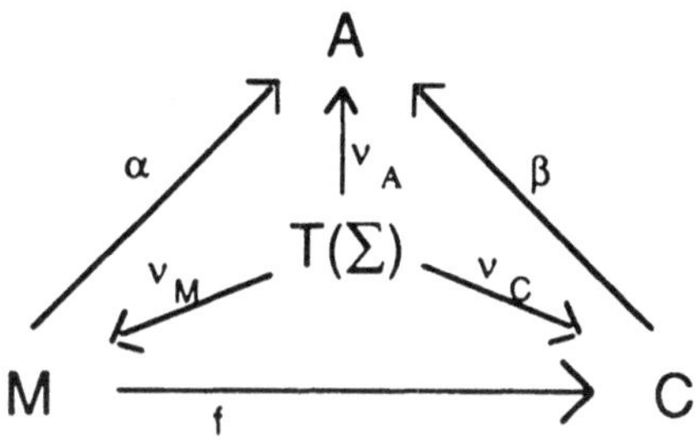

All algebras have signature Σ. C is an arbitrary coordinatization of A, M a minimal coordinatization (this makes A minimal too). The only difference between a proof for single-sorted or many-sorted algebras is a host of indices. Therefore we assume Σ single-sorted.
We have to construct a recursive function f such that $\alpha = \beta \circ f$. We fix an effective enumeration of $T(\Sigma)$. Take a number $m \in M$. Let t be the first term in the enumeration with $\nu_M(t) = m$. Now define $f(m) = \nu_C(t)$. $\nu_C(t)$ can be determined effectively as the functions in C are recursive. ⊠

Minimal coordinatizations are therefore equivalent and lead to the same conclusion about the computability properties of the target algebra. The same holds for semicomputable coordinatizations as follows from the next theorem. This theorem replaces the uniqueness lemma 3.10 in [BT1].

Theorem A semicomputable coordinatization of a minimal algebra recursively reduces to every coordinatization.

Proof The picture in the previous proof still applies, but M is now semicomputable instead of minimal. We have to construct a recursive function f such that $\alpha = \beta \circ f$. We fix an enumeration of the terms of $T(\Sigma)$. Take a number $m \in M$. Now we can not necessarily find a term t with $\nu_M(t) = m$. What we can find is a term t such that $\alpha(\nu_M(t)) = \alpha(m)$ because A is minimal. In order to find it in an effective way we start the enumeration of $T(\Sigma)$ and for each element in this enumeration we start an enumeration of the r.e. set E_α defined by

$$E_\alpha = \{ (x, y) \in M \times M \mid \alpha(x) = \alpha(y) \text{ in } A \}$$

doing one step in each of the running enumerations of E_α at each new element of the enumeration of $T(\Sigma)$. Now define $f(m) = \nu_C(t)$ where t is the first term with $\alpha(\nu_M(t)) = \alpha(m)$.⊠

3.5 Not all coordinatizations of a minimal algebra are equivalent. There may be noncomputable coordinatizations, even in the presence of a computable one. For the following example we are grateful to J. A. Bergstra.

Example Let B be the algebra of booleans, with one universe, containing the two constants T and F and the function ¬, the logical not. Let V be a subset of ω containing one element of each pair (2n, 2n+1). Let α be the coordinatization mapping that maps the elements of V to T, the others to F. The function that corresponds with the not is of course the mapping $2n \to 2n+1$, $2n+1 \to 2n$. If we choose V recursive, then the coordinatization is computable, if we choose it non-computable, then the coordinatization is also non-computable. These two facts are easy to prove.

The importance of minimal coordinatizations has become clear in the previous pages. This raises the following question : does every coordinatization of a minimal algebra have a minimal kernel (the largest minimal subalgebra) which is still a coordinatization ? The question easily reduces to : does the minimal kernel (the largest minimal subalgebra) of a recursive number algebra still have recursive universes ? Freek Wiedijk gave a very simple counter-example with two universes ω and a recursive function f from one universe to the other with f(ω) not recursive.

4. One hidden sort suffices.

4.1 This section mainly consists of the statement and proof of the many-sorted version of theorem 5.3 in [BT1].

Theorem Every minimal semicomputable algebra has a specification with a finite number of non-conditional equations and only one hidden sort.

The idea of the proof is as follows. We denote the algebra by A and its signature by Σ. It has a semicomputable coordinatization (G, γ_A) based on a Gödel numbering. This number algebra G will be transformed into an algebra O that does the same job as G does, but in addition it is specifiable without the use of hidden functions or sorts, has only one sort and contains functions g_i and h_i that enumerate the inverse image sets under γ_A of the equality relations on the universes of A. Then we construct the algebra D as the disjoint union of A and O together with the functions γ_A. The algebra D happens to be specifiable, just by adding some equations for γ_A to the equations that specify O. No infinite enumeration of all the pairs of elements for which γ_A is equal is necessary because of the enumeration functions g_i and h_i.

The main problem of formulating the proof consists of giving names to all the objects that are hanging around in this proof. For instance, the functions in A occur in four versions : in A, in O and in the subalgebras A and O of D. And the same holds for the corresponding function names in the signatures.

We will say that an expression E *has sort s* if s is the image sort of the outermost function of E. We say that an equation has sort s if both expressions in the equation have sort s.

Proof We will use indices i for sort names and indices k for function names of Σ. According to [BT1] (lemma 3.11), there exists a coordinatization (G, γ_A) of A, based on a Gödel numbering γ_* of the term algebra $T(\Sigma)$, such that :

- each universe in G equals ω
- $\gamma_A = \nu_A \circ \gamma_*$, $\gamma_* \circ \nu_G = id_{T(\Sigma)}$ (but $\nu_G \circ \gamma_*$ not necessarily $= id_G$)
- the sets

$$E_i = \{ (x, y) \in G_i \times G_i \mid \gamma_{A_i}(x) = \gamma_{A_i}(y)\}$$

are r.e.

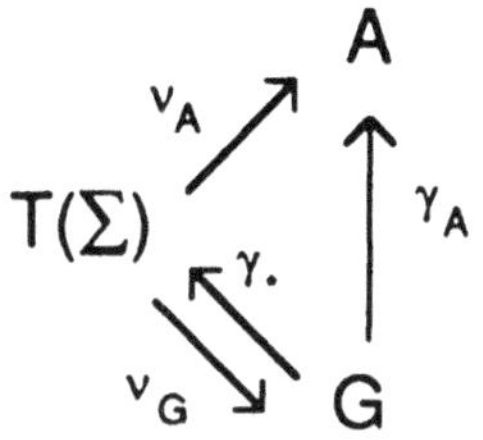

The transformation of G into the algebra O with signature Ω is done by the following steps :

- the signature Ω is equal to Σ apart from the collapsing of the sort names into a single one and apart from the additions in the following steps.
- recursive functions g_i, h_i such that (g_i, h_i) enumerates E_i, are added.
- extra functions are added to make O specifiable, according to the main theorem of [BT2]. Among these functions are the constant 0 and the function succ (+1 on natural numbers).

The sort collapsing signature morphism $\Sigma \to \Omega$ will be called $\sigma_{\Sigma\Omega}$. The canonical morphism $O \to G$ is an example of an opposite algebra morphism. The set of equations for the specification of O is called E_1. So, $T(\Omega, E_1) \cong O$ ($\cong$ means isomorphic). We should give other names to $\gamma_* : O \to T(\Sigma)$ and $\gamma_A : O \to A$ but we don't. We won't need the old meanings any more.

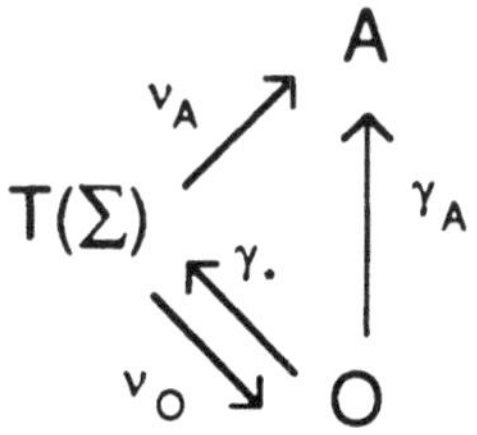

Now we can form the algebra D with signature Δ. It is the disjoint union of A and O together with the functions γ_{A_i}. Δ is defined accordingly, as the disjoint union of Σ and Ω, together with symbols for γ_{A_i} which we will denote by $\underline{\gamma}_i$ (these constructions can be made precise as unions with overlap). The type of $\underline{\gamma}_i$ is less difficult to guess than to describe. It is clear that D is minimal (A and O are) and that $D_{|\Sigma} \cong A$ (where Σ is mapped into Δ in the canonical way which is called $\sigma_{\Sigma\Delta}$).

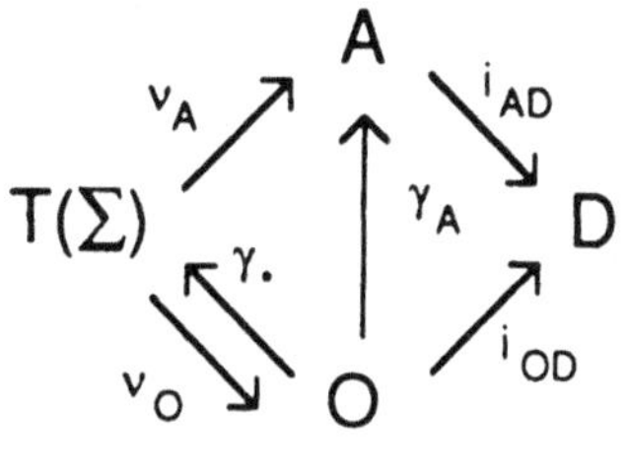

The functions i_{AD} and i_{OD} are just the monomorphic embeddings that do not overlap with each other. The next picture shows us the signatures :

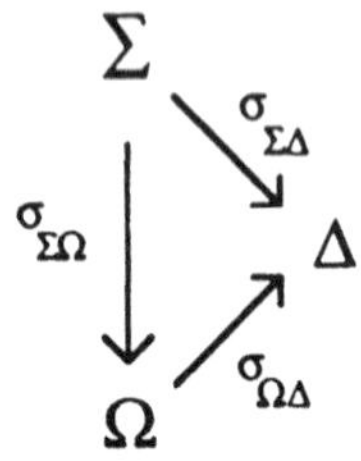

The morphism $\sigma_{\Sigma\Omega}$ is the above mentioned sort collapsing morphism, the other two are just the monomorphic non-overlapping embeddings.

Now some naming conventions. $f^{\Sigma}{}_k$ will denote a function name of Σ. $f^{A}{}_k$ a function of A. Analogously $f^{\Omega}{}_k$ and $f^{O}{}_k$ for the algebra O. Their counterparts in Δ respectively D will be distinguished by underlining : $\underline{f}^{\Sigma}{}_k$, $\underline{f}^{A}{}_k$ etc. Likewise, the symbols for succ, 0, g_i, h_i and γ_{A_i} in D will look like $\underline{succ}$, $\underline{0}$, $\underline{g}_i$, $\underline{h}_i$ and $\underline{\gamma}_i$. Of course, there are now equalities like $\sigma_{\Sigma\Delta}(f^{\Sigma}{}_k) = \underline{f}^{\Sigma}{}_k$.

Only the functions $\underline{f}^{A}{}_k$ and γ_{A_i} remain to be specified. Once the γ_{A_i} are specified, we can specify the $\underline{f}^{A}{}_k$ by the equations :

$$\underline{f}^{\Sigma}{}_k \circ \underline{\gamma} = \underline{\gamma} \circ \underline{f}^{\Omega}{}_k \qquad E_2$$

Again the composition operator relieves us here from the dreadful job of writing out the proper components of $\underline{\gamma}$ as required by $\underline{f}^{\Sigma}{}_k$. In case $\underline{f}^{\Sigma}{}_k$ is a constant, the left hand side is of course just $\underline{f}^{\Sigma}{}_k$. The reader should convince himself that in each concrete case these equations can be written in the usual form with variables.

The functions $\underline{\gamma}_i$ can be specified by

$$\underline{\gamma} \circ \underline{g} = \underline{\gamma} \circ \underline{h} \qquad E_3$$

We abbreviate $E_1 \cup E_2 \cup E_3$ by E. Let us prove that $T(\Delta, E) \cong D$. The equations E hold in D. The evaluation $v_D : T(\Delta, E) \rightarrow D$ is therefore well defined and surjectivity follows from the minimality of D.

In order to prove injectivity we start with two pure Σ-terms t_1 and t_2 in $T(\Delta)$ that evaluate to the same value in A_i in D. Are they $=_E$ equal ? ($=_E$ denotes provable equality in $T(\Delta)$ by the equations E). Their Ω-counterparts t_1' and t_2' (in $T(\Delta)$) can be evaluated in O (in D), yielding two numbers m, n. As $\gamma_{A_i}(m) = \gamma_{A_i}(n)$, there exists a number p such that $m = g_i(p)$ and $n = h_i(p)$. Any equation in $T(\Omega)$ that can be proven with the set E_1, has a Δ-counterpart that still can be proven. This means we can prove (using E_1 and E_3) :

$$\underline{g}_i(\underline{succ}^p(\underline{0})) = \underline{succ}^m(\underline{0})$$

$$\underline{h}_i(\underline{succ}^p(\underline{0})) = \underline{succ}^n(\underline{0})$$

$$\underline{\gamma}_i(\underline{succ}^m(\underline{0})) = \underline{\gamma}_i(\underline{succ}^n(\underline{0}))$$

$$\underline{\gamma}_i(t_1') = \underline{\gamma}_i(t_2')$$

From the latter equation we can derive the desired equation by means of the set E_2.

If you take two arbitrary terms t_1 and t_2 in $T(\Delta)$ that evaluate to the same value in D, they must either be of the universe of O or of one of the universes of A. If they are of the universe of O, they must be pure Ω-terms and can be proven equal with equations E_1. Otherwise they may contain (or consist of) terms with γ_i as head. With the equations E_2 this can be replaced by pure Σ-terms. This means that if t_1 and t_2 are of a sort of Σ, they can be replaced by pure Σ-terms. We saw above how to prove them equal. ⊠

References.

[BT 1] Bergstra, J.A., J.V. Tucker, *Algebraic specifications of computable and semicomputable data types*, Theoretical Computer Science, 50,1987.

[BT2] --------, *The Completeness of the Algebraic Specification Methods for Computable Data Types*, Information and Control, 54, (1982), pp.186-200.

[BT3] --------, *A characterisation of computable data types by means of a finite, equational specification method*, in J.W. de Bakker and J. v. Leeuwen (eds.) *Automata, Languages and Programming, Seventh Colloquium, Noordwijkerhout, 1980*, Springer Verlag, Berlin, 1980, pp. 76 - 90.

[BW] Bloom, S.L., E.G.Wagner, *Many-sorted theories and their algebras with some applications to data types*. In Algebraic Methods in Semantics, edited by M.Nivat, J.C.Reynolds, Cambridge University Press, 1985, pp. 133-68.

[EM] Ehrig, H., B. Mahr, *Fundamentals of Algebraic Specification 1*, EATCS, Monographs on Theoretical Computer Science 6, Springer-Verlag, Berlin, 1985.

[M] Mal'cev, A. I., *Constructive algebras, I.*, Russian Mathematical Surveys 16 (1961) pp. 77 - 129.

[MacL] MacLane,S., *Categories for the Working Mathematician*,Springer-Verlag, New York Inc., 1971.

[MG] J.Meseguer, J.A.Goguen, *Initiality, induction and computability*. In Algebraic Methods in Semantics, edited by M.Nivat, J.C.Reynolds, Cambridge University Press, 1985, pp. 459 - 541.